W9-CRN-234

ART AND TECHNOLOGY

A Symposium on Classical Bronzes

ART AND TECHNOLOGY

A Symposium on Classical Bronzes

Edited by

Suzannah Doeringer
David Gordon Mitten
Arthur Steinberg

Published for

The Fogg Art Museum, Harvard University
and the
Department of Humanities, M.I.T.
by
The M.I.T. Press
Cambridge, Massachusetts, and London, England

Edited by Suzanna Doeringer.

Set in Linotype Palatino and printed by Verlag Philipp von Zabern, Mainz, West Germany.

Bound in the United States of America by The Colonial Press, Inc. Clinton, Massachusetts.

ISBN 0 262 04030 1 (hardcover)

Library of Congress catalog card number: 70-1113372

Foreword

Cyril Stanley Smith

When Professors John Coolidge and George M. A. Hanfmann were planning the exhibition of "Master Bronzes from the Classical World" at the Fogg Museum, the existence of the neighboring institution known as the Massachusetts Institute of Technology resulted naturally in the extension of the accompanying symposium on the art-historical aspects of these beautiful pieces of metal to encompass also the technology behind their production.

Note that this symposium is not on *science* and art — it is on *technology* and art. The intellectual's natural concern with abstract matters has led to far more concern with the relation of art to science than with its relation to technology, which is certainly closer and, I at least believe, more important. To be sure, science in the creative sense is related quite intimately to art (for there seems to be little difference between what goes on in the mind of a scientist and in that of an artist at their critical moments of insight), and science provides modern techniques for the characterization of materials that help the museum curator in the identification and dating of works of art,[1] but with technology art is in intimate and continual contact. The main sources for the historical study of early technology are not written words but are the three-dimensional objects in art museums, for the artist's knowledge of many of the properties of materials far preceded any scientific enquiry into their nature.[2] Conversely, technology is a prerequisite for the existence of a work of art. Even poetry needs paper, ink, and press for permanency, and music its instruments. The recent trend to nonobjective painting has been accompanied by a wider enjoyment of the decorative arts. It is probably true that throughout most of history the principal aesthetic experience for the majority of people has been with objects fashioned of ceramic, wood, or metal for the decoration of temple or church or for common use. The elevation of painting to the finest of arts may not be beyond its merits, but it has resulted in an unbalanced picture. There is plenty of evidence that this is changing, and with the change has come an increased interest in the quality of materials.* Although a decade ago few art museums would have had any interest in a detailed exploration of techniques, there have been a number of recent art exhibitions the catalogues of which devote almost as much space to an examination of the technique by which the objects were made as to the customary type of stylistic and historical analysis. Perhaps it is no accident that two of the best of these have dealt with metals — both the basest metal (iron), in a superb exhibition in Houston, Texas,[3] and the noblest metal (gold), in the sumptuous glitter of Greek jewelry.[4] To these can now be added bronze. The technical essays in the catalogues of these exhibitions all show how techniques of production intimately affected form and in some cases have dictated essential features of the design, or at least the realization of the artist's idea led to his selection of a given material.

Though admittedly technology is on a lower level of human creation than is the vision of an artist, the conversion of the vision into a visible work of art *is* a technological process. The artist must constantly adjust his ideas to the nature of the material as it takes shape beneath his fingers — whether paints of differing viscosity and reflectivity on various surfaces, stones that chip or abrade variously, clays of differing plasticity, or fluid

* A similar change is happening within science: Physics is beginning to return to a concern with real materials after centuries of preoccupation with idealized matter.

and malleable bronze. Without such "feedback" from the subtleties of behavior and texture of the material, the products of an artist's industry rarely possess an integral aesthetic quality. A technical tour de force, the coercion of a material into a shape unnatural to it, is no more satisfying than is the overly exuberant use of a given technique. There can be effective technology without art (as our environment today constantly reminds us), but art that ignores technique lacks integrity.

This symposium will explore the nature of the processes used in fabricating the bronzes, their aesthetic background, the growth and diffusion of style and styles, and the cultural modification of form. If the connection between these various aspects has not always been obvious, it has nevertheless always existed, and the mere bringing together of people of diverse interests in this symposium and the focusing of their attention on the same objects is certain to provide an enriching experience.

This conference will prove valuable also to historians of technology, who are increasingly turning to museums for some of the basis of their studies. No one would take very seriously a history of art that was based only on what people had written about it: it is necessary to see the objects themselves. Literary sources are equally inadequate for technology. Though Pliny, for example, is of immense use, he cannot be believed with confidence unless there exists some contemporary object to confirm what he says. People who make things, people whose knowledge is practical and not intellectually ordered, usually do not write down what they know. Conversely, in the rare event that a literary gentleman has any interest at all in technological details, he is likely to misunderstand them. Moreover, a sufficiently precise vocabulary is often lacking. Prior to the twelfth century there is not a single written source of information on the metallic arts that can be used except as a basis for detective or deductive exercises. The earliest clear writing is the *De Diversis Artibus* of the Benedictine priest Theophilus,[5] written in Germany about 1123 A.D. — this almost carries the very smells and sounds of the workshop. Technical things, of course, are mentioned by writers long before this, and even some workshop recipes exist, but they are usually garbled beyond recognition. Scholars have traced the continued transmission of some glass and color-making recipes inscribed on tablets from Nineveh and Babylon, through a second-century A.D. papyrus to some manuscript compilations that circulated in the seventh to tenth centuries and later. The sequence provides fascinating information about how manuscripts were compiled and circulated, but it is virtually unrelated to what was going on in contemporary workshops. For most of its history, technology can be reconstructed far better on the basis of laboratory studies of objects than from the scraps of written information in which the historian of ideas properly delights. The laboratory examination can often tell more about some aspects of the way objects were made than the man who made them could have conveyed, however hard he tried. Not only was the detailed terminology lacking, but modern analysis of the composition and structure of materials can give quantitative data on many things that the earlier workers knew only qualitatively, if at all.

The technical historian is, of course, dependent upon the archaeologist and museum curator to provide him with properly authenticated objects for study, and he can be tolerably sure of his deductions only after the examination of many objects and of every scrap of other evidence regarding raw materials and equipment.

A technical man who enters a museum laboratory does so because he likes works of art. His desire for knowledge in this area is secondary to aesthetic enjoyment. He does, however, need to have material to work on, and his studies are sometimes destructive. The metallographic study of a metal object, for example, is a certain means of distinguishing between cast and worked metal, and it indicates how much heat was used, but to be conclusive the examination should be done on a complete cross section cut out of the piece. There are, however, many authentic objects so badly damaged as to be of no aesthetic value, and the loss of the integrity that remains is more than balanced by the knowledge that is gained by exhaustive study. Dealers could doubtless produce many such pieces were the market for them known, but excavated pieces are certainly to be preferred. Even beautiful things will often have some broken or missing parts that have to be restored, and it does little harm to remove a small sample adjacent to the remaining edges.

The significance of a given technique, as of a work of art, can be appreciated only when its social and cultural background is understood. The art historian must eventually go far beyond the technical historian. Yet at the present moment, thanks to the growing concern with the real history of technology based on new methods of laboratory analysis, the two are asking almost identical questions and can interact most fruitfully.

For most people the aesthetic enjoyment of a work of art is greater the more is known about its background and the more the viewer can share the experience of the man who shaped it in the first place. At the end of this symposium connoisseurs, museum directors, and curators will, I hope, agree that technical examination contributes directly to the interest and beauty of these objects and perhaps eventually to a better understanding of man himself.

Notes

1 *Application of Science in Examination of Works of Art,* ed. W. J. Young (Boston: Museum of Fine Arts, 1967).

2 C. S. Smith, "Materials and the Development of Civilization and Science," *Science,* CXLVIII (1965), 908—917. *Idem,* "Matter versus Materials, a Historical View," *Science,* CXLII (1968), 637-644.

3 *Made of Iron,* ed. Dominique de Menil, catalogue of an exhibition at the University of St. Thomas, September to December, 1966 (Houston, 1967).

4 H. Hoffmann and P. F. Davidson, *Greek Gold, Jewelry from the Age of Alexander,* ed. A. von Saldern, catalogue of an exhibition at the Museum of Fine Arts, Boston; The Brooklyn Museum; and the Virginia Museum of Fine Arts (n.p., 1965).

5 *On Diverse Arts, The Treatise of Theophilus,* trans. J. G. Hawthorne and C. S. Smith, (Chicago, 1963). The best version of the Latin text is in the edition by C. R. Dodwell (London, 1958).

Arthur Steinberg

Cyril Smith has singled out as one of the important reasons for studying the technology of works of art the pleasure a viewer derives from understanding the workman's experience. There is undoubtedly a certain kind of aesthetic in the intimate knowledge of and appreciation for the handiwork of an artisan or group of workmen. If enough such studies could be amassed, we might well achieve a marvelous sense of the creative and reproductive processes in ancient art, which we have not been able to attain thus far through stylistic studies alone.

But another area in the study of technology is equally important and can give us a different kind of knowledge of antiquity. This approach consists of viewing a particular technology in its cultural context. While it still departs from the individual artifact, it treats it only as one member of a larger group; the workshop becomes the new point of focus. The following areas are central to such an approach: the definition and description of the processes (what the technology is), the social organization of the technology or industry (how it works and who does it), and, broadly speaking, the relationship of the technology to society, including the relations of this technology to other technologies and the social values governing its practice (the external social forces that make a technology function).

For the bronze industry, which preoccupies us here, the description of the technology might involve sources of the metal (mines, scrap, trading); its processing (smelting, refining); designing the object; building the molds, making the alloy and casting the work (foundry work, though it is not clear that this is distinct from designing the piece); finishing the piece (an especially important aspect if the bronze is made in several pieces); marketing or other distribution of the product (the free market versus the patron-client arrangement); and the maintenance of the product, especially relevant for larger statues. All of these stages need careful examination in as many examples as possible in order to determine the industrial practices used in antiquity.

On the social side is the complex organization needed to make the technology function. Questions must be asked about the organization of the labor in the areas of trade, refining, casting, finishing, and maintenance. Was there any kind of internal hierarchy in this organization; was the social status of the founder higher than that of the copper-miner, joiner, or trader? What were the relationships among apprentices, expert craftsmen, common laborers, or specially skilled foreign masters importing new techniques? Were there distinctions in the bronze industry according to the kinds of objects made? Were works of art cast in different foundries from furniture decoration or other utilitarian objects such as arms and armor? Were repoussé and raised pieces (armor, vessels, decorative objects) produced in still other workshops? Were there social distinctions along functional-artistic lines? Were social or other valuational criteria used to determine where a particular kind of technology should be located in a city or town, or was location decided on the basis of function? What were the interrelationships of the various parts of the bronze industry? Where, for instance, did invention and innovation come from — were they made in the casting of works of art or more utilitarian objects, or did they come from outside (see pp. 103-106)? Were the standards for casting art different from those for other work? Were there any outside controls on quality? — a question that brings us to the general consideration of the relation of the technology to society.

The social role of technology has several aspects, which might be illustrated by the bronze industry. What is the relationship of the bronze-worker to other metallurgists — goldsmiths, blacksmiths, and so forth — and to other craftsmen? Was there also a social hierarchy here? Furthermore, how was the bronze industry related, both socially and technically, to the making of iron or other metals? What was the nature of the interaction between various technologies in antiquity? Was there any kind of patronage — state or private — that distinguished some phases of bronze-working? Did religion play any special role, as, for example, the emphasis on ritual did in the manufacture of the Japanese steel sword? In short, what kind of social and religious pressures were exerted on bronze-working, and what effect did they have on the technology; and conversely, did the technology have any shaping effect on the society?

Finally, in considering the relationship of bronze-working to society we must look at the values placed by society on the products of the industry. There appears to be a clear correlation between the quality of a piece, its function, and the importance of that function to the society. Thus, it is significant that in the archaic period Etruscan grave gifts, especially bronzes, are generally of higher quality than the votive material in temple deposits. Perhaps the samples from these two areas merely represent different socio-economic levels, but more likely they indicate a cultural emphasis on tomb gifts rather than votives. On the other hand, in archaic and classical Greece the best bronzes seem to come from temple deposits and inferior ones from tombs. Is this again mere chance, or is the quality of workmanship dictated by function, bound up with the political and religious ideologies of the areas? Are the Etruscans more interested in perpetuating themselves in death than the Greeks, who seem to prefer to dedicate their fine objects to the gods, the embodiment of their *poleis*? In Rome, where we have relatively little funerary material, the situation is less clear, though it appears that "state art," whether religious or political, was the finest in execution.

Embodied in this social view of art is not only the implication that on the whole the best art of a culture is that which is the most "useful" to the state but also that the technology producing socially or politically useful Establishment art is also the most important in that society (tomb architecture and gifts in Etruria, religious architecture and sculpture in Greece). Thus, we might expect the greatest technological advances to be made in the industry that produced the most "useful" art and artifacts for the society.

Some of the preceding questions about the operation of the bronze industry can surely be answered, but many of them still cannot, and among the latter are the broader questions of the social role of technology. When archaeology makes such problems the objects of its research, when areas are investigated that will show large-scale enterprises and small workshops, their location in cities and their material contexts, then we may be able to see more clearly not only the individual experience of the artisan-founder-joiner but also the relationship of his trade to the rest of ancient society.

Preface

Suzannah Doeringer
David Gordon Mitten
Arthur Steinberg

"Master Bronzes from the Classical World," the first international exhibition of Greek, Etruscan, and Roman bronze sculpture, opened at the Fogg Art Museum on December 3, 1967. To heighten the awareness of casual museum-goers and scholars as well of the intricate problems involved in the study and preservation of classical bronzes, it was decided that a symposium should be held that would focus on both the art-historical and the technological aspects of the subject. This volume makes a permanent record of the events of that colloquium, which took place in Cambridge, December 2 and 4, 1967.

From the outset the symposium was conceived of not as a self-contained art-historical monologue but as a dialectic between the art historians and the technologists who work daily with the same objects, but too often without interaction and only from their disparate vantage points. Its aim has been to meld the "two worlds," at least to such an extent that each can come to understand the basic methodologies of the other, its strengths and weaknesses, and the sorts of results it can hope to attain. Through the papers presented, the discussion sessions, and also in informal conversation over coffee or luncheon or in the exhibition galleries, students, collectors, and scholars from diverse disciplines found a common ground in their desire to probe the questions posed by classical bronzes.

Planning such an interdisciplinary symposium was a co-operative effort from the first. The idea was born in the minds of Professor Cyril Stanley Smith of M.I.T. and Professor George M. A. Hanfmann of Harvard, and the project remained a joint endeavor of the two universities. Significantly, the technological papers were presented at the Fogg Art Museum, while a number of the art-historical presentations were made at M.I.T.

Interest in the symposium far surpassed the anticipations of its planners. Nearly 400 persons attended the Saturday sessions, and about 250 came to the Monday meetings. Scholars, collectors, and museum curators made up a large segment of the audience, but numbers of interested museum-goers also attended. Students from Boston area institutions came, and special funds were provided to bring thirty-two particularly interested students from a dozen more distant schools to Cambridge for the event.

The meetings each day were divided into morning and afternoon sessions, separated by a luncheon for symposium participants and invited guests. A banquet on Monday evening preceded the last two papers. On that occasion Professor John Coolidge, at that time the Director of the Fogg Art Museum, made the following remarks.

Two years ago our government underwrote a statistical survey of museums in the United States and Canada. The pamphlet in which the results are published tells a story of popular boom and intellectual bust. Two new museums are founded every week. On the average, every American, young or old, who is physically able to do so, visits one museum or another at least twice a year. On the other hand, to quote the report, "scholarly museum staffs are often smaller than they were thirty years ago; scholarly publication and research have almost disappeared."

These are unpalatable facts. We are reluctant to face them. As intellectuals we are apt to place excessive emphasis on small, indeed trivial, evidence of countertendencies. I submit that if we are intellectually honest we must recognize that the decline in the intellectual life of museums is international and that it is almost certainly irreversible — that conditions are likely to get worse rather than better.

This is an impossible situation. If this symposium has proved anything, it is that you can study bronzes in a multitude of ways but that there is only one way in which you cannot study them. You cannot study them exclusively in the library. You must look at the originals, and that takes you at once into a museum. Research must go on in museums.

Traditionally in the West since the Renaissance cultural enterprises have been the result of co-operation between two groups: patrons and humanists. The Master Bronzes exhibition and this symposium are obvious examples. They would have been impossible without the wholehearted support we have received from private collectors — from people like Leon Pomerance, Norbert Schimmel, and George Ortiz — and all of us here must be grateful that they have not only lent their objects to the exhibition but have also encouraged other collectors to lend, that they have given us of their time, that they have come and participated in the symposium. May I express our collective thanks to them and to all the lenders for their multiple acts of generosity.

The irrefutable facts in this new pamphlet suggest that the happy co-operation between collectors and curators is no longer sufficient. We need a broader base, and the largest significance of this symposium may be to suggest that we have found a way out of this dilemma. This exhibition and this symposium are remarkable for three reasons.

First, on the whole it is an overwhelmingly academic occasion. Depending on how you look at it, you can say that the universities are supplying the scientific staff, of which museums are so short, or you can say that the professors have rushed in where the curators feared to tread.

Second, this occasion is remarkable because it has been so inter-institutional. The Master Bronzes exhibition would have been impossible for the Fogg alone; we required the constant, continuous, and generous support of the Museum of Fine Arts and of professors and museum curators across the country, who offered advice and information at every stage of our preparations. The symposium would have been impossible for Harvard alone. It came into being only because of the enthusiastic help of the Department of Humanities of the Massachusetts Institute of Technology.

Finally — and here we come to the third factor that has made this occasion so remarkable — the symposium was made possible only because it was underwritten by two great American corporations, corporations whose names are household words: Phelps Dodge and Kennecott. We have been used to thinking of big business supporting popular culture. It is gratifying, but hardly surprising, that Eastern Airlines should pay for a middle-brow wow such as von Karajan's performance of Wagner's *Ring*. But surely it is unique for great corporations to support advanced scholarship in the humanities. Their underwriting this gathering is the counterpart in humanistic terms of pure research.

This occasion was inconceivable before the age of the airplane. Cambridge has become the place where a little-known lion from Seattle can be flanked by a vase handle from the Louvre and a votive plaque from Berlin. Cambridge has become a place where a professor from Australia can confer with a curator from Denmark. But if the age of the airplane has created opportunities, it has also clearly created greater problems: more intricate intellectual problems, as the talks during the symposium have clearly indicated, and — more serious — problems of patronage, the co-operative contribution of many kinds of institutions. Your participation and interest in this symposium, for which we are all most grateful, shows that even these exciting challenges that the new age has posed can, with human good will, be creatively overcome.

As Professor Coolidge pointed out, a project of the scope of this symposium necessarily requires considerable financial support. We are deeply grateful to the Phelps Dodge Corporation and, in particular, to its president, George B. Munroe; to the Kennecott Copper Corporation, especially to Dr. Ewan Fletcher and Dr. Arthur L. Loeb of its Ledgemont Laboratory. The keen interest and generous financial assistance of these two sponsors enabled us to realize the plans for the symposium and to present the proceedings in the present format. Our gratitude goes also to The Old Dominion Foundation, which provided a significant grant.

In addition we wish to thank Mr. Alexander Abraham, Mr. James Boyd, Mr. George P. Livanos, Mr. David Miller, Mr. and Mrs. Leon Pomerance, Mr. Norbert Schimmel, Mr. Edwin L. Weisl, Jr., the School of Humanities and Social Science of M.I.T., and an anonymous donor for their support.

The gift from the Kennecott Copper Corporation was designated for the publication of the proceedings, and it is thanks to it that this volume could be so thoroughly illustrated, with the use of color where necessary, and yet be offered for sale at a fraction of its actual cost.

We wish to extend our sincere gratitude to Professors Cyril Stanley Smith and George M. A. Hanfmann, our mentors in this entire project, for providing not only conceptual ideas but also concrete suggestions and willing intercession when called upon. We also thank Mr. James Reynolds, Mr. Howard Brooks, and Mr. William Olney of the Harvard Office for Development, who were instrumental in drawing the project to the attention of industrial sponsors.

The staff of the Fogg Art Museum, and particularly its director at the time, Professor John Coolidge, co-operated magnanimously, both in contributing the museum's facilities to the symposium and in welcoming the visitors. We are most grateful to Mrs. Charles Fuhrmann, who attended cheerfully and competently to the myriad critical minutiae of the planning, and to Mrs. Wellington Scott for helpful ideas and sound advice at every stage. Mrs. Horace Frost and Miss Sharon Foster provided both practical information and willing hands, and Mr. Henry Berg was of untiring aid in making arrangements for the out-of-town students.

We also extend our thanks to Dr. Charlotte Moore, Miss Ellen Thurman, Mrs. Emily G. Lort, and Miss Naomi Lustig for their help in preparing the manuscript. The good-natured and patient co-operation of the printer, Mr. Franz Rutzen, has made the production of the book a pleasure.

The papers in this volume are arranged in the order in which they were presented at the symposium, the more technologically oriented papers coming first and the more art-historical ones following. Each group of papers, representing a morning or afternoon session, is followed by an abbreviated summary of the discussion that followed it. The introductory sections, prepared after the symposium by the editors, attempt to interrelate the papers presented in each session, to raise some of the broader questions, and to outline some avenues for future study.

References to the Master Bronzes catalogue are to David Gordon Mitten and Suzannah F. Doeringer, *Master Bronzes from the Classical World* (Mainz, 1967), the catalogue of an exhibition at the Fogg Art Museum (December 4, 1967 to January 23, 1968), City Art Museum of Saint Louis (March 1 to April 13, 1968), and The Los Angeles County Museum of Art (May 8 to June 30, 1968). Objects in that exhibition are referred to here by their catalogue numbers, for example "(No. 23)." Other abbreviations used are those listed in the *American Journal of Archaeology*, LXIX (1965), 20 ff. A work is cited in full the first time it occurs in each paper. Subsequent references are abbreviated, i.e., Jantzen, *Bronzewerkstätten* (n. 45), 7 ff.

Contents

Foreword v
Cyril Stanley Smith
Arthur Steinberg

Preface xi

Part 1

Introduction to Part 1 1
David Gordon Mitten

Bronze Joining: A Study in Ancient Technology 5
Heather Lechtman
Arthur Steinberg

Chemical Composition of Greek and Roman Statuary Bronzes 37
Earle R. Caley

Discussion Session 1.1 51
Cyril Stanley Smith

Patina: Noble and Vile 57
Rutherford J. Gettens

The Conservation of Bronze Objects 73
R. M. Organ

Authentication of Works of Art 85
William J. Young

Discussion Session 1.2 95
Harold J. Plenderleith

Part 2

Introduction to Part 2 103
Arthur Steinberg

Technical Note 107
Arthur Steinberg

Near Eastern Bronzes in the West: The Question of Origin 109
Oscar White Muscarella

Panoplies from Afrati 129
Herbert Hoffmann

The Artistic Context and Environment of Some Greek Bronzes in the Master Bronzes Exhibition 145
Mogens Gjødesen

Discussion Session 2 167
David Gordon Mitten

Part 3

Introduction to Part 3 173
Arthur Steinberg

Etruscan Bronzes in the British Museum: New Acquisitions and Old Possessions 177
Sybille Haynes

Etruscan Votive Bronzes of Populonia 195
Hans Jucker

Observations on Selected Roman Bronzes in the Master Bronzes Exhibition 221
Heinz Menzel

Discussion Session 3 235
Cornelius C. Vermeule, III

Part 4

Introduction to Part 4 241
Arthur Steinberg

Ancient Bronzes: Decline, Survival, Revival 245
Elaine K. Gazda
George M. A. Hanfmann

Some Thoughts on the Collecting of Bronzes 271
Herbert A. Cahn

Contributors to This Volume 279

Index 283

PART 1

Introduction to Part 1

David Gordon Mitten

The papers in the first half of this symposium discuss and summarize some of the most compelling problems encountered in the growing joint effort of scientists, art historians, and archaeologists to comprehend the technological context in which ancient bronzes — implements, vessels, armor, and large and small statuary bronzes — were produced. They amply demonstrate that fully as much can be learned about a given metallic object by examining how it was made as through the traditional archaeological and art-historical approaches of aesthetics, chronology, and workshop attribution. New apparatus and new techniques are rapidly expanding the types of data that can be recovered and are increasing its accuracy. Awareness of the dividends that can accrue from such analysis has also stimulated growing concern on the part of field archaeologists to record and sample properly both the products of ancient metallurgy and their contexts: the furnaces, tools, and by-products such as slag and casting rejects. Archaeologists are increasingly enlisting the co-operation of chemists, geologists, physicists, metallurgists, mineralogists, and conservators to analyze and interpret their finds. An indication of this trend, which will surely become one of the predominant features of interdisciplinary archaeological research in the future, is the increasing number of analyses of ancient objects published not only in technological journals but in archaeological and anthropological periodicals as well, generally under joint authorship.

In archaeology, as in many other fields, one often finds what one is prepared to recognize. Response to the material one encounters is conditioned by and dependent upon the basic premises and questions with which one approaches the excavation of an archaeological site. How radically these premises and questions have changed in less than a century is clear when we contrast the search for spectacular art objects by Schliemann, his contemporaries, and immediate successors, with the detailed, painstaking recovery and analysis — physically, chemically, and in the aggregate statistically — of faunal and floral material at sites of formative culture like Beycesultan, Hacilar, Suberde, and Çayönü Tepesi in Turkey; Saliagos, Franchthi Cave, Nea Nikomedeia, and Asprochaliko in Greece; Tepe Sarab and Tal-I-Ilbis in Iran, and Jarmo in Iraq. For the total picture of cultural dynamics and processes at work in these early sites, a sample of carbonized grain or a lump of slag may be far more significant than the most sophisticated art object, providing data of profound importance for the history of technology and the development of culture itself.

When an object has been separated from its archaeological context, however, what can it tell us of itself, of the processes by which it was made and the environment through which it has passed? Much of its initial value for the scholar — its context, position, and precise location — is irretrievably lost. If it has appeared on the art market, its protective (and informative) coat of corrosion products has in many cases been stripped away, and it may be encumbered or distorted by restorations or additions. In such cases, among which must be numbered most ancient bronzes in American and Western European museums and private collections, analysis and technical examination are all the more important, often supplementing or correcting judgments made on purely stylistic or aesthetic grounds. In many instances technical analysis can assist the scholar decisively in resolving questions of authenticity.

The papers here make clear the ways in which technological investigation can contribute to an understanding of the particular bronze in question — how it was made, approximately when and where it was made (which implicitly involves a judgment on its authenticity), its present condition and hence the kind of treatment and conservation it should receive. They also suggest the more general questions that may be illuminated — particularly as the number of related bronzes undergoing technical study increases. Knowing how a number of specific bronzes were made will produce insights into the history of technological development, the social organization of workshops, and to some extent the customs and structure of various cultures in general (see pp. VI-VII). Being able, on the basis of technological criteria, to reinforce or revise stylistically based judgments on the approximate date and locale of manufacture of objects will provide a firm groundwork on which to base discussion of stylistic development, workshops, trade routes, and the like. The possibilities are endless. Also, through study of the condition of an object the scholar can learn much about its ecological habitat during the centuries since its manufacture, even when it has been separated from an archaeological context. Let us look at the specific areas of investigation to be pursued.

Important studies of the methods of manufacture and assembly of monumental bronze statuary in classical antiquity are only beginning to appear. Bronze, if we are to believe ancient writers such as Pliny the Elder, Pausanias, and others, was by far the most important medium of sculpture in classical antiquity. All but a very few bronze statues were soon melted down for their metal at the collapse of classical civilization or in medieval times; those that have come to light have not until recently been studied from a technological point of view. This situation has been brought about as much by the failure to appreciate the importance of such studies for the history of art and technology as by the understandable reluctance of museum authorities to allow their treasures to be disassembled and sampled.

However, recent studies such as Lechtman and Steinberg's (pp. 5-35), and others by D. E. L. Haynes,[1] B. S. Ridgway,[2] and T. Dohrn,[3] have attempted to focus upon this important technical aspect and its contribution to the aesthetic appreciation and total understanding of the work of art. They reveal that the manufacture of large bronze statues during classical antiquity was a far more complex process than had been thought and that methods formerly considered to have originated much later were well-known to classical foundrymen. Many more investigations of this sort are needed, especially of major groups like the Piraeus bronzes, so that eventually a body of closely documented studies of dated bronze statues will emerge that will serve as the framework for a history of bronze-casting in the ancient world.

Analyses of bronzes, be they wet-chemical, spectrographic, or other, may help both in authenticating the pieces and in indicating the regions or workshops in which they were made. If a bronze is found to contain large quantities of a metal that we are certain was not used in antiquity, it should be suspect (see Caley and Young papers). Furthermore, trace elements and certain ratios of basic components may eventually aid in determining the provenience of an object. So far these kinds of studies have not proved successful because of the difficulties encountered in the proper sampling of bronzes and the need to acquire a large body of comparative data, which has thus far proved unfeasible. As Caley has shown, the problem is further compounded by the widespread use of scrap metal in statuary bronzes, which tends to reduce the differences that might appear in compositions from different workshops. Nevertheless, if enough bronzes are sampled, reasonably sound statistical methods may yield helpful results.

Another important area of study is the corrosion products of bronzes. As Young illustrates, forged patinas, often difficult to discern with the naked eye, can be detected in thin sections examined under the microscope. When we learn more, too, about the mechanics of corrosion — the growth of new minerals over a long period of time — we will be able to use the corrosion products as indices of both the environment in which the piece was buried and possibly also the age of the object (see Gettens paper).

Since corrosion products are potentially such important sources of information, cautious treatment of a bronze after excavation must become an urgent concern of archaeologists, curators, dealers, and collectors alike. The environment in which the bronze has lain since its final disappearance in antiquity — whether a layer of burned debris from the destruction of a sanctuary, the waterlogged fill of a grave, a submerged location such as a well or sea bottom, or the open surroundings of a sealed tomb chamber — has allowed the metal to reach a relatively stable state. As Gettens and Organ point out, the course of cleaning and treatment should be considered carefully for each individual bronze on the basis of its condition. Hasty or drastic cleaning can destroy valuable and scientifically significant corrosion products as well as the original surface of the bronze, along with whatever fine decoration may be present, and also runs a serious risk of exposing the object to disastrous and rapid corrosion. Thus not only must the bronze be cleaned and treated with utmost care, but the environment in which it is exhibited must also be carefully controlled and kept as stable as possible so that no new destructive corrosion will take place. Bronze is a highly sensitive and unstable alloy and must be handled as such in both cleaning and storing.

What should be the long-range goals in the technological and metallurgical study of classical bronzes? These goals cannot be formulated apart from their place within the development of the over-all study of ancient metallurgy, which in turn is part of an even larger new field, the study of the history of technology. Moreover, it is clear that technological investigation is essential to any complete study of an object or a site and that the results of such an investigation can offer valuable evidence toward resolving the questions that an art historian or an archaeologist asks of an object.

In the foregoing it has been pointed out repeatedly that the broader implications of technical study can be realized only when significant numbers of objects have been studied. Caley's paper has made clear both the paucity of analyses available in print and the appalling state of the documentation of the objects on which these analyses have been done. The development of new nondestructive or virtually nondestructive techniques for metallurgical analysis, such as X-ray fluorescence and the laser-microscope (see pp. 91, 93 f.), should be an immense boon in overcoming the understandable reluctance of museum curators and private owners to have samples removed from their works of art for analysis. It should become routine procedure to have a metallurgical study of a bronze done at the time it is first published, and the results should be incorporated into the publication. It is essential, of course, that in all published analyses the object be carefully identified as to date, provenience, and the like, as otherwise the value of the analysis is severely circumscribed. The eventual availability of a body of metallurgical analyses in the literature will provide the data from which fundamental trends in the development of bronze technology during classical antiquity will become visible.

Crucial for realizing such an ambitious program of technical investigation is the establishment of modern, well-equipped and well-staffed analytical laboratories in the countries where archaeologically documented bronzes continually come to light. Invariably these countries severely restrict or prohibit the export of ancient materials, including specimens for scientific analysis; for this reason, central research and conservation laboratories that could undertake the analysis and preservation of excavated materials are urgently needed. Such laboratories would increase by many times the amount of analytic data that would become available; they would also ensure that excavated bronzes are properly treated and preserved, a goal that it is sometimes difficult to achieve under present conditions.

Accompanying this must come increasing interest in technological processes as revealed by excavation. Bronze foundries and workshops, such as the casting pits in the Athenian Agora[4] and the south slope of the Athenian Acropolis, the recently discovered bronze foundries at Corinth,[5] foundry debris from workshops at Enkomi, Cyprus,[6] and the hoard of bronze statuary scrap from Augst[7] are of primary importance, for both the over-all environmental study of the workshops and their industrial debris and detailed analyses of samples of metal and slag. Particular attention should be paid to casting rejects or other incomplete objects, such as the incomplete griffin protomes from the Heraion at Samos published by U. Jantzen.[8] Search for technologically significant sites, such as workshop or foundry sites, mining establishments, and so forth, should be increasingly undertaken, and promising ones should be excavated carefully.

It is the purpose of this symposium to survey the major areas of problems and potential research, to suggest approaches and possible solutions. Above all, it attempts to demonstrate ways in which historians of metallurgy, scientists, archaeologists, and art historians can contribute data and can work together for the solution of fundamental problems in the study of ancient bronzes.

Notes

1 D. E. L. Haynes, "Some Observations on Early Greek Bronze-Casting," *AA* (1962), cols. 803-807.

2 B. S. Ridgway, "The Bronze Lady from the Sea," *Expedition*, X:1 (1967), 2-9; "The Lady from the Sea: A Greek Bronze in Turkey," *AJA*, LXXI (1967), 329-334, pls. 97-100. *Idem*, "The Bronze Apollo from Piombino in the Louvre," *Antike Plastik*, VII (Berlin, 1968), 43-75.

3 Tobias Dohrn, "L'Arringatore, capolavoro del Museo Archeologico di Firenze," *BdA*, XLIX (1964), 97 ff.

4 H. A. Thompson, "The Excavation of the Athenian Agora, Twelfth Season: 1947," *Hesperia*, XVII (1948), 171 f., pl. 48 : 1, fig. 7.

5 James Wiseman, "Excavations at Corinth, the Gymnasium Area, 1966," *Hesperia*, XXXVI (1967), 402 ff., esp. 409.

6 C. F. A. Schaeffer, *Enkomi Alasia*, I (Paris, 1952), 3-4, 16; H. W. Catling, *Cypriot Bronzework in the Mycenaean World* (Oxford, 1964), 278 ff., *passim*.

7 Alfred Mutz, "Über den Metall-Massenfund von Augusta Raurica," *Ur-Schweiz*, XXXVI : 1 (1962), 18-24.

8 U. Jantzen, *Griechische Greifenkessel* (Berlin, 1955), 16, 57 ff., pls. 17, 18 : 1-2.

Bronze Joining: A Study in Ancient Technology

Heather Lechtman
Arthur Steinberg

The exhibition of Master Bronzes from the Classical World is for the most part an assembly of bronze objects that are castings in both concept and execution. It is remarkable, therefore, to witness the extent to which auxiliary techniques of joining bronze to bronze were employed in the fabrication of many of these castings. We have examined in detail some of the methods of joining used by Greeks, Etruscans, and Romans as they are manifest in particular objects in the exhibition selected largely on the basis of the variety of such techniques that they illustrate.

The examination of the technical processes involved in the realization of these objects is fundamental to their full appreciation. Certainly a deeper understanding of the techniques of making, repairing, and finishing a work lends a whole new dimension to the aesthetic of the piece, a dimension that stems, quite simply, from a delight in workmanship, in manual skill and dexterity. As Professor Smith has pointed out in his introductory remarks, it leads to an awareness and appreciation of what it means for the individual's mind, eye, and hand to work together harmoniously. The product of such a successful concert of faculties may be not only a work of art but a "master bronze" in the fullest sense of that term.

The constraints of time, the relative accessibility of the objects, and the size of the show with its 325 individual pieces imposed limitations upon the number that could feasibly be chosen for careful examination. We were unable to give all the bronzes the same thorough attention that they merit and may have missed some important examples of joining techniques that should be investigated. This paper, then, should serve merely as the prolegomena to a larger study of ancient joining methods pointing out the variety of technical inquiry pertinent to such a study and the kinds of conclusions that may be drawn from the results. Above all, illustration of the technological mastery and beauty of some of these objects should stimulate larger questions about ancient technology and the artistic process that ought to be considered more fully. Ultimately we may be able to reconstruct more reasonably how the artist conceived his work and how, through a consummate control of materials and techniques and through the co-operation of other artisans, he created a work of art. We may never know to what extent a "master bronze" is the work of one man or of several but, proceeding from the end product back to its conception, we may at least see clearly the various stages that went into its execution.

The Necessity for Joins in Cast Bronzes

The casting of complex shapes in bronze is fraught with many difficulties even today. It appears that one solution often resorted to in antiquity was casting several portions of an object separately and subsequently joining them to produce the finished whole. Since the process of casting involves a mold and often a core, as well as molten metal, the problems that develop may arise from the refractory material or from the bronze itself and not infrequently from the interaction between the two. The mold must be thoroughly dry before the metal is introduced. Unless it is baked slowly and uniformly, it is quite likely to crack. If it is not dry enough or if it is insufficiently porous, it will generate gases when the hot metal is poured in, and an unsound casting full of gas pockets and blow holes will result. The bronze itself must be devoid of dross and other impurities so that it will solidify evenly and produce a reasonably uniform surface. It too must be as

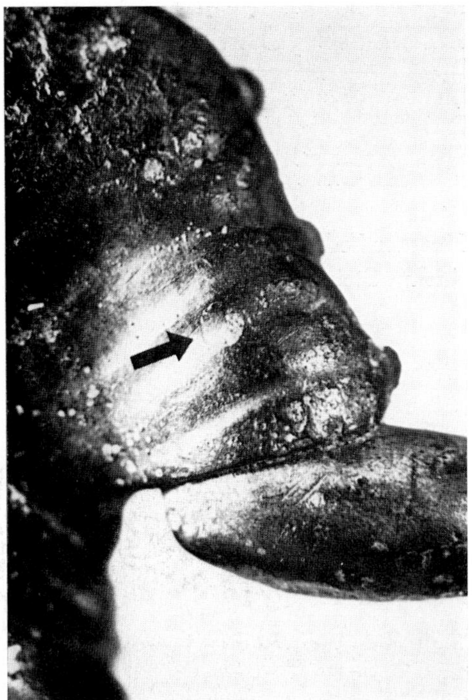

Fig. 1: Etruscan lady with a dove (No. 185). Detail of proper right arm seen from the rear; arrow indicates round end of dowel that holds the arm within the socket.

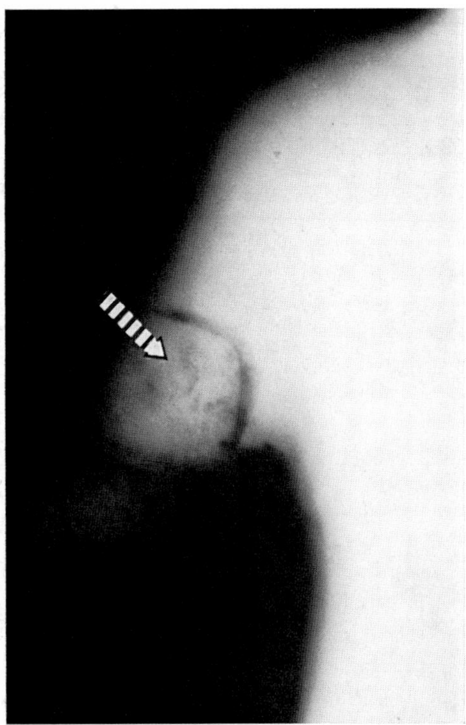

Fig. 2: Etruscan lady with a dove (No. 185). X-radiograph detail of socket-and-tenon join of proper right arm; the arrow points to the dowel, which can be distinguished on the film.

free as possible of gases which are easily absorbed during the melting process. Perhaps the most important requirement, however, is good mold design. The proper placement of the gate through which the metal is poured, the judicious arrangement of vents to allow gases to escape and of risers to permit the metal to fill the mold efficiently and to compensate for shrinkage, the fixing in place of the core so that it does not shift, thereby avoiding a casting of uneven thickness, are all fundamental to a successful result.

In the case of large castings considerable quantities of molten bronze must be available so that a continuous, virtually uninterrupted pour can be achieved. The bronze must be hot enough so that it will run freely into all parts of the mold no matter how far they are from the pouring gate; otherwise misruns are likely to occur. When the mold is large and of intricate design, the metal often has to flow through spaces of varying cross section and over broad areas of mold surface. Upon cooling, the solidifying metal requires continuous feeding from the melt to compensate for the change in volume in going from liquid to solid. Insufficient feeding may result in the formation of shrinkage cavities. As the metal cools and shrinks, it will crack or "tear" if it hangs in the mold and the mold is too hard to yield. Many of these impediments to sound castings are less severe when objects are made on a small scale, yet even in such cases the casting of relatively long projections, such as arms and legs, integrally with the body poses real difficulties that apparently were often insurmountable.

Given the variety of complications that may arise during the casting process, it is not surprising to find many ancient defective castings which the artist or foundryman salvaged by employing, in addition to general repair, a number of joining techniques to attach new parts to the incomplete objects. Ancient joins, as we observe them, are therefore either a result of the purposeful production of an object in several sections in order to avert the foreseen complications of casting it in one piece, or they are the result of the repairs made on defective castings that were originally conceived as single castings.

Types of Bronze Joins

Ancient joins basically fall into two categories, mechanical and metallurgical. A mechanical join consists of interlocking parts. The interlocking is achieved by

1. Locally shaping pieces of metal in the area of the join through the application of a physical force such as hammering, bending, twisting, crimping, peening, and so forth. In such cases the join may be produced through the agency of an additional element such as a rivet, dowel, or peg.

2. Designing cast pieces in such a way that, once solidified, they can be fitted together without any additional materials and with little further working.

3. Casting together the members of a join which has been designed in such a way that those members become locked when the molten metal solidifies. A good example of such a mechanical join is the "interlock casting" used in the manufacture of Chinese bronze vessels.[1]

A metallurgical join, on the other hand, consists of parts that are bonded together by interatomic forces so that they become a single, continuous piece. Such bonding is produced either by locally melting the surfaces to be joined or by introducing molten metal between them. In soldering, this added metal must completely wet the two solid surfaces so that upon cooling the intermediate "adhesive" layer is metallurgically continuous. Fusion welding, alternatively, is the process in which the two surfaces to be joined are locally melted together without any change in chemical composition. This is achieved either by applying concentrated external heat or by adding superheated molten metal of similar composition.

Fig. 3: Etruscan tripod (No. 195). Detail of one of the U-junctions showing the positions of the vertical rods.

Mechanical Joins

The most common mechanical joins are made with rivets, dowels, or pegs. In the Master Bronzes exhibition there are many examples of such joins among the mirrors and vessels, where they are characteristically used in the application of handles. A more unusual example of the use of the dowel appears on the proper right arm of the fourth- or third-century B.C. Etruscan lady holding a dove (No. 185), illustrated in Fig. 1. This join is either the result of a defective casting in which the right arm was damaged and a new arm subsequently had to be attached, or it is intentional, apparently made because it was felt that the position of the projecting right arm would constitute a technical casting problem. The figure and the added arm are solid cast. A radiograph of the area in question (Fig. 2) reveals the presence of a roughly cylindrical socket in the right upper arm into which the tenon of the added lower arm was inserted. To fasten the arm more securely within the socket, a bronze dowel was later driven through the upper arm, from the rear, into the tenon of the added member. The fit of the arm in the socket is so tight and accurate that only close visual examination reveals that the arm was not, in fact, cast integrally with the rest of the piece. Upon further inspection of the back of the arm, however, the carefully finished round end of the dowel can be seen (see arrow, Fig. 1).

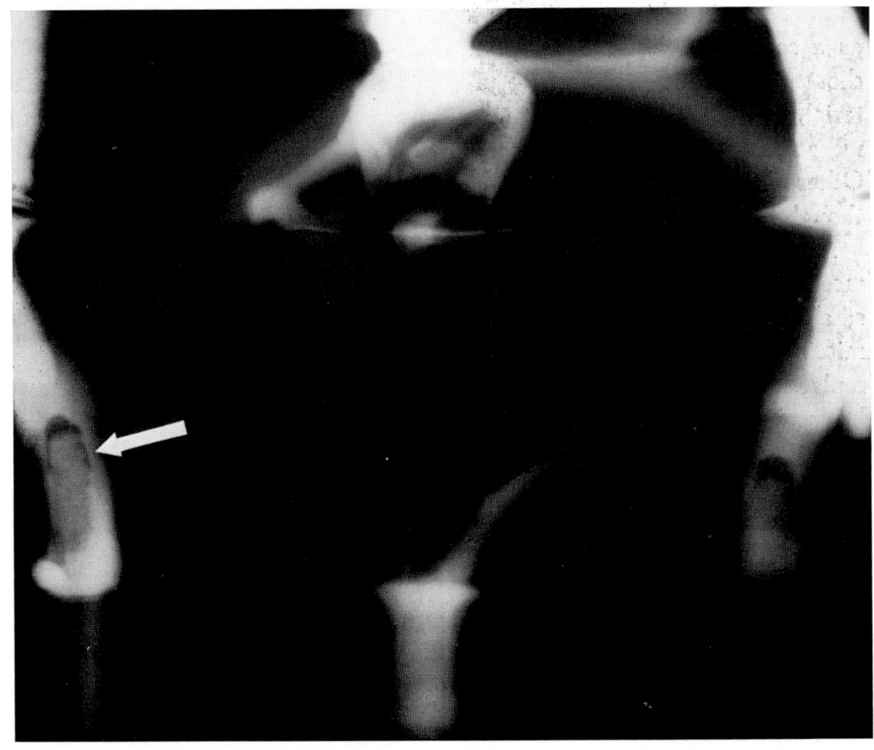

Fig. 4: Etruscan tripod (No. 195). X-radiograph detail of the joins between the U-junctions and the vertical rods; the arrow indicates the toothed surface of the tapered end of one of the rods.

Fig. 5: Etruscan tripod (No. 195). Detail of one foot, illustrating the entry of five individual rods into the circular top; the hollow foot was filled with lead from below.

Noteworthy of this join is the precision and care with which it was executed and the craftsman's apparent desire to mask or disguise the fact that he had to make a join here.

Similarly fine precision work is exhibited on a sixth-century B.C. Etruscan rod tripod (No. 195). Examination of the exterior of this object provides no evidence of the method of attachment of the vertical rods to the highly decorated, inverted U-shaped junctions at the top of the tripod (Fig 3). Once again, a radiograph taken of the area of the join and reproduced in Fig. 4 reveals the joining technique employed. A single rod-and-junction join from each of two U-junctions is shown at the extreme right and left of the radiograph. The join at the center of the radiograph is of the same variety but involves only one vertical rod. Holes were cut, perhaps by drilling and reaming, into either end of each solid-cast U-junction. The ends of the rods were fitted to the diameters of the holes, tapered, and roughened by cutting small teeth into the metal to produce a serrated surface.[2] The serration on the end of one of the rods can actually be seen on the radiograph (see arrow, Fig. 4). It is worthy of note that no auxiliary fastening devices were used to supplement the simple tightness of fit that effects this join.

A different method was selected for joining these same rods to the feet of the tripod (Fig. 5). The feet, unlike the U-junctions, are hollow cast. The circular top of each foot was provided with a series of holes into which the rod ends were placed. Molten lead was then poured into the hollow cavity of each foot from the underside and, when solid, secured the rods into position. This method allowed for some variation in the length of each rod.

The addition of lead to the feet of this tripod illustrates the last form of mechanical join we wish to discuss. Although the lead is introduced in a molten state, it is not hot enough for any appreciable interaction to take place between it and the bronze. Thus no metallurgical join is made here, in the sense in which we use the term. The lead simply acts as a filler, not as a solder.[3] A low-melting-point metal such as lead was undoubtedly chosen because it is so easy to prepare, it is a reasonably permanent material, and it will create a firm, solid join that will withstand the kind of wear and stress likely to be placed upon a supporting member of this kind. Other materials, such as plaster, could have been used to produce a similar though less strong join.

Fig. 6: Roman Diana (No. 253). Detail of the socket in the proper right arm; the lead within the socket can just be discerned.

A more common utilization of lead as a filling material to produce a mechanical join is found on several small statuettes in the exhibition. A small, first-century A.D. Roman Diana (No. 253) with her right forearm missing is a hollow casting from which the core has been removed and replaced with lead. An X-radiograph of this figure shows that the proper left arm is solid bronze. It would appear, however, that the right arm was not cast with the figure but that a hollow socket was prepared in the original casting that was later to accept the separately cast extremity. The arm was fitted into the socket and the entire figurine filled with lead, which served to hold the arm in place. It is quite possible that the missing arm of the Diana was originally cast with the figure, broke off, and was later reattached to the piece by the leading method. The shape and smoothness of the edge of the socket, shown in detail in Fig. 6, strongly suggest, however, that the socket is an as-cast feature of the piece and that an arm was appended to it subsequently.

A similar example is to be found in the third- or fourth-century A.D. Roman votive hand (No. 313) which supports a separately cast figure in its palm. A tang protrudes from the seat of the small, seated man through a hole in the palm of the hand and down into the hollow interior of the casting. The position of this tang is indicated in Fig. 7. Lead, poured into the hollow from the open base of the hand, solidified around the tang holding the figure in place (see arrow, Fig. 8). This same method may have been used on the Etruscan *kouros* (No. 167), which now lacks both its arms. Unlike the other two hollow pieces, this is a solid casting with sockets left in the shoulders for the insertion of separately cast arms. It seems possible, since examination and radiography have revealed no traces of dowels or other mechanical means of attachment, that the arms were secured to the figure by the addition of lead to the sockets. Analyses of samples removed from the interior of the sockets might confirm this speculation.

Whether these kinds of joins are the results of defective castings or are, in fact, intentional cannot be determined without a much larger sample of sound pieces. For there is ample evidence that castings were repaired in a great many different ways in antiquity, and the use of lead as a filler would have been a convenient way of making certain types of repairs. It is significant, as has been pointed out previously, that most of these mechanical joins are so well executed, so carefully finished, that they are often invisible to the eye. It was clearly the intention of the artist or foundryman to produce an object that appeared to be a single, integral casting. If joins had to be made, they were made as invisible as possible.

Fig. 7: Roman votive hand (No. 313). Detail of the area where the small seated man is joined to the palm of the hand; the arrow points to the tang emerging from the figure and entering the palm.

Metallurgical Joins — Soldering

We distinguish between two primary types of ancient metallurgical joins on bronze — soldering (soft and hard) and fusion welding. Although the pieces in the exhibition have not presented clear examples of either soft-

Fig. 8: Roman votive hand (No. 313). A view looking into the hollow interior of the casting from the underside; the arrow points to the lead that has surrounded the tang and locked it in place.

or hard-soldering, studies such as those of Drescher and Gettens[4] indicate that soldering was indeed an important joining technique in antiquity.

A solder is a metal with a melting point lower than that of the metal to be joined. To produce a successful soldered join, the metal surfaces must be thoroughly clean so that the solder can completely wet them. In order for any kind of wetting and bonding to take place, the oxide that forms on bronze (as on most metals), especially when it is heated, must be removed. This is usually accomplished by scraping, filing, or by other abrasive action, after which a flux is spread over the area to dissolve the residual oxide and prevent the formation of more.

Soft and hard solders differ primarily in their melting points, but they differ also in the strength of the join they produce. The alloys of copper with tin or with silver (silver solder) that were used in antiquity for hard-soldering are in themselves harder and stronger than those tin-lead alloys used for soft-soldering and are also closer to the strength of bronze itself. The greater heat required in hard-soldering accelerates interalloying and diffusion between the solder and the bronze and gives a better bond. The fact that hard solders are closer in composition to bronze than soft solders lessens the likelihood of electrolytic corrosion in the join, thus making it more permanent.

We illustrate the structural difference between hard- and soft-soldered joins with two photomicrographs of modern joins produced in copper with materials that were also used in antiquity.[5] Figure 9 shows a cross section of a soft-soldered join made with a 50 — 50 weight per cent tin-lead solder which melts at 215° C. (See the Sn-Pb constitution diagram, Fig. 10.) The thorough wetting of the copper by the solder is characterized by the forma-

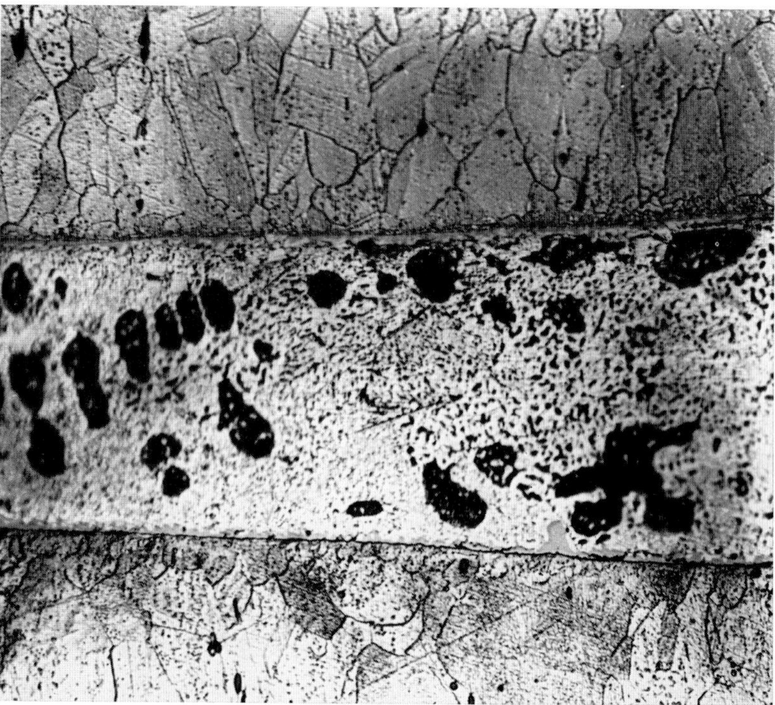

Fig. 9: Microstructure of a soft-soldered join made between two pieces of copper with a 50-50 Sn-Pb solder. The thin gray zone along both edges of the join is an intermetallic compound. x *500 Etch: Ammonium hydroxide-water-hydrogen peroxide (5:5:2) over ammonium persulphate.*

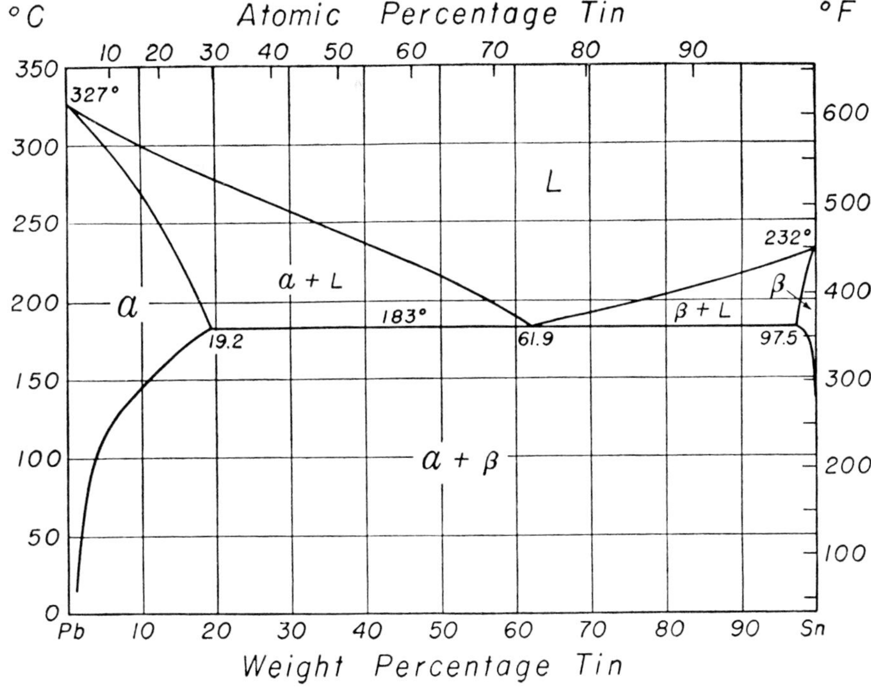

Fig. 10: Constitution diagram for tin-lead alloys. (From Metals Handbook, *American Society for Metals, 1948 edition.)*

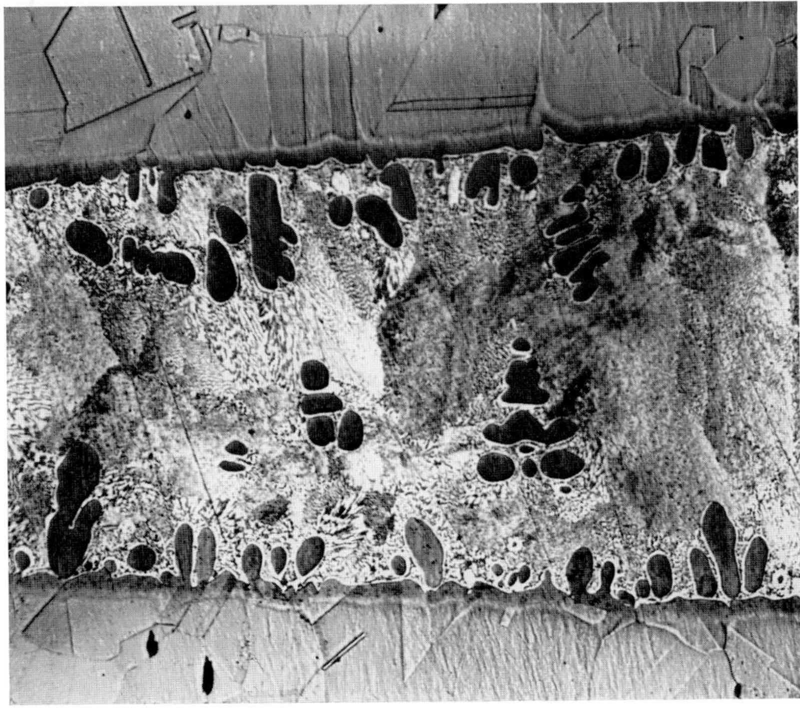

Fig. 11: Microstructure of a silver soldered join made between two pieces of copper with a 72-28 Ag-Cu solder. Note the continuity of structure between the grains of copper and zone of diffusion. x *500 Etch: Potassium bichromate.*

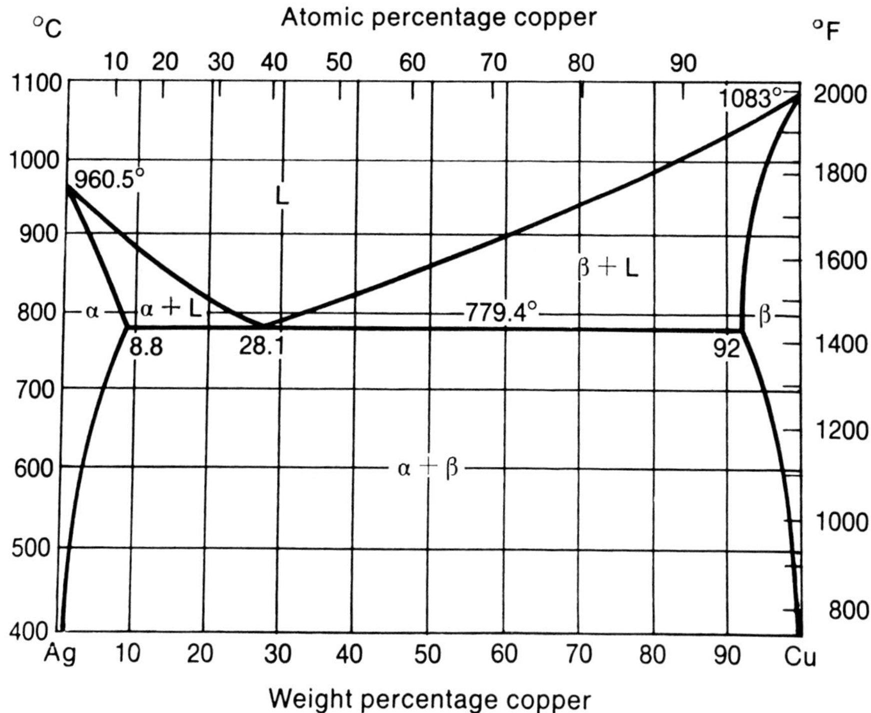

Fig. 12: Constitution diagram for silver-copper alloys.

tion of a thin, brittle layer of gray intermetallic compound (Cu_6Sn_5) along both interfaces of the join. The abrupt change in structure between the copper and the solder is also clear along the interfaces. The photomicrograph reproduced in Fig. 11 illustrates the structure of a join made with a 72 — 28 weight per cent silver-copper solder. In this case the melting temperature of the solder is approximately 780° C. (See the Ag-Cu constitution diagram, Fig. 12.) In contrast to Fig. 9, the interfaces of this join are characterized by a fairly broad zone of diffusion between the solder and the metal which, when etched, appears as a band of various shades of gray. Some of the orientation relationships of the grains and twins in the copper continue into this zone, showing structural continuity between the two.

The proximity of the melting point of hard solder to that of bronze must

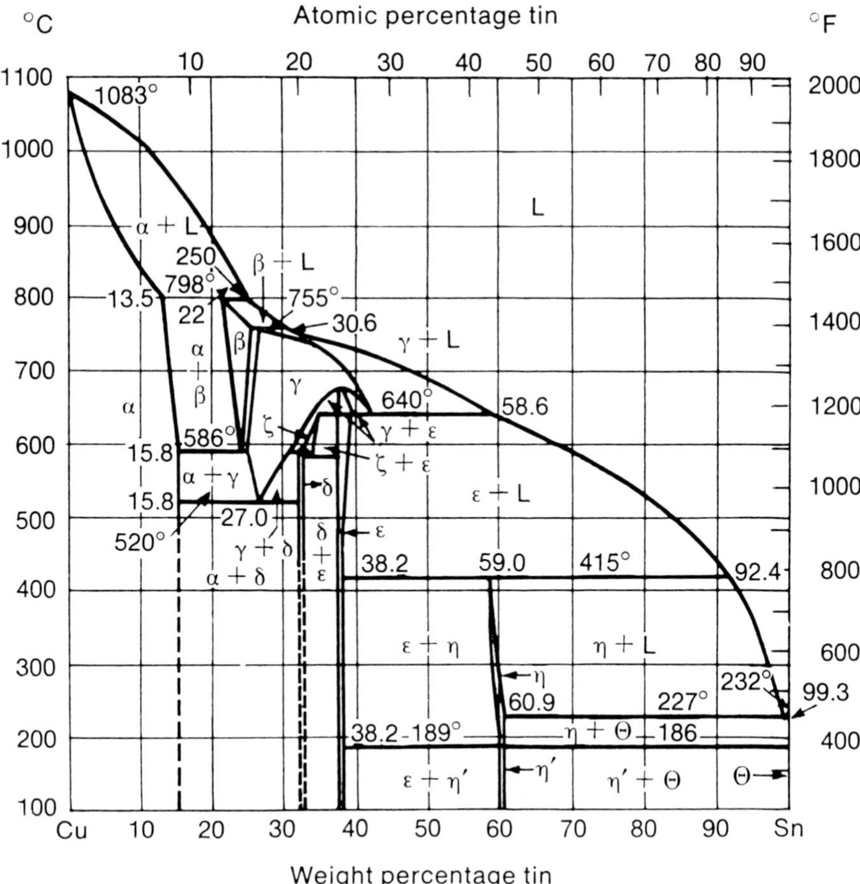

Fig. 13: Constitution diagram for copper-tin alloys. The dotted lines below 450° C. show the conditions to be expected under normal metallurgical treatment; under true equilibrium conditions additional changes would occur. (From C. S. Smith, "The Interpretation of Microstructures of Metallic Artifacts," in Application of Science in Examination of Works of Art *[Boston: Museum of Fine Arts, 1967.])*

have made it more difficult to hard-solder joins than to soft-solder them.[6] Quite apart from the general heating of the parts to be joined, a much more highly concentrated heat had to be applied locally to the join itself. Thus there was the twofold problem of producing the right amount of heat and of avoiding overheating and accidental melting of the bronze. Such joins are made with ease today, but we wonder what the source of heat was in antiquity and how it was directed. Would a simple mouth blowpipe directing a stream of air against a red-hot piece of charcoal have been adequate to melt the solder? Probably so, if the parts to be joined were sufficiently preheated.

We cite here three examples of what we believe to be ancient soft-soldering, but we would like to stress that solder is frequently used in modern restorations and is often difficult to distinguish from its ancient

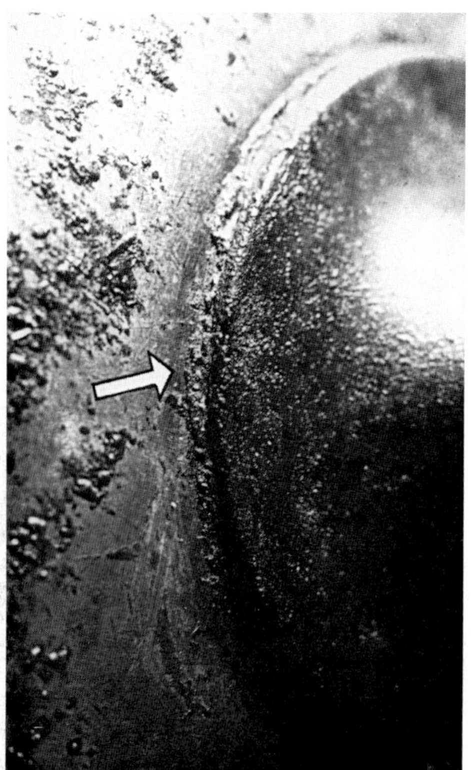

Fig. 14: Greek hydria (No. 109). Detail of the juncture between the handle and the body of the vessel; the arrow points to the layer of material, possibly a soft solder, within the join.

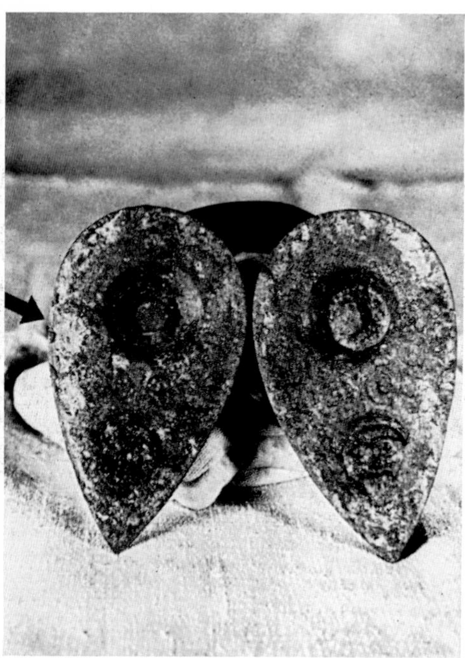

Fig. 15: Etruscan stamnos handle (No. 201). A view of the backs of the two attachment plates of the handle; the arrow indicates the grayish discoloration at the edges of the plates, possibly the remains of a soft solder.

counterpart. Our attributions are, therefore, merely suggestions. The handles of the fifth-century B.C. Greek hydria (No. 109) appear to be soldered to the body of the vessel. There are no traces of rivets or other mechanical forms of attachment, but there is a gray material between the handles and the vessel that looks like a tin-lead solder. Figure 14 is a detail of the area where the handle meets the body of the hydria. The rather thick layer of intermediate material can be seen. The fifth-century B.C. Etruscan or Campanian krater handles (No. 200) also show no trace of any kind of mechanical attachment to the vessel, and we assume that here too the handles were somehow soldered to the krater. The same is true of the fifth- or fourth-century B.C. Etruscan stamnos handle (No. 201) which still has a grayish-white discoloration along the edges of the rear of the attachment plates (see arrow, Fig. 15). This coloring, presumably the corroded remains of a tin alloy, and the absence of any other means of joining, again point to the probable use of a soft solder. Once again, removing selective samples from such areas for analysis ought to determine whether solder is present in these joins.

Soft-soldering is an effective and relatively simple method of joining bronze, and it is tempting to suggest that it was used relatively early in Greece. We know that it was much used by Roman craftsmen for all kinds of joins.[7] We have been unable to find clear examples of hard-soldering among the objects in the exhibition, however. It is difficult to recognize because the soldering material and its corrosion products are usually similar in color to the metal of the joined parts.

Metallurgical Joins — Fusion Welding

In fusion welding a bond takes place between the welding material and the metal to be joined because their surfaces melt, fuse, and solidify integrally. Iron, it may be recalled, can be welded simply by bringing the surfaces to be joined to a white heat and then hammering them until they bond. Bronze, however, is brittle when hot, excessively so above 800 °C., and shatters on continued deformation. Oxide formation on the surfaces of iron does not interfere with the welding because iron oxides fuse at a temperature below that at which the surfaces bond. But the oxides of bronze, which are still present at these elevated temperatures, prevent intercrystalline contact between the two surfaces. The only way to make autogenous bronze welds is to heat the surfaces to be joined until they melt and actually flow together. As in hard-soldering, introducing enough heat to the area is the primary problem.[8] One solution used in antiquity was to pour molten metal onto the area of the join. The added metal had to be hot enough to cause the surfaces to melt, to fuse with one another and with it.[9] This technique is not as easy as it sounds, however, for obviously the temperature of this added metal, which serves as the primary source of heat, must be higher than that at which the metal being joined melts. Thus a continuous stream of metal, more than is actually needed to fill the join gap, must be used, and it has not only to be introduced to, but must also be conducted away from, the join until the entire area has reached the temperature of fusion. Furthermore, the join has to be cooled fairly slowly to avoid failure from shrinkage and cracking. In fact, joins of this kind that have failed are generally the easiest to study.

One of the most interesting examples of an attempted metallurgical join is found between the tail and body of an eighth-century B.C. Greek bird

(No. 25).[10] Its most striking feature is the combination of metallurgical and mechanical elements employed to ensure that the tail would remain attached to the body. But because of weakness of the body metal in the neighborhood of the join and the effects of corrosion within the join, the bond has not held, the two sections of the bird have come apart, and we have been able to study the nature of the join itself.

The bird was lost-wax cast around a refractory core which remains and has yet to be studied. The core was centered in the mold by a single bronze chaplet that passes through the thickest portion of the body. One end of the chaplet can be seen in Fig. 16, embedded in the center of the core. It would appear that this single chaplet was insufficient to hold the core in place during the pouring of the bronze. The core must have shifted to one side, creating a considerable disparity in the thickness of the two sides of the final casting, which is apparent from the exposed cross section of the broken edges. It was probably this circumstance that caused the heavy, solid tail to break away from the thin, fragile metal of the body. The tail, as it appears in Fig. 16, was photographed in a position corresponding to its original placement with respect to the body of the bird.

The bird was repaired and a new tail provided in the manner described here, but presumably as a result of corrosion it broke a second time and is now once again a separate unit. On the second occasion of breakage, a portion of the rear of the bird's body also broke away and has remained inside the tail. A view into the broken end of the tail (Fig. 22) shows the remnants of this body metal inside it. The metal toward the bottom of the photograph, corresponding to the proper left side of the bird, is quite thick, whereas that to the right and left of it is amazingly thin.

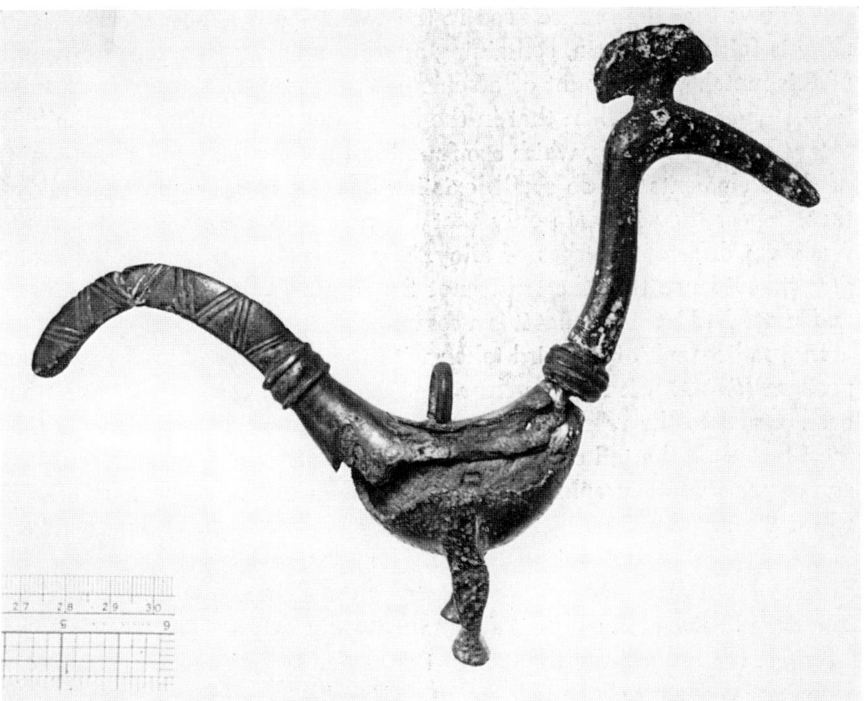

Fig. 16: Greek bird (No. 25). The tail, now separate from the body, has been propped into its original position.

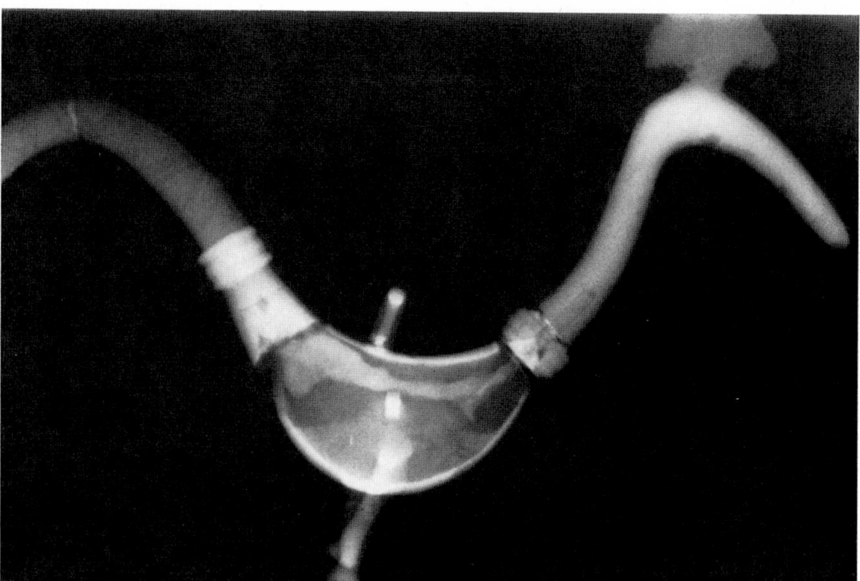

Fig. 17: Greek bird (No. 25). X-radiograph of the bird with the tail propped into place.

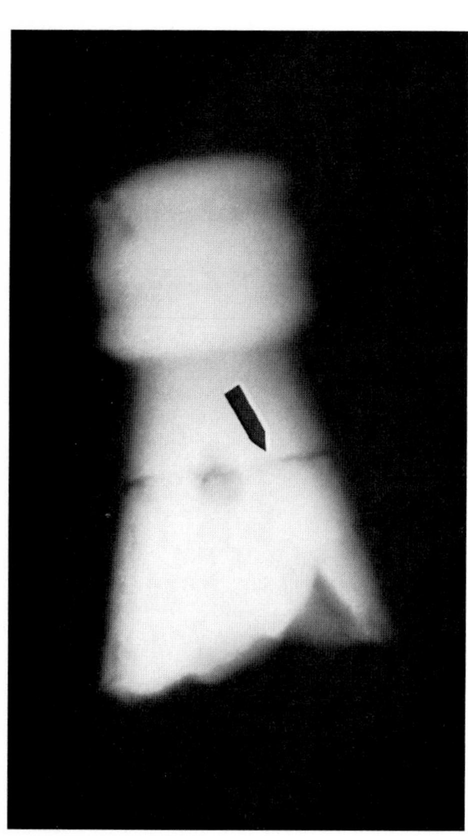

Fig. 18: Greek bird (No. 25). Detail of the X-radiograph shown in Fig. 17; the arrow points to the space, seen as a dark line, between the cast-on tail and the metal of the body still within the tail.

Whether the original break actually occurred during casting or subsequently we cannot say. Because the restored head is still in place, we have not been able to determine whether it broke off, as did the tail, or whether this break is the result of some other accident. In any case, at some point in the bird's history a new tail was cast onto the rear of the body. There is no reason to believe that this was not done at the time of the original casting. Table 1,[11] which presents the results of quantitative analyses carried out on a number of metal samples removed from both the body and tail, shows that the bronze used in the two cases is almost identical. The alloy is fairly rich in tin, containing approximately 11 per cent by weight of this metal. The amount of arsenic in the tail appears to be from three to ten times greater than that in the body, and the body metal lacks both bismuth and antimony, which are found in the tail metal. But the amounts of these elements are so small, existing only as traces within the alloys, that at best they indicate only that the metal used for the two castings was from different batches of alloy. The analyses corroborate the radiographic evidence that the tail is not the original one cast with the body and reattached later but that it is a completely separate casting.

In a radiograph of the bird taken with the tail propped into its original position (Fig. 17), it is quite clear that the tail is a separate unit that has been joined to the rear of the body. This is indicated by a dark line on the film inside the tail close to the point at which the tail abuts the body and appears more graphically in the detail in Fig. 18. The dark line to which the arrow points is actually a thin space between the metal of the bird's body and the metal of the tail. The tail was attached to the bird by casting it onto the body. We reconstruct the entire procedure along the following lines and illustrate it diagrammatically in Figs. 19 and 20.

1. The tail broke from the rear of the bird, leaving a jagged and uneven area there with part of the core emerging (Fig. 19, detail 1).

2. The broken edges of the rear of the body were filed down to receive the new tail (Fig. 19, detail 2). This rather smooth, filed area can still be

TABLE 1. COMPOSITION OF BRONZE SAMPLES REMOVED FROM THE GEOMETRIC BIRD (NO. 25)[11]

Sample No.	Site of Sample	Element (Weight per cent)														
		Cu	Sn	Ag	Al	As	Bi	Ca	Co	Fe	Mg	Mn	Ni	Pb	Sb	Si
1	Tail: smooth surface of join	90.34	9.72													
2	Body: thick metal at broken edge	88.95	10.98													
3	Body: thick metal at broken edge	87.10	12.96													
4	Body: thick metal at broken edge			0.007	0.01	0.003	—	0.007	0.004	0.08	0.004	0.001	0.005	0.008	—	0.04
5	Tail: base of long tang			0.01	0.01	0.03	0.003	0.005	0.006	0.08	0.006	0.004	0.009	0.05	0.007	0.05
6	Tail: smooth surface of join			0.01	0.006	0.01	0.003	0.007	0.004	0.03	0.01	0.003	0.005	0.07	0.006	0.008

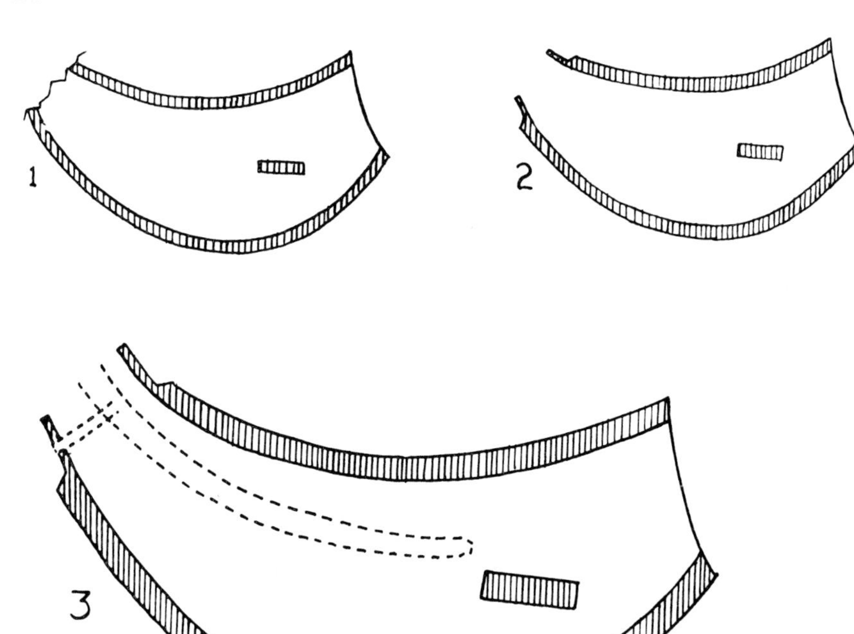

Fig. 19: Diagrammatic reconstruction of the casting-on procedure used to join the tail to the body of the bird: (1) Loss of the tail leaves a jagged area of metal at the rear of the body. (2) The metal at the broken rear of the body is filed and smoothed to prepare it for the new tail. (3) Channels are dug into the core within the body along which the molten bronze will flow and solidify. (Drawing by Marjorie Benedict Cohn.)

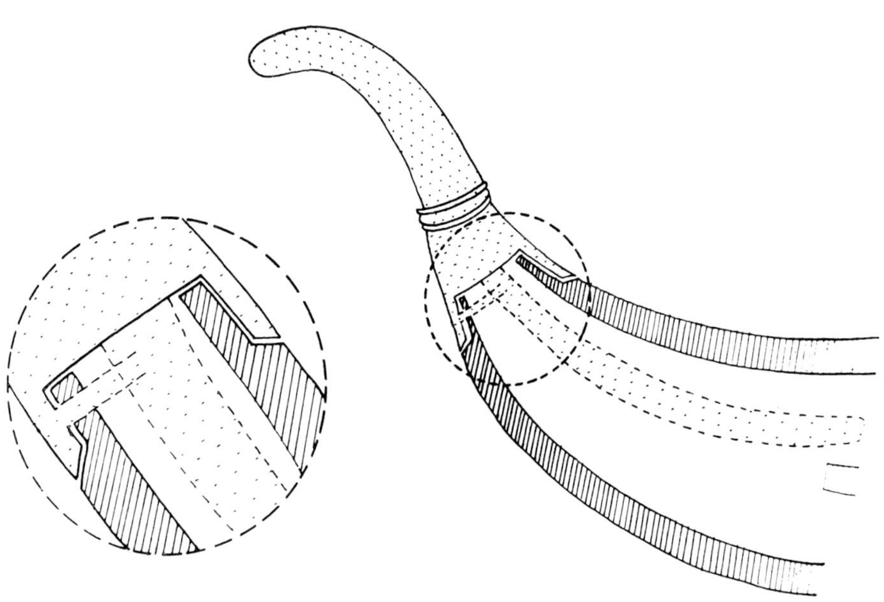

Fig. 20: Diagrammatic reconstruction of the casting-on procedure used to join the tail to the body of the bird. The cast-on tail is shown in place on the rear of the bird; the stippled areas indicate solid bronze of this second casting; the enlarged detail illustrates the function of the shorter bronze pin. (Drawing by Marjorie Benedict Cohn.)

seen on the left side of the body, as indicated in Fig. 21. The result was a roughly conical shape onto which the new casting would be made. It was not symmetrical because the uneven thicknesses of metal at the rear of the body forced the artisan to accommodate himself as best he could by filing some areas and not others. The appearance of the exterior of the tail and of the radiograph is deceptive in this detail.

3. Probably because the bird's body was so fragile, it was felt that the casting-on must be guaranteed by some mechanical means as well. Channels

were dug into the core of the body along which the molten metal would eventually flow and solidify (Fig. 19, detail 3). One long channel ran well toward the front of the body but always along the outer surface of the core near the metal on the right side of the bird. The bronze on this side was so thin that when the new casting was made, the metal that flowed into this long groove actually fused with the bronze on the surface of the bird's body, resulting in a tang that was intimately bonded with the metal of the body. This long tang, which proceeds from the tail anteriorly along the right side of the body and almost reaches the neck, appears in Fig. 16 and in the radiograph in Fig. 17. A second, much shorter channel was excavated in the core, running from the center of the opening in the rear out through the thin bronze wall of the body. When the new casting was made, the metal that solidified in this channel formed a kind of bronze pin that ran through a small portion of core, through the wall of the bird's body and connected with the tail (Fig. 20). In effect this produced a continuous "loop" of tail metal running through a portion of the core and the bird's body. In Fig. 22 the core that was originally present has been removed to facilitate study of this area. It shows the relative positions of the long tang and the short pin, the latter indicated by the white arrow.

4. After the filing of the body and excavation of the channels, the tail was probably modeled in wax against the rear of the body and covered with clay to form the mold for the casting. It is likely that the whole complex of bird and mold was then heated to a considerable temperature to melt or burn out the wax, to dry the clay, and to facilitate the joining. After the bronze was poured in, the new casting was allowed to cool slowly, the mold was removed, and the joined area was carefully scraped, filed, and polished.

Although the join was presumably meant to be a metallurgical one, it is only in the immediate area of the junction of the long tang with the tail

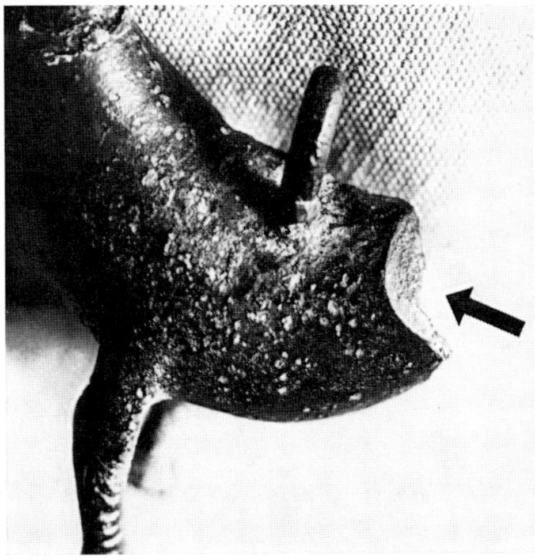

Fig. 21: Greek bird (No. 25). The body of the bird seen from the proper left side; the arrow points to the filed-down edge of the metal at the rear of the body.

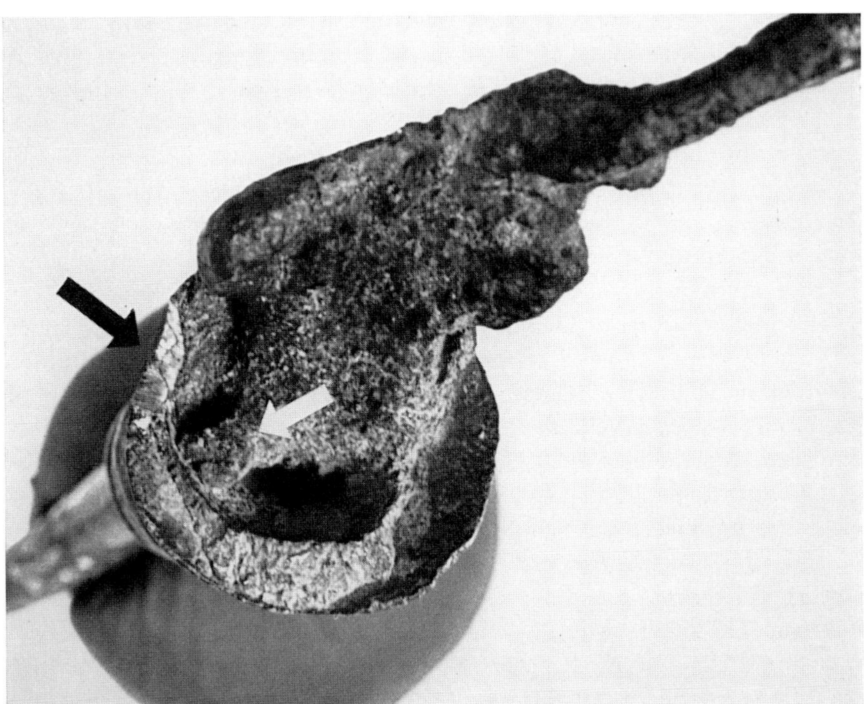

Fig. 22: Greek bird (No. 25). A view looking down into the broken end of the tail; the long tang projects out at the top of the photograph; the white arrow points to the shorter pin, while the black arrow indicates the site from which a section was removed for metallographic study.

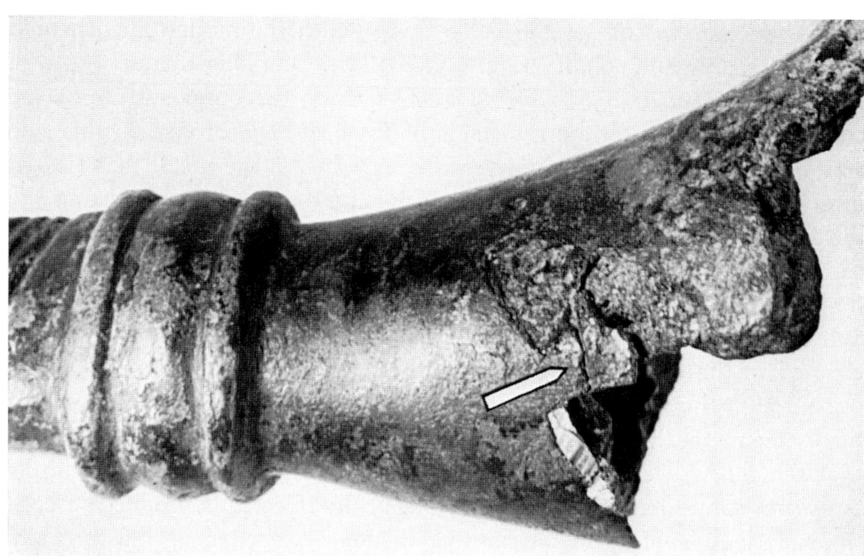

Fig. 23: Greek bird (No. 25). A detail of the broken portion of the tail; fusion has taken place between the tail and the metal of the bird's body at the top of the photograph; the arrow indicates an area where no fusion has occurred.

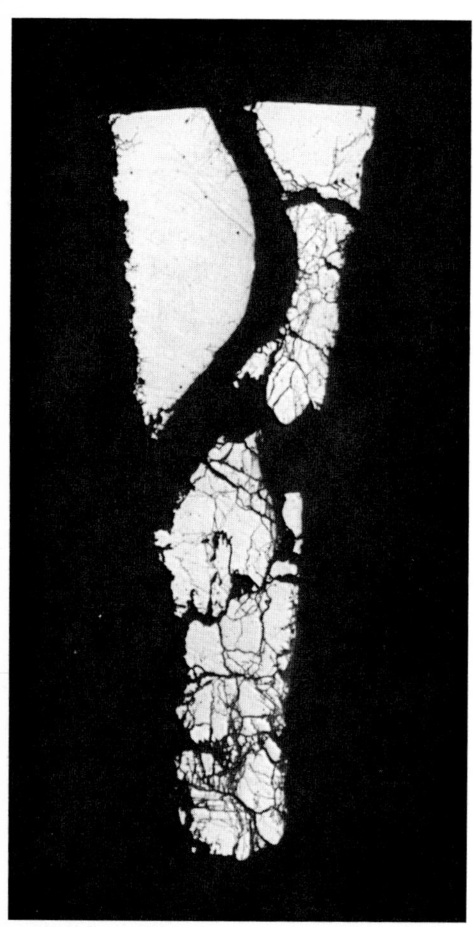

Fig. 24: Photomacrograph of the section removed from the tail. Tail metal at the left, body metal at the right; between the two is a wide gap filled with corrosion products, x 22 as polished.

proper, as well as at the far extremity of the long tang, that the molten bronze of the tail actually fused with the metal of the body. The fusion of the base of the tang with the body metal can be seen in Fig. 23. The metals of the tang, tail, and body are indistinguishable at the uppermost portion of the tail. Immediately below this rather limited zone of fusion, however, the arrow points to a pronounced, roughly vertical line that establishes the end of the tail at this position. A fragment of the body metal can be seen to lie inside the tail here. There is virtually no bond between the two. Except for this small area, then, the cast-on tail simply abuts onto the rear of the bird, and it is only by means of the mechanical tangs that the join is made.

A section through the join itself illustrates more exactly what has taken place. The black arrow in Fig. 22 indicates the site from which the section was cut. The dark line of corrosion between the inner metal of the bird's body and the outer metal of its tail can be seen in the shiny area of freshly sawed metal. Figure 24 shows a magnified view of this same section after it has been polished. The outer tail metal appears at the left, the inner body metal at the right. The wide, dark gap between the two is filled with corrosion products. Figures 25 and 26 show the section after etching. It is immediately apparent that there was never any fusion between the two metals. No continuity of structure exists, and the two must always have been separated by an appreciable space now accentuated by the corrosion.

The microstructure of the body metal (Fig. 25) reveals large, well-formed crystals of the alpha solid solution of tin in copper. (See the constitution diagram in Fig. 13.)[12] The large crystal size is the result of slow cooling of the bronze casting. We suspect also that the metal has been subsequently annealed, for there is relatively little segregation or coring within the grains, and no alpha-delta eutectoid, which generally forms in castings of this composition but which can go into solid solution on prolonged heating. The surface of the body metal along the corrosion-product-filled gap between it and the tail shows a somewhat different structure, however. The small, twinned grains along this edge indicate that the metal was superficially worked, probably by filing, and then heated to a temperature above the recrystallization temperature of the bronze.

The tail has the microstructure of a casting (Fig. 26) similar to that of the body, except that there are obviously no recrystallized twinned grains along the surface that joins with the body. There was no opportunity for any kind of working of the metal in this area. The tail was merely cast against the prepared surface of the body. On the other hand, the twinned grains on the *outside* surface of the tail (which also appear elsewhere on the exterior of the bird's body) are the result of the superficial tooling that went into the finishing of the final casting.

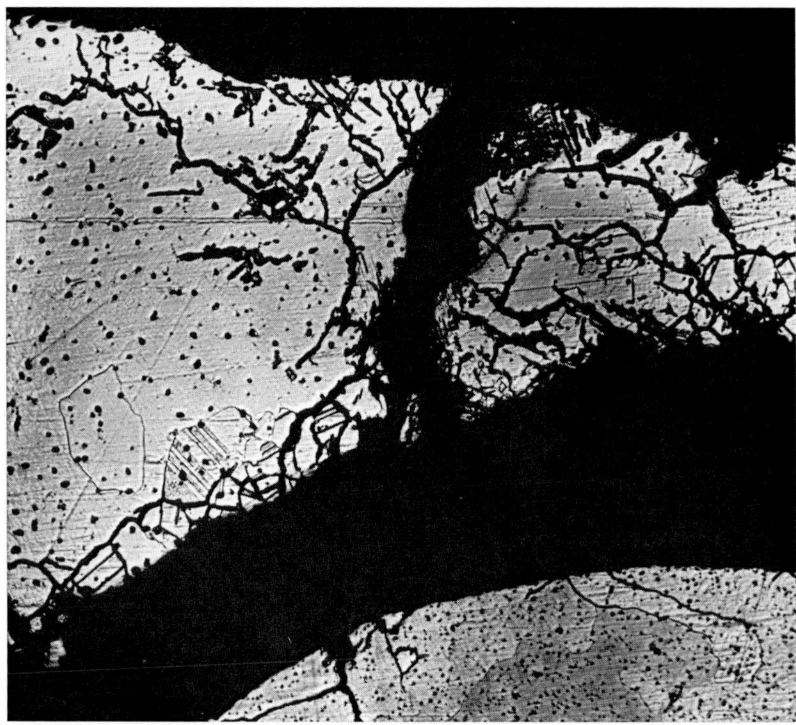

Fig. 25: Microstructure of the metal of the bird's body (from the section shown in Fig. 24). Note the small, twinned grains along the edge of the metal that is contiguous with the corrosion-field gap. x 100 Etch: Potassium bichromate.

Fig. 26: Microstructure of the metal of the bird's tail (from the section shown in Fig. 24). Note the large grain size, the absence of twinned grains along the edge that meets the gap, and the presence of twins along the outer surface. x 100 Etch: Potassium bichromate followed by copper ammonium chloride.

There are three structural phenomena present in both body and tail that are due to annealing: homogeneity within the grains, lack of eutectoid, and presence of twinning. We are not certain at what stage the annealing took place. It seems likely that, for the body, this heating occurred during the preparations for casting-on the new tail, in which case the microstructure of the tail is due to heating subsequent to the finishing of the entire piece. It should be noted, however, that such a final prolonged heating is unusual in finishing castings. Furthermore, the similarity in size of the twinned grains on both body and tail suggests that they may have been formed as a result of the same heating. If further study shows that the latter was the case, then certain details of our reconstruction of the casting-on procedure might need modification.

In summary, we have here a fine example of a combined metallurgical and mechanical join that we have called casting-on. The join might have succeeded metallurgically if more or hotter metal had been poured around the critical area. Casting-on, a form of fusion welding, is accomplished by pouring a large quantity of molten metal past the edges to be joined so that they actually melt and fuse with the liquid metal. But the mechanical part of the join was effective, and it is only the burial and attendant corrosion of two thousand years that have caused the join to fail and to become visible.

The last type of join to be considered is a well-executed fusion weld on a life-size, hollow-cast fragment of Roman drapery of the late second century A.D. (No. 237). This drapery represents one side of a standing male figure, the missing head having been attached separately. At the back of the drapery there seems to be a finished edge that is turned outward, forming a shallow ledge along the entire length of the figure. It has been tentatively suggested that the drapery fragment might be part of a large relief in which each bronze figure was fastened to a stone or wooden background by inserting such a shallow ledge into an appropriate cutting.[13] The join bisects the drapery horizontally midway between the torso and the legs, roughly at the level of the hips. The outer surface of the piece is well

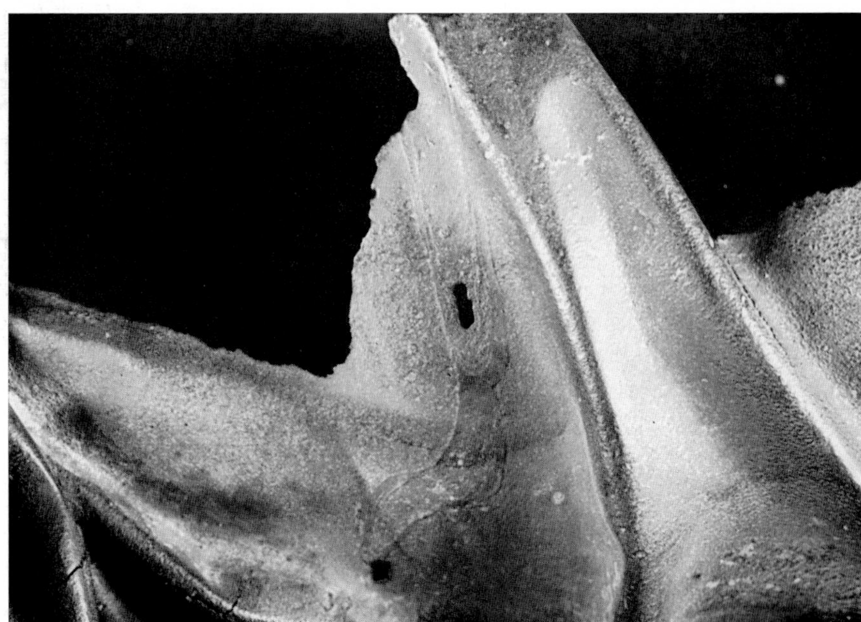

Fig. 27: Roman draped male statue (No. 237). Detail of the join on the exterior surface. Note the long oval configurations that run along the join and follow the drapery contours.

preserved, with a fine green patina, and has obviously been very thoroughly finished. The interior is rough, probably much the way it came out of the mold. It is very revealing to study the inside of this large bronze, for we can learn a great deal about ancient foundry practice from it.

We cannot be certain about the precise method of manufacture of this piece, however, until we have made some further analyses and have actually reproduced in the laboratory the method of joining it exhibits. How was the casting made? What were the number of molding stages? Was wax used? How was the mold oriented during casting? Where were the gates and risers situated? All these questions still remain unanswered. In fact, we cannot even be certain whether the drapery was cast in one piece and later cracked at the middle, necessitating an elaborate repair, or whether it was cast in two pieces that were intended to be joined in this way. We can suggest, however, that the remarkably uniform thinness of the bronze, its large size, and the analogy of other large Roman bronzes[14] all support the view that the drapery was intentionally cast in two pieces that were later welded together.

On the exterior the join is characterized by a number of ovals and circles in the bronze which have slightly raised borders and in some cases raised concentric ridges within them (Fig. 32). These configurations follow along the entire length of the join. A portion of the join illustrating two such oval patches is shown in Fig. 27. Some of the ovals contain rectangular holes and plugs, and it is likely that the holes are simply areas where the plugs have fallen out. The circular and oval areas are not always contiguous throughout the join, though their ends generally abut on each other. Another characteristic of these configurations is that they closely follow the contours of the surface of the drapery. This is particularly clear in Fig. 27. Thus a single large oval may begin on one side of a prominent fold in the drapery and continue over its apex onto the other side. Similar oval and round areas, observable on the exterior where joins have been made, appear on the Bacchus from Avenches (No. 246, see Fig. 28) as well as on a large bronze from Agde recently studied in the

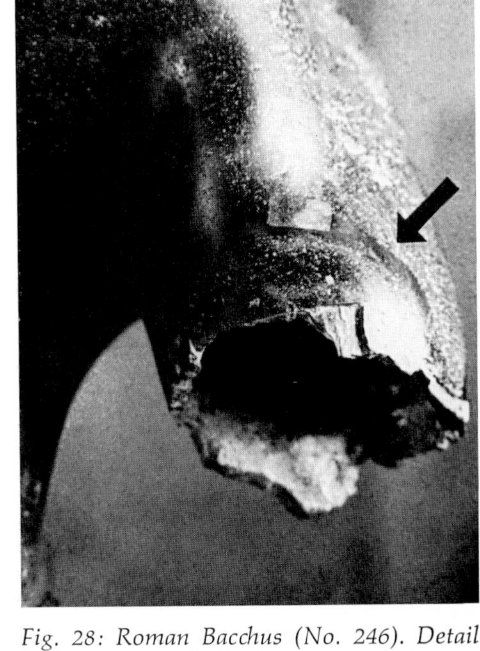

Fig. 28: Roman Bacchus (No. 246). Detail of the join of the broken proper left arm; the arrow points to the roughly circular configuration that occurs at the join.

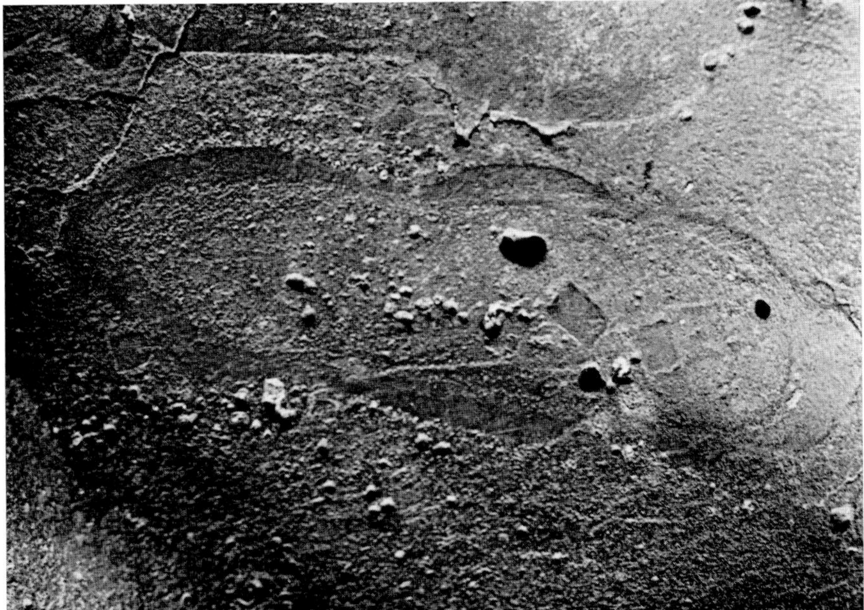

Fig. 29: Roman draped male statue (No. 237). Detail of a single oval patch in the neighborhood of the join. Note the rectangular metal fills used to plug holes along the edges of and within the oval itself.

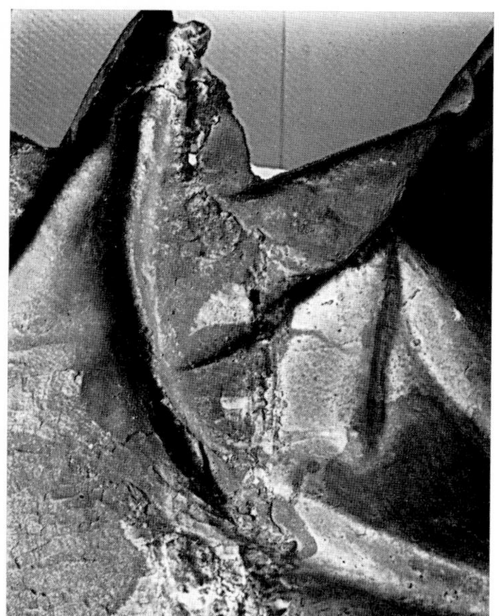

Fig. 30: Roman draped male statue (No. 237). Detail of the join on the interior surface; the area shown here corresponds to that portion of the join shown on the exterior surface in Fig. 27. Note the thickness and irregularity of the accretions of weld metal along the join.

laboratory of the Louvre.[15] One of these oval areas on the Roman drapery should be noted in particular, for it is not on the line of the join itself but at some distance below it (Fig. 29). It seems to be a large patch made in an area so weak or cracked that it required welding to strengthen it. This weld is especially interesting because of the several small rectangular metal patches still embedded in it which must have been added to fill holes that were left even after the weld was completed. Clearly the whole exterior of the drapery, including the weld, was heavily cold-worked (scraped, filed, polished) to give it such an even and clean appearance.

The interior of the join is different in appearance from the exterior (Fig. 30). It consists of a number of rough accretions of weld metal (generally corresponding in position to the ovals on the exterior) that look as though they have been pushed along the surface with a tool while the metal was in a pasty condition, although it is not very likely that this technique was actually used here. The weld metal is thicker in some areas than in others and displays a tendency to crack. Little more appears on visual examination alone, but we were kindly allowed by the Museum of Fine Arts, Boston, to make a more thorough study of this join. Such a study is of considerable importance since most large Roman and some Greek bronze sculptures have been assembled or repaired by this method, to judge from the telltale oval patches that appear on many of them. But the technique has never been properly described or analyzed. Our description of the nature of the join in this one piece of drapery may serve as an introduction to a closer look at Roman, and possibly Greek, fusion welding.

Six different samples of the bronze were analyzed, including several removed from the area of the join. The results are given in Table 2.[16] The

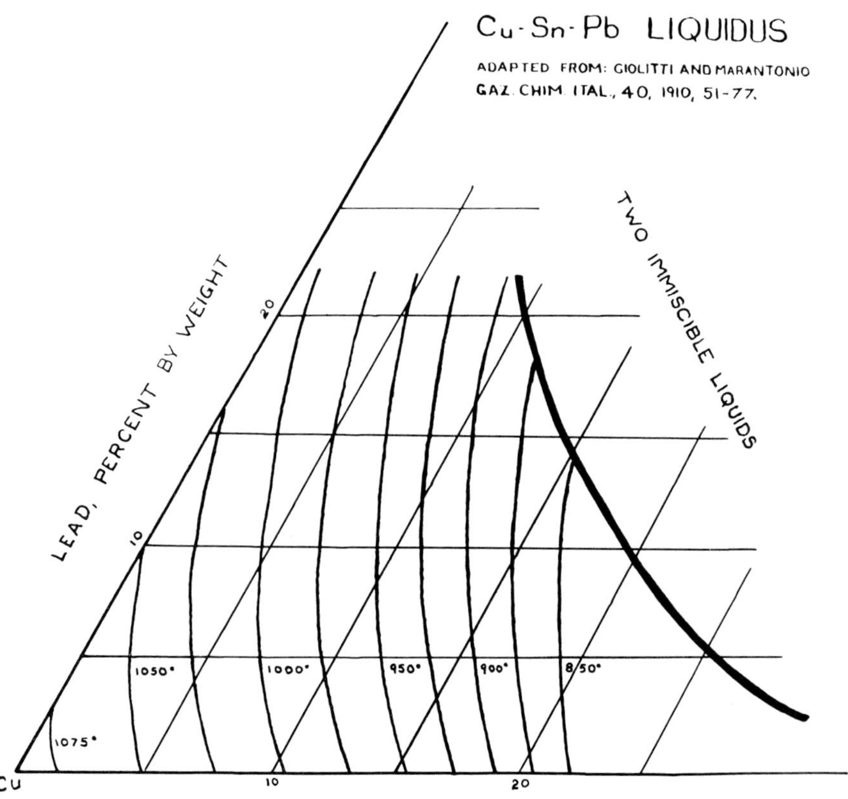

Fig. 31: Liquidus Isotherm diagram for copper-tin-lead ternary alloys.

TABLE 2. COMPOSITION OF BRONZE SAMPLES REMOVED FROM THE ROMAN DRAPERY FRAGMENT (NO. 237)[16]

Sample No.	*Site of Sample*	*Element (Weight per cent)*															
		Cu	Sn	Pb	Ag	Al	As	Bi	Ca	Co	Fe	Ga	Mg	Mn	Ni	Sb	Si	Zn
1	Added metal appearing on inside of left shoulder*	68.5	4.8	19.5	0.04	0.004	0.006	0.005	0.008	0.05	0.05	0.001	0.01	0.005	0.05	0.007	0.007	—
2	Weld metal from join; interior surface	67.7	3.1	19.9	0.04	0.006	0.006	0.005	0.006	0.05	0.07	0.001	0.01	0.005	0.05	0.007	0.007	—
3	Metal from upper piece of casting; interior surface	65.6	3.5	21.9	0.007	0.004	0.01	0.003	0.01	0.05	0.08	0.001	0.009	0.006	0.06	0.007	0.007	0.01
4	Metal from lower piece of casting; interior surface	65.7	6.6	23.8	0.007	0.003	0.007	0.003	0.005	0.05	0.08	0.001	0.005	0.004	0.06	0.007	0.005	0.01
5	Metal from upper piece of casting, removed from section used for metallographic examination (see Fig. 24)	65.5	6.6	24.8	0.02	0.005	0.008	0.004	0.003	0.05	0.07	0.004	0.005	0.003	0.05	0.006	0.004	0.01
6	Metal from lower piece of casting, removed from section used for metallographic examination (see Fig. 24)	54.1	3.7	38.5	0.02	0.005	0.01	0.004	0.005	0.05	0.07	0.004	0.008	0.003	0.05	0.006	0.004	0.01

* It appears that hard-soldering or welding was performed at places on the drapery other than the major join itself, such as at the base of the neck and at the back of the proper left shoulder. Some of this added metal remaining inside the shoulder was sampled for analysis to serve as a comparison with the weld metal of the primary join.

Fig. 32: Roman draped male statue (No. 237). Detail showing the edge from which the section (Fig. 34) through the join was removed for metallographic examination; the raised ridges of two contiguous ovals can be seen on the exterior surface.

Fig. 33: Roman draped male statue (No. 237). The interior surface of the drapery, showing the edge where the section through the join was removed.

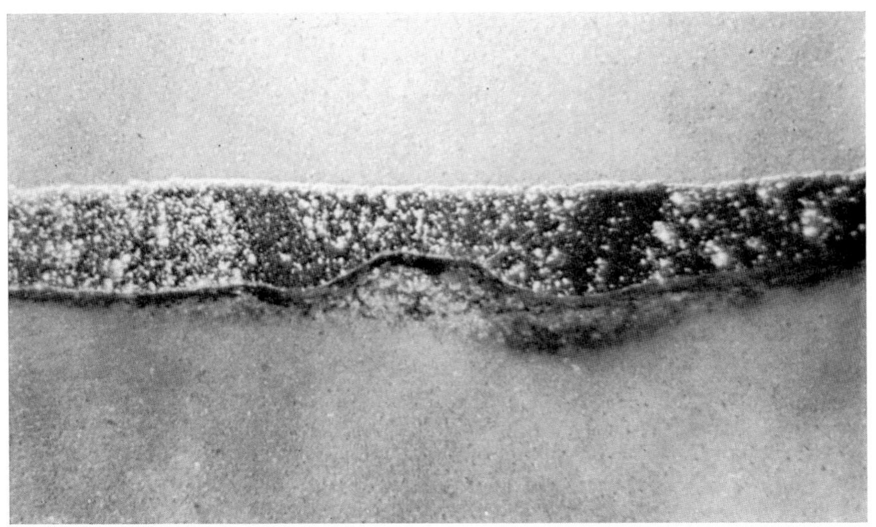

Fig. 34: Roman draped male statue (No. 237). The mounted and polished section of the join removed for metallographic study; the smooth exterior surface is at the top, and the indented, irregular interior surface is at the bottom of the section.

analyses show most clearly that the metal of the upper and lower portions of the main casting and the metal added to achieve the join are virtually identical in composition. This compositional identity would be expected in a true fusion weld. The metal in all the samples is a ternary alloy of copper, tin, and lead with copper the main constituent, about 20 to 25 per cent lead, and only 3 to 7 per cent tin.[17] The melting temperature of this alloy is in the vicinity of 950° C., as is evident from the copper-tin-lead liquidus diagram in Fig. 31. The diagram also shows that a bronze containing approximately 5 per cent tin and no lead has a melting temperature of approximately 1050° C. Thus the large quantity of lead added to the drapery bronze served to lower the melting point of the alloy by about 100° C. Further, it must have made it much easier to cast (the alloy being more fluid and less gassy), probably also easier to weld, and certainly simpler to tool in the finishing operations.

In order to study the actual structure of the metal at the join, a section that included metal from both upper and lower castings was cut from one edge of the drapery through the join.[18] The site of this section on the drapery is shown in Figs. 32 and 33 (the arrows indicate the sawed edge where the section was removed). As is clear in Fig. 32, which shows the outside surface of the bronze, the section was cut through one end of one of the oval patches of the join. Figure 33 gives the corresponding view of the inside of the drapery. A photomacrograph of the mounted and polished section itself, taken with oblique illumination, is illustrated in Fig. 34. The upper part of the cast drapery appears at the left, the lower part at the right, with the weld itself between them. The smooth exterior of the drapery is at the top, the interior below. The small, diffuse white patches throughout the section are globules of lead that have scattered the incident light. The contour of the join is roughly that of a funnel, decreasing in width from the exterior to the interior of the drapery. This is undoubtedly due to the heat gradient that existed across the section at the time that the join was made and indicates that the metal was hotter on the exterior than on the interior surface in this local area. It suggests that the welding was done from the exterior, where the greatest amount of heat was concentrated. The metal in the join must have begun to cool from the inside, gradually solidifying toward the outside surface.

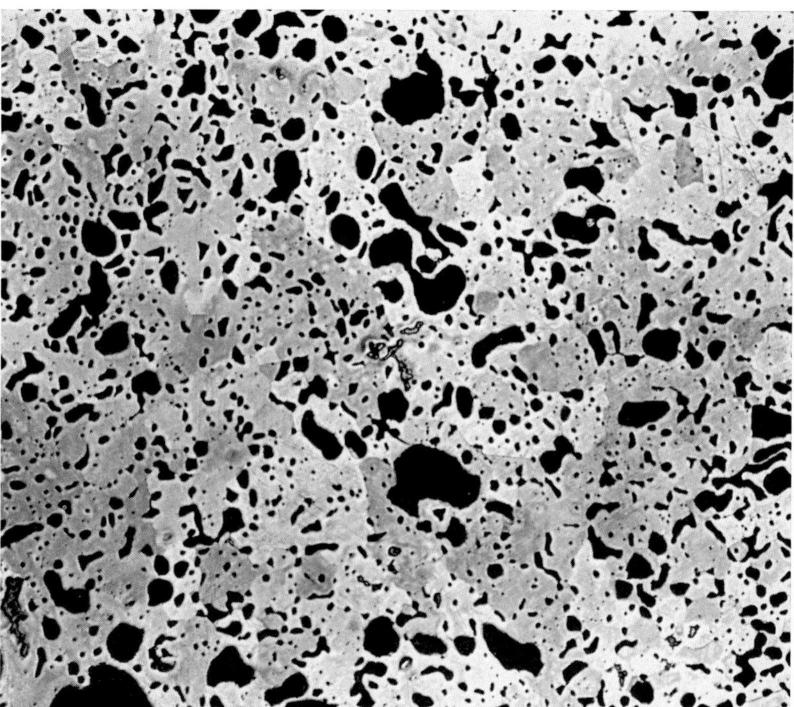

Fig. 35: Photomicrograph of the metal in the cast drapery. Small, cored grains of alpha solid solution of tin in copper are separated by large globules of lead; one patch of eutectoid appears at the center of the field. x *100 Etch: Potassium bichromate.*

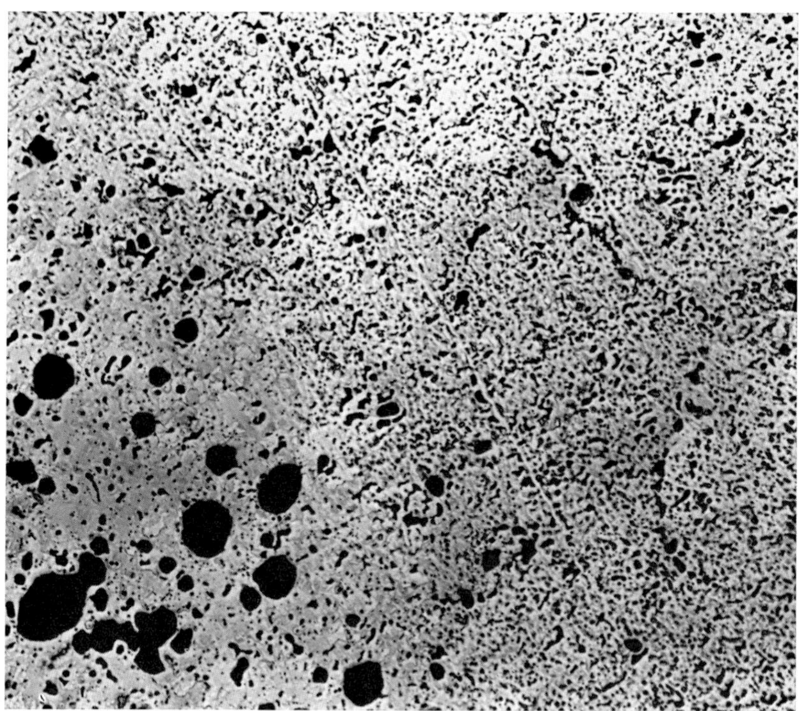

Fig. 36: Photomicrograph of the transition zone between the cast metal of the drapery and the weld metal of the join. Note the complete fusion of the weld metal with the cast metal. x *100 Etch: Potassium bichromate.*

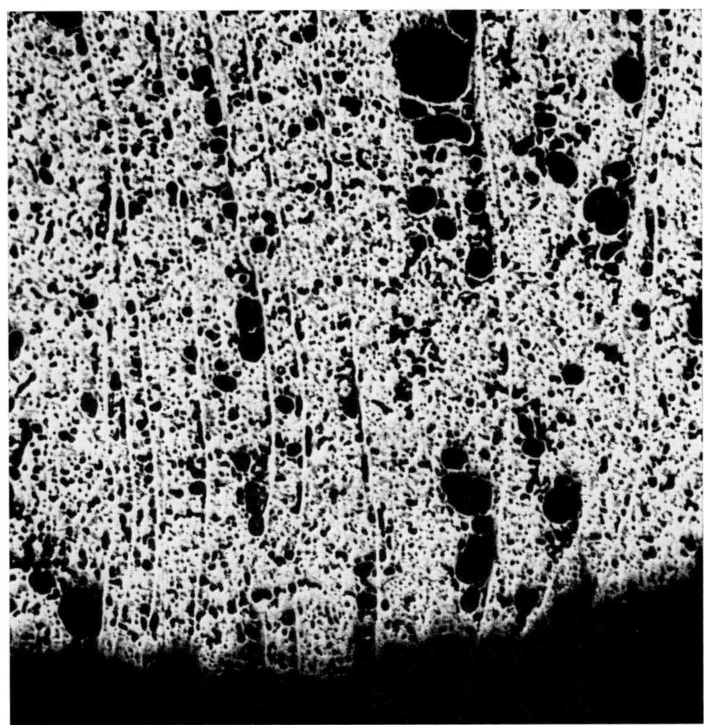

Fig. 37: Photomicrograph of the weld metal within the join at the interior surface of the drapery. Note the fine structure and the "stringers" that run from the surface up into the bulk of the weld metal.

Figures 35 through 38 illustrate the microstructures of the metal at the join. The metal of the drapery itself (Fig. 35) is composed of small, cored grains of the alpha solid solution of copper and tin with the lead, essentially immiscible in the copper-tin solid solution, segregated intergranularly in large globules. The metal is in the as-cast condition. There is very little eutectoid present (one light gray patch of eutectoid can be seen at the center of the field), which indicates that the casting was cooled relatively slowly after it was poured or that it was reheated for the welding.

Between the cast metal and the actual weld metal there is a narrow transition zone where the microstructure is similar to that of the casting, except that the grain size is smaller and there is more eutectoid present than in the cast metal. (Figure 36 shows the microstructure of the casting, the transition zone, and the weld.) Both these phenomena are the result of more rapid solidification of the metal in this zone and would seem to indicate that in the process of welding the edges of the casting at the join melted and then resolidified more rapidly than had the original casting. The most significant aspect of this photomicrograph, however, is the complete fusion of the cast and weld metals, characterized by the continuity of structure between the two. Nowhere can one delineate the precise boundary between them. The microstructure confirms the analytical results and establishes the fact that the join is a true fusion weld.

The weld metal itself (Figs. 37 and 38) shows a similar structure, but it is still finer than that of the transition zone and contains much more eutectoid. It is a structure obtained by quite rapid cooling of the metal. The photomicrograph in Fig. 37 shows the weld metal at the interior surface of the drapery. Both this photograph and Fig. 38 demonstrate that the area of the weld closest to the original edge of the casting is characterized by long, thin "stringers" that grow up and outward from the interior to the exterior surface of the join (i.e., from the region of least

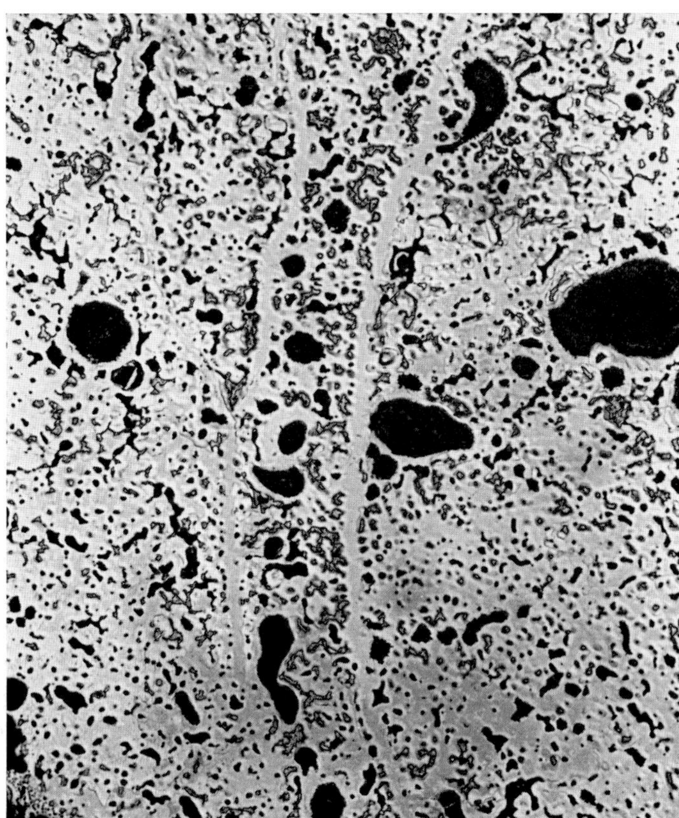

Fig. 38: Photomicrograph of the weld metal within the join. Note the fineness of structure and the density of eutectoid within the weld; the "stringers" appear to be the backbones of dendritic plates that run through the join. x 200 Etch: Potassium bichromate.

heat and more rapid solidification to that of greatest heat and of slower cooling). The more highly magnified detail in Fig. 38 suggests that these "stringers" are actually the backbones of dendrites with small, vestigial arms present along their length, an unusual structure. A section of the weld metal made at right angles to that described here revealed an identical microstructure, indicating that these "stringers" are actually a form of dendritic plate which runs through the join. We assume that the series of concentric ridges, visible in Fig. 32, that appears at the edges of the oval patches as well as within them, bears a close relation to the zone within which the plates occur. We further suppose that the plates themselves represent some form of discontinuity in the cooling and solidification of the weld metal.

Finally it should be pointed out that the grains at the exterior surface of the weld contain slip bands which are apparent because corrosion has penetrated along the slip planes. (These structures are not illustrated here.) These slip bands are the result of cold-working on this surface of the drapery. It is to be expected, of course, that the weld was carefully cleaned after it had cooled so as to be as smooth and unobtrusive as possible.

The evidence of analyses and microstructure demonstrates that this join is a well-fused weld that bonds the upper and lower parts of the drapery with the same metal that was used to fabricate the original casting. It was probably made from the exterior surface and with sufficient heat to melt the edges of the drapery, enabling the liquid weld metal to fuse with those edges and to alloy with them. It appears that at least a portion of the weld metal in the join may have undergone a series of solidifications and remeltings in the course of the joining operation, cooling each time from the edges nearest the casting toward the center. This may have caused the characteristic platelike structure noted above to form, for surely these irregularities within the structure, as well as the ovals themselves, are indicative of some peculiarity of the welding technique.

As for the actual procedure employed for executing the join, we can suggest two alternatives at the moment but hasten to add that until we have tried to duplicate these techniques and others in the laboratory our suggestions must remain hypotheses. The first possibility is that the weld metal was introduced at the join in a solid or pasty state and then heated *in situ* until it melted. The method might have been somewhat as follows.

The two cast pieces of drapery to be joined were clamped together leaving about 0.5 to 1 cm. of space between them. The entire drapery was then supported horizontally, with the exterior surface uppermost, above a charcoal fire placed beneath the general area of the join. A clay channel to contain the weld material had previously been fitted under the area to be joined. Once the edges of the drapery were sufficiently hot, the weld metal was introduced. Greater heat was then concentrated at the join by means of a blowpipe and a small portable heat source, such as pieces of red-hot charcoal. The continuous blasts of heat directed onto the weld metal melted it and the surrounding bronze. If this local heating continued long enough, passing from place to place along the length of the join as each new batch of pasty metal was introduced, all the metal at the join would gradually melt and fuse. The work was done progressively, one small section after another, and the individual ovals might then be explained as puddles caused by the localized application of intense heat to each batch of weld metal. It might further be argued that the concentric ridges within the ovals and the stringlike plates evident in the microstructure of the join are discontinuities in solidification caused by interruptions in heating with the blowpipe. If the heat were applied roughly at the center of each oval, the weld would be alternately melted and solidified with successive blasts of hot air. The metal farthest from the center would cool and solidify first. The next blast of air, however, would again melt the edges of this already solid zone but would not melt all of it. Thus solidification would proceed gradually toward the center of the oval. Since the greatest heat was presumably concentrated at the center of the oval, this region might easily have overheated and burned or cracked on final cooling. Alternatively, shrinkage of the last metal to solidify at the center of each oval may have caused shrinkage cavities to form. Either explanation may account for the numerous holes and the metal plugs used to fill them that exist throughout the join roughly along a line that runs through the centers of the ovals.

An alternative method that would also account for most of the characteristics of this join might be called "puddling," a variant of the kind of casting-on referred to in the discussion of the geometric bird.[19] With this method a channel of some refractory material would again have been fitted underneath the join. But, in addition, a series of molds would have had to be built on top of the join area, with entry and exit openings such that the molten weld metal could be run through each mold continuously until it had melted the edges of the drapery. When in each individual puddling procedure the edges of the drapery had melted, the exit was closed and the weld was allowed to cool. In this way the join might have been "tacked" in a number of places, initially fastening the two pieces of bronze. Afterward the intermediate areas were similarly fused until the work was complete. The considerable length of some of the ovals might be better explained by this method than by the former explanation. But the cooling discontinuities are more difficult to account for in the puddling process unless we can assume that the pouring was not rapid or continuous enough, so that the metal actually solidified in a series of stages, and the melting-back previously described occurred as each new flow of metal was introduced.

In either method, plugs were inserted in the damaged areas of the join, and the whole region was heavily worked to remove uneven areas in the weld. Finally the join was polished so as to be even with the rest of the casting and to blend with it visually. The patina of the join is similar to that of the rest of the bronze. Only the raised concentric ridges in the ovals are somewhat browner than the surrounding areas, due perhaps to some kind of segregation in the alloy in these places that has caused this metal to corrode slightly differently from the rest.

The competence with which this join was made, and by virtue of which it has lasted so long, is testimony to the considerable metallurgical knowledge and skill of the Roman artisans who are responsible for it. They must have had an intimate familiarity with alloys of bronze, with their melting and solidifying properties, with the ways in which the alloys "handled," and they must also have been capable of working with temperatures of the order of 1,000° C. over extensive areas of metal but in a carefully controlled fashion. As with all the other joins we have discussed, the finishing of this one is expert. In fact, the join is only visible on fairly close inspection of the piece and in a favorable light. If the drapery was originally placed at any height from the spectator or at a distance in excess of about ten feet, it would scarcely have been visible.[20] We can probably safely say that it was a feature of the aesthetic of large-scale Roman statuary that joins had to be used for technical reasons but were not to be visually apparent.

Interrelationship of Art and Technology

It seems, then, that it was often thought necessary or desirable to make a bronze statue or statuette in several pieces, which were to be joined after casting. In some respects this reflects the necessity that the artist give way to the foundryman, which is still true today. If it was considered easier to make something in several pieces this was done, and the joins were later made as inconspicuous as possible. The artist may well have added his own finishing touches to the piece by doing some of the final tooling, which would help mask the joins. But the question must then be raised, and will remain unanswered for the present, as to what extent the artist participated in the design of the casting procedure to be used in the production of his work. Were artist, foundryman, and joiner one man, or were they all different individuals with different skills? Over how many of these processes did the artist actually have control? In fact, to what extent is a "master bronze" the product of the work of one man or the collaboration of a team of artist and highly skilled technicians who carried out his designs? Are we even justified in talking about an "artist" in the sense in which we generally use the word and the concept today? What were the arrangements made for large-scale production of vessels, tripods, figurines, in short any of the bronzes that appear to have been made in considerable quantity? To what extent was the choice of a particular method of casting and/or joining dictated by the organization of the workshop, even by the division of labor? To what degree are certain procedures simply the result of traditional practice, and to what degree do they seem innovative? We would hope that insights into at least some of these very large but really fundamental questions can be reached through technical studies — the examination of more and more objects, the reproduction in the laboratory of ancient techniques — which are only one of many avenues of approach open to us.

Even our circumscribed technical examinations of the joining procedures exhibited by the few bronzes we have discussed have already raised questions of a different sort. What governed the type of join used on an object? Why, for example, were the handles of hydrias and other large vessels often soldered instead of riveted to the bodies? The choice must often have been dictated by aesthetic requirements, for each kind of joining process has shapes that are natural and unnatural to it, and often by economic considerations. What factors influenced the use of soft-soldering, hard-soldering, or welding as the metallurgical procedure of choice? Clearly one of the factors was an understanding of the metallurgical properties of alloys. Was this metallurgical knowledge based on practical experience alone, or was it aided in any way by a primitive science of materials? In other words, can we through such studies contribute to an understanding of the interrelationship between ancient science and technology?

All these questions really point to a single area of concern which was, after all, the fundamental reason for the calling of this symposium — the crucial interaction of art and technology. It is to a fuller understanding of and delight in this vital relationship that our efforts are directed.

Acknowledgments

We would like to thank for their cooperation and help during the course of this study the organizers of the exhibition "Master Bronzes from the Classical World," the Conservation Department of the Fogg Art Museum, the Research Laboratory of the Museum of Fine Arts, Boston, and the Ledgemont Laboratory of the Kennecott Copper Corporation. In particular we wish to thank the following individuals for their thoughtful assistance and for the many long hours of discussion of the bronzes in which they cheerfully participated: Mr. Edwin H. Backman, Mr. Arthur C. Beale, Professor Merton C. Flemings, Mrs. Judith E. Moore, Professor Cyril Stanley Smith, and Mr. William J. Young.

H. L.

A. S.

Notes

1 R. J. Gettens, "Joining Methods in the Fabrication of Ancient Chinese Bronze Ceremonial Vessels," *Application of Science in Examination of Works of Art* (Boston: Museum of Fine Arts, 1967), 205-212.

2 Mr. Joseph Ternbach of New York, who found that this technique was used on a similar tripod (in the Virginia Museum of Fine Arts) that he restored in 1964, suggested to us the possibility of its occurrence on this piece.

3 Lead was similarly employed in antiquity as a filler to secure metal clamps set into stone building blocks. The clamps were used in fitting the blocks.

4 H. Drescher, *Der Überfangguss* (Mainz, 1958), especially 165-181; "Untersuchungen zur römischen Löttechnik," *Technische Beiträge zur Archäologie*, I (1959), 65-77; Gettens, "Joining Methods . . ." (n. 1), 212-217.

5 Tin-lead soft solders: Drescher, *Der Überfangguss*, and ". . . *Löttechnik*" (n. 4), *passim*; A. Lucas, *Ancient Egyptian Materials and Industries* (4th ed.; London, 1962), 216, 253, 254; silver solders: *ibid.*, 216; copper-tin hard solders: Gettens, "Joining Methods . . ." (n. 1), 212-217.

6 For example, in the case of the silver solder discussed above, the melting point of 780° C. is quite close to 840° C., the temperature at which a typical bronze containing 10 per cent tin by weight begins to melt (see the copper-tin constitution diagram, Fig. 13), but the bronze is not completely molten until approximately 1020° C.

7 Drescher, ". . . *Löttechnik*" (n. 4), *passim*; he also claims (p. 75) to have seen soft solder on the Vix crater.

8 The temperature required to melt the bronze depends, of course, on its composition. For example, adding increasing amounts of tin or lead to copper will progressively lower the melting point of the alloy (Figs. 13 and 31). If it is foreseen that considerable fusion welding will be needed on the finished casting, the foundryman may choose an alloy that not only melts at a lower temperature but also has good working properties. It is probably because leaded bronze alloys combine these features that they were used for Roman statuary.

9 For an extensive discussion of casting-on and related techniques see Drescher, *Der Überfangguss* (n. 4), *passim.*

10 We were able to study this piece in such detail due to the generosity of its owner, Mr. Norbert Schimmel. He wished the modern restoration removed before the bird was exhibited, and as a result of this the complicated fabrication of this object came to light. It was also found that the head and neck, both legs, and the ring on the back were broken and repaired at some time.

11 All samples were obtained by drilling deeply into the metal of the body and tail. Any corrosion products remaining in the drillings were carefully removed before analysis. Samples 1, 2, and 3 were analyzed by spectrophotometry through the courtesy of Mr. Lawrence P. Zopatti at the Ledgemont Laboratory of the Kennecott Copper Corporation. The maximum error in the tin analyses by this method is ± 5 per cent. Samples 4, 5, and 6 were analyzed by emission spectrography by Mr. Walter Correia at the Central Analytical Laboratory, Department of Metallurgy and Materials Science, M.I.T. The results are semiquantitative for the minor and trace elements present.

12 For a concise explanation of the microstructures of archaeological metal artifacts, see C. S. Smith, "The Interpretation of Microstructures of Metallic Artifacts," *Application of Sciene in Examination of Works of Art* (Boston: Museum of Fine Arts, 1967), 20-52.

13 Miss Judith Garb of Radcliffe College suggested this during discussion in a seminar at Harvard College.

14 K. Kluge and K. Lehmann-Hartleben, *Die Antiken Grossbronzen* (Berlin and Leipzig, 1927), I, 160-169.

15 S. Delbourgo, "L'étude au laboratoire d'une statue découverte à Agde," *Bulletin du Laboratoire du Musée du Louvre*, 1966, 7-12. The composition of this bronze statue (Delbourgo, 10-11) is very similar to that of the Roman drapery from the Museum of Fine Arts, Boston (see Table 2).

16 Samples 1, 2, 3, and 4 were obtained by removing a number of the many nodular protuberances of solid metal on the inside of the casting. Samples 5 and 6 were relatively large pieces of metal sawed from either end of the section removed from the join. The determination of copper was by electrolytic deposition, of lead by the standard methods of gravimetric analysis, and of tin by volumetric analysis. The maximum error in the tin and lead values is of the order of ± 10 per cent. The analyses were made by Mr. Donald L. Guernsey at the Central Analytical Laboratory, Department of Metallurgy and Materials Science, M.I.T. The trace element composition was determined by emission spectrography, and the results are semiquantitative. The analyses were made by Mr. Walter Correia at the M.I.T. Laboratory.

17 As is clear from Professor Caley's analyses of Roman statuary bronzes (see pp. 43 ff.), this is a rather common alloy during the Empire.

18 The section was removed by Mr. William Young at the Museum of Fine Arts, Boston, and it was through his courtesy that we were able to examine it metallographically.

19 Since this paper was written, some experiments have been conducted using the puddling method with the same alloy as that of this drapery. The results show that this method is feasible for producing this kind of join.

20 The many joins present on the famous "Lady from the Sea," found near Bodrum, Turkey, are even less evident than is the join on the Roman drapery. It was only discovered on very close scrutiny and by looking inside the hollow bust that this statue was made from several pieces that were carefully joined. See B. S. Ridgway, "The Lady from the Sea: A Greek Bronze in Turkey," *AJA*, LXXI (1967), 329-334. Had the arms on the Bacchus from Avenches (No. 246) not broken off, the joins would hardly have been visible. In fact, the proper left leg of this statue is almost certainly attached to the body in the same way that the arms were once attached, and one sees at the junction of the leg and the body the characteristic ovals that follow the line of the join.

Chemical Composition of Greek and Roman Statuary Bronzes

Earle R. Caley

In contrast to the abundance of knowledge about Greek and Roman statuary bronzes from the standpoint of form, little is known about them from the standpoint of chemical composition. Less than 25 quantitative analyses of the metal of such bronzes have previously been published,[1] and the reliability of some of these analyses is open to question. One element of uncertainty common to most of the analyses is the lack of information as to how the sample for analysis was obtained. Apparently almost all the analyses were made on single samples taken from some one part of a statue or statuette. If a large statue is so sampled, especially one cast in piece molds, the analysis may well represent the composition of that one part of the statue but not the average composition of the statue as a whole. On the other hand, a single sample taken from a small statuette may well represent its average composition. From this standpoint it is fortunate that over half the analyses were made on samples taken from statuettes or small statues.

Another less important element of uncertainty in respect to sampling procedure is that the size of the sample is never stated. In view of the general heterogeneity of ancient statuary bronzes, especially those containing high proportions of lead, a sample that is too small may not be representative of average composition. However, since all the analyses appear to have been made on a macro scale with analytical samples weighing around a gram, this possible source of error is probably not serious. The possibility that corrosion products were included in the samples seems unlikely since most of the analysts indicate or state that clean metal was analyzed.

One serious defect of some of the analyses is that no determinations were made of the minor components or impurities present in the bronzes. In the other analyses most of the usual ones were determined, but the accuracy of the methods employed for some of the determinations is questionable. Hence valid comparisons among the analyses in respect to the reported percentages of the lesser components are not possible. In view of this, and in view of the doubtful accuracy of some of the determinations, only the totals of the reported percentages of these components are listed in the tables. These serve as approximate indications of the purity of the bronzes. Accurate individual percentages obtained in a few recent analyses are listed in the references to the analysts and publications.

The reported percentages of the main components, tin, lead, and copper, cannot be uncritically accepted as being without error. All the analysts used a method for the determination of tin that is known to yield high results.[2] In this method the sample of bronze is treated with nitric acid to produce a residue of insoluble hydrated tin oxide that contains all the tin. This residue is filtered off and weighed after proper heat treatment. The weight of the tin present is then calculated on the assumption that the tin oxide is pure, though as a matter of fact it contains adsorbed metal oxides, principally copper oxide. The average relative error in the percentage of tin found in this way is about 10 per cent for the range of proportions of tin found in statuary bronzes; i.e., if the reported percentage of tin is 11 per cent, the real percentage is only about 10 per cent. However, since the reported percentages of tin are all about equally in error, a comparison of the analyses among themselves with respect to proportions of tin will lead to essentially the same conclusions as would a comparison based on the exact percentages.

Since the positive error in the determination of tin is largely caused by the presence of copper in the tin oxide, the reported percentages of copper will be too low if this is the sole source of error in the determination of the copper. But this is often not the sole cause, for in about half the analyses the copper was apparently estimated by difference, i.e., by subtracting the determined percentages of the other components from 100 per cent. When the minor components or impurities were not determined at all, or when not all of them were determined, the reported percentages of copper tended to be too high. Therefore, the reported percentages of copper are either too high or too low, unless by a fortunate compensation of errors the figures happen to be exact. Since the methods used for the determination of lead are fairly accurate, the reported percentages of this component should be less in error than those of tin or copper. In general fine distinctions with respect to the stated proportions of the main components cannot be made when the analyses are compared with one another.

Most of the analysts give very little descriptive information about the statues or statuettes they analyzed. Often they say nothing about their location, general appearance, or state of preservation. Even exact statements about their size are sometimes lacking. Except for one analyst who included photographic views of the objects he investigated, the analytical reports are without illustrations. Although many of the objects evidently came from, or were in, museums at the time they were analyzed, the information is so meager that the museums cannot now be identified and the present location of most of the objects is unknown. Information about the provenance of most of the statues or statuettes that were analyzed is also meager or entirely lacking. Possibly more information on this point was available at the time but was either not given to the analysts or not reported by them. Most of the objects appear to be classified as Greek or Roman on stylistic grounds alone. The findspots of the few excavated objects are given, but these of course are often not the places where the objects were made. Even more uncertain are the dates of manufacture of these objects. Although the dates of burial of such objects may often be approximated by their position in strata or by the dates of associated objects, such as coins, the dates of manufacture may be much earlier. In the tables in this paper I indicates that the provenance of a given object is known approximately, II that the findspot is known but not the date, and III that the provenance is unknown.

In spite of the defects in the analyses and the gaps in the information about the objects that have been analyzed, a considerable residue of important facts remains. The following discussions of the several analyses are largely based on these facts, but certain supplemental facts from other sources are introduced for the purpose of properly interpreting the analytical data.

Greek Statuary Bronzes

There is no unequivocal evidence that any of the statues or statuettes that have been analyzed are of earlier date than the third century B.C., but it seems probable that four of the objects are earlier, though not as early as the fifth century. The analyses of these objects are listed in Table I. As is indicated, only the first analysis in the table is of an object of definite provenance. This object was part of a bronze hoard consisting of the arms and parts of the arms of at least two statues, found on the island of Antikythera. All the pieces were much corroded. The sample for analysis was taken from the uncorroded metal core of a separated hand. On the basis of the archaeological evidence the date of this hoard is third century B.C., but since the hoard consisted of bronze scrap, the original statues from which the various pieces came were probably much older. A fourth-century B.C. date seems very likely. Rhousopoulos also made a qualitative analysis of a sphericle of unaltered metal taken from the interior of a large intact bronze statue found in the sea in the neighborhood of the island of Kythera. Although he does not so state, the photographic illustration in his report shows beyond doubt that this is the famous large statue of an athlete now in the National Museum in Athens.[3] On the basis of style this statue is generally agreed to be fourth century B.C. in date, and some consider it to belong to the first half of the century. The only metals found by the qualitative analysis were tin and copper. Some minor components or impurities that must have been present evidently escaped detection. It will be noted that tin and copper were the only components reported in the bronze from Antikythera. This bronze is remarkable for containing the highest proportion of tin so far found in any Greek or Roman statuary bronze.

TABLE I

Composition of Greek Statuary Bronzes

No.	*Certainty of Provenance*	*Tin* %	*Lead* %	*Copper* %	*Other Metals* %
1	I	14.29	none	84.74	—
2	III	11.46	none	88.54	—
3	III	10.13	none	88.51	1.36
4	III	9.22	none	89.96	0.82

Analysts and Publications

1. O. A. Rhousopoulos. Published in P. Diergart, *Beiträge aus der Geschichte der Chemie dem Gedächtnis von Georg W. A. Kahlbaum* (Leipzig and Vienna, 1909), 187.
2. F. Göbel, *Über den Einfluß der Chemie auf die Ermittelung der Völker der Vorzeit oder Resultate der chemischen Untersuchung metallischer Alterthümer* (Erlangen, 1842), 23.
3. E. von Bibra, *Die Bronzen und Kupferlegierungen der alten und ältesten Völker* (Erlangen, 1869), 88-89.
4. E. von Bibra, *ibid.*

The second analysis listed in Table I is of a female figure said to be of fine style, but whether it is a statue or a statuette is not stated. The third analysis is of a statuette 6.2 cm. high, which is not otherwise described, and the fourth analysis is of a fragment of a statuette.

That lead was entirely absent from all five of these bronzes is very improbable. Its apparent absence is probably due to the use of analytical methods not sensitive enough to detect very low proportions. However, it is clear that lead was not an intentional component of any of these bronzes, which may be taken as evidence of early date, for lead has not been found to be an intentional component in Greek bronze objects of any kind made before the Hellenistic period. The average proportion of lead found by Davies[4] in twelve corroded pins, earrings, and shapeless fragments from the Argive Heraeum was only 0.66 per cent, and this, when recalculated for the uncorroded metal, is still only about 0.73 per cent. Lead was apparently absent from three of these objects. The same investigator found an average of only 0.17 per cent lead in five miscellaneous early objects from five other Greek sites, and this, when recalculated for the uncorroded metal, is only about 0.21 per cent. Lead was apparently absent from two of the objects. All these bronzes were of various early dates, and none was as late as the fourth century B.C. The occurrence of lead in low proportion in objects known to be of fourth-century date is shown by the composition of the bronze coins of Alexander the Great. Results of all the known analyses are listed in Table II. It will be seen that only one of the results for lead content exceeds 1 per cent. Even this exceptional result is probably not an indication of the intentional addition of lead. The average lead content of the coins is only 0.55 per cent. Also of some significance is the high tin content of some of them and their high average tin content of 11.86 per cent. The average tin content of the four bronzes of Table I is 11.29 per cent. Perhaps there is no sound reason for drawing conclusions about the composition of early Greek statuary bronzes from what is known about the composition of other contemporaneous bronzes, but it seems to be more than a coincidence that lead is not present as an intentional component in these other bronzes or in the few Greek statuary bronzes so far analyzed. Apparently the practice of adding lead in bronze manufacture was a later development. Therefore, it seems reasonable to conclude from all the present evidence that statuary bronzes made before the Hellenistic period do not contain lead as an intentional ingredient. Another less certain characteristic of early Greek statuary bronzes seems to be their generally high tin content.

TABLE II

Analyses of Bronze Coins of Alexander the Great

No.	*Tin* %	*Lead* %	*Copper* %	*Other Metals* %
1	14.34	0.30	85.04	0.32
2	13.14	0.02	86.52	0.14
3	13.02	none	86.87	—
4	13.02	0.06	86.67	0.26
5	11.81	0.04	87.81	0.35
6	11.70	trace	87.72	0.65
7	9.71	1.00	88.25	1.04
8	8.15	2.97	88.52	0.36

Analysts and Publications

Nos. 1, 6, and 7 were analyzed by E. von Bibra, *Bronzen und Kupferlegierungen* (Table I, n. 3), 86-87, and No. 3 by J. A. Phillips, *Journal of the Chemical Society*, London, IV (1852), 268-269. Nos. 2 and 4 were analyzed by E. R. Caley and P. J. Elving, No. 5 by R. L. McEwen, and No. 8 by T. L. Moore. These were published by E. R. Caley, "The Composition of Ancient Greek Bronze Coins," *Memoirs of the American Philosophical Society*, XI (Philadelphia, 1939), 16.

TABLE III

Composition of Uncertain Greek or Hellenistic Statuary Bronzes

No.	*Certainty of Provenance*	*Tin* %	*Lead* %	*Copper* %	*Other Metals* %
1	II	11.05	7.91	80.61	0.43
2	III	10.13	5.25	80.91	0.43
3	II	7.00	0.13	92.28	0.43
4	II	6.09	4.87	89.04	—

Analysts and Publications

1. L. R. von Fellenberg, *Mitteilungen der Naturforschenden Gesellschaft in Bern* (1861), 173-187, Analysis No. 91.
2. E. von Bibra, *Bronzen und Kupferlegierungen* (Table I, n. 3), 88-89.
3. W. H. Deebel. Published by E. R. Caley, *Ohio Journal of Science*, LI (1951), 6-12. The following results were obtained for the minor components or impurities: Iron = 0.16%; Nickel = 0.05%; Zinc = 0.22%; Gold, Silver, Arsenic, Sulfur = none.
4. K. Natterer, *Monatshefte für Chemie*, XXI (1900), 256-262.

Four other analyses have been made of a statue and three statuettes that seem to be Greek in origin. These analyses are listed in Table III. The first analysis in the table is of a statuette of Artemis, 10 cm. high, found at Pagonda on the island of Euboea. Except for the findspot, evidence of Greek manufacture is lacking. The rather high lead content indicates that it was not made before the Hellenistic period, and in fact its lead content is high enough to suggest a Roman origin. Possibly this statuette was made late in the Hellenistic period. The second analysis is of a fragment of a statuette not otherwise described. Here again the lead content does not indicate a date before the Hellenistic period. The third analysis is of the metal core of a severely corroded female statuette about 10 cm. high, found in the filling of an abandoned well in the Athenian Agora along with various other bronze objects. The results shown are weighted figures from analyses of two cross sections of the core. Although the date of the deposit is about the middle of the second century A.D., the very low proportion of lead in the metal of this statuette does not indicate manufacture in Roman times, for Roman statuary bronze almost invariably contains moderate-to-high proportions of lead. On the other hand, the rather low proportion of tin does not indicate that it was made before Hellenistic times. Manufacture in the Hellenistic period therefore seems likely. The fourth analysis is of metal from a corroded fragmentary statue of an athlete found in the Roman Forum at Ephesus. In spite of the findspot this object has been ascribed to the fourth century B.C. The results of the analysis do not indicate such an early date, for the tin content is too low and the lead content too high. It may even be Roman, though manufacture in the Hellenistic period is not unlikely.

Any comparison of the analyses of Table III with the composition of a variety of bronze objects made in the Hellenistic period is impossible because virtually no other kinds of such objects, except coins, have been analyzed. Many analyses have been made of coins of various dates. The composition of one group of coins of the third century B.C., for example, is shown in Table IV, in which are listed all known analyses of bronze

Table IV

Analyses of Bronze Coins of Antigonus Gonatas

No.	Tin %	Lead %	Copper %	Other Metals %
1	13.77	1.34	84.53	0.36
2	11.66	0.46	87.80	—
3	8.24	4.66	86.80	0.33
4	8.12	1.17	90.78	—
5	7.01	3.18	89.02	0.66
6	6.88	1.82	90.78	0.52
7	6.48	4.45	88.68	0.54

Analysts and Publications

Nos. 1 and 6 were analyzed by E. von Bibra, *Bronzen und Kupferlegierungen* (Table I, n. 3), 86-87, and the others by E. R. Caley, *Mem. Amer. Phil. Soc.*, 1939 (Table II), 16.

Table V

Analyses of Late Hellenistic Bronze Coins of Athens

No.	Tin %	Lead %	Copper %
1	8.54	9.93	81.25
2	8.25	15.31	75.13
3	7.96	12.33	78.42
4	6.59	17.49	74.99
5	7.54	18.82	73.16
6	6.02	17.72	75.73
7	6.89	18.68	73.60
8	6.29	22.73	70.25

Analysts and Publication

No. 6 was analyzed by R. L. Wicinski and the others by E. R. Caley. Published in M. Thompson, *The New Style Silver Coinage of Athens* (New York: The American Numismatic Society, 1961), 640.

coins of Antigonus Gonatas of Macedon (277—239 B.C.). A comparison of these analyses with those in Table II shows the chronological changes in the composition of the coinage bronze in one particular series. In those struck in the third century B.C. the tin content is generally lower and the lead content generally higher. The lead content of coins struck later in the Hellenistic period is often much higher, as is shown by the analyses of new style bronze coins of Athens listed in Table V. If these chronological changes in the composition of coinage bronze are any indication of the changes in the composition of bronze of all sorts, it would seem that Hellenistic statuary bronze should have a lower tin content and a higher lead content than earlier statuary bronze. The actual existence of such a difference in composition can be established only by analyses of statuary

TABLE VI

Composition of Roman Statuary Bronzes — Group A

No.	*Certainty of Provenance*	*Tin* %	*Lead* %	*Copper* %	*Other Metals* %
1	II	10.77	10.24	78.33	0.66
2	III	10.72	2.01	87.16	traces (?)
3	II	10.02	9.30	78.36	0.72
4	I	9.44	7.68	80.70	1.72
5	III	6.23	6.20	87.36	0.21

Analysts and Publications

1. L. R. von Fellenberg, *Mitteilungen der Naturforschenden Gesellschaft in Bern* (1863), 135-142, Analysis No. 143.
2. W. Flight, *Journal of the Chemical Society, London*, XLI (1882), 134-135.
3. W. Flight, *ibid.*
4. Arnaudon, *Bulletin de la Société chimique de France*, I (1860), 245.
5. E. von Bibra, *Bronzen und Kupferlegierungen* (Table I, n. 3), 72-73.

bronzes known beyond question to be of Hellenistic date. At present no such analyses are available.

Roman Statuary Bronzes

In an attempt to bring some order into the analyses of Roman statuary bronzes, they have been rather arbitrarily divided into three groups. Group A (Table VI) includes those bronzes in which the ratio of the percentage of lead to the percentage of tin is less than one, Group B (Table VII) includes those in which the ratio is at least one but less than two, and Group C (Table VIII) includes those in which the ratio exceeds two. As will be shown later, this grouping may have some chronological significance.

The first analysis listed in Table VI is of metal from a large gilded statue found at Finthen, Germany. An adequate description is lacking, and its date is uncertain. The alloy of this object contains the highest proportion of tin so far found in Roman statuary bronze. The second analysis in this table is of a statue of a boy holding a bunch of grapes. At the time of the analysis, at least, this object was in the Blacas Collection of the British Museum. The alloy of this statue is remarkable because it contains by far the lowest proportion of lead so far found in Roman statuary bronze. The third analysis is of a part of a statue of Mercury found on the site of the Old India House, Leadenhall Street, London. Although its date is uncertain, it probably belongs to the period of the early Roman occupation of Britain. The fourth analysis is of considerable importance because the provenance of the object is virtually certain. The analyst simply stated that the analysis was of a statue of Victory found at Brescia, Italy, but in all probability this is the famous statue of Victory found in the Roman Forum at Brescia in 1826.[5] Its date is very probably first century A.D. The last analysis in Table VI is of a fragment of an animal statuette, probably that of a lion. Its provenance is completely unknown.

TABLE VII

Composition of Roman Statuary Bronzes — Group B

No.	Certainty of Provenance	Tin %	Lead %	Copper %	Other Metals %
1	II	9.33	9.34	81.23	0.10
2	III	9.03	12.07	78.77	0.13
3	III	8.99	10.03	79.83	0.34
4	III	8.13	10.00	80.65	1.22
5	I	8.10	11.41	79.05	0.05
6	III	7.33	12.11	76.03	4.43
7	II	6.44	9.97	80.70	—

Analysts and Publications

1. L. R. von Fellenberg, *Mitteilungen der Naturforschenden Gesellschaft in Bern* (1865), 1-20, Analysis No. 198.
2. E. von Bibra, *Bronzen und Kupferlegierungen* (Table I, n. 3), 72-73.
3. E. R. Caley, not previously published. The following results were obtained for the minor components or impurities: Iron = 0.30 %; Nickel = 0.04 %; Zinc = trace.
4. E. von Bibra, *(supra,* n. 2), 72-73.
5. E. R. Caley and W. H. Deebel, not previously published. The following results were obtained for the minor components or impurities: Iron = trace; Nickel = 0.05 %; Zinc = trace; Gold, Silver = none.
6. E. von Bibra (*supra*, n. 2), 72-73. Zinc was found to be 3.03 %.
7. Wingham. Published by W. Gowland, *Journal of the Institute of Metals*, VII (1912), 24.

TABLE VIII

Composition of Roman Statuary Bronzes — Group C

No.	Certainty of Provenance	Tin %	Lead %	Copper %	Other Metals %
1	II	8.19	19.01	72.63	0.17
2	III	7.67	22.62	65.95	0.46
3	II	6.77	24.46	68.62	0.15
4	III	4.22	9.13	85.64	1.00
5	I	3.74	34.45	60.40	1.14

Analysts and Publications

1. L. R. von Fellenberg, *Mitteilungen der Naturforschenden Gesellschaft in Bern* (1865), 1-20, Analysis No. 199.
2. E. R. Caley, not previously published. The following results were obtained for the minor components or impurities: Iron = 0.40 %; Nickel = 0.06 %; Zinc, Gold, Silver = none. Considerable oxygen was present in the form of cuprous oxide.
3. L. R. von Fellenberg (*supra*, n. 1), 1-20, Analysis No. 197.
4. E. von Bibra, *Bronzen und Kupferlegierungen* (Table I, n. 3), 72-73.
5. V. Sheipline. Published by E. R. Caley, *Ohio Journal of Science*, LI (1951), 6-12. The following results were obtained for the minor components or impurities: Iron = 0.33 %; Nickel = 0.09 %; Zinc = 0.40 %; Silver = 0.22 %; Gold, Arsenic, Sulfur = none.

The first analysis listed in Table VII is of metal taken from the base of a statue of a youth, found at Bern, Switzerland. As in the last analysis listed in Table VI, the proportions of tin and lead are almost identical. The second analysis of Table VII is of a statuette of Minerva only 5.5 cm. high. The third analysis in this table is of a statuette of Diana 31 cm. high, which was submitted for technical study by the Toledo (Ohio) Museum of Art.[6] The sample for analysis was drilled from an inconspicuous place under the tunic. Slightly corroded metal was present in the drillings that were analyzed. The fourth analysis is of a statuette 8.4 cm. high, not otherwise described. The fifth analysis in the table is of a sample of metal weighing eight grams taken from the body of a horse that was part of a gilded equestrian group of large size recently excavated at Ancona, Italy. This group is first century A.D. in date. Because of the certain provenance of the object this analysis is of considerable importance. The sixth analysis is of a statuette of Victory only 6.0 cm. high. The zinc content of the alloy is unusually high. The last analysis of Table VII is of a figure of Apollo. Unfortunately, the report of this analysis is inadequate in various ways. The size of the figure is not given, so that it is uncertain whether it is a sizeable statue or a statuette. It is listed as a Gallo-Roman bronze, from which it would appear that it was found in France, but no site is named. Finally, its date is stated to be first century A.D., but no evidence for this is given.

The first analysis listed in Table VIII is of a votive figure bearing the inscription: DEAE NARIAE REG. ARVRE. CUR. FEROC. L. It is believed to have been found at Bern, Switzerland. The second analysis is of a heavily patinated, solid female bust 5.0 cm. high, provided with a small central hole in the underside for attachment to a support of some sort. It is now in the author's collection. The sample for analysis was taken by drilling into this hole. The drillings showed that this object is much corroded internally. The third analysis is of the base of a votive figure bearing the inscription: DEAE ARTIONI LINCINIA SABINILLA. It was excavated at Bern, Switzerland. The fourth analysis is of statuette 8.0 cm. high, not otherwise described. The last analysis in Table VIII is of the solid core of a severely corroded animal statuette, probably that of a stag, about 6.0 cm. long and 4.5 cm. high. This was found in the filling of an abandoned well in the Athenian Agora along with various other bronze objects. The date of the deposit is about the middle of the second century A.D., and this statuette may be of second-century manufacture, though an earlier date is not improbable. The results shown in the table are weighted averages from analyses of two cross sections of the core. The alloy of this object is remarkable for containing the lowest proportion of tin and the highest proportion of lead so far found in any Roman statuary bronze.

Certain significant data taken or derived from Tables VI, VII, VIII, and the corresponding descriptive matter are listed Table IX. The increasing ratio of percentage of lead to percentage of tin is the basis for the serial arrangement of the data in this table. Contrary to what might be expected, the percentages of tin do not decrease in regular order as this ratio increases. However, the general trend toward an inverse relationship is obvious. The ratios of lead to tin in the bronzes of Group A are, with the exception of the one very low figure, rather close to each other, and the ratios in Group B are regularly spaced. A considerable gap exists between the last ratio of Group B and the first ratio of Group C, and the ratios in this latter

TABLE IX

Summary of Selected Data on Roman Statuary Bronzes

Group	*No.*	*Tin* %	*Lead/Tin Ratio*	*Size*	*Century A.D.*
A	2	10.72	0.19	Medium	
	4	9.44	0.81	Large	I
	3	10.02	0.93	Medium (?)	
	1	10.77	0.95	Large	
	5	6.23	0.99	Small	
B	1	9.33	1.00	Medium (?)	
	3	8.99	1.12	Medium	
	4	8.13	1.23	Small	
	2	9.03	1.33	Small	
	5	8.10	1.41	Large	I
	7	6.44	1.55	?	I (?)
	6	7.33	1.65	Small	
C	4	4.22	2.16	Small	
	1	8.19	2.32	?	
	2	7.67	2.95	Small	
	3	6.77	3.61	?	
	5	3.74	9.24	Small	II (?)

group differ much more widely than those of the other two groups. Possibly the bronzes of Group C reflect a different practice in statuary bronze manufacture, or it might be that they were made in a different region or at a different period. However, these irregularities in the distribution of the ratios may be a mere accidental effect arising from the insufficient data obtained from the few analyses so far made. It is entirely possible that the ratios of percentages of lead to percentages of tin would take the form of a continuous regular series if a large number of bronzes were analyzed.

From the data of Table IX it would appear that the percentage of tin is usually higher and the ratio of percentage of lead to percentage of tin is usually lower in statuary of large and medium size than in small statuettes. This may indicate that the composition of the bronze employed for the manufacture of these hollow-cast objects was usually different from that employed for making solid small objects. There is a slight indication from Table IX that the larger objects with their lower lead to tin ratios are of earlier date.

The Bronze Recipes of Pliny

The recipes given by Pliny in his *Natural History* are the only ancient sources of information on the quantitative composition of Roman bronzes. Although this author often mixes fact with fable, there would seem to be little room for the latter in simple factual recipes. It is therefore likely that his statements on this particular subject correspond to actual practice in Roman bronze manufacture at the time that he wrote, i.e., around the middle of the first century A.D. However, his recipes are by no means free from ambiguity. One reason for this ambiguity is that his word *aes* denotes both copper and bronze, and another is that his word *plumbum*, when unmodified, denotes both tin and lead. Fortunately, lead is usually distinguished as *plumbum nigrum*. Another ingredient is *plumbum argentinum*, or simply *argentarium*, which was not an alloy of lead and silver, as these terms seem to imply, but an alloy composed of equal parts of tin and lead. In the following translations the term "tin-lead alloy" denotes this ingredient. These translations are of the most pertinent passages in Book XXXIV, sections 95 to 98, of the *Natural History*.

Recipe A

Of the other kinds Campanian carries off the palm, and is in high favor for utensils and vessels . . . ten pounds of Spanish tin-lead alloy are added to each hundred pounds of copper.

Recipe B

A variety which resembles Campanian is made in many parts of Italy and in many provinces, but they add eight pounds of tin (lead?).

Recipe C

The same alloy is used for tablets as for statues, and is made in this way: The metal (copper?) is first fused and one-third as much scrap bronze, from old vessels that have been bought, is added . . . twelve and a half pounds of tin-lead alloy are added to each hundred pounds of molten metal.

Recipe D

The name mold-bronze is given to that blend which produces the most delicate product, for the addition of a tenth part of lead and a twentieth part of tin-lead alloy enables it to acquire the so-called Greek color.

The theoretical composition of the bronzes produced by the use of these recipes may be readily calculated if various assumptions are made. A necessary general assumption is that the proportions of the ingredients were the same before and after melting, in spite of losses from oxidation and volatilization. Certain special assumptions, which are mentioned, were also used in calculating the compositions.

Recipes A and B are of importance only for calculating the composition of the statuary bronzes produced by Recipes C and D. The bronze produced by the use of Recipe A would contain about 4.5 per cent tin and 4.5 per cent lead if the copper used as the main ingredient was entirely pure. On the same assumption, the bronze produced by the use of Recipe B would contain about 7.4 per cent tin and no lead, if the unmodified word *plumbum* in the recipe denotes tin, which seems very probable. If it denotes lead, then the alloy would contain about 7.4 per cent lead and no tin, but this would not be a bronze, at least in the modern sense. Since small percentages of tin, lead, or both were always present in what the Romans considered to be pure copper, these theoretical percentages are slightly lower than they were in the real alloys produced by the use of Recipes A and B.

If the main ingredient for Recipe C was pure copper and the scrap bronze added in the form of old vessels had the theoretical composition of the alloy of Recipe A, then the statuary bronze produced by the use of Recipe C would contain about 6.6 per cent tin and 6.6 per cent lead. These percentages are close to the percentages of tin and lead in analysis No. 5 of Table VI. If the scrap bronze had the composition of that made by Recipe B with tin as the alloying ingredient, the statuary bronze produced by the use of Recipe C would contain about 7.2 per cent tin and 5.6 per cent lead. These percentages do not correspond to any found up to now by analysis.

Copper is not actually named as the main ingredient in Recipe C. It could very well have been that this ingredient was often a mixture of copper and miscellaneous scrap bronze such as that left over from the previous casting of bronze statuary. If it is assumed, for example, that the main ingredient consisted of half copper and half statuary bronze of the composition of analysis No. 2 of Table VI and that the scrap vessels had the theoretical composition of the alloy of Recipe A, then the resulting statuary bronze would contain about 9.7 per cent tin and 9.1 per cent lead. These percentages are fairly close to the percentages of these metals in analysis No. 3 of Table VI. Or again, if it is assumed that half the main ingredient was statuary bronze of the composition of analysis No. 6 of Table VII, and that the other ingredients were as before, then the resulting statuary bronze would contain about 8.7 per cent tin and 10.0 per cent lead. These percentages are close to those of analysis No. 2 of Table VII. On the basis of reasonable assumptions of this sort, the calculated theoretical compositions come close to the real compositions found by analysis for those statuary bronzes in which the ratio of percentage of lead to percentage of tin is around one. For analyses in which this ratio is as much as two, no such agreement is possible for theoretical compositions calculated for Recipe C.

The use of Recipe D would produce bronzes in which the ratio of percentage of lead to percentage of tin is as high as any found by analysis. This recipe seems defective because no main ingredient is mentioned. It could not have been copper alone, for the theoretical composition of an alloy with this as the only main ingredient is 2.2 per cent tin and 10.9 per cent lead, percentages that differ widely from those found by analysis in Roman bronze of any kind. The main ingredient could have been a mixture of copper and bronze, probably scrap bronze, or scrap bronze alone. Another possibility is that the main ingredient for Recipe D was statuary bronze prepared by means of Recipe C and that Recipe D was merely the finishing step in the preparation of certain statuary bronzes. As to the first possibility, if it is assumed that the main ingredient was half pure copper and half statuary bronze of the composition of analysis No. 2 of Table VI, the bronze produced by the use of Recipe D would contain about 6.8 per cent tin and 11.8 per cent lead. These percentages are similar to those of analysis No. 6 of Table VII. If it is assumed that the main ingredient was entirely scrap bronze having the composition represented by analysis No. 6 of Table VII, then the statuary bronze produced by the use of Recipe D would contain about 7.8 per cent tin and 19.5 per cent lead, percentages not very different from those of analysis No. 1 of Table VIII. On the basis of such assumptions as to the identity of the main ingredient, the calculated theoretical compositions come close to the real compositions as found by analysis for statuary bronzes in which the ratio of percentage of lead to percentage of tin approaches three. Theoretical compositions with higher ratios are possible if it is assumed that the main ingredient used in Recipe D was a high lead bronze that had previously been produced by means of this recipe. For example, if the main ingredient in the first run was composed of half copper and half bronze of the composition represented by analysis No. 4 of Table VI, the resulting bronze would contain about 6.3 per cent tin and 14.2 per cent lead. If this bronze was then used as the main ingredient in a second run, the final bronze would contain about 7.6 per cent tin and 23.2 per cent lead, percentages that are rather close to those of analysis No. 2 of Table VIII.

If the bronze of moderately high lead content needed for the manufacture of statuary bronze of very high lead content by means of Recipe D was scrap statuary bronze, which seems not unlikely, it necessarily follows that the statuary bronze of very high lead content is later in date than the one containing the lower proportion of lead. Therefore, a relatively late date of production for a Roman statuary bronze may be indicated if its analysis shows the ratio of percentage of lead to percentage of tin to be very high. This possibility lends support to the chronological indications of the data of Table IX.

Concluding Remarks

Present knowledge about the chemical composition of Greek and Roman statuary bronzes is fragmentary, and any conclusions based on this knowledge are only tentative. Many more analyses are obviously needed, especially accurate and complete analyses of bronzes of known provenance.

Notes

1 The author is aware on the basis of private communications that an uncertain number of unpublished chemical analyses have been made, especially in connection with questions of authenticity, but unfortunately the data of these analyses are not available for consideration in this paper. A few qualitative or semiquantitative spectrographic analyses have been published, but these have failed to yield information of much significance, one reason being that they usually represent the composition of surface metal, not the composition of the unaltered original alloy. Quantitative wet-chemical methods were used for all the analyses listed in this paper.

2 E. R. Caley, "Critical Evaluation of Published Analytical Data on the Composition of Ancient Material," in *Application of Science in Examination of Works of Art* (Boston: Museum of Fine Arts, 1967), 167-171.

3 No. 13396. S. Papaspyridi, *Guide du Musée National d'Athènes* (Athens, 1927), 218 f., with bibl.; V. Staïs, *Marbres et bronzes du Musée National*, I (Athens, 1910), 302-304, ill., with bibl.

4 O. Davies, "The Chemical Composition of Archaic Greek Bronze," *BSA*, XXXV (1934-1935), 131-137.

5 K. Kluge, K. Lehmann-Hartleben, *Die antiken Grossbronzen* (Berlin and Leipzig, 1927), II, 106, figs. 1, 2 and III, pl. 33.

6 Acc. no. 55.75. First quarter of second century A.D.? Illustrated: *Toledo Museum News*, n.s. V, No. 3 (Autumn, 1962), 56.

Discussion Session 1.1

Cyril Stanley Smith,
Discussant

The discussant, Professor Cyril Stanley Smith, initiated the discussion with the following remarks. "I rather wish that Dr. Caley had more strongly emphasized, as he has on other occasions,[1] the necessity of treating chemical analyses with skepticism unless the procedures of sampling and analysis are fully known. The taking of a sample is extremely important, particularly in castings of bronzes with high lead content which are subject to the egregious segregation, and many samples are needed to reveal the nature of the casting. Further uncertainty may arise as a result of oxidation during annealing and especially as a result of corrosion, during which both major and minor components can be added or lost. Though it is often desirable to analyze corrosion products, their composition is not that of the original metal. Generally speaking any superficial samples are highly suspect, and only deep drillings from solid metal should, in general, be sent to the analyst.

"Dr. Caley mentioned the value of trace element analyses. Here too caution is needed in interpretation. The amount of various elements in an ore may vary from place to place within a given deposit, and additional ones may come from the refractories, fuels, and fluxes that are used in metallurgical processing. The amount of impurity that is present in the final metal depends far less upon its ubiquity than upon the intensity of its reactions with oxygen, nitrogen, and sulphur during smelting, melting, and annealing. Further complications arise from the impurities that are introduced with tin or other alloying elements, perhaps of widely different origin. Moreover, metal scrap was in continual circulation. Old metal diluting the new not only changed the main composition, as Dr. Caley has shown, but also sometimes introduced contamination from decorative finishes and occasional freak compositions from experiment or accident. Since the composition was also modified by reduction, drossing, and reactions with slag or sulphides during remelting, it is not surprising that the analyses of a few samples by themselves are of a rather limited value. Nevertheless a statistical study of a large number of analyses as Pittioni and Junghans have done is valuable, for it can eventually establish the definite probability that a bronze of known composition belongs to one or another group.

"I would like to add some rather random remarks on techniques of quite different kinds to illustrate the dependence of form on the way in which things are made.

"The greatest problem that a historian of techniques faces is, perhaps, to avoid jumping to the conclusion that an object was made in the way that he himself would find natural to make it! At the present state of our knowledge a critical laboratory examination will often upset "obvious" conclusions. When I first saw the geometric bird (No. 25) I thought that it was clear how it had been made — and that it was rather uninteresting. Yet as soon as Miss Lechtman and Professor Steinberg began their close examination (see pages 14 to 22) they revealed one exciting thing after another. The defects and the joins, the patching of a simple casting instead of remaking it, give insight into the technical, economic, and aesthetic environment in which the foundryman worked.

"The evidence of technical processes disclosed in an alert examination of a work of art will often enhance the aesthetic reaction to it. In the field of painting there are probably few surprises of this kind to be uncovered, but the detailed study of ceramics, bronzes, and other metalwork has hardly begun. The red and black of Attic vases depend intimately on a controlled sequence of kiln atmospheres.[2] Sung and Ming ceramics owe their beauty not only to the potter's eye but equally to the behavior of metallic ions in unusual environments in the glaze and to most subtle variations of surface tension, viscosity, and crystal formation.

"A complete reassessment of the aesthetics of Chinese bronzes was necessitated by the realization, little more than a decade ago, that the bronzes were not made by the lost-wax process (as had been unthinkingly assumed because in the West this process alone could have given such complicated castings) but that they were made in multiple piece molds (Fig. 1). The main features of the design originate directly from mold joints and other exigencies of the technique.[3]

"Castings can be made without using any mold at all, and this was once an important form of casting, used mainly for jewelry granulation and for coins. The earliest Lydian coins and many later ones throughout the Middle East and Europe — even some in seventeenth-century Japan — have a pleasant irregular shape arising from the effect of surface tension, which draws any mass of molten metal into a smooth drop as nearly spherical as gravity with allow. In making coins it is necessary to adjust the weight exactly. Numismatists have assumed that somehow drops of molten metal of the appropriate weight were poured out of a crucible into a mold cavity, but to a worker of metals it seems far more likely that the coin-maker assembled a small pile of metal fragments, adjusted when cold to the correct weight, and then heated these on a nearly flat refractory surface until they melted and flowed together. The resulting sessile drop became a finished coin after merely being struck with appropriate punches or dies.[4]

Fig. 1: Chinese bronze of type ting, *eleventh to tenth century B.C. Note the flanges that occur at major divisions in the mold and the decorative details which, if coarse, were molded or, if fine, were cut into the inner surface of the mold. The legs were separately cast and inserted in the mold for the main casting. Diameter 20.3 cm. Fogg Art Museum, 1943.52.100.*

"Surface tooling, whether for producing a desirable finish on an already shaped surface or for adding pictorial or decorative detail, is another area in which technology and aesthetics are closely linked. Most of the objects in the Master Bronzes exhibition are castings that were finished simply by scraping and filing, followed by some kind of abrasive polishing process. The superb armor in the exhibition (Nos. 29-32), however, was shaped from hammered sheets of bronze by raising, then the three-dimensional design executed by repoussé, and finally the linear decoration applied with a tracing tool.

"The quality of a traced or engraved line is almost as sensitive to the tool and the manner of its use as are the lines produced by pencil or brush. Examination under the microscope of the decorative lines on the Cretan helmet (No. 29), in the few places where details are not hidden by the white filling or by corrosion, shows that they had been traced, using, for the most part, a tool that was squarish, about 0.3 by 0.5 mm. in size, and slightly rounded at the end. The impressions, of which there are three to four per millimeter of line length, can be seen, at slight magnification, in Fig. 2. Tracing tools are generally more chisel-shaped than this, and the line they make tends to be composed of a series of overlapping straight sections that give an interrupted quality to sharp curves; the Cretan tracer could follow the curvature of the design with a uniformly wide line. The individual dots shading the lion's skin were produced with a very small lenticulate chisel-shaped tool, and still another tool was used for outlining the repoussé snakes and legs. It is possible that some sort of die was used for producing the parallel lines on the border of the *mitra*, No. 31. Special tools, of course, were common, and later smiths had an arsenal of nar-

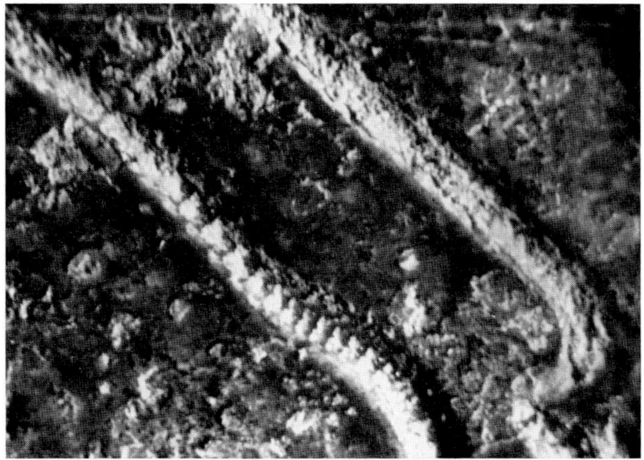

Fig. 2: Magnified detail showing traced line in archaic Cretan bronze helmet (No. 29). The area shown is the lion's leg in the lower center of the right panel (see illustration in the Master Bronzes catalogue, pp. 46, 47). Oblique illumination. x 17 (photo by Heather Lechtman).

row, broad, curved, vee, round, rectangular, and ring-shaped tools to produce innumerable effects.

"Herbert Maryon, the great authority on ancient metalworking techniques, reproduced two eighth-century B.C. Greek gold fibulae that were engraved[5] but pointed out that most linear decoration in antiquity was done by tracing. Engraving clearly was used in decorating one of the most attractive pieces in the Master Bronzes exhibition — the geometric fibula, No. 26. When examined under slight magnification (Fig. 3), the lines show the occasional slips of the tool and the variation in width (from 0.25 to 0.40 mm. in the main lines and 0.1 to 0.2 mm. in the minor ones) that characterize the use of the burin or graver. The little circles and semicircles were obviously cut with a special tool having a cutting point at a fixed distance from a center point inserted in a punch mark around which it was rotated, like a compass. A quite different pattern of series of segmental curves, probably produced by a rocking scorper, was cut on one of the contemporary gold fibulae described by Maryon.[6]

"This session of the symposium, though it exposes many gaps in our knowledge, has displayed some of the richness of the material already available for the historian of technology to work with. I hope it will equally serve the scholarly needs of art historians and contribute to the enjoyment of those who react to a work of art with their whole being, both intellectually and sensually."

The session was then opened to questions from the floor.

Professor H. W. Janson of New York University began by asking whether information is available about the methods of manufacture of ancient bronzes that would indicate how many individuals were involved in the production of an object. He felt that many of the speakers oversimplified in referring to "the artist" as a single man who made the model, made the mold, did the casting, and then finished the object. He suggested that the more technically complex and artistically inventive the object, the greater was the likelihood that there would be some division of labor between the man who created the model and finished the cast product and the man or team that did the casting.

Professor Steinberg agreed that, although there is no clear evidence for the methods used in antiquity, the production of statuettes was clearly the work of a team of men. The artist would have made the model and may have taken a hand in making the mold, particularly if a complicated series of positives and negatives was to be made from the original. He

Fig. 3: Magnified detail showing engraved lines in bronze fibula (No. 26). x 2 (photo by Arthur Steinberg).

would also have done the extensive tooling and finishing on the cast object. The ingenuity of both the foundrymen, who did the casting, and of the joiners, who put the pieces together, should not be overlooked, however. (See also pp. 174 f.)

Professor George M. A. Hanfmann suggested that, indeed, the whole history of art could be re-examined from the point of view of the degree to which the artist was involved in the technological process. One important document for Greek practices, he pointed out, is a representation of a sculptor's workshop on a cup by the Foundry Painter,[7] which implies that the artist also ran the foundry. The literary tradition, in Greece at least, bears out this impression. For example, even though the Colossus of Rhodes took twelve years to make, Philo Byzantinos[8] suggests that Chares managed the technological as well as the artistic aspect. Thus, much as did Ghiberti in the Renaissance, the sculptor usually ran his own shop, the result being a close relationship between the artist and the craftsman. The relationship undoubtedly varied for different quality levels of work. For example, a foundryman casting common figurines for dedication en masse probably did everything himself. For the Roman period there is very little evidence,[9] and the closeness of association between artist and craftsman probably varied at different periods, although in general during antiquity there was a greater involvement of the artist in the technological process than in subsequent periods.

Professor Brunilde Ridgway of Bryn Mawr College asked whether Professor Steinberg could enlarge upon the technology of making a large object such as the fragmentary life-size so-called bust of Demeter[10] found in the sea near Bodrum.

Professor Steinberg said that he had not been able to examine the object thoroughly but that it was clearly cast in several pieces which were then joined. He suggested that the model was made of clay or wood and that piece molds (in clay or plaster) were then taken from it. The system of piece molds was surely very elaborate: a single drapery fold or even part of a fold might have had an individual mold. The molds (or refractory molds made from them) would then have been baked to dry them, coated on the interior with wax, and filled with core material. After the wax had been melted out, the pieces were then cast in their individual molds, and finally the separate pieces were joined to create the finished statue.

Alternatively, it is possible that the model was partitioned before piece molds were made from it. The undercutting and complex configurations of some of the drapery folds point to some such procedure. But after piece molds had been made from the model pieces, the process would have been the same as that just described.[11] In any case, this piece warrants a much closer look to determine the details of its manufacture.

Further examination and analyses would also be necessary to determine how the various pieces were joined to form the finished bust. Professor Steinberg suggested tentatively that a hard solder or braze might have been used. But if the material of the joins was very close in composition to the bronze of the casting, the technique would be a kind of fusion welding such as that used on the Roman drapery fragment, No 237 (pp. 22 ff., figs. 27 ff.). The joins on the "Demeter," which has been dated fourth century B.C., are still finer than those on many Roman objects and are virtually invisible on the exterior.

Mr. Gettens noted that although Professor Caley has studied the use of zinc in Roman coinage,[12] he did not discuss zinc in his paper. Professor Caley replied that the percentage of zinc in Roman statuary bronzes which he has analyzed is always less than one per cent. In fact, he has used the absence of zinc as a test of authenticity in Roman bronzes. Brass, which includes zinc, was used for Roman coinage, but its manufacture appears to have been a monopoly of the government and its use was strictly limited. It is possible that at a late date larger objects containing zinc might have been made from coins that had been melted down. He also suggested that archaeologists may possibly yet discover examples of genuine Roman bronzes in which zinc is a principal component. Professor Steinberg observed that he and Mr. William J. Young of the Museum of Fine Arts, Boston, had analyzed a number of objects, including fibulae, excavated at the large tomb MMT at Gordion. Independently they both found a very high zinc content and low tin content to be characteristic of this group. Undoubtedly the metalworkers who made them were unable to refine zinc metal, but they must have used ores that were rich in zinc. Analyses for zinc are not very accurate over 10 per cent, but they indicate that the metal of the Gordion objects contains at least 10 per cent zinc, approximately 2 to 3 per cent tin, and very little lead. This unusual alloy, which is a kind of brass, is peculiar to Gordion.

Professor Hanfmann asked Professor Caley whether the rise in lead content in Roman bronzes over time could be attributed solely to the reuse of scrap metal in the melt. Professor Caley said that this alone could not cause the increase but that additional lead must have been added, in accordance with Pliny's second formula (see p. 47).

Professor Merton C. Flemings of M.I.T. suggested that perhaps the decreasing amount of copper in the alloy used by the Romans was a result of their problems with joining. As copper content goes down, the melting point becomes lower, so that welding, as opposed to soldering or mechanical joining, becomes easier.

Professor Steinberg hypothesized that the change in the composition of bronze was probably brought about to meet a combination of metallurgical needs, such as the joining problem, and economic ones. Tin was extremely rare in the ancient world, coming primarily from Spain and Britain and possibly also from the Sinai area, so that it was an economically significant discovery that lead, which was more readily available, could be used to alloy with copper in place of some tin.

Professor Smith suggested that it is also possible that high lead alloys, when properly finished, developed an attractive patina and may have been aesthetically more pleasing to the ancients. Professor Flemings added that high-lead bronze was undoubtedly easier to work and tool after casting, strengthening Professor Smith's observation that technological decisions are usually the result of a complex series of factors, rather than any single one.

Professor Hanfmann had also inquired whether any finds of Roman scrap are known. Dr. Herbert A. Cahn offered the information that a large hoard of bronze scrap, certainly coming from statues, has been found at Augst (Augusta Raurica), near Basel.[13]

Dr. Cahn then questioned Professor Caley's use of analyses of coins as evidence for the composition of bronze statuettes. He pointed out that coins were not made in the same workshops as statuary bronzes, the former being controlled by the state and the latter being privately run.

Professor Edith Porada of Columbia University pointed out that different types of objects demand different alloys — weapons, for example, generally have a higher tin content than do statuary bronzes.

Professor William Samolin of Columbia University explained that in ancient Chinese vessels, where the percentage of lead and tin combined is often close to 20, it is not the percentage of either lead or tin that determines the ratio but the combination of the two. He pointed out that adding lead increases the fluidity of the bronze, which would be helpful in a complex casting such as a Chinese ritual vessel. Certain types of Chinese weapons, particularly in the late Chou period, are almost pure copper, but they are work-hardened, which makes them very hard on the edge yet gives them a great amount of shock resistance. Metal so treated is tough and ductile.

A further question was asked as to whether structural and chemical analyses had been used to help solve controversial problems regarding the origin of certain classes of objects — such as griffin protomes — during the Orientalizing period in the eighth and seventh centuries B.C.

Professor Steinberg replied that he had studied griffin protomes and siren attachments analytically, having done about 300 spectrographic analyses of Orientalizing Greek, Etruscan, Phrygian, and Urartian bronzes. But the questions of manufacture are so complex that he felt more work ought to be done on the microstructure of these objects before definite conclusions could be drawn.

Notes

1 E. R. Caley, *Analysis of Ancient Metals* (Oxford and New York, 1964).

2 J. V. Noble, *The Techniques of Painted Attic Pottery* (New York, 1965).

3 Noel Barnard, *Bronze Casting and Bronze Alloys in Ancient China,* Monumenta Serica monograph No. XIV (Canberra, 1961). R. J. Gettens, *Catalogue of Chinese Bronzes in the Freer Collection,* II, *Technical Studies* (Washington, D. C.: The Freer Gallery, in press).

4 R. F. Tylecote, "The Method of Use of Early Iron-Age Coin Moulds," *NC,* II (1962), 102-109. C. S. Smith, "The Early History of Casting, Molds, and the Science of Solidification," *Proceedings of the Second Buhl International Conference on Materials,* 1966 (New York: Gordon and Breach Science Publishers, Inc., 1968), 3-52. For a contrary view on flan casting see D. G. Sellwood, "Some experiments in Greek minting techniques," *NC,* III (1963), 217-231.

5 Herbert Maryon, "Metal Working in the Ancient World," *AJA,* LIII (1949), 93-125.

6 See also Mr. Young's discussion on the use of the scorper, p. 87-89.

7 Beazley, *ARV* (Oxford, 1963), I, 400-401, no. 1; II, 1651.

8 Philon Byzantinos, *De septem orbis spectaculis,* chap. 4, quoted in H. Maryon, "The Colossus of Rhodes," *JHS,* LXXVI (1956), 68-69.

9 Pliny *N.H.* XXXIII. 157.

10 Brunilde S. Ridgway, "The Lady from the Sea: A Greek Bronze in Turkey," *AJA,* LXXI (1967), 329-334, pls. 97-100; "The Bronze Lady from the Sea," *Expedition,* X:1 (Fall, 1967), 2-9.

11 D. E. L. Haynes, *AA* (1962), cols. 803-807.

12 Earle R. Caley, *Orichalcum and Related Ancient Alloys,* Numismatic Notes and Monographs, No. 151 (New York: American Numismatic Society, 1964).

13 Alfred Mutz, "Über den Metall-Massenfund von Augusta Raurica," *Ur-Schweiz,* XXXVI:1 (1962), 18-24.

Patina: Noble and Vile

Rutherford J. Gettens

The great majority of the master bronzes in the Fogg exhibition do not look now as they did when they came fresh from the foundry or while they were in use. Copper, the principal metal of bronze, is not a noble metal; it does not long retain its salmon-red color, even in pure country air. The same is true of bronze, the alloy of copper with the element tin. The unprotected surface of both copper and bronze in a few weeks grows dull or tarnishes from formation of a thin coating of black compounds resulting from chemical reaction with components of the atmosphere. Over a period of years in open air, even in nonpolluted air, the bronze surface begins to take on a green bloom and eventually turns green all over. The reactants in the air are, first, its normal components, oxygen and carbon dioxide; second, its occasional impurities from natural sources like ozone, oxides of nitrogen, and salt particles carried inland in ocean spray along coastlines; and lastly, pollutants, mainly of industrial origin, like sulphur dioxide, sulphur trioxide, and hydrogen sulphide. Copper roofs in country air turn green in 50 to 100 years; but in sulphur-polluted urban air the change to green takes about half that time because of the formation of basic copper sulphate. Bronze statues out of doors first tarnish black, then become streaked black and green, especially in urban atmospheres.

When a bronze is buried in soil or immersed in water, the corroding environment is vastly different. Here in particular the change at the surface is dependent upon many factors, including composition of the metal, kind and concentration of the chemically active agencies (especially of oxygen and of salt anions), pH or degree of acidity or alkalinity, temperature, seasonal changes, and finally the physical character of the products of chemical change. A free metal in many environments is less stable than the minerals or ores from which it was originally derived. Corrosion basically is an attempt of the metal to revert to a mineral form that is stable in the ambient conditions.

Because of their economic implications, many of the corrosion factors have been studied intensively in modern times by chemists and chemical engineers, quite in proportion to the economic importance of each metal. Naturally iron comes first, and then aluminum, and copper and its alloys follow.

Mineral Alteration Products

The products of chemical change are identical with many of the copper minerals that make up the ores in whose form copper and its alloy constituents originally existed in the earth's crust. While some purists among mineralogists refuse to use mineral terminology for metal compounds formed on artifacts, other mineralogists have no hesitancy, and they themselves have invented the term "mineral alteration products."

Most mineral alteration products unfortunately do not enhance the surface appearance of metals; rust on iron, black tarnish on silver, and white crusts on tin and lead are an abomination; but on the other hand under certain circumstances the appearance of copper and bronze is actually enhanced by thin mineral alteration crusts. A thin fairly uniform green crust of copper basic carbonates with splashes of the related blue mineral azurite is admired by collectors, who call it "patina." (The dictionary says the word is Italian but of uncertain origin.) If especially good in appearance and stable, it is sometimes qualified as "noble patina."

Patina is more than a tarnish. It connotes not merely a specific color but also a more or less continuous surface layer of measurable thickness which may have some protective value. It has come also to mean evidence of age and use. The fine smooth pale green surface on Chinese bronzes is called "water patina." Such noble patinas are so admired that they are often imitated and produced artificially by paint or by chemical means.

There are, on the other hand, agencies in air, soil, and water that can eat deeply into the metal surface and transform it into undesirable and unsightly compounds, weaken it internally, and eventually destroy it. They are mainly water-soluble chloride and sulphate salts in the soil. These agencies, which we will treat in some detail later, produce what a curator or collector may call "malignant patina" or more commonly "bronze disease," but for emphasis I choose to call it "patina vile." All transformations, good or bad, may be lumped under the unromantic technical term "metal corrosion." Whether we call it patina or corrosion, it is important because locked in it is some evidence of the environment in which the bronze has lain in the past. It may give evidence of geographical or regional origin; it is always important when authenticity is considered.

Some of the chemical transformations at the surface of a bronze appear to be quite simple; for example, the direct union of copper with oxygen to form black cupric oxide or the direct attack by carbonic acid and water to form copper carbonate. Other mechanisms, however, are more complicated; some are electrochemical, in which transfer of electric energy between elements of unlike polarity exists. Under some conditions corrosion proceeds from the surface toward the interior along a well-defined front, but in others it is highly selective and penetrates along grain boundaries. In some forms of corrosion a single product is formed, but in others a layered struture made of minerals of different composition develops.

Let us now examine in some detail the more important patina constituents.

Copper Oxides

There are two kinds. Black cupric oxide, which goes by the mineral name *tenorite*, CuO, is a form that is easily produced artificially simply by heating copper in air. The occurrence of tenorite, however, is only occasionally mentioned in examination reports on bronze objects. It may be present more often than we realize as one of the constituents of black tarnish, perhaps mixed with black cupric sulphide, both being partially concealed by dirt and soot. It never seems to form a distinct thick layer.

The lower oxidation form, red cuprous oxide or *cuprite*, Cu_2O, however, is very common. It is usually seen as a distinct brick-red layer underlying green and blue surface layers. Hence it appears to be an intermediate oxidation product in the conversion of metal to the fully oxidized salts. Cuprite is often revealed when the outer green crusts are removed from bronzes by mechanical and some kinds of chemical cleaning. In some places where the green has flaked off, the cuprite beneath has a sugary appearance caused by glistening facets of numerous cube-shaped crystals. When cast bronzes are examined in cross section, it is often seen that cuprite has penetrated along grain boundaries and along seams that run deep into the metal core. In advanced corrosion the entire core may be converted to cuprite, sometimes interlaced with seams or lenses of white tin oxide.

Bronze converted internally to cuprite is brittle and easily shattered. One interesting point: in the transformation of copper to cuprite the calculated volume increase is nearly 1:2.[1] In spite of this substantial theoretical volume increase, the original shape of a fairly heavily corroded bronze object is often well retained in the cuprite layer. The increase in volume appears to be accommodated by transfer of copper from within to outside the original surface, where some of the copper is deposited as low density basic salts. Patches of hard red cuprite revealed by partial cleaning of a bronze often add color and variety to the patina and thus increase interest in the eyes of collectors.

Copper Sulphides

A variety of black copper sulphide minerals including *chalcocite*, Cu_2S; *chalcopyrite*, $CuFeS_2$; *bornite*, Cu_5FeS_4; and *tetrahedrite*, $(Cu,Fe)_{12}Sb_4S_{13}$, were observed in the late nineteenth century by the French mineralogist Daubrée on Roman bronze coins and medals recovered in French mineral springs.[2] He also noted the occurrence of indigo blue *covellite*, CuS.[3] Covellite seems to be an especially abundant corrosion product on copper and bronze artifacts recovered from wrecks of old wooden ships found at the edge of the sea. This may seem strange because there is little or no sulphide ion in sea water. The sulphide ion, however, appears to come from sulphate-reducing bacteria harbored in decaying wood, which act on sulphates in sea water. Sulphate ion makes up about 7.7 per cent of the salt content of sea water. Another early investigator, Lacroix, observed covellite mixed with chalcocite on copper nails from a Roman shipwreck found in 1907 off Mahdia in Tunis.[4] Unfortunately sulphides seldom enhance the looks of a bronze; hence they are probably quickly removed by zealous cleaners.

Copper Carbonates

Basic copper carbonates are among the most desirable constituents of bronze patina. There are two kinds, *malachite*, $Cu_2(OH)_2CO_3$, and *azurite*, $Cu_3(OH)_2(CO_3)_2$, the first being the more abundant. Carbon dioxide dissolved as carbonic acid in humid air or in ground waters reacts slowly with copper and its alloys to form these two basic salts. The initial product of carbonic acid attack seems partially soluble in water, and in this way copper ions can be transported some distances over the surface of an object, even into the surrounding soil. Carbonated bronzes seem mostly to have lain long in humid closed spaces such as underground tombs. The initially soluble cupric compounds are slowly changed to a colloidal gel with banded structure, which is formed in blisterlike and rounded concretions sometimes described as botryoidal or mamillary malachite. The rounded masses of malachite found in secondary ore deposits of copper are reproduced in miniature on the surfaces of bronzes. Occasionally malachite deposits thinly and smoothly on bronze like green enamel paint and on this account is sometimes suspected of being artificial. Malachite ordinarily produces a very fine patina on bronzes; the beautiful surface of the *mitra* from Crete (No. 31) shown in color on the cover of the catalogue of the Master Bronzes exhibition appears to contain much of this mineral.

The blue basic carbonate of copper called *azurite* contains slightly less water of constitution and has a distinctly different crystalline structure and habit. Its color on bronzes varies from bright blue to dark indigo. Azurite is slightly less stable and hence not nearly so abundant as malachite. It seems more often to form on the interior surface of vessels or on bronzes long confined in small spaces, such as tombs, where the environment is perhaps a little drier and in stable equilibrium. As previously mentioned, cuprite often underlies both malachite and azurite, and where all three are present and exposed at the surface, the effect can be quite colorful and interesting.

Tin Oxide

Since we are still concerned mainly with patina that is admired, let us at this point digress to discuss a kind of noble patina that is peculiar to cast bronzes of high tin content. Under conditions little understood the copper constituent of such bronzes can be leached out, apparently by carbonic acid, and transported into the soil or redeposited on the surface as malachite. The tin constituent which is in solid solution with the copper does not go into solution but appears to be transformed directly *in situ* to tin oxide (stannic oxide, SnO_2), a product quite similar to the tin ore called *cassiterite*. Unlike copper and lead, both of which form several compounds, tin forms only this one. There may be intermediate products, but so far tin dioxide, the end product, is the only one known.[5] Another interesting feature is that the oxide of tin forms from a tin-rich phase in the alloy without apparent increase in volume, with the result that the original surface is unmarred and unblemished; and because the tin oxide replacement is hard and compact, the surface of an ancient bronze, even though deeply altered to a depth of 1 mm. or more, is still lustrous. The replacement of copper-tin solid solution with compact stannic oxide is very close, if not identical, to the pseudomorphic replacement of one mineral by another, a phenomenon well known to mineralogists. The tin oxide corrosion product, which is white or light yellow-gray when pure, is usually tinged green or bluish-green by a small amount of retained copper salts. Tin oxide patina occurs commonly on Chinese bronzes of all types but especially on mirrors, which usually have extra high tin content. But the phenomenon is not exclusively Chinese, as viewers of the Master Bronzes exhibition will appreciate. Fine-quality copper-stained tin oxide patinas are found on Etruscan mirrors (Color Plate I). The very beautiful patina on the huge bronze krater found at Vix in France[6] seems to be mainly tin oxide. I have observed it directly on a Bronze Age bracelet in the Duchess of Mechlenberg Collection at the Peabody Museum of Harvard University. W. Geilmann in Germany has described several Bronze Age artifacts in which brownish tin oxide is now the principal constituent and copper the minor.[7] He notes that this type of patina seems to be found principally on bronzes buried in sandy soils where carbonic and humic acids play an important role in dissolving out the copper, leaving the tin as stannic oxide.

The X-ray diffraction patterns of tin oxide from bronzes are identical in spacing to those of naturally occurring cassiterite, but the lines are broader and more diffuse, which indicates that the bronze corrosion product is much more finely divided than the cassiterite of tin ore deposits.

Furthermore, it has been observed that the X-ray diffraction patterns of the tin corrosion product closely resemble a complex tin mineral, discovered in the Belgian Congo about 1945 by N. Varlamoff,[8] that contains metastannic acid, stannic oxide, ferric oxide, silicon dioxide, and water. This mineral, which also occurs in the tin deposits of Cornwall, England, has been named *varlamoffite,* after its discoverer. I am tempted at times to call this very noble patina formed from tin oxide "varlamoffite patina," but to this point I have held myself in check. Whether we call it "water patina," "varlamoffite patina," or simply tin oxide, we can agree that it beautifies the surface of an ancient bronze.

Copper Chlorides

We have been discussing mainly the products of copper and tin corrosion, which by consensus of taste add interest and luster to the surface of an ancient bronze. Corrosion crusts, however, commonly entrap earthy accretions, foreign materials (charcoal, sand, shell, and vegetable remains), and sometimes rust from adjacent corroding iron objects, all of which harm surface appearance and are sometimes difficult to clean away (Color Plate II). The worst that can happen to an ancient bronze, however, is that it be buried in the saline soils or sands of desert regions, like those of Egypt, Arabia, and Mesopotamia. Long contact with sodium chloride eventually transforms copper to a mineral called *atacamite,* which gets its name from the province of Atacama in Chile. It is basic cupric chloride with the formula $Cu_2(OH)_3Cl$. A bronze deeply encrusted with atacamite is usually fissured and distorted. The surface is covered with dark green multifaceted crystals that glisten in the light. A cross section of such a bronze reveals a complex structure. (Color Plate III). If the original shape of the bronze is recognizable, there is probably a core of uncorroded metal. The grain boundaries of alloy near the core surface are stained black. Farther out there may be islands of metal surrounded by initial corrosion product; next comes a ring of light grayish translucent material, something like paraffin wax in appearance, which is known to be cuprous chloride, a lower oxidation form of copper. It is called by its mineral name *nantokite,* CuCl; it is a rare mineral named from its first noted occurrence at Nantoko, also in Chile. Beyond this is a hard compact layer of red cuprite already described. The red layer may be interlaced with veins or pockets of white tin oxide. Beyond this is a thick and usually banded green layer of the ultimate oxidation product, atacamite, but the atacamite may be mixed with some malachite. At various points within the cuprite layer there may be tiny scales or rounded deposits of elemental copper, also a corrosion product, which is formed by a reverse electrochemical reaction. Often crystalline atacamite, which has orthorhombic crystal structure, is associated with a paler green product of identical chemical composition, a dimorph called *paratacamite* which crystallizes in the hexagonal system. The inner layer of nantokite is important to collectors because, as it is unstable, it is the cause of "bronze disease." Under ordinary circumstances it is in equilibrium, contained between the inner core of bronze and the surrounding shell of cuprite; but if by accident it is exposed to humid air, even to air with a relative humidity as low as 50 per cent, it quickly absorbs water, turns moist, oxidizes to green basic cupric chloride in the process, and swells up in lumps and blisters. In dry air the pale green product eventually turns to a powder that gives X-ray diffraction patterns of paratacamite (see Color Plate III). Bronzes in advanced stages of chloride corrosion may break out with greenish beads of moisture after standing long in humid summer air, but when the air becomes dry in autumn from central heating, the affected areas turn powdery pale green, and eventually grains of the green collect at the base of the bronze. That is why such a patina may appropriately be called "patina vile." A simple remedy, of course, is to keep a bronze suspected of harboring base patina in a dry environment.

The complex chemical reactions that bring about this transformation were first explained by the French chemist Berthelot in 1894.[9] G. A. Rosenberg in Copenhagen (1917),[10] and later Professor Earle R. Caley, who worked with corroded bronze artifacts of known Greek source,[11] made notable contributions to knowledge on this special aspect of bronze corrosion. Robert Organ has contributed to an understanding of the mechanism of corrosion action.[12] In my article on the corrosion of Chinese bronzes of some years ago,[13] I drew upon the observations of Berthelot, Caley, and others to construct a table of reactions which I believe in part explains step-wise the chloride-stimulated corrosion processes. If not accurate in all respects, they can at least serve as points of departure for discussions.

My remarks on "patina vile" may sound foreboding, but the fact is that in my own experience I have observed little damage by chloride-bearing patinas on bronzes kept in a normally dry environment, even in non-air-conditioned galleries and storage areas. There is great benefit to bronzes in long dry winters, overheated galleries and dwellings, and in nearly airtight exhibition cases. I have seen evidence of patina vile on only a few bronzes in the Master Bronzes exhibition for the simple reason that they were well chosen. Most of them came from the better-watered areas on the north side of the Mediterranean, where salt concentration of the soil seems to be fairly low. In addition most have been cautiously acquired by collectors and in turn carefully selected for this exhibition, not only for their artistic merit but also because of their splendid condition.

Other Copper Minerals

The mineral alteration products just described seem to be the principal ones seen on bronzes found in Greece and Italy. There are others, however, which we might expect to find under certain circumstances, especially on those Greek and Roman bronzes that were transported to the arid regions of the Near East and Egypt. I have already briefly mentioned basic copper sulphate, identical with the bright green mineral *brochantite*, $Cu_4(SO_4)(OH)_6$, which occurs so commonly on outdoor bronze statuary and on copper roofs exposed to the urban atmosphere.

This circumstance is rather peculiar because it was long held that the green (often misnamed verdigris) so commonly seen on park bronzes and on architectural trim of public buildings is basic copper carbonate, identical with malachite. Two investigators in England, W. H. J. Vernon and L. Whitby, in the early 1930's concluded from their analyses of many samples of green from public buildings in London and elsewhere that it is mainly basic copper sulphate.[14] Their conclusions have been confirmed several times in the analysis of green from bronze and copper roofs in urban areas of this country. Just a short time ago analysis made of the green patina of the Statue of Liberty in New York Harbor showed that it is not basic carbonate as some had guessed but, in fact, is principally basic sulphate. It contains copper basic chloride only as a minor constituent. Sulphur compounds from burning fuels in the region of New York Harbor are more active as corroding agents than salt ocean spray.

Rare Copper Minerals

Of special interest to me are the very rare minerals that are occasionally found on ancient bronzes. I find it good sport looking for them. Some years ago Professor Clifford Frondel of the Department of Mineralogy, Harvard, observed on the inside of the base of an Egyptian bronze figurine of the deity Bastet in the Fogg Museum (1943. 1121 b) a blue-green deposit which he identified as the very rare copper basic chloride mineral *botallacite*, $Cu_2(OH)_3Cl \cdot H_2O$. Both Frondel and I later described as a new mineral species a bluish-green chalky crust we discovered on the hollow interior of the base of another Egyptian bronze figurine, of the deity Sekhmet, also in the Fogg Museum (1943. 1121 a). It is a double carbonate of sodium and copper, $Na_2Cu(CO_3)_2 \cdot 3H_2O$, to which we gave the name *chalconatronite*.[15] This rare mineral might some day be found on a classical bronze recovered in certain districts of Egypt where alkali carbonates occur abundantly in the soil. Elsewhere I have described several of these rare minerals occurring on antiquities including *connellite*, a complex basic sulphate and chloride [$Cu_{19}(SO_4)Cl_4(OH)_{32} \cdot 3H_2O$?], and *libethenite*, a basic copper phosphate, $Cu_2(PO_4)(OH)$.[16] There is also some evidence of the existence of a basic copper nitrate, not yet fully described or named, among corrosion products on bronze vessels found by University of Pennsylvania archaeologists in a royal tomb at Gordion in Anatolia.

Mineral Alteration of Lead

Another important constituent of many ancient bronzes is lead. Unlike tin, lead does not alloy easily with copper but mostly segregates in a copper-tin solid solution in the form of rounded inclusions. Unfortunately I have little precise data on the amount of lead in classical bronzes, but if they are like the Chinese bronzes we have met with, the lead content varies over a wide range, from nothing to over 25 per cent. I have seen on some of the bronzes in the Master Bronzes exhibition evidence of *cerussite*, white lead carbonate, $PbCO_3$, which is the most common lead alteration product. Cerussite is not usually seen as a distinct layer on bronzes but in patches or pockets in contact with malachite crusts. I suspect it is sometimes a minor constituent of light colored tin oxide patina; it sometimes occurs deep in the corrosion crusts, next to the metal core, in little rounded pockets where it is obviously the alteration product of lead globules formed in lead segregation.

Some rather interesting rare lead minerals have been found, like the *cotunnite*, lead chloride, $PbCl_2$, reported by A. Lacroix on lead plates in the sunken Roman ship found off Mahdia, Tunis, in 1907, previously mentioned.[17] Lacroix also noted *phosgenite*, lead chloro-carbonate, $Pb_2(CO_3)Cl_2$, on a Roman lead pipe from the same source. I had the good fortune to find phosgenite on the column of an old Persian lamp now in the Freer study collection. I also found on the same object, in contact with the phosgenite, deep blue crystals of the even more rare mineral, *cumengite,* a complex copper-lead basic chloride, [$Pb_4Cu_4Cl_8(OH)_8 \cdot H_2O$?].

Brass

Among late Roman bronzes it is possible to find copper alloyed with zinc, now commonly called brass. Although apparently not yet reported, we might expect to find on objects made from copper-zinc or copper-tin-zinc both *smithsonite,* zinc carbonate, $ZnCO_3$, and *hydrozincite,* $Zn_5(OH)_6(CO_3)_2$, as well as other interesting minerals in the corrosion crusts, providing these have not already been scraped off and thrown away in premature cleaning.

I mention these rare minerals because they reflect the environment and even remotely the geographical origins of the bronzes on which they are found. For example we would expect to find chalconatronite (p. 63) on a bronze long in contact with a highly alkaline soil, like that of certain parts of Egypt, or phosgenite on a lead object long submerged in sea water. Even if mainly of academic interest, rare minerals should be searched out and reported.

Conclusion

I have said elsewhere, but it does no harm to repeat it here, that the knowledge of mineral alteration products has practical as well as academic value. Although it is rarely possible to estimate age, provenience, and authenticity solely on the basis of the patina of a bronze, this information does supplement stylistic, historical, and epigraphic evidence. Identification of the composition of the metal and of the patina constituents is necessary for the complete description of a bronze. Such facts are notably missing in the descriptions of individual pieces in the beautiful catalogue of the Master Bronzes exhibition. Such data are necessary for the comparison of objects of unknown provenience with objects whose age and source are known. Lastly, knowledge of the kind and character of corrosion products on an object is necessary for choosing a rational method of conservation and cleaning.[18]

Projects for Study

I do not want to leave the impression that patina, either noble or vile, is fully understood. We are vastly ignorant on many points. To improve the state of our knowledge the following projects ought to be considered:

1. Because we are greatly hampered in the technical study of such bronzes as are included in the Master Bronzes exhibition by the reluctance among private owners and even curators to permit sampling, probing, and general laboratory study, I propose that a study and reference collection of metal artifacts and specimens for the area generally called the West be established in some museum or other cultural center. Gathered here would be odd fragments, broken bits, unexhibitable material, duplicates, fragments cast off from archaeological digs, and even fakes and forgeries. The collection, containing some prime teaching material, would be obtained through gifts and by purchase. Perhaps some of it could be acquired

through arrangements with foreign governments, many of whom have a great surplus of such material in their museums. I have already proposed to the ICOM Committee on Conservation that it foster a working group to deal with "Reference Materials." This group has been authorized, and when it gets under way I hope it will assist in the world-wide collection of study material. The study material should be held free for complete technical study, with no prohibitions against sampling objects for analytical purposes, cutting them up, melting them down, or using them for experimental cleaning. We have established a special study collection for Oriental bronzes and ceramics in the Freer Gallery of Art, and we have already been richly rewarded by the results. This is quite a drastic proposal, but I am dead serious about it. I think I fully realize all the problems of administration that such a collection might entail, but the end results will repay the trouble.

2. The following specific problems deserve further attention:

a. More chemical analyses on dated bronzes are essential.

b. Further work should be carried out on the phenomenon of the pseudomorphic replacement of copper with tin oxide at the surface of buried bronzes of high tin content, especially to learn about the corroding agencies that cause it and the mechanisms of reaction. There is apparently little or no mention of this phenomenon in the metallurgical or chemical literature.

c. What are the dark products of initial intergranular corrosion attack on bronzes? What is the mechanism of corrosion? Modern analytical research instruments like the electron-beam microprobe might be directed to the problem.

d. What is the composition of the thin black patina on many ancient bronzes? It is generally assumed that it is a mixture of black oxides and sulphides of copper, but is this so? Again, modern instruments like X-ray fluorescence spectrography or the electron-beam microprobe might be brought to bear.

e. What is the critical relative humidity and temperature for transformation of cuprous chloride to paratacamite? A critical study of the physical chemistry of cuprous chloride might be in order.

With these problems we can begin.

Notes

1

$$\begin{array}{lccc} & Cu_2 + [O] & \rightarrow & Cu_2O \\ \text{MW} & 127.1 + 16 & \rightarrow & 143.1 \\ \delta & 8.9 & \rightarrow & 6.0 \\ \text{Vol} \left(\frac{\text{MW}}{\delta}\right) & 14.3 & \rightarrow & 23.8 \end{array}$$

2 A. Daubrée, "Cuivre sulfuré cristallisé (cupréine), formé aux dépens de médailles antiques, en dehors de sources thermales, à Flines-les-Roches, département du Nord," *Comptes Rendus hebdomadaires des séances de l'Académie des Sciences*, XCIII (1881), 572-574. This journal is hereafter abbreviated as *C. R. Acad. Sci., Paris.*

3 *Ibid.*

4 A. Lacroix, "Sur quelques minéraux formés par l'action de l'eau de mer sur des objets métalliques romains trouvés en mer au large de Mahdia (Tunisie)," *C. R. Acad. Sci., Paris*, CLI (1910), 276-279.

5 Since these words were written, Mr. Robert Organ informs me (personal communication) that he and Mr. J. A. Mandarino at the Royal Ontario Museum, Toronto, found growing on a tin bowl, fifteen feet under river water, black crystals of stannous oxide SnO, and white crystals of stannous oxide hydrate $5SnO \cdot 2H_2O$. These compounds have been accepted as minerals under the names *romarchite* and *hydroromarchite* respectively by the Commission on New Minerals and Mineral Names, International Mineralogical Association.

6 R. Joffroy, *Le trésor de Vix* (Paris, 1954); *La tombe princière de Vix* (Chatillon-sur-Seine, 1961).

7 W. Geilmann, "Chemie und Vorgeschichtsforschung," *Die Naturwissenschaften*, XXXVII (1950), No. 5, 97-102; No. 6, 121-128.

8 S. Gastellier; "Note sur un minéral jaune trouvé par M. Varlamoff," Institut Royal Colonial Belge, *Bulletin des Séances*, XXI (1950), 412-419.

9 M. Berthelot, "Sur l' altération lente des objets de cuivre au sein de la terre et dans les musées," *C. R. Acad. Sci., Paris*, CXVIII (1894), 768-770.

10 G. A. Rosenberg, *Antiquités en fer et en bronze; leur transformation dans la terre contenant de l'acide carbonique et des chlorures, et leur conservation* (Copenhagen, 1917).

11 Earle R. Caley, "The Corroded Bronze of Corinth," *ProcPhilSoc*, LXXXIV (1941), 689-761.

12 Robert M. Organ, "Aspects of Bronze Patina and Its Treatment," *Studies in Conservation*, VIII (1963), 1-9.

13 Rutherford J. Gettens, "The Corrosion Products of an Ancient Chinese Bronze," *Journal of Chemical Education*, XXVIII (1951), 67-71.

14 W. H. J. Vernon and L. Whitby, "The Open-Air Corrosion of Copper. I. A Chemical Study of the Surface Patina," *Journal of the Institute of Metals*, London, XLII, No. 2 (1929), 181-182; "II. The Mineralogical Relationships of Corrosion Products," *ibid.*, XLIV, No. 2 (1930), 389-408.

15 Rutherford J. Gettens and Clifford Frondel, "Chalconatronite: an Alteration Product of Some Ancient Egyptian Bronzes," *Studies in Conservation*, II (1955), 64-75.

16 Rutherford J. Gettens, "The Corrosion Products of Metal Antiquities," *Smithsonian Annual Report for 1963*, 547-568.

17 Lacroix, *Ibid.*

18 At the moment of sending this manuscript to the editor, there has appeared a remarkably complete bibliography compiled by S. Z. Lewin and S. M. Alexander on "The Composition and Structure of Natural Patinas. Part I. Copper and Copper Alloys. Section A, Antiquity to 1929. Section B, 1930 to 1967; Part II. Zinc and Zinc Alloys, 1872 to 1965; Part III. Tin, Lead and their Alloys, 1873 to 1964." It is published as a Supplement to *Art and Archaeology Technical Abstracts*, VI, No. 4 (1967), 201-283; VII, No. 1 (1968), 279-366; VII, No. 2 (1968), 151-190. (Published at the Institute of Fine Arts, New York University.)

Selected Bibliography

Bass, George F. "The Cape Gelidonya Wreck: Preliminary Report," *AJA*, LXV (1961), 267-276, ill. See also G. F. Bass, "Cape Gelidonya: A Bronze Age Shipwreck," *TransPhilSoc*, LVII (1967), part 8. See also Peter Throckmorton, "Oldest Known Shipwreck Yields Bronze Age Cargo," *National Geographic Magazine*, CXXI (May 1962), 697-711.

Berthelot, M. "Sur l'altération lente des objets de cuivre au sein de la terre et dans les musées," *C. R. Acad. Sci., Paris*, CXVIII (1894), 768-770.

Caley, Earle R. "The Corroded Bronze of Corinth," *ProcPhilSoc*, LXXXIV (1941), 689-761.

Collins, William F. "The Mirror Black and Quicksilver Patinas of Certain Chinese Bronzes," *Journal of the Royal Anthropological Institute*, LXIV (1934), 69-79.

Daubrée, A. "Sur la formation contemporaine, dans la source thermale de Bourbonne-les-Bains (Haute-Marne), de diverses espèces minérales cristallisées, notamment du cuivre (chalkopyrite), du cuivre panaché (philippsite) et du cuivre sulfuré (chalkosine)," *C. R. Acad. Sci., Paris*, LXXX (1875), 461-469.

______. "Formation contemporaine dans la source thermale de Bourbonne-les-Bains (Haute-Marne) de diverses espèces minerales, galène, anglésite, pyrite et silicates de la famille des zéolithes, notamment la chabasie," *C. R. Acad. Sci., Paris*, LXXX (1875), 604-607.

______. "Cuivre sulfuré cristallisé (cupréine), formé aux depens de médailles antiques, en dehors de sources thermales, à Flines-les-Roches, département du Nord," *C. R. Acad. Sci., Paris*, XCIII (1881), 572-574.

Evans, Ulick R. *The Corrosion and Oxidation of Metals. Scientific Principles and Practical Applications.* New York: St. Martins Press, Inc., 1960

Fink, C. G., and Polushkin, E. P. "Microscopic Study of Ancient Bronze and Copper," *Transactions of the American Institute of Mining and Metallurgical Engineers*, CXXII (1936), 90-117.

Frondel, Clifford. "On Paratacamite and Some Related Copper Chlorides," *Mineralogical Magazine*, XXIX (1950), 34-45.

Gastellier, S. "Note sur un minéral jaune trouvé par M. Varlamoff," Institut Royal Colonial Belge, *Bulletin des Séances*, XXI (1950), 412-419.

Geilmann, W. "Chemie und Vorgeschichtsforschung," *Die Naturwissenschaften*, XXXVII (1950), No. 5, 97-102; No. 6, 121-128.

______. "Verwitterung von Bronzen im Sandboden," *Angewandte Chemie*, LXVIII (1956), 201-211.

Geilmann, W., and Meisel, K. "Röntgenographische Untersuchungsmethoden in der Vorgeschichtsforschung: Libethenite, ein Mineral der Patinabildung," *Nachrichtenblatt für Deutsche Vorzeit*, XVIII (1942), 208-212.

Gettens, Rutherford J. "Tin Oxide Patina of Ancient High-tin Bronze," *Bulletin of the Fogg Museum of Art*, XI, No. 1 (1949), 16-26.

______. "Mineralization, Electrolytic Treatment, and Radiographic Examination of Copper and Bronze Objects From Nuzi," *Technical Studies in the Field of the Fine Arts*, I (1932), 118-142.

______. "La corrosion récidivante des objets anciens en bronze et en cuivre," *Mouseion*, XXXV-XXXVI (1936), 119-138.

______. "The Corrosion Products of Metal Antiquities," *Smithsonian Annual Report for 1963*, pp. 547-568.

______. "The Corrosion Products of an Ancient Chinese Bronze," *Journal of Chemical Education*, XXVIII (1951), 67-71.

Gettens, Rutherford J., and Frondel, Clifford. "Chalconatronite: an Alteration Product of Some Ancient Egyptian Bronzes," *Studies in Conservation*, II (1955), 64-75.

Lacroix, A. "Sur un nouveau cas de formation de chalcosite aux dépens de monnaies romaines immergées dans une source thermale," *Bulletin de la Société Française de Minéralogie*, XXXII (1909), 333-335.

______. "Sur les quelques minéraux formés par l'action de l'eau de mer sur des objets métalliques romains trouvés en mer au large de Mahdia (Tunisie)," *C. R. Acad. Sci., Paris*, CLI (1910), 276-279.

Olshausen, Otto. "Über chemische Beobachtungen an vorgeschichtlichen Gegenständen. 4. Zinn und Bronze," *Zeitschrift für Ethnologie*, XVI (1884), 524-533.

Organ, R. M. "Aspects of Bronze Patina and its Treatment," *Studies in Conservation*, VIII (1963), 1-9.

______. "The Examination and Treatment of Bronze Antiquities," in *Recent Advances in Conservation;* Contributions to the IIC Rome Conference, 1961, Ed. G. Thomson. London: Butterworths, 1963, pp. 104-110.

Otto, Helmut. "Das Vorkommen von Connellit in Patinaschichten," *Die Naturwissenschaften*, L, No. 1 (1963), 16-17.

______. "Röntgen-Feinstrukturuntersuchungen an Patinaproben," *Freiburger Forschungshefte*, Vol. B 37 (1959), 66-77.

______. "Über röntgenographisch nachweisbare Bestandteile in Patinaschichten," *Die Naturwissenschaften*, XLVIII (1961), 661-664.

Périnet, G. "Sur les produits de corrosion du blindage de plomb de l'épave antique du grand Congloüe," *Revue Mensuelle Saint Germain-en-Laye*, XXXVI, No. 436 (1961), 454-458.

Plenderleith, Harold J. *The Conservation of Antiquities and Works of Art.* London: Oxford University Press, 1956.

Rooksby, H. P., and Chirnside, R. C. "The Formation of Basic Copper Chloride and Its Identity with Atacamite," *Journal of the Society of Chemical Industry*, LIII (1934), Part I, pp. 33t-35t.

Rosenberg, G. A. *Antiquités en fer et en bronze; leur transformation dans la terre contenant de l'acide carbonique et des chlorures, et leur conservation.* Copenhagen, 1917.

Russel, Sir Arthur, and Vincent, E. A. "On the Occurrence of Varlamoffite (Partially Hydrated Stannic Oxide) in Cornwall," *Mineralogical Magazine*, XXIX (1950-52), 817-826.

Vernon, W. H. J. "The Open-air Corrosion of Copper. III. Artificial Production of Green Patina," *Journal of the Institute of Metals*, London, XLIX (1932), 153-167.

Vernon, W. H. J., and Whitby, L. "The Open-air Corrosion of Copper. I. A Chemical Study of the Surface Patina," *Journal of the Institute of Metals*, London, XLII, No. 2 (1929), 181-182. "II. The Mineralogical Relationships of Corrosion Products," *ibid.*, XLIV, No. 2 (1930), 389-408.

Color Plate I: This Etruscan mirror, third to first century B.C., in the Fogg Art Museum (CC 2311) was apparently willfully damaged in antiquity. It has an extraordinarily smooth and fine blue-green "noble" patina which consists mainly of compact tin oxide stained with copper salts. Height 26.3 cm. Composition, Cu, 87.7; Sn, 11.0; Pb, 0.3; total 99.0 per cent. Trace elements not estimated. (Analysis by Mrs. I. V. Bene, Freer Gallery of Art. Photo by Freer Gallery of Art.)

Color Plate II: Egyptian bronze aegis inlaid with blue glass and gold, which dates from the XXVI-XXX dynasties (Freer Gallery 08.51; height 20.6 cm.), is deeply corroded, presumably by long contact with saline soil which has caused it to be encrusted with basic copper chloride identical with the mineral atacamite. As shown below in the detail of the top of the crown (x 2), the green is unevenly spotted with limey (calcium carbonate) accretions. (Upper photo, Freer Gallery of Art, lower photo, W. T. Chase.)

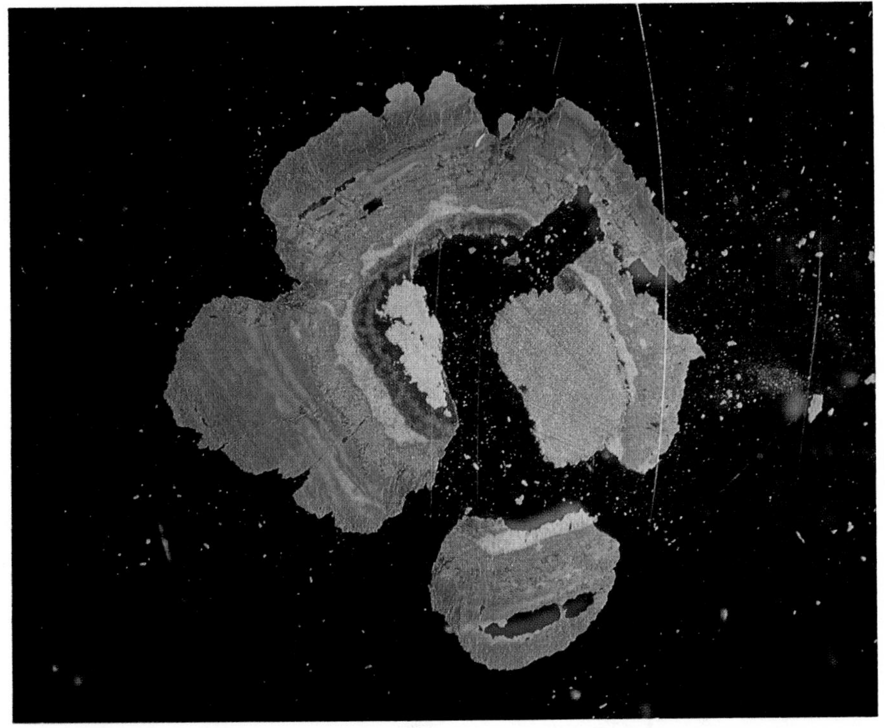

Color Plate III(A): A thin cross section of the spike of a copper door-studding nail, brought from Nuzi in Iraq by the Harvard-Baghdad School Expedition in 1928, shows a well-layered structure caused by extensive corrosion during approximately 3500 years of burial in saline soil. At the center is a remnant of the original copper spike. Beyond, between the copper and the red cuprite layer, is a zone of nantokite or cuprous chloride; the inner part of this zone has bands of black and red-brown impurities, perhaps silver and iron salts respectively. Beyond these the cuprous chloride is crystalline, nearly white, and presumably quite pure. The outer green zone is atacamite, the final product of corrosion. This thin section was described in greater detail in Technical Studies in the Field of Fine Arts, *I: 3 (January 1933), 118-142. The thin section split and fragmented during its original preparation because of its fragile nature. Macrograph, dark field,* x *10, by W. T. Chase.*

Color Plate III(B and C): Illustrations B and C were taken from a portion of this same spike mounted in plastic and polished for metallographic study. B shows the specimen in freshly polished condition. C was taken after the specimen had stood some months in open air. The inner zone of unstable cuprous chloride has oxidized to pale green paratacamite. The behavior is identical with the phenomenon known as bronze disease. Macrographs, dark field, x *4, by W. T. Chase.*

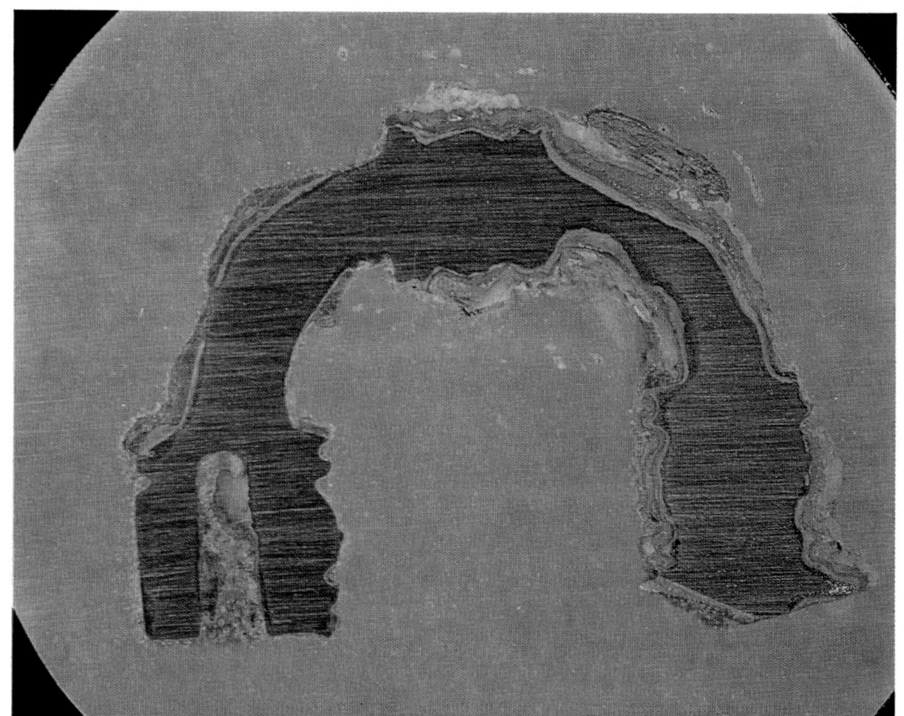

Color Plate IV(A): Unpolished longitudinal section of a bronze fibula from Gordion in Anatolia dated eighth to sixth century B.C. The metal of a similar fibula in the same series contains about 11 per cent tin and less than 1 per cent lead. Next to the metal core is a narrow gray zone of cuprous chloride; beyond is a red zone of cuprite, and on the exterior an irregular zone of green atacamite. Courtesy of the University Museum, Philadelphia.

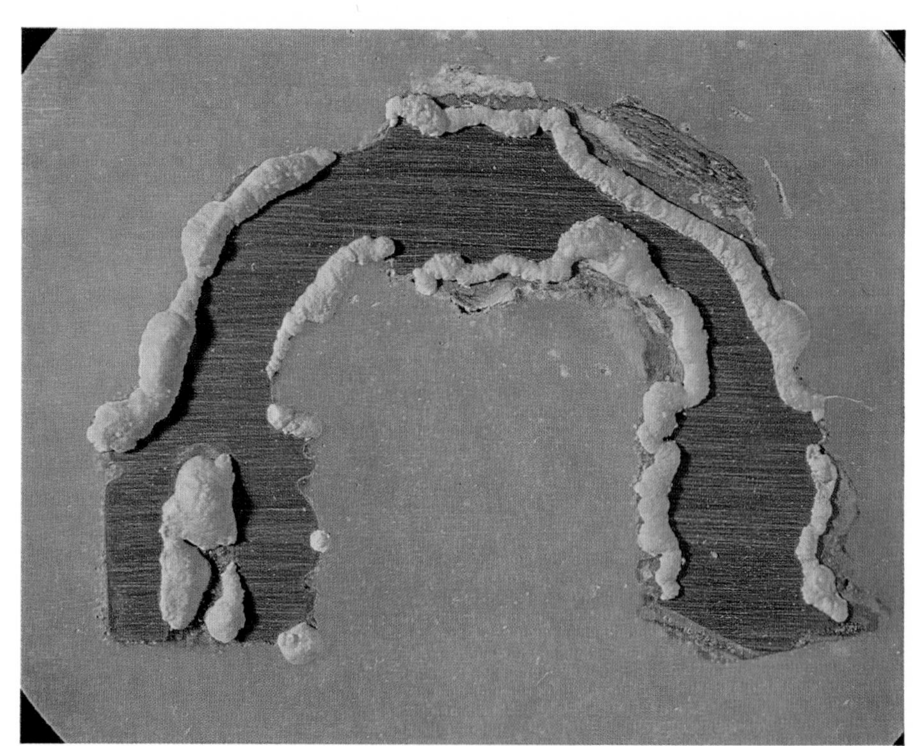

Color Plate IV(B): The same section after exposure to water-saturated air under a bell jar at room temperature. The inner zone of unstable cuprous chloride has reacted with air and water to form a pasty mass of green oxidation product. On drying, the moist green becomes a powdery mass of paratacamite. This is another example of bronze disease. Specimen, courtesy of Miss Ellen Kohler of the University Museum, Philadelphia. Macrograph, dark field, x 3, by W. T. Chase.

The Conservation of Bronze Objects

R. M. Organ

Definitions

In introducing this subject, we must first define those terms that may be a little unfamiliar. Because the term "conservation" probably has connotations of natural resources, it should be defined here as "actions leading to the prolongation of the life" of bronze objects. This definition, which originated with Paul Coremans,[1] should be contrasted with that of "restoration," which involves a certain amount of surgery — for example, surgery preliminary to the addition of a recreated limb — and with "preservation," which calls to mind rows of sealed bottles containing pallid medical specimens immersed in a preservative liquid.

Objectives of the Conservator

Although the conservator's ultimate objective, prolonging the life of an object indefinitely, requires immediate far-sighted consideration of details, this needs to be followed by unremitting attention over a protracted period. Here, however, we shall take only a short-term view of this same objective, directed to the appearance of the object, considering in particular the objects in the Master Bronzes exhibition.

Origins of Change in Appearance: External Causes

Let us now consider the nature of possible changes in appearance. Clearly, the appearance of a bronze is dependent on the nature of its surface: the light by which we see it assumes its particular qualities at that surface — becomes warm brown by reflection at bare metal or assumes various shades of red, green, or blue at a patinated surface. Some of the changes in appearance that we should wish to prevent may therefore be listed as change of surface, including the following: (1) darkening, caused by handling, acquisition of dust, or chemical reactions; (2) separation or loss of repairs, or alteration in the appearance of the paint that obscured their presence; (3) loss of so-called "noble" patina from certain areas; (4) outbreaks of bronze disease, or Gettens' "vile patina" (see pp. 57 ff.).

Internal causes

Although in the short-term view we are most concerned about superficial changes, we cannot entirely neglect consideration of the inner structure of a bronze, for this supports the surface, supplying its characteristic shape, and also influences our choice of the processes of conservation that can be applied safely for the cure of various ills of the surface.

In order to reveal the consequences for conservation of these various features of a bronze — superficial and internal — we must review some of the discussion elsewhere in this volume on both patina (perhaps better termed "corrosion crust" if it happens to be unpleasant in appearance) and internal structure, as they existed originally and as they have become altered during the passage of time.

Internal structure, "Macro"

Considering first the internal structure of a bronze, this may vary considerably on what may be called the "macro" scale. As an example we may consider one of the hydrias in the catalogue. In an imaginary cross section,

Fig. 1, this may be seen to contain five or six differing materials: first, a lip and neck that have been cast in one with the body — which itself has perhaps been expanded into its final shape by working after casting; second, two handles separately cast from two "pours" of metal that could well differ in composition; third, a foot that has been cast separately; fourth, the layers of solder employed to join handles and foot to the body. These several materials may alter differently as they age in corrosive conditions, perhaps buried in earth or exposed to dripping saline water. Thus it may happen that the wrought areas resist corrosive attack longer than the cast portions that have remained unworked. In addition, the solder, if it consists of a lead-tin alloy, will eventually become mineralized, with consequent weakening of the joint and possible separation of the component.

Other forms of construction that have been described in other papers at this symposium may present difficulties during some of the processes of conservation necessitated by decay. For example, while a solid casting presents few problems, a porous casting, a figure that has been cast hollow or one cast around a clay core that was left in place, cannot safely be immersed in solutions because of the risk that these may enter the interior through some unnoticed pore or crevice and there set up unwanted corrosion processes at some later date.

The superficial appearance of these various components of a bronze object begins to alter from the moment of their creation: when the mold is broken from around a still-hot casting, the metal immediately begins to oxidize in the air and to develop a film that is initially protective. Later, as a result of the normal fettling and finishing processes applied by a founder to the cold casting, this initial film of oxide may be abraded away or dissolved away, only to be replaced immediately by another. This second process of atmospheric tarnishing is familiar as the natural darkening of bright copper, which would eventually become green in color if not continuously cleaned by abrasion in use. Such a natural process is often hastened in modern times, at the request of the artist, by exposing a bronze to chemical reagents. Whatever the initial cause of its formation, the conservator always has to deal with a corroded surface, whether noble or vile.

Internal structure, "Micro"

If there are inhomogeneities within bronzes on the macro scale — observable to the informed naked eye — there are others on the micro scale that can usually be observed only after preparation. For this purpose we cut a cross section through part of the object, then polish it to a mirror finish, and finally etch chemically in readiness for observation under the microscope. Actual cutting through the object is often not permissible, but in this event the metallographer can sometimes find a convenient protuberance and can level this off in order to observe features at some slight depth inside the metal.

The result of this kind of examination is exemplified in Fig. 2, in which the circle represents the field of view in a microscope of a minute polished area of a surface. Here is displayed the metallic structure present at various depths beneath the surface of the metal. The imaginary cross section shown alongside the circle illustrates how the leveling process has cut through surface irregularities. Visible differences exist between the lower portion of the circular view, representing the area nearest the surface, and the upper portion, representing a greater depth into the interior of the metal. In both

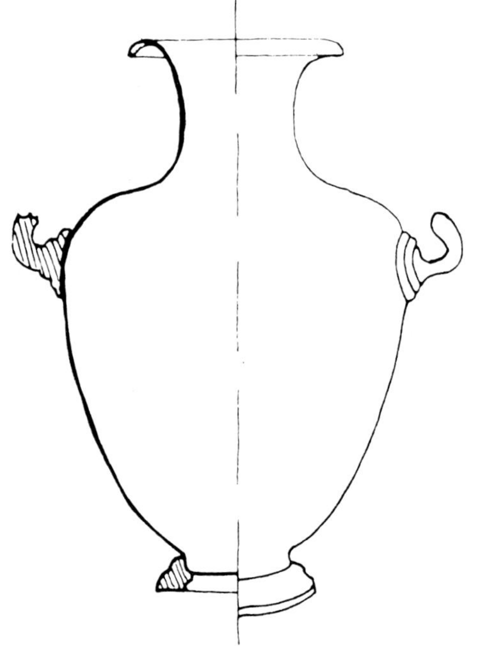

Fig. 1: A hydria, showing on the left the several components in cross section.

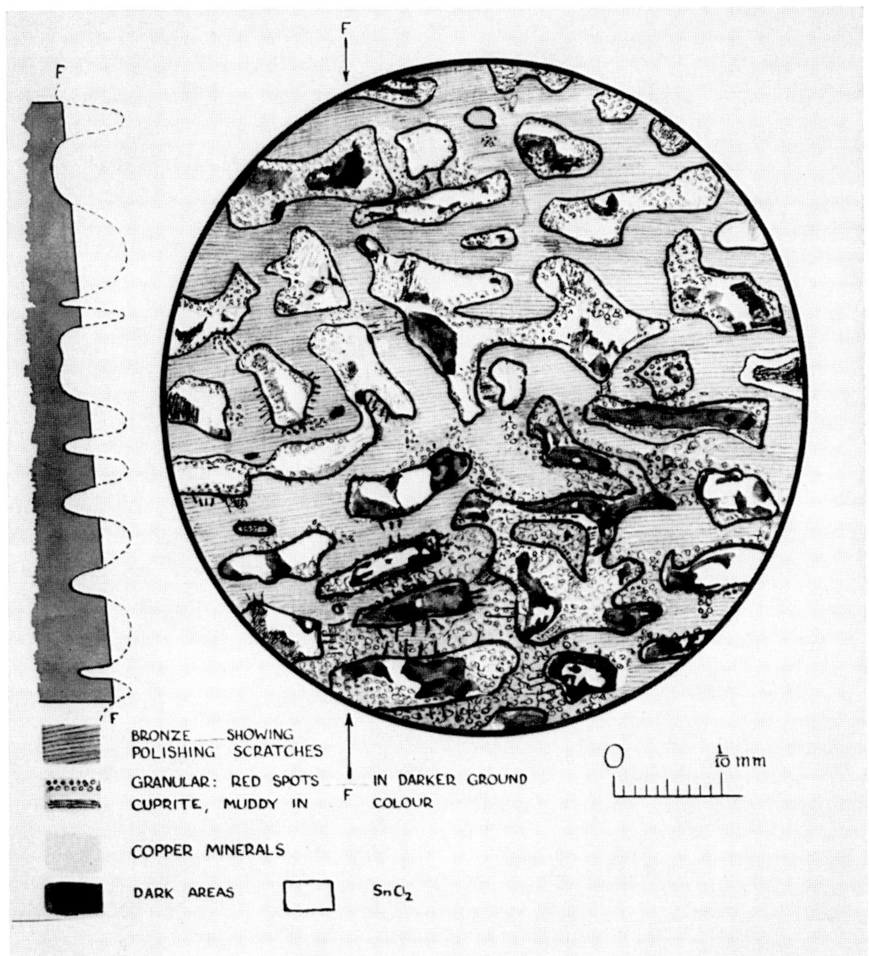

Fig. 2: The circular field of view through a microscope of a polished surface of bronze, showing diagrammatically the mineralized crystal structure present at various depths below the surface. The cross section at the left represents a section made along the line FF and shows how the plane of polishing can be arranged to cut through the corroded surface at varying depths.

surface (bottom) and interior (top) areas a discontinuous crystalline structure can be observed. In the areas near the surface this is penetrated by corrosion products, principally cuprous oxide, which in the unprepared object was continuous with any corrosion crust that happened to cover the surface.

This example came from a bronze that had suffered only light corrosion, not very apparent on casual inspection. The next object to be considered, Fig. 3, was marked externally by deep fissures, and it is instructive to learn what lay within. It was a droplet of bronze found in the remains of a Romano-British funeral pyre. When it was cross-sectioned along its greatest dimension (amounting to about one-half inch) across the superficial fissures, the structure shown in Color Plate V A was revealed. Here it can be seen that unchanged metal remains only at the right. Outside this on one side the metal is coated with a thin corrosion crust, but on the other side it has changed into a series of strata in which several corrosion products — including red cuprous oxide and white stannic oxide — alternate some sixty times. The edges of these strata correspond roughly with the external fissures.

Fig. 3: One of many striated green objects, about one-half inch long and roughly cylindrical, that were found at the site of a Romano-British funeral pyre.

Perhaps the most important feature of this cross section for our present purposes is the presence of pale green powdery material along the line separating metal from mineral strata. This material had not been present when the droplet was first sectioned but had developed as a result of deliberate exposure of the section to water vapor. If this had suddenly appeared on the outside of a bronze in a museum, it would have been considered a case of "bronze disease." It is important to note that the location of whatever mineral reacted with water vapor to generate this "disease" lay at the interface between the metal and the mineral crust.

The foregoing represents one extreme example of the corrosion of a copper alloy. Another extreme is represented by an early copper chisel from Jericho, about 8,000 years old, shown in Fig. 4. It was sectioned along the line indicated and appeared when viewed between crossed polars as shown in Color Plate V B, the height of the object in the print representing about one-fourth inch. Here the only metal that remains is represented by an indented rectangular shape in the center. This shape is outlined by a dark line of gray waxy mineral, identifiable as cuprous chloride, which is the recognized source of bronze disease. Beyond this is a thick crust of pink cuprous oxide that is bounded at the surface by a thin green crust. Evidently the chloride now present in contact with the metal has been trapped at some earlier stage of the corrosion process, and as the crust thickened it has penetrated more and more deeply into the metal.

Another important feature of this cross section is represented by the dark line halfway through the thickness of the cuprous oxide. This line encloses a rectangular shape with rounded corners and clearly represents the original surface of the chisel, now both overlaid and undermined by a growth of cuprous oxide. This cross section provides another example of the preservation of an original surface, described elsewhere in this volume by Gettens (see p. 59).

Condition of Objects in a Collection

Now that we have been alerted to the end results of prolonged processes of corrosion, we are in a better position to appreciate the condition of many of the bronzes in museums. These objects have seldom entered collections directly from an excavation. More usually they have been excavated under uncontrolled conditions and have then been prepared for the market by someone who first cracked off from above the original surface that part of the corrosion crust that obscured the more significant areas and then applied a little wax in order to restore a metallic sheen. Subsequently these objects have passed through many hands. Occasionally a new owner has the remainder of the crust cracked away but then dislikes the result and has the object repatinated. Finally it comes to rest on the shelf of a display case, exposed to light, heat, dust, and air containing varying amounts of water vapor. What can happen next?

Fig. 4: Two copper chisels from Jericho, corroded together, which had suffered damage in transit sufficient to expose the metal remaining uncorroded within a thick outer crust.

Chemical Processes of Decay

The metal of an object, protected by a complete outer crust of minerals, is shown in diagrammatic form in Fig. 5. In any one actual bronze the original complete crust depicted may no longer be present because of the treatment to which it has been subjected since its excavation. Alternatively, the crust may have a striated structure; or it may have been removed almost completely or altered into some other chemical form by various kinds of treatment; or perhaps it has been partially removed and the residue saturated with synthetic resin or wax. In whatever way the corrosion crust has been altered, so long as even a microscopically thin layer of the cuprous chloride mineral remains and is partially protected in some manner, we may expect the reactions shown in Fig. 5, or their variants, to progress, with the net result that under the combined influence of atmospheric moisture (relative humidity above about 45 per cent) and oxygen the cuprous chloride moves steadily into the remaining metal, leaving a thickened mineral crust behind. The rate at which this movement occurs is determined by the rapidity with which oxygen and water can penetrate: in our example from the dry climate of Jericho, Color Plate V B, the layer moved inward a distance of about one millimeter in 8000 years; in the example taken from the moist climate of England, Color Plate V A, a penetration of about seven millimeters occurred in less than 2000 years.

If the cuprous chloride layer happens to lose the protection of overlying mineral, we may expect a totally different reaction to occur with a resulting rapid oxidation to basic cupric chloride. This is the green powdery material found externally in examples of bronze disease or in compact form as the outer green corrosion produced on an ancient bronze. Internally it may be found sometimes as a small mass left behind by the advancing corrosion front and now surrounded on all sides by cuprous oxide.

The outbreak of bronze disease in small spots is pictured in cross section in Fig. 6, occurring at some location on the bronze where the protection afforded by the crust has been weakened, perhaps by a crack or by pollution with a spot of some hygroscopic substance that has locally increased the concentration of water. This drawing should not be accepted too literally, but it serves to illustrate the principal features of the occurrence.

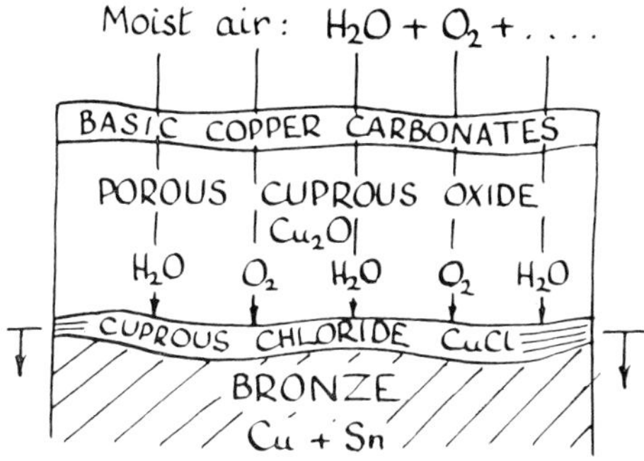

Fig. 5: Diagrammatic representation of a cross section through the surface of a mineralized bronze, suggesting a mechanism by which the mineral crust can thicken at the expense of the bronze, which corrodes away under the influence of atmospheric moisture and oxygen.

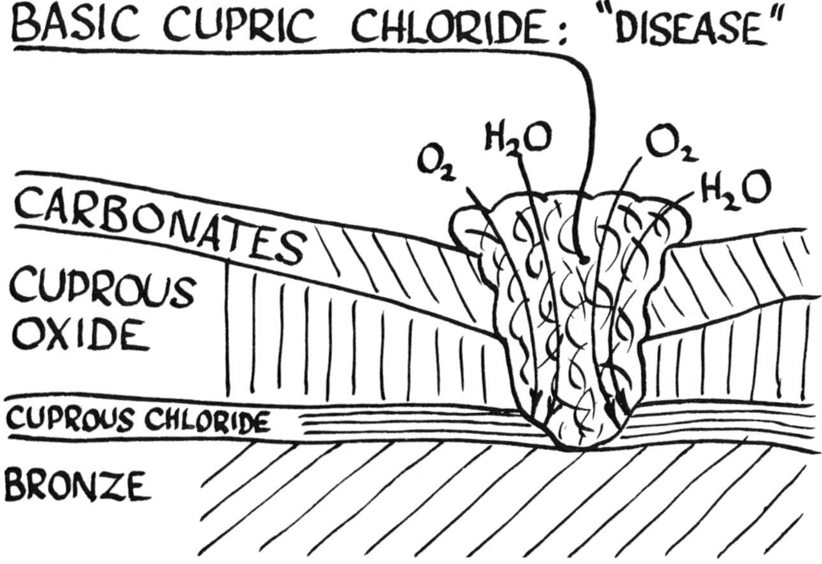

Fig. 6: Diagrammatic representation of another reaction between cuprous chloride and atmospheric oxygen in the presence of moisture. When there is little restriction to access of oxygen, a pale green powder is formed that consists of basic cupric chloride and is the symptom of active bronze disease.

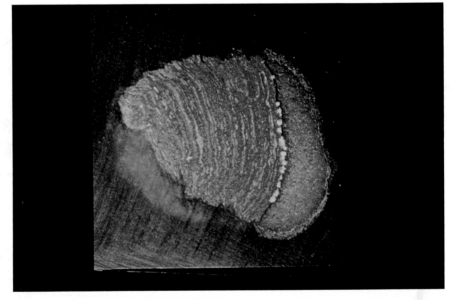

Color Plate V(A): Cross section of another object like that shown in Fig. 3. Note the stratified corrosion products to the left of the remaining unchanged metal and the narrow line of pale green bronze disease induced experimentally along the interface between metal and mineral crust by exposure to moisture vapor.

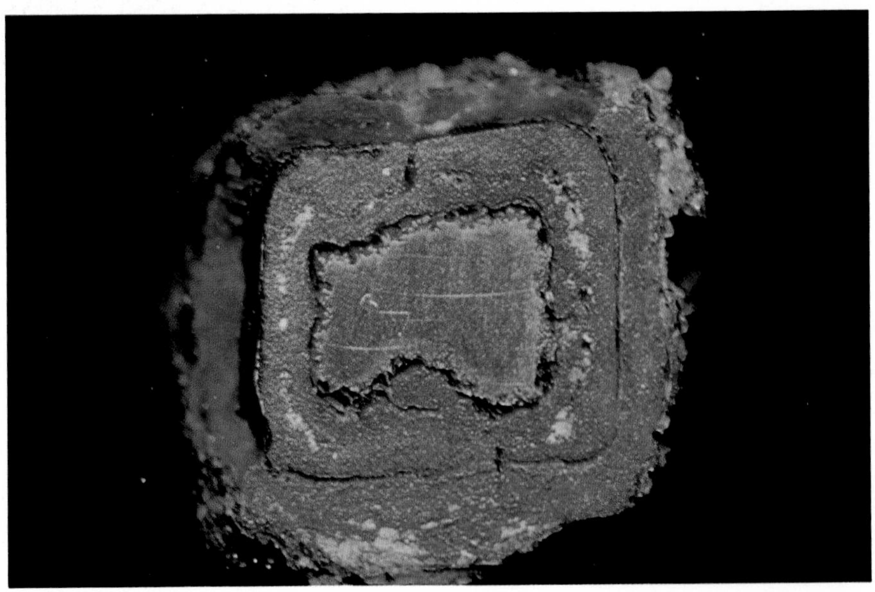

Color Plate V(B): Cross section made through the Jericho chisel at the plane marked by a line at the right side of Fig. 4. An inner core of unchanged metal is surrounded by a dark line identifiable as cuprous chloride and a double outer crust of red cuprous oxide. The rounded square between the two crusts represents the original surface of the uncorroded chisel.

Visible Evidence of Change

The least amount of harm that can occur to a bronze as a result of a history of exposure is an accumulation of grease and dust caused by handling without gloves and by lack of protection. Externally this results in loss of color contrast between, for example, a pink copper inlay and an originally yellow-bronze figure. Internally the dust falling from a polluted atmosphere may also encourage corrosion processes that start on areas of exposed metal.

A crust of smooth patina that at first sight appears to be protective — and may have been consolidated at some time with a coat of preservative lacquer or varnish in order to enhance this property — may commence to crack and to lift and then to fall away, exposing a rough surface of pitted metal. This can result from careless handling of, for example, an arm, whose ductile metal core will merely bend while its more brittle corrosion crust will crack. Then moisture vapor enters and activates unstable minerals within. On the other hand a layer of smooth corrosion crust that is obviously not protective may begin to flake away and thus permit moisture to activate unstable minerals and to form a white or pale green edging to the islands of crust that remain.

We can also recognize what may be termed "collection bronze" — objects that appear to have been partially stripped of their corrosion crust to a level below the original surface and then repatinated skillfully to blend together the appearance of the untouched and the bared surfaces. This condition can be recognized by observation under a hand lens at a magnification of about ten diameters. For example, on the right thigh of the athlete (No. 83) shown in Fig. 7, a dendritic structure (shown magnified in Fig. 8) is visible which is quite different in nature although similar in appearance to a structure that is often observable in noble so-called water patina. (See Gettens, p. 58). Unlike Gettens' example, this structure contains individual metal crystals standing in slight relief as a result of the conversion of the surrounding metallic matrix by prolonged corrosion processes into mineral, now removed.

Fig. 7: Athlete pouring a libation, 7 inches tall (No. 83). The metal has a dendritic structure that is typical of fabrication by casting.

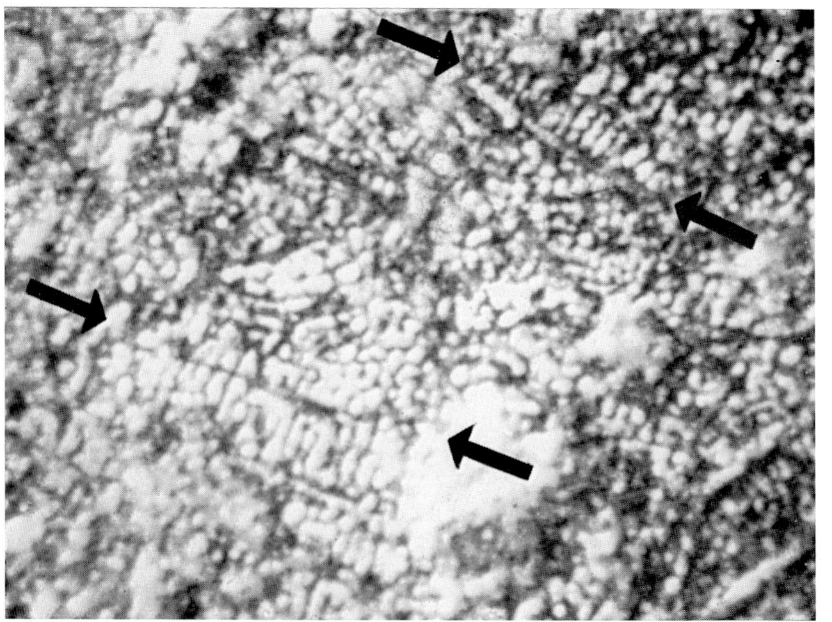

Fig. 8: Magnified view of the unprepared surface of the thigh of the athlete shown in Fig. 7. The full height of the illustration represents about 1/8 inch on the bronze. The ladder-like ("dendritic") structure of the metal crystals is visible at two areas. The quality of the picture is poor partly because the surface was not polished and etched and partly because a microscope was not used for observation.

Another example of collection bronze will be found among the hydrias, one of which (No. 110) has suffered damage in the past and has later been straightened, its fractures repaired, and its surface made uniform in appearance by some over-all application that has left evidence of dripping liquid on one side.

Fig. 9: The proper right arm of a statuette of Aphrodite with a dove (No. 93). The arm is bent at the wrist, and excessive thinning of the arm beginning just below the elbow could have resulted from incautious mechanical cleaning undertaken for cosmetic reasons.

Processes of Conservation

Next let us consider the techniques that are available to the conservator, remembering that his ultimate purpose is to prolong the life of the objects.

Cleaning

One common task is cleaning in order to remove old discolored and dulling wax. In the case of a small figure, but only if examination indicates that overpaint is absent, this process may be carried out conveniently in a chemist's Soxhlet extractor by means of an organic solvent that boils at a low temperature and is free from chlorine. Alternatively, fuller's earth mixed to a pasty consistency with toluene may be applied and left to dry until it falls off, carrying the wax with it. Old and discolored shellac can sometimes be removed by a similar method, employing alcohol in place of toluene. On the other hand, if museum dust has been allowed to collect on an unwaxed and patinated bronze, then removal may prove difficult, and in the very last resort a method of spraying gently with a feebly abrasive material may become necessary. As abrasive one may select sodium bicarbonate, which is softer ($2^1/_2$ on Mohs' scale) than any of the copper and tin minerals that are usually found in bronzes (all above $3^1/_2$ on Mohs' scale).

Clearly, there is little direct risk of shortening the life of any bronze as a result of carefully applying one of these cleaning treatments. Nevertheless there is always the additional risk of accidental damage inseparable from the necessary handling.

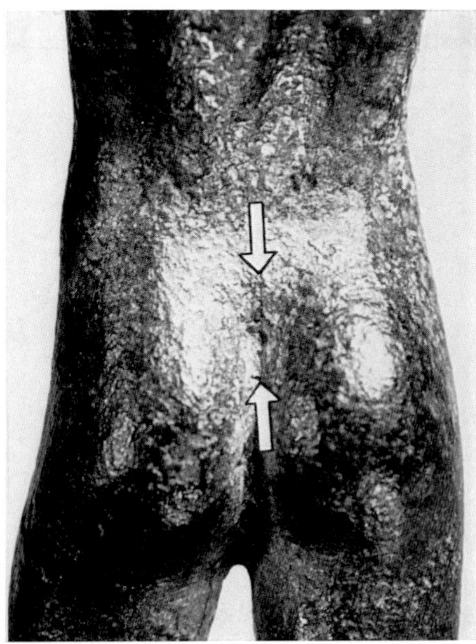

Fig. 10: A deep vertical scratch made by a slipping graver just above the buttocks of an Etruscan discobolus (No. 176).

Cosmetic

Another group of treatments may be described as "cosmetic" because their primary purpose is to improve appearance. Among these may be listed the removal of excrescences, using mechanical methods, in order to expose an original surface. When skillfully applied, these methods are effective, and little evidence of their application remains. However, in unskillful hands, especially on thickly encrusted bronze comparable to Color Plate V B, where the original surface lies midway through the incrustation, a disastrous change in appearance may result. For example, the excessive thinning of the upper right arm of the Aphrodite (No. 93) shown in Fig. 9 could well have resulted from such treatment.

As a means of reducing the risk of such an unfortunate result, some workers prefer to use tools made of materials such as ivory (about 5 on Mohs' scale) which are softer than those made of the more usual steel (about $6^1/_2$ on Mohs' scale), although not necessarily softer than the bronze on which they are required to operate. Nevertheless, it is not uncommon to find the mark of a slipping tool on a bronze, as for example in Fig. 10.

In our consideration of cosmetic treatment we have so far considered only methods of removing unsightly crusts. What precautions should we take when consolidating good surfaces that are in danger of falling off? In selecting a consolidant it is good to avoid those synthetic resins or lacquers that produce an unnatural glossy surface on a crust of mineral. It may also be argued that if a crust is in danger of detachment because a moisture-activated expansive chemical reaction is taking place beneath it, then it would be better not to employ a relatively impermeable consolidant. A more permeable layer such as Maranyl soluble nylon[2] would enable moisture to pass more easily and thereby allow measures taken to dry the bronze with the object of halting the reaction to take effect more rapidly.

Stabilization by Control of the Environment

None of the above treatments has much effect on the chemical stability of a bronze because each is concerned with the outer surface not with the interface between metal and mineral incrustation. (Figure 5 serves as a reminder of the situation that is possible.) Let us next consider what can be done to enhance stability, first considering methods that do not require treatment of the object itself.

One of the most important measures is to control the atmospheric pollution to which a bronze is exposed. For example, sulphide from vehicle exhausts tarnishes any bare bronze that happens to be exposed in the same manner as it tarnishes silver and also causes films of metal sulphides to thicken; the volatile acetic acid, present near museum cafeterias where vinegar is supplied, forms acetates that could be almost as potent a source of continuing corrosion as cuprous chloride; dust present in industrial atmospheres is usually a vehicle for ammonium sulphate, which is not only the source of obscuring bloom but can also act as a corrosive electrolyte in the presence of moisture. In view of the fact that few, if any, museums are equipped with air-conditioning systems capable of eliminating all pollution from galleries, both pollution from outside and pollution introduced by visitors themselves, local control of the environment of individual bronzes would appear to be essential. This control can be exercised by selection of a properly airtight display case open to the outer air only through a dust filter and through activated charcoal for the removal of polluting gases.[3]

The design not only of the case but also of its contents should be given attention. Figure 11 serves as a warning of the possible consequences of neglect. It represents a bronze object that was placed in a well-aged display case. After only a few years on display it was observed that white "hairs" were growing over the surface. These were identified as crystals of lead salts, which appeared to be growing from the globules of lead that are always present in leaded bronze. It is almost certain that the cause of their growth was the accumulation in the closed case of volatile organic acids liberated by the new wood of which the stand for the bronze had been constructed. Clearly, inclusion within cases of sources of injurious vapors such as new wood, new fabrics, newly applied paint, neoprene, and vulcanized rubber sealing strips should be avoided. Almost anything that has an odor perceptible to a sensitive nostril should be considered suspect until proved to be harmless.

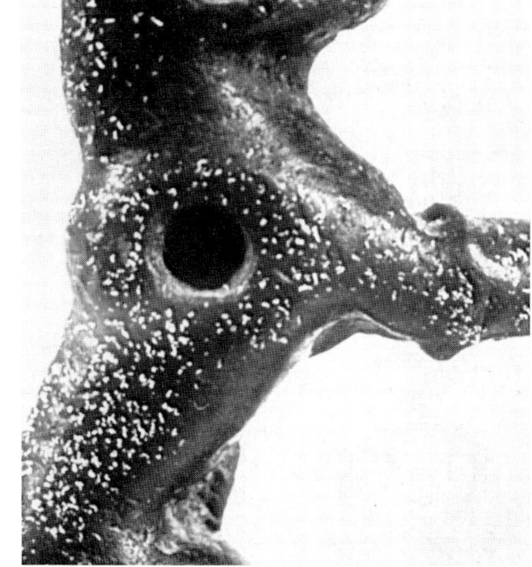

Fig. 11: The forelegs and body of a Chinese leaded-bronze animal that developed white whiskery growths of crystalline lead salts after exposure in a sealed display case. The growth was attributed to the use of a mounting block made of ill-seasoned wood.

The next important measure for stabilization without treatment of the object itself is the control of relative humidity. Figures 5 and 6 remind us that the presence of water is essential to the chemical reactions that are the sources of instability. Experiment suggests that these reactions cannot occur if the ambient relative humidity is below 35 per cent. In practice it is found that bronze disease does not occur in museums where the relative humidity only infrequently and briefly rises above 50 per cent.[4] As in the case of atmospheric pollution, if the galleries themselves cannot be conditioned satisfactorily, then the interior of the appropriately designed display cases should be dried, either by periodic insertion of freshly regenerated desiccant (silica gel, activated alumina or Drierite) or by attachment of an automatically controlled, electrically operated "Rotaire" unit.[5]

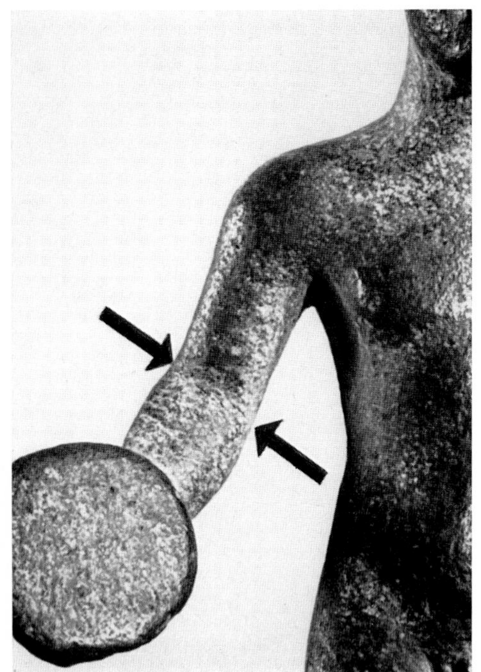

Fig. 12: The proper right arm of the discobolus (No. 176). Hairline cracks in the brittle mineral crust are visible inside the elbow.

Stabilization by Local Treatment

Let us next consider methods of stabilization that involve treatment of the object.

An example of one common problem is presented by the Discobolus shown in Fig. 12 (No. 176). The mineral crust on his right arm has developed three cracks, presumably as a result of a fall, that, unless filled, will permit free access of moisture vapor to the cuprous chloride layer, if it happens to be present in this area. Bronze disease will then develop. An obvious choice of material for use as a filler is wax, to be applied only after drying the bronze thoroughly, preferably over a desiccant *in vacuo*. Treatment of this nature has usually been reported to be not lastingly effective, but the chances of success will be enhanced if a microcrystalline wax is used in place of plain paraffin or beeswax, both of which have appreciable permeability to moisture vapor.[6] The appearance of the bronze need not be altered appreciably by this treatment, especially if a suitably colored pigment is incorporated into the wax.

Chemical methods are also available for restricting access of water vapor to the cuprous chloride exposed either at cracks in the crust or at cavities left open after the mechanical excavation of bronze disease (Fig. 13). Two of these[7] are in current use, both making use of silver salts for the purpose of reacting with chloride in order to form a seal of silver chloride. At least one of these methods has been found to be effective over a prolonged period, and again very little alteration need be made in the appearance of the surface as it had been before the outbreak of the disease.

Another local treatment[8] that has been employed at the site of disease spots is electrochemical in nature and makes use of a zinc nib wired through a milliammeter to the body of the bronze. The nib is wet first with hydrochloric acid and applied to the spot until the electric current flowing through the meter fails to increase further. The process must then be repeated at the same spot successively with phosphoric acid and sodium carbonate instead of the hydrochloric acid.

Yet another electrochemical local treatment[9] makes use of zinc filings applied to the spot of disease in strong sulphuric acid, with the object of reducing the unstable salts to stable metal.

All of the methods of local treatment noted here may be applied to any bronze, however fabricated, unless it should happen that a hollow object with core still in position has an exceptionally thin wall. In all cases, any alteration in appearance is localized and slight.

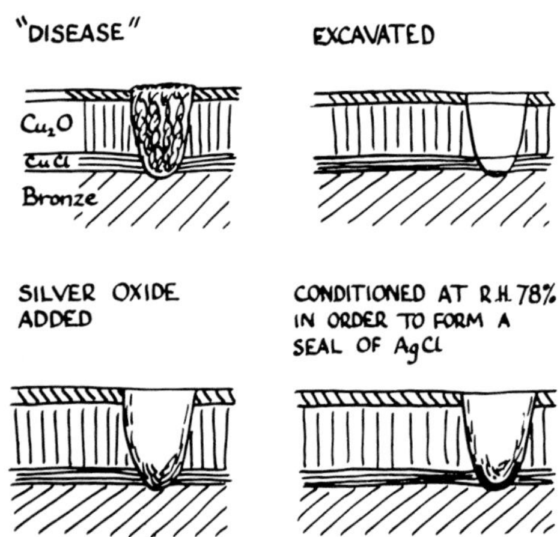

Fig. 13: A diagrammatic representation of one of the processes available for the treatment of bronze disease. The most recent method, using benzo-triazole, is described by Madsen, Studies in Conservation, *XII (1967), 163-167.*

Stabilization by Complete Immersion

Another group of stabilizing treatments involves complete immersion but causes either no change or only slight and acceptable change in appearance. These methods clearly should not be applied unthinkingly to bronzes that either are hollow or retain a porous core into which liquids may penetrate.

In one of these methods[10] the object is made the cathode in an electrolytic cell containing only distilled water. Ions sufficient to conduct small currents of electricity are provided by the more soluble portions of the mineral crust to which the water is able to gain access. These are the areas containing either active or imminent disease, and the resulting localized reduction appears to seal them off satisfactorily.

In another method the object is immersed in a weak solution of sodium sesquicarbonate, without an applied electric potential. Again, the more soluble portions of the mineral crust to which the solution is able to penetrate react with it, and the liberated chloride ions diffuse out into the liquid. The liquid is changed frequently until no more chloride ions can be detected. The great disadvantages of this method are its prolonged duration and the unwanted reactions that occur if the bronze happens to be heavily leaded.

A third and most recent method, reported by H. Brinch Madsen, *Studies in Conservation* XII (1967), 163-167, requires vacuum impregnation of the degreased and dry object in a 3 per cent by weight solution of benzotriazole in denatured alcohol. After exposure sufficient to allow the solvent to evaporate and the removal of any residual white patches of excess benzotriazole, the object may be considered to be stable.

None of these stabilizing treatments permits any guarantee by the conservator that unwanted corrosion will never recur. There is one general method that does permit such a guarantee, but it is one that should never be applied lightly to an object of art. This method involves complete removal of the corrosion crust, including the cuprous oxide layer, under controlled conditions, completed by intensive washing.[11] Naturally, if an original surface had been preserved within this crust, it will be irretrievably lost as a result of the treatment, but this is the price to be paid for complete removal of the cause of bronze disease. It may be considered to be not excessive if it happens that the original form, not surface detail, is important. The surface exposed by this treatment need not acquire a bright appearance; it is more usual for the full treatment to yield a dark, oxidized surface.

As a result of this brief discussion, the would-be conservator may ask which is the best method of treatment to select. A simple general answer cannot be supplied because of the varying circumstances surrounding the question. The most rigorously conservative treatment would be to establish the bronze in a safe environment and then never to handle it again. Such a procedure is impracticable. Let us revert to the beginning of this paper and sum up the treatments permissible for the short-term objective of allowing only a minimum of change in the appearance of the bronze. First, if darkening should have resulted from handling and from dusty or polluted atmospheres, then cleaning is necessary, but let it be skillful and indulged in no more frequently than, say, at intervals of twenty years. Second, if repairs fail or noble patina commences to flake away, then action must be taken to repair or to halt the change, bearing in mind the internal condition of the patina that supports it. Third, if bronze disease should strike — and it can be prevented altogether by provision of a suitable environment — then again immediate action must be taken. Of the several treatments noted, one should be selected that will cause little alteration in appearance. In this manner the life of the object can be prolonged and the objective of the conservator be attained.

From the preceding discussion it will be clear that a conservator cannot be only a scientist. While he must be able to understand the chemical origins of the various ills of a bronze, he must also be willing to estimate the aesthetic results of the various treatments that are possible. Conservation of professional quality therefore necessitates both access to laboratory facilities and also close collaboration by the conservator with the curator who bears responsibility for the integration of the particular bronze into his collection and who for this reason will favor one of the permissible treatments above the others.

Notes

1 Paul Coremans in *The Organization of Museums*, UNESCO Museums and Monuments, IX (Paris, 1960), 106.

2 Grade 109/P from I. C. I. (America) Inc., 151 South Street, Stamford, Conn.

3 A description of the details involved in the design of such a case was given by Padfield at the IIC London Conference on Museum Climatology, 1967, appearing on p.119 of the Preprints. (The Proceedings of this conference are available from the IIC office, 176 Old Brompton Road, London, S.W. 5, England.)

4 G. Thomson, *Recent Advances in Conservation* (London: Butterworths, 1963), 108.

5 Cargocaire Ltd., Broadway Chambers, Ilford, Essex, England and New York, San Francisco, etc.

6 Thomson, *Recent Advances* (n. 4), 143, 178.

7 H. Nichols, *Restoration of Ancient Bronzes and Cure of Malignant Patina* (Chicago: Field Museum, 1930); R. M. Organ, *Museums Journal*, LXI (1961), 54-56.

8 U. R. Evans, *Chemistry and Industry* (London, 1951), 710.

9 H. J. Plenderleith, *The Conservation of Antiquities and Works of Art* (London: Oxford University Press, 1962), 193.

10 R. J. Gettens, "La corrosion récidivante des objets anciens en bronze et en cuivre," *Mouseion*, XXXV-XXXVI (1936), 119-138.

11 R. M. Organ, *Museums Journal*, LV (1955), 112-119.

Authentication of Works of Art

William J. Young

Pliny first wrote, "We can but marvel at the fact that fire is necessary for almost every operation; by fire is iron born and by fire it is subdued; by fire gold is purified." In ancient times the sole means of attaining the heat necessary for smelting ores and melting solder for gold, silver, copper, or bronze, was probably a charcoal fire, and for small work a blowpipe was used. Depending upon the size of the work and the temperature required, the fire could be excited by a draft from a chimney or a bellows, or by fanning or using a mouth blowpipe (Fig. 1).

Originally metallurgy implied a knowledge of the art of extracting metals from their ores in sufficient purity to enable them to be employed for practical purposes. In nature metals occur in ores that require special preparation before they are submitted to smelting operations. Copper ore is often associated with more or less extraneous matter, termed the matrix or gangue. The essential character of the ore depends on the nature and condition of the contained metal. Many metals occur in the earth as sulphides. As these are often converted into oxides and carbonates by the action of air and moisture, many sulphides are found with a cap of oxide or carbonate.

While gold and silver were, perhaps, the first metals to be used by the ancients, copper was also one of the first metals to be used by them (Fig. 2). Copper-working is the earliest branch of metallurgy and is looked upon as a most dramatic stride forward in the history of mankind. It was with copper that ancient man learned to experiment and discovered the astonishing changes that could be brought about by fire and the miraculous transformation of "colored stones" into a metal; he also created the possibility of producing other metals. Armed with experience gained during centuries of transition from the early Stone Age to the metal age, he then mixed metals and ores to obtain more useful alloys.

As early as 2500 B.C., the Sumerians and their successors in Mesopotamia had developed skill in the use of gold, silver, copper, and bronze. They were not only skillful in metalworking but had also developed the art of metal coloring (Fig. 3). For instance, they developed a technique whereby a high copper alloy strongly heated with white arsenous oxide acquired the whiteness of silver (Fig. 4).

The ancients knew the value of tin, and many bronzes vary in their tin content from 2 to 30 per cent. In general, on analysis one finds Greek

Fig. 1: Metallurgical scene, part of wall painting from the tomb of Rekhmire, ca. 1450 B.C. (Drawing by Norman Davies.)

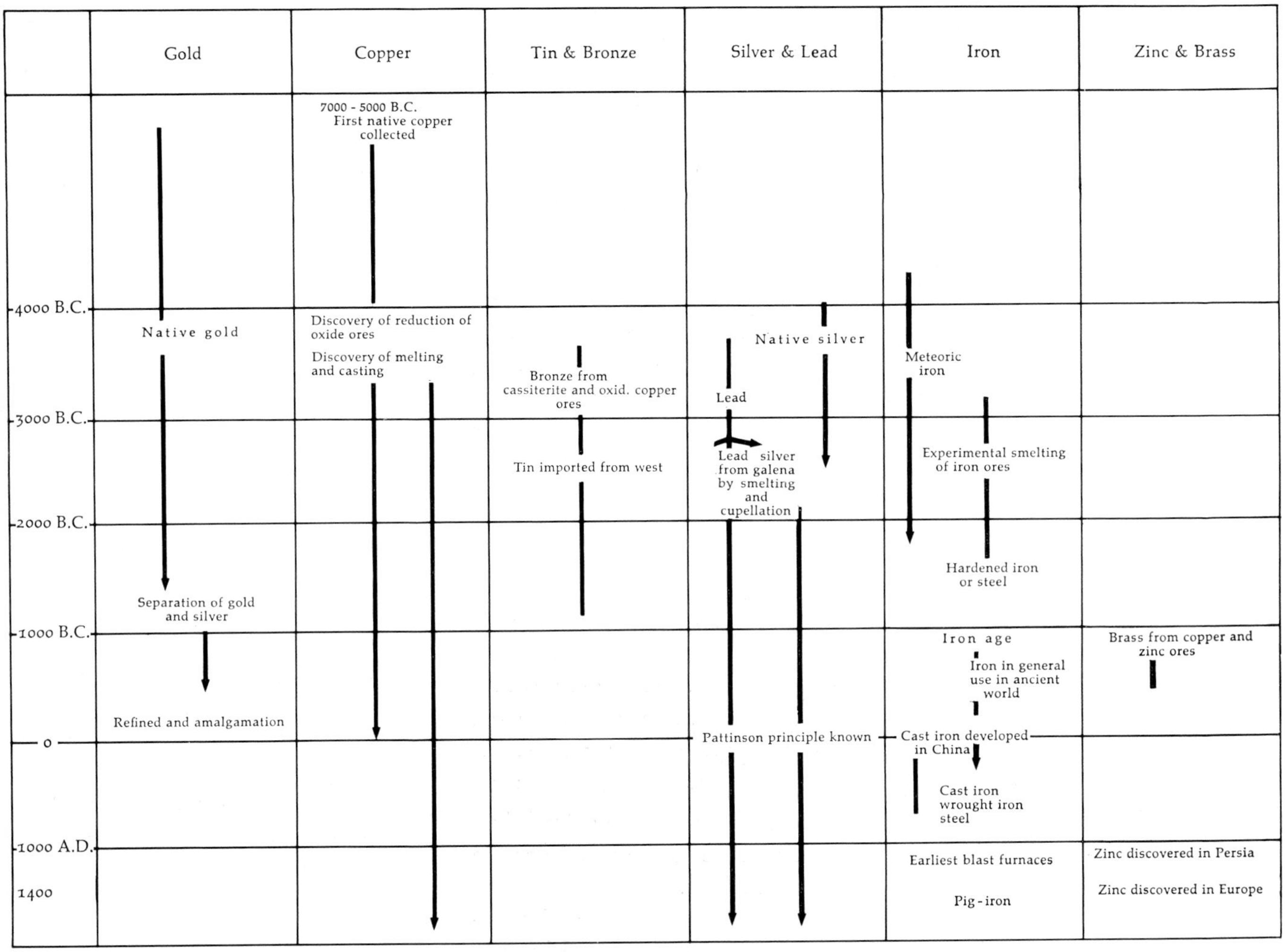

	Gold	Copper	Tin & Bronze	Silver & Lead	Iron	Zinc & Brass
		7000 - 5000 B.C. First native copper collected				
4000 B.C.	Native gold	Discovery of reduction of oxide ores Discovery of melting and casting	Bronze from cassiterite and oxid. copper ores	Native silver Lead	Meteoric iron	
3000 B.C.			Tin imported from west	Lead silver from galena by smelting and cupellation	Experimental smelting of iron ores	
2000 B.C.	Separation of gold and silver				Hardened iron or steel	
1000 B.C.	Refined and amalgamation				Iron age Iron in general use in ancient world	Brass from copper and zinc ores
0				Pattinson principle known	Cast iron developed in China Cast iron wrought iron steel	
1000 A.D.					Earliest blast furnaces	Zinc discovered in Persia
1400					Pig-iron	Zinc discovered in Europe

Fig. 2: Chart showing approximate dating of the use of metals.

Fig. 3: Anatolian bulls, pre-Hittite, ca. 2100 B.C. Left: Before electrolysis. Right: After electrolysis. Museum of Fine Arts, Boston.

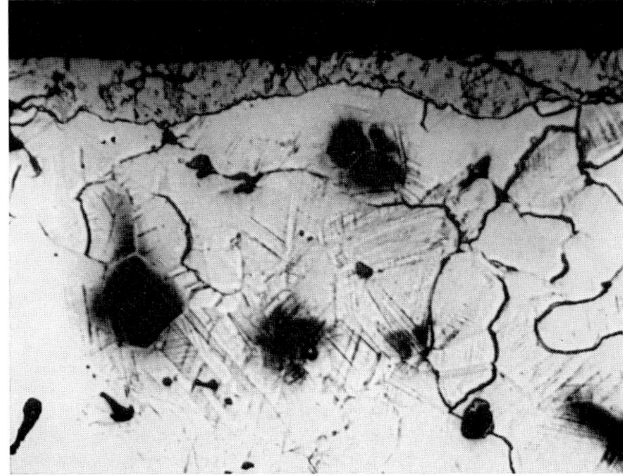

Fig. 4: Polished cross-section of Anatolian bull showing layer of arsenic on the surface of the bronze. Arsenic layer varies from 0.015 to 0.005 mm. in thickness. x 500 Etch: Potassium bichromate. (Photomicrograph by. C. S. Smith.)

metal objects to be fairly high in tin while containing a low percentage of lead. Etruscan mirrors are usually made of a high reflecting alloy containing 20 to 30 per cent tin, a tin content similar to that of Chinese mirrors.

However, in metal objects of Roman provenance one finds a lower percentage of tin and a higher percentage of lead. The Romans found that copper could be deprived of its original red coloring and acquire the yellowness of gold by prolonged heating with a mixture of charcoal and calamine. In this way a new alloy was created which gave the appearance of gold.

Today the authentication of works of art becomes increasingly difficult because as objects find their way into museums and private collections a scarcity of fine works is created. This scarcity, along with today's high market values for works of art, gives rise to a very lucrative field for the forger. Today in many cases the forger is a skilled craftsman who also avails himself of the specialized knowledge of the art historian and the chemist. Let us now examine some of the ways in which the authenticity of an ancient bronze can be determined.

Physical Examination

In the examination of a bronze figure the first approach should be a physical one. It must be determined how the bronze was fabricated, whether the object was cast by the lost-wax (*cire-perdue*) or the piece-mold method, or was hammered. Most ancient Greek and Etruscan bronzes lack mold marks, as they were cast by the *cire-perdue* process which requires a one-piece mold. The next step in the authentication of an object would be to examine the fractures to determine if they are natural or were made during casting (Fig. 5). A cast fracture would naturally arouse suspicion. Often forgeries that are stylistically correct can be readily detected by a metallurgical examination (Fig. 6). For example, a figure of Zeus that was cast in a lead alloy was subsequently given a surface plating of copper, which simplified the patination process of the surface.

Fig. 5: Piece-mold casting with cast fractures, bronze, forgery.

Incised designs were practiced from Minoan times. When a bronze has an incised design, it is important to ascertain the type of tool that was used,

Fig. 6a: Figure of Zeus. Left: forgery. Right: original.

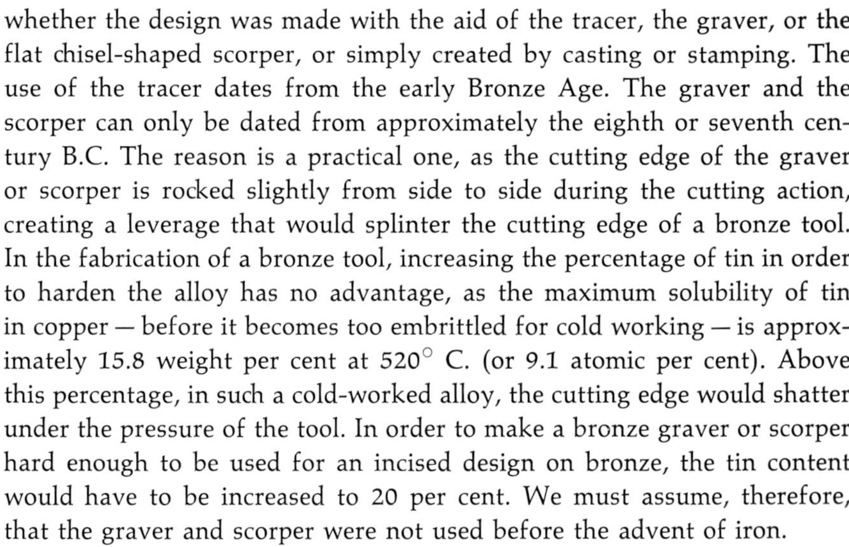

whether the design was made with the aid of the tracer, the graver, or the flat chisel-shaped scorper, or simply created by casting or stamping. The use of the tracer dates from the early Bronze Age. The graver and the scorper can only be dated from approximately the eighth or seventh century B.C. The reason is a practical one, as the cutting edge of the graver or scorper is rocked slightly from side to side during the cutting action, creating a leverage that would splinter the cutting edge of a bronze tool. In the fabrication of a bronze tool, increasing the percentage of tin in order to harden the alloy has no advantage, as the maximum solubility of tin in copper — before it becomes too embrittled for cold working — is approximately 15.8 weight per cent at 520° C. (or 9.1 atomic per cent). Above this percentage, in such a cold-worked alloy, the cutting edge would shatter under the pressure of the tool. In order to make a bronze graver or scorper hard enough to be used for an incised design on bronze, the tin content would have to be increased to 20 per cent. We must assume, therefore, that the graver and scorper were not used before the advent of iron.

The tracing tool is similar to a small chisel with a slightly beveled cutting edge (Fig. 7). The tool is held between the thumb and the finger and tilted at an angle in the direction opposite to the planned direction of travel of the design. The tracer tool is then given rapid, light blows to create an incised line in the metal. Where the metal is depressed, one finds on examination a small mound on each side of the incised line no metal is removed. The graver is a diamond-shaped tool that is pushed forward with a slight rocking motion making a "v" cut in the metal. A small amount of metal is removed in this process. At the bottom of the groove one usually finds a telltale track left behind by such a tool.

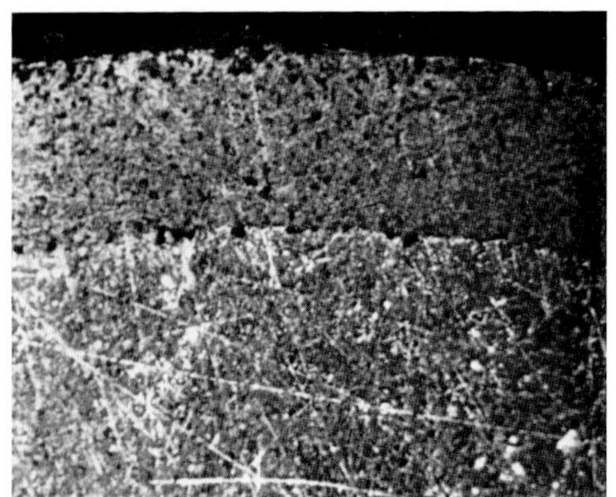

Fig. 6b: Microstructure of forgery of Zeus showing surface plating of copper. x 20.

The scorper can vary in shape. The characteristic design usually observed (Fig. 8) is made by a flat-edged, chisel-shaped tool cut at an angle. When in use it is held between the thumb and forefinger with the handle situated in the hollow of the palm of the hand. The tool is driven forward by pressure, with an angular side-to-side rocking motion that creates a zigzag design (Fig. 9) and removes a small amount of metal.

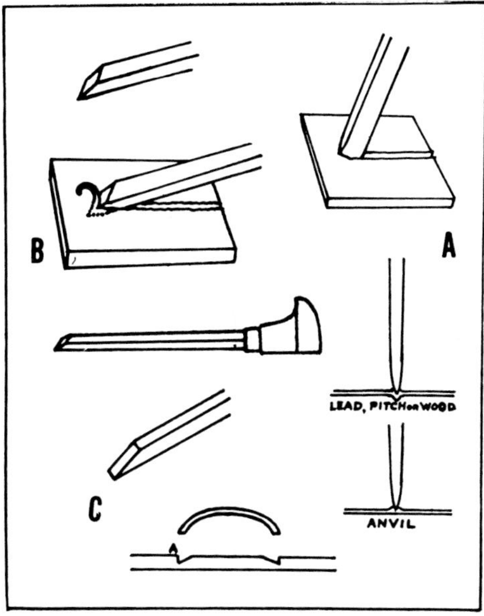

Fig. 7: *Drawing of (A) tracer tool, (B) graver, and (C) scorper. (Drawing by Herbert Maryon.)*

Corrosion

Factors affecting the rate of corrosion of metals are numerous: the nature of the metal; the presence and amount of impurities, both hemophase and heterophase; the presence of cavities, of internal stresses, and of grains physically different from the rest or in contact with other metals.

The initial corrosion may be observed to be either incipient or selective, depending in part on the constituents of the alloy and the environment to which the bronze was exposed. In incipient corrosion (Fig. 10) one observes the corrosion penetrating into the grains themselves, while in selective corrosion (Fig. 11) the initial corrosion follows the grain boundaries. At the initial corrosion stage cuprite is formed along with the oxide, tenorite. The carbonates usually observed are malachite and azurite. In an ancient bronze one can often observe a color change in the eutectoid caused by infiltration by a liquid during burial. The more noble metals, such as gold and silver, have a low affinity for oxygen; their stability is an essential character of the metal itself. When a metal such as copper, iron, silver, or gold is alloyed with another metal and subjected to burial, it is exposed to various chemical agents of corrosion, organic acids, and carbonated waters, along with electric currents that greatly influence the course of corrosion.

Electrochemical Series

Gold	Cobalt
Platinum	Cadmium
Silver	Iron
Mercury	Zinc
Copper	Aluminum
Lead	Magnesium
Tin	Sodium
Nickel	Potassium

Fig. 8: *Fibula with decorated catchplate, showing design made by scorper. Greek geometric, ca. 800-700 B.C., said to have come from Thebes. Museum of Fine Arts, Boston, 98.643.*

Fig. 9: *Fibula with decorated catchplate, enlargement showing use of scorper.*

Fig. 10: Incipient corrosion penetrating the grains, Thai Buddha, ninth to tenth century A.D. Dark field illumination. x *20.*

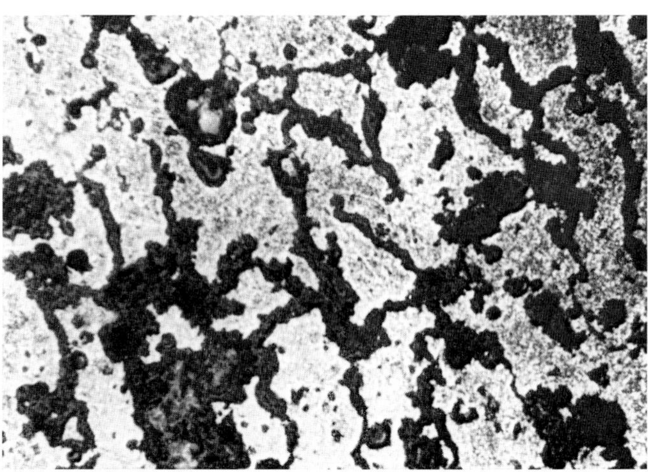

Fig. 11: Selective corrosion following grain boundaries, Egyptian rivet. Dark field illumination. x *20.*

Fig. 12: Korean Ewer Basin, eleventh century A.D., before electrolysis.

Fig. 13: Korean Ewer Basin, after electrolysis, revealing a silver basin, gold plated by gold/mercury amalgam.

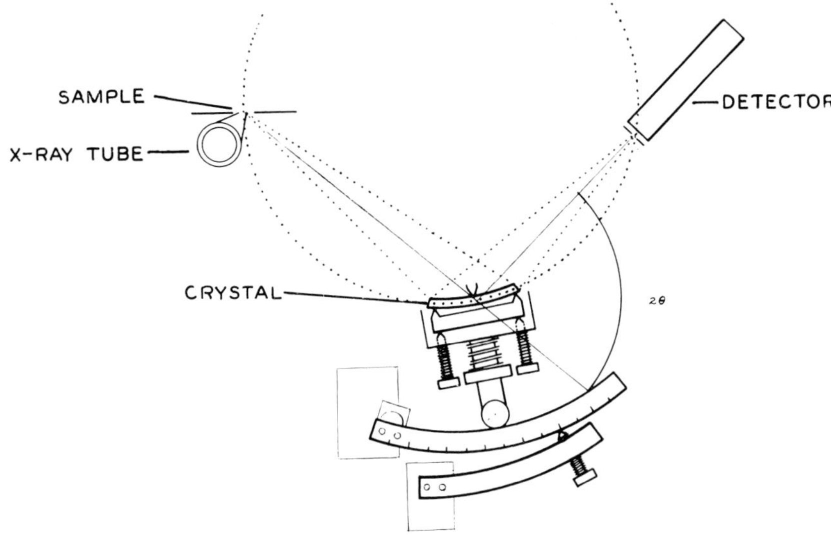

Fig. 14: X-ray mini-probe with curved crystal optics.

Corrosion, as we understand it, is mainly an electrochemical action, and an alloyed metal is affected according to its position in the electrochemical series. Mother Nature is very orderly. The noble metals are more easily reducible but are not easily corrodible. The reactive metals, reducible with difficulty, are very easily corrodible. If an alloy consisting of a solid solution of one metal in another is subjected to anodic treatment under conditions of potential that would allow the more reactive metal to pass into the ionic state, it would leave the more noble metal undissolved. Under certain circumstances "parting" (Fig. 12) takes place, the result of the reactive metal passing into solution and the noble metal remaining (Fig. 13). This action continues until the constituents of the metal have turned into their own oxides, with eventual enrichment at the surface.

Such a condition can be measured nondestructively by X-ray fluorescence analysis using the mini-probe technique (Fig. 14). The X-rays are collimated down to a diameter of 0.5 mm. An object or a cross section of one can be made to travel across the beam from the outer surface into the center of the bronze. At definite points a signal is registered, giving a semiquantitative analysis of the enrichment of copper, tin, etc. (Fig. 15).

From this description it is evident that alterations occur within the bronze itself. The patination, therefore, should be part of the bronze. Much information can be obtained if a minute piece of the surface patina of a bronze, including original metal, is removed from the object to ascertain whether the malachite layer is in contact with a cuprous oxide layer or lies directly on the surface of the metal. In the latter case, unless the bronze is of a high lead content or another satisfactory reason is found, the condition would arouse suspicion.

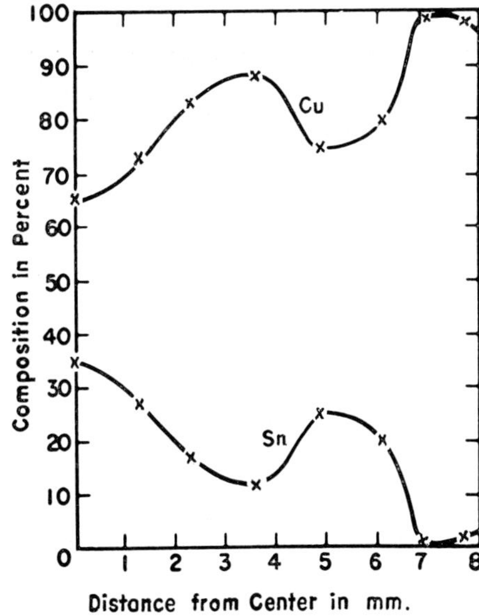

Fig. 15: Surface enrichment of copper in a tin bronze.

The Metallurgical Microscope

To the untrained eye a metal object would appear to be made of a structureless noncrystalline material. As the properties of any metal are altered when it is alloyed with another, the metallurgist would observe the same object in a more sophisticated manner under a microscope, where he would try to determine the composition of the alloy.

Metals are solid and opaque. The metallurgical microscope is designed to examine the surface of a metal by reflected light. When a small polished section of metal is etched with a weak acid, it reveals that metals are built up of innumerable small grains. When a molten alloy begins to solidify, minute crystals form at various points in the liquid, and these grow by developing branches. These treelike formations are known as "dendrites." When a polished specimen of a pure metal is examined under the microscope, no evidence of dendrites can be observed. However, when a cast alloy is examined microscopically, the dendrites can usually be seen. A skilled metallurgist can learn a great deal about the structure and history of an object from the polished section — whether the object was cast or was made by hammering, or whether the metal was first cast, then hammered, and subsequently heated (Fig. 16).

A metallurgical examination is one of the most reliable tests for the authentication of a metal object. Under the microscope the initial corrosion in the metal can be observed, which, along with the study of the corrosion products, supplies scientific proof of genuineness (Fig. 17).

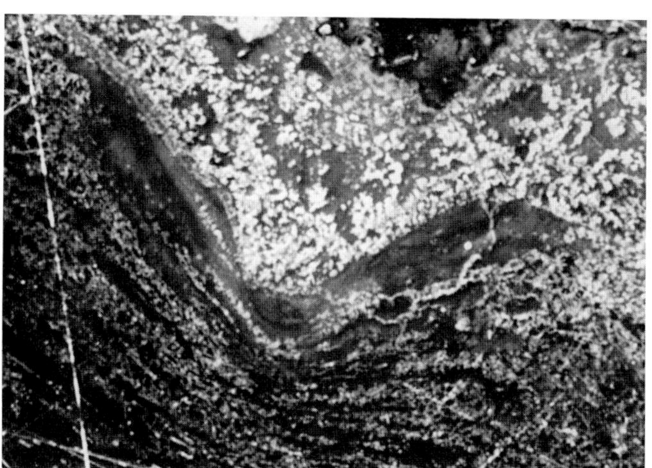

Fig. 16: Cross section of Greek helmet showing cold-worked structure by hammering. Dark field illumination. x 20.

Fig. 17: Cross section of Greek helmet showing surface and intermediate corrosion zones. Dark field illumination. x 20.

Chemical Analysis of Bronzes

Determination of the chemical composition of a metal object is important in order to ascertain the presence or absence of certain elements. For example, while the Romans were successful in producing a high zinc alloy, which they used mainly for coinage and rarely for statuary, nineteenth-century copies of Greek originals are usually found to be of high-zinc-content bronze or brass.

Spectrochemistry is an instrumented method for performing chemical analyses, a method for defining what elements are present in a material and how much of each. It is practiced most commonly by making the sample or object the pole of an electrical circuit, so that the sample is burned in an arc or spark discharge. The light produced contains the characteristic frequencies or light wave lengths of all elements present, and when these are separated into an orderly array of wave-length progression by a spectrograph, an optical emission spectrum is produced. Optical spectrochemical analysis is a widely practiced technique and indeed has been used in the archaeological field for over thirty years.

The recent invention of the optical laser (Fig. 18) led to proposals that energies to produce optical emission from a sample might be derived from a light beam in place of an electric discharge. Furthermore, it was postulated that this method might permit direct sampling with little damage to the object. In the Museum of Fine Arts Research Laboratory analyses have been carried out with the aid of the laser microscope on bronze, corrosion films, and other metals and materials. The laser beam used during these experiments was produced from a ruby crystal which has reproducibility comparable to that obtained with a spark emission spectrum. Recently a more advanced version of the laser has been developed using a neodymium-doped glass rod that produces an emission at 1.06 microns. As the neodymium-doped rod is not as temperature-sensitive as a ruby crystal, when exposures are spaced fifteen to twenty-five seconds apart, good reproducibility is attained with an improved output of better than ± 3 per cent.

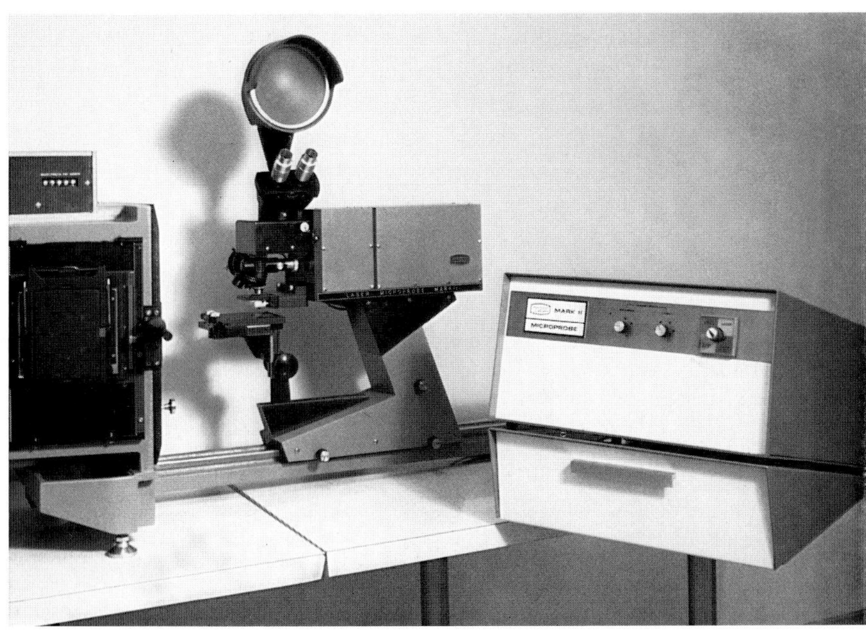

Fig. 18: Optical laser microprobe.

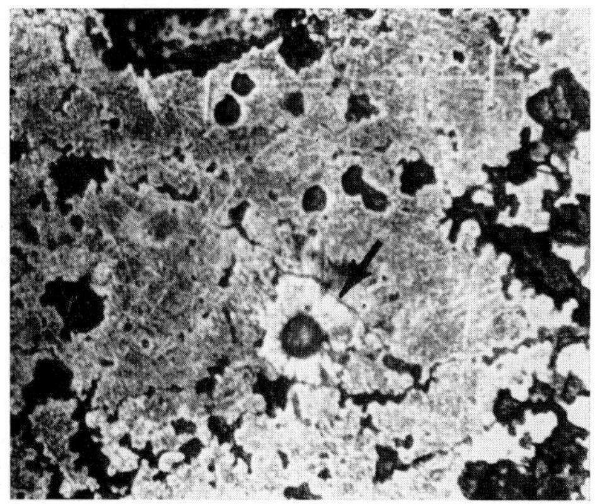

Fig. 19: Impact area of laser on Egyptian rivet. x 6.5.

The laser microscope is mounted on the optical bar in front of the spectrograph. Its optics are so arranged that the pulse of coherent radiation, which leaves the rod in a horizontal direction, is turned through 90 degrees by a prism. It then passes through the microscope objective, which focuses the radiation. Without preliminary preparation a sample or an object may be placed on the microscope bench and located in the focal plane in readiness to receive the laser beam. The binocular eyepiece of the microscope has an optical system at the same axis as the laser beam. The exact impact area may be chosen by the aid of a cross-hair eyepiece. The crater left by the laser beam is a function of the photon density in that particular focal site. A low energy beam produces smaller craters. By means of a variable control, it is possible to limit the impact area crater to 5 microns in diameter. Luminosity of the resulting vapor plume is low; therefore, in order to produce satisfactory results for spectrographic analysis, the resultant vapor plume from the sample is raised in temperature by making it pass through a charged electrode gap. The plume provides a short circuit that raises the temperature by stored energy in the electrode gap and in so doing increases the luminosity necessary for successful spectrographic analysis.

In general, the laser removes a sample slightly larger than a human hair, 50 to 80 microns in diameter, with an average depth of 80 to 100 microns (Fig. 19).[1]

Fig. 20: Photograph taken under ultraviolet rays of Chinese bronze chia, Shang Dynasty, indicating restored areas (light areas).

Examination under Ultraviolet Rays

Many materials will fluoresce under ultraviolet light, as they absorb light at a certain wave length and re-emit much of this absorbed energy as light at a longer wave length. If a bronze that has had a false pigmented patina applied to the surface is put in the path of these invisible light rays, energy will be absorbed and immediately re-emitted as visible light or fluorescence, and since no two materials will produce the same fluorescence, such an examination is often a rapid way of determining the heterogeneity of an object (Fig. 20).

In the past in the examination of a work of art it was customary to rely mainly on visual observations made either by the unaided eye or with the aid of a lens or low-power microscope. While this method of approach cannot be superseded, it can often be profitably supplemented with more specialized investigations. Scholarship cannot be overemphasized. A stylistic judgment can be a rewarding one, but it has certain shortcomings when not supported by scientific fact.

Note

1 F. Brech and W. J. Young, "The Laser Microprobe and Its Application to the Analysis of Works of Art." *Application of Science in Examination of Works of Art* (Boston: Museum of Fine Arts, 1967), 230.

Discussion Session 1.2

Harold J. Plenderleith, *Discussant*

Dr. Harold J. Plenderleith, the discussant, opened the discussion with the following remarks.

"The papers in this session seem to have fitted together very well with a minimum of overlapping to give us an interesting and satisfactory picture of some of the ways in which science can be of service to art.

"Mr. Gettens began in Cambridge many years ago and made an early reputation for himself in studying the pigments used in fresco paintings and easel paintings. It is a very natural transition from this to the study of the minerals found in decomposing bronzes. Having lived for a number of years in the nirvana of the Freer Gallery in Washington, among a collection of wonderful specimens, he is completely spoiled and always looks for minerals of gemlike quality on any bronze find. So much is this the case that we did not hear much about the "vile" constituents from him, but Mr. Organ made up for that.

"The study of Chinese bronzes is one of the most absorbing studies that any technologist can take up in a museum because these objects have been very well preserved and because they have such satisfactory patinas. For a man like Mr. Young, who looks into questions of genuineness, they offer the possibility of gaining information, not only from the metal itself and the technical workings of the alloy but also from the minerals that derive from the same. The condition of a mineral is often a very good indication of the authenticity of the specimen. Mr. Gettens mentioned copper oxide and cuprite, and when he discussed the patina of metal roofs in Washington, he emphasized the green brochanite [$Cu_4SO_4(OH)_6$] which is so characteristic, not only in Washington but also in Boston. But it is of interest that the churches that are covered with copper in Switzerland, where the atmosphere is pure, are patinated in cuprite, which is a rich brown-red color. They don't get as far as the brochantite; in fact, they might provide a useful source of aged copper with cuprite on it.

"The oxides of copper are a much more complicated subject of study than we may admit. The black surfaces were described as being in the vile category, but very satisfactory black surfaces do exist on copper alloys, particularly those used in mirrors, where there is a burnished surface. Burnishing may have something to do with the growth of the very thin black lacquerlike layer found on these objects, which is almost like niello in character.[1] Much of it must be tenorite, but this alone does not account for the surface. In my early days I was once set to analyzing some Korean speculum metal which had this black surface. I was unable to dissolve it in any of the normal acids and alkalis. I could dissolve the high tin alloy from a broken edge but not through the black coating, until by chance I came across an old book about silicon bronzes and just as a matter of course splashed some hydrofluoric acid on the metal. The black came off like paint! It therefore appears possible that there is some silicon or silica constituent in that black layer.

"I was amused also to hear Mr. Gettens talk about his sporting hunt for unusual minerals. That reminds us of the dogged integrity of his work in this connection. All these years he has worked with these minerals in the laboratory and missed nothing.

"These papers have all been dealing with the ultimate constitution of things — the minerals, materials themselves, and how they age with time. Mr. Organ has considered what should be preserved and what should not be preserved when one is charged with the responsibility of conserving an object, as well as what method it is best to use. In the textbooks many methods for dealing with corroded metals are described. By no means are they all essential or necessary. Some are very necessary, and we cannot do without them. But it must be confusing for a beginner to select the best method for the job at hand. A very careful laboratory study must be made before one begins, before one makes the actual decision as to what method to use. People sometimes tend to use one single method far too much. If you ask a young man how to clean a bronze he will probably say at once, without any hesitation, "Oh, I'll reduce it." Of course, that is usually the way to wreck it. It certainly would destroy any patina that it had.

"I remember once going into a laboratory that was full of jars in which there were corroded bronzes in sodiumsesquicarbonate. This man had the idea that sodiumsesquicarbonate is a safe thing to use for bronzes, so when a bronze came along it went straight into the sodiumsesquicarbonate. But he did not take account of the fact that the normal treatment of a bronze in sodiumsesquicarbonate may last eight months or a year, or two years. In the meantime the archaeologists are digging up more bronzes all the time, and the results are stagnating in the laboratory.

"One has to think not only of the method with which one is most experienced but also of the characteristics of other methods. Indeed, Alfred Lucas,[2] who did a lot of work in Egypt on Tutankhamen's tomb, latterly came to the conclusion that the best method of all was the mechanical picking method. I am quite sure he would not argue that now. Professor Gustav A. T. Rosenberg of the National Museum, Copenhagen, came to the conclusion that the ultimate answer to cleaning spotty bronzes was to treat them with a mixture of agar-agar, glycerine, and aluminum.[3] I have tried that, and it made a frightful mess of the bronze. It seemed to cure the spots, but it was almost impossible to get rid of the resulting aluminum chloride dust afterward. One would make a special plea, therefore, for those who are interested in beginning this work to study the methods, choose a few that are reliable, and get to know the best conditions under which they can be used.

"Mr. Organ and Mr. Gettens were dealing with the tangibles and Mr. Young mostly with the intangibles. He has first to study the genuine specimen in order to recognize what its characteristics are. But I think it is seldom possible to prove that an object is genuine. One can very often prove that it is fake, but to prove it is genuine is much more difficult. One may even prove that a bronze is old, but it might not be genuine, that is, it might be of a different date or from a region other than that to which it had been attributed. This study of instrumentation as applied to the investigation of authenticity is entrancing, and in this particular field Mr. Young is a pioneer. Few people have the facilities that he has to marshal an arsenal of equipment to solve particular problems like this, and we all wish him very well in these studies."

General discussion then followed. Dr. Herbert A. Cahn asked Mr. Organ whether electrolytic reduction should be used on bronzes. Mr. Organ replied that this depends on the problem. Electrolytic reduction might be used, under carefully controlled conditions, to recover the original surface of an object embedded in a heavy layer of mineralization. Once the object has been cleaned in this way, it can be chemically repatinated to give its surface the appearance it had before corrosion. In some cases, he added, electrolytic reduction is the only possible method for obtaining the desired result; for example, it would be essential for regenerating silver from metal corroded almost completely to silver chloride without losing the shape of the object.

Mr. Organ cautioned that the electrolytic method should be used only by a person experienced with the materials on which he is asked to work. The conservator should bear in mind that a variety of methods is available to meet specific problems, and no one method should be used exclusively. If for some reason only a single method can be employed, he suggested that it should be a mechanical one. Mechanical cleaning can be the safest method if done by a skilled person, although untrained persons can make the mistake of going too far (see p. 80, Fig. 9).

He then discussed the silver oxide method, used to treat bronze disease on patinated surfaces when it is desirable not to lose the patina. The diseased spot is excavated, and silver oxide is put into the surface and compacted at about 78 per cent relative humidity to form an impermeable seal over the area, so that the cuprous chloride which has not yet been activated will be sealed off from contact with the air. Another method involves the use of silver nitrate, although Mr. Organ has not found this to be successful, and yet another, developed by Henry Nichols in Chicago, uses silver sulfate. This method is successful in some parts of the world but not in places such as London, possibly because of the humidity of the climate. In fact, the corroded bronze droplet (Organ, Fig. 3) had been treated with silver sulfate, followed by baryta-water, before sectioning, but outbreak of the disease under deliberately humid conditions had not been prevented.

Dr. Plenderleith asked Mr. Young whether examples are known of bronzes plated with arsenic or antimony, mentioning that the Near Eastern bull in the Museum of Fine Arts, Boston (Young, Fig. 3) was the only such example of which he knew. Mr. Young said that he knew of no other examples of arsenic plating, although arsenic often occurs in copper ores. Dr. Plenderleith pointed out that although careful analysis had proved that this was not the case with the bull, a novice using the electrolytic tank without cleaning the electrolyte could accidentally plate an impurity such as antimony onto a bronze.

It was asked what impact both the heat and the deposition of hydrocarbons and resins that would result from a wood fire would have on bronzes. Dr. Plenderleith explained that heat would melt the cuprous chloride on a corroded bronze and cause certain deformations that would result in a reorientation of the corrosion in a different direction, especially if there were moisture involved.

Mr. Organ added that an early treatment for bronze disease, based on the misconception that it was caused by germs, was cauterization; a red-hot wire was plunged into the diseased area. He speculated that perhaps this treatment might serve a useful purpose, as cuprous chloride melts at about 420° C., and the heat might thoroughly dry out the cuprous chloride layer and postpone further outbreaks of disease for perhaps a decade.

It was then asked whether any assumptions could be made about the rate of formation of patina or corrosion and whether any experimentation on the rate had been done under controlled or simulated conditions.

Mr. Young replied that some objects have been buried for a period of time in order to form an accelerated patina. Even the patinas on Chinese bronzes have been accelerated. It is usually possible to detect an accelerated patina with enough experience. He suggested that perhaps the most certain way to find out if a patina is original is to polish a small section of the object down to the metal in order to see the initial corrosion and the enrichment of the surface — to see the copper and tin actually leaving the object and going to the surface to create a patina.

Mr. Gettens described an experiment now in progress at the Freer Gallery of Art. About five years ago they had cast a series of discs of sixteen different compositions, one-quarter inch thick and four inches in diameter. Pure copper, pure tin, and pure lead were included, as well as alloys of copper-tin and copper-tin-lead, graduated in 5 per cent steps — i.e., 95 per cent copper-5 per cent tin, 90 per cent copper-10 per cent tin, etc., down to about 75 per cent copper. Twelve sets of these discs were made, several of which are in the process of being subjected to accelerated corrosion under different conditions. Among the locations are a Maryland barnyard, a fountain at the Freer Gallery of Art, the Freer garden, and a tide-level site at Wilmington Beach, N.C. There will be no significant data from this experiment for at least ten years, however. Mr. Gettens mentioned that one of the most important studies on the corrosion of Greek bronzes was published by Professor Caley in 1941.[4]

Mr. Organ stated that the National Bureau of Standards has a publication on the underground corrosion of modern metals.[5] He pointed out that unless one knows precisely the environmental conditions to which an object has been subjected and is certain that these conditions have remained unchanged for a given period of time, it is extremely difficult to draw any conclusions about the rate of patina formation. The Jericho chisel (Color Plate V B) grew a crust of cuprous oxide about a millimeter thick in 8,000 years, whereas the bronze droplet (Color Plate V A) grew a series of layers of corrosion products about seven millimeters thick in less than 2,000 years.

Mr. George Ortiz asked Mr. Young whether the pattern on the Boeotian or Thessalian fibula he discussed (Young, Fig. 8) was made with a rounded chisel, as D. K. Hill suggested in discussing a class of similar objects,[6] or with a flat chisel. Mr. Young replied that the tool used was a scorper — or engraving tool — which actually removes metal, rather than a tracing tool, which makes a characteristic broken line at the bottom of the groove but displaces the metal rather than removing it. On the fibula in question one can see where the scorper was twisted. One side is a very light line and the other a heavy scoop.

Mr. Gettens was asked whether tenorite is found only between the bronze core and cuprite or whether it could exist above the malachite surface, as it seemed to in the Egyptian bronze aegis (Color Plate II). He replied that he had not examined that object in detail but that the patches of tenorite and malachite alternate. Tenorite is generally the product of the heat decomposition of malachite, although he could not say that this was the cause of the tenorite formation in this example.

Mr. Thomas Morton asked about the use of niello to heighten the effect of engraving. Dr. Plenderleith recommended a study on the subject by A. A. Moss.[7] The speakers pointed out that niello is not used on bronze but on brass, silver, and possibly copper.

Mr. Young asked Professor Cyril S. Smith about the action of arsenic in copper. Arsenic was used instead of tin in early copper alloys, he said, and has been proved to serve as a protective agent against corrosion. He inquired whether the presence of arsenic in two metals would facilitate their joining.

Professor Smith replied that in the transition from the use of copper alone to the extensive use of bronze there was a period of several hundred years in which arsenic was used extensively as an alloying element.[8] Copper-arsenic alloys, though inferior to copper-tin alloys, are superior to copper in many ways: they melt more easily, are harder, and produce sounder castings. The principal disadvantage of these alloys is that men who work with them do not live very long! Copper-antimony alloys are also archaeologically important. They have fairly good properties, although they get brittle before they get very hard. He explained that the relatively uncorroded surface of the bull (Young, Fig. 3) resulted from the presence of a thin layer of the intermetallic compound Cu_3As formed on the surface, apparently by a low-temperature cementation operation. Small amounts of arsenic in solid solution in copper improve its corrosion resistance somewhat, but the compound is in a different class.

Notes

1 John D. Cooney, "On the Meaning of Black Bronze," *ZAeS*, XCIII (1966), 43-47.

2 Alfred Lucas, *Ancient Egyptian Materials and Industries*, ed. and revised by J. R. Harris (4th ed.; London, 1962).

3 Gustav A. T. Rosenberg, *Antiquités en fer et en bronze* (Copenhagen, 1917), 87 ff.

4 Earle R. Caley, "The Corroded Bronze of Corinth," *ProcPhilSoc*, LXXXIV (1941), 689 ff.

5 Melvin Romanoff, "Underground Corrosion," *National Bureau of Standards Circular* 579 (1957).

6 Dorothy K. Hill, "Six Early Greek Animals," *AJA*, LIX (1955), 39, no. 1

7 A. A. Moss, "Niello," *Studies in Conservation*, I:2 (1953), 49-62.

8 For the properties of Cu-As alloys see J. R. Maréchal, *Reflections upon Prehistoric Metallurgy* (Lammersdorf, 1963), 24 ff. J. A. Charles, "Early Arsenical Bronzes — A Metallurgical View," *AJA*, LXXI (1967), 21-27.

PART 2

Introduction to Part 2

Arthur Steinberg

Since these papers deal mainly with Oriental and Orientalizing bronzes, they raise the difficult and critical question of the transmission or diffusion of subjects, motifs, and techniques from one culture to another. What we should like to know more about, of course, is how these elements were passed on, by whom, and why. Bound up with these questions is the whole renaissance of Greek culture in the eighth century, for not only were techniques and styles adopted from the Near East at this time, but so were the alphabet, currency, and probably a good many precepts of commerce, politics, and even religion, of which we know much less. There appears to have been a large-scale diffusion of Near Eastern (Syrian, Phoenician, Urartian, Assyrian, Egyptian, etc.) cultural elements to receptive and reawakening Greece, resulting in a synthesis that produced the archaic period in Greece. Clearly Greece makes something new out of what it has borrowed (as Hoffmann observes about the Cretan armor), but we should not lose sight of the fact that there is wholesale borrowing that must be satisfactorily explained. For in the mechanics of this transmission lie some of the basic elements of artistic and technological creation and organization.

Muscarella deals with the fascinating problem of the griffin protomes that decorated cauldrons. The iconography of these griffins is Oriental (I do not want to take sides in the dispute over whether they are Urartian or North Syrian), and presumably the religious connotations of the griffin were also adopted from the Orient, but in both cases the questions "how" and "why" arise. We cannot go very far in determining why these elements were adopted until we have many more of them in excavated contexts in both the Orient and Greece, but there are some interesting speculations that arise regarding the "how" of the adaptation.

It is not at all clear how these protomes and cauldrons came to Greece and Etruria — whether they were traded or made there by itinerant craftsmen who brought both techniques and styles with them from the Near East and then adapted them to their local clients' demands. What makes these protomes of particular interest is the technique in which they were first produced, an extremely skillful high repoussé. This is an unusual technique (Fig. 1), with a limited distribution in the Near East that includes situlae imported to Gordion and material in the Iranian and North Syrian sphere of influence, including pieces at Hasanlu and from Luristan as well as earlier high-repoussé vessels in northern Iran. That this technique should be spread to the West in typically Oriental objects (cauldron-and-stand ensembles and dishes) is not unlikely, and because of the immense skill involved in the technique, it is relatively likely that the technique was brought along with the motifs by itinerant craftsmen, who then trained locals in this work (see p. 241). There seems to be a close relationship between style and technique here, the one transmitted with the other, but something happens to both shortly after adoption: the motif is adapted to Greek taste and needs, and the griffins become cast rather than repoussé! What happens to the style is more a problem for the art historian and has been discussed at some length, but the technical assimilation has not been examined.

What little we can tell from the chronological development of the griffin protomes seems to show that they are only made in repoussé at the very beginning of their introduction into the Greek (and Etruscan) world but are soon produced by lost-wax casting, probably beginning around the third quarter of the seventh century.[1] This is a striking example of a motif and

Fig. 1: Detail of high repoussé relief on a "North Syrian" bowl in the University Museum, Philadelphia, Pa.

technology being imported together, probably by individual craftsmen, but then soon being dismembered and executed differently, probably by locals. The reason for this change in technique is not clear, though repoussé may have been found too difficult and cumbersome, while casting from a single model might have proved more efficient. Furthermore, in Greece the making of such bronze ornaments may have fallen in the realm of the bronze-founder rather than the armorer or other worker in repoussé, whereas this had not been the case in the Near East. In short, we have only a few random examples that hold out a tantalizing story of the complex process of technological adaptation and development.

It is not clear whether the same high-repoussé-raising tradition that produced the griffins is responsible for the Cretan armor discussed by Hoffmann, but the large amount of tracing and low repoussé on this material and other Cretan bronzes suggests that the tradition is different. Hoffmann and others have discussed the iconographic and stylistic problems of Cretan bronze-working at length, but again there are technical distinctions that seem worth making. Already in the hoard of bronzes from the Idaean Cave there are differences in technique corresponding to differences in style. The famous tympanum is not only in higher relief than most of the other shield fragments, but it is also stylistically more closely related to the cauldron stands and vessels that are considered by some to be North Syrian (some of these are found among the Nimrud bowls, too). On the other hand, not only many of the Idaean shield fragments but also a few of the other early fragments of Cretan bronze work are in a technique that relies less on the relief of high repoussé and more on linear decoration by tracing and punching, where only a few of the decorated areas are raised in shallow relief and outlined with tracing (Fig. 2). This technique is used throughout the Assyrian Balawat Gates, where there is engraving in addition, and on a good many of the Nimrud bronze bowls (though it is not clear where they were made), as well as on most of the other "Phoenician bowls," especially the gilded silver ones in the Etruscan tombs.

This technique, relying heavily on tracing and only slightly on low repoussé to render the surface undulating, is used on the Cretan armor discussed by Hoffmann. It is easily distinguishable from the high repoussé and coarser tracing of the Idaean tympanum and its related pieces and must also be associated iconographically and stylistically with pieces outside of that group. To what extent motifs, themes, and style were imported to Crete with this technique is not clear and should, I think, be studied using the technical criteria as the initial distinguishing features of the workshop — or possibly workshops — that could thus be established (Hoffmann's parallels to the Axos bronzes, for example, are in an identical technique). Surely finer technical distinctions could be made among the various pieces of the Afrati hoard, but closer study of the various kinds of objects will be required before we can isolate a distinct workman's hand in the fabrication of these bronzes, basing our judgment on his technological rather than his artistic style.

Here again a technique has been adopted from the Levant, though surely from a different area and intermediary than in the case of the griffin protomes. The themes and motifs introduced with it were subsequently turned into a distinctive local idiom. This apparently represents a different stage of adaptation from the griffin protomes, for the idiom of the Cretan material is distinctly local and "Greek"; it is also later in date than the adaptation of the griffin protome. Whether in this instance motifs and technique were imported coupled and then somehow separated, as in the case of the griffin protomes, is not clear.

Hoffmann and Gjødesen show an interesting tendency in their stylistic analysis that bears on precisely this question. In order to place the armor in an artistic context, they draw heavily for parallels on Attic, Corinthian, and Cretan vases, Cretan sculpture, and other bronze work. As Gjødesen points out, when the metalworker and potter work in physical proximity, which may have been the case at Afrati, stylistic interaction is likely; on the other hand, we must ask how foreign styles (in this case Attic and Corinthian),

Fig. 2: Detail of traced and punched decoration accentuated by low relief on a bowl from Nimrud in the British Museum. Photo courtesy of the British Museum.

in the same or other media, might influence local craftsmen in a certain area. It has been observed that even when apparent itinerants worked in Greece (or Crete?), they adapted their work to local needs and tastes. Again we must ask how. Did the itinerant metalworker look at local pottery and imitate it in his own medium, or did both the metalworker and the potter work from similar models (a sketchbook, textile designs, or some other easily destructible material)? Why, in fact, are the parallels often so close? It is certainly unlikely that the same man decorated pots and bronze helmets! It is striking how much of a decorative *koine* did exist in Greece from the seventh century on (palmettes on architectural members are comparable to those on vases and bronzes, and so forth).

What kind of organization must have existed among the craftsmen of the various technologies that kept them sharing in the development of motifs in bronze-working, vase painting, architectural carving, and so forth, in a striking kind of lock step? Does this tell us something about social or religious pressures that dictated the taste and artistic usage of the Greek city-states? Possibly the sharing of large sanctuaries and festivals by all the Greek city-states made for some kind of unanimity among them in the decoration of their artifacts. One of the most vexing questions in this apparently closely controlled system is that of decorative, or artistic, innovation: how were new elements introduced into the workshops? The invention of red-figure from black-figure painting in Athens poses one such problem. It took some time before the artists, and probably their clients, became convinced that the new method was better than the old, but then everyone seems to have adopted the new process without returning to the old. This is yet another of the knotty questions that can only be posed and not properly answered until far more research has been done.

Note

1 It is of particular interest to note several examples of failed castings of griffin protomes from the Heraion at Samos that indicate that these were made by *indirect* lost-wax casting (see p. 107) or possibly plain piece-mold casting, since the telltale fins of the mold joins are in clear evidence. Furthermore, it is fairly likely that some of the siren-and-bull attachments that decorated many cauldron complexes were also cast with the use of piece molds at some point and might thus have been the models for the griffin-casters.

Technical Note

Arthur Steinberg

Virtually all the bronzes discussed in the following papers were made by the lost-wax casting method, but under this general heading are subsumed a number of procedural variants that require some discussion. Once a model or pattern has been fashioned, the central problem in bronze casting is how to make a negative form (the mold) that accurately represents the model, from which the model can be removed, and that is also strong enough to resist the thrust of many pounds of hot metal. The obvious geometrical problem underlying mold-building is the removal of the model from the mold. In the lost-wax method this is done by making the model out of wax, which can easily be melted out of the mold — destroying the model in the process.

In making a mold for *direct* lost-wax casting a core is built to the approximate shape of the statue, then covered with wax to form a model in exactly the shape desired in bronze, and finally invested with a clay mold. The wax is melted out and the bronze poured in. By thus building the mold directly on the model, the model will be destroyed as it is melted out of the mold. In this method the artist who makes the model has complete freedom of design, since there is no problem of drawing the mold from the model; the mold is broken off the finished bronze after the metal solidifies. Since the model is destroyed in the process, the finished bronze is unique.

Since there were occasions on which this destruction of the model was undesirable, a variant form of mold-building, the *indirect* lost-wax method, which allowed for reproducibility, was devised. In this method piece molds are built over the artist's model, which can be of any material. These piece molds (negatives) are then removed from the model, which is thus preserved. The interior of the piece molds is coated with wax either by pressing strips of wax into the separate pieces of the molds, reassembling them, and then smoothing over the joins in the wax or by first reassembling the piece molds and then slush-casting liquid wax into the mold until the desired thickness is built up, the excess wax being poured out. This wax positive is then filled with core material, the piece molds are removed, and the exterior of the wax (positive) is invested with a clay mold. From this stage on, the process is the same as for direct lost-wax casting. The indirect method has more steps (making more positives and negatives from the model), and it can only be used on models from which the piece molds will draw. Either the artist must limit the amount and depth of undercutting he uses, or the piece-mold builder must be ingenious. The distinct advantage of this method, however, is that it allows unlimited reproduction of the original model, either by casting several wax models in the piece molds or by forming several sets of molds from the original model. Furthermore, this method can be employed even if complex undercutting or a very large statue are involved, since individual groups of piece molds can be made of the various parts of the model, reassembled separately, coated with wax and cored, without reassembling the mold of the whole statue. The parts thus cast separately can subsequently be joined by any number of different methods to build up a particularly large or complex statue (see p. 22 ff.). Thus either for mass production of small, relatively simple pieces or for individual castings of great size or complexity the indirect lost-wax method has advantages over the less complicated direct method.

Probably all cast classical bronzes are molded in one of these two methods, most of them — except for a few larger pieces — in the direct method. Even the various techniques used in the Renaissance, referred to by Hanfmann and Gazda, are essentially only variants on these two fundamental mold-building procedures.

Near Eastern Bronzes in the West: The Question of Origin[1]

Oscar White Muscarella

In the history of Western civilization the early centuries of the first millennium B.C. remain one of the most exciting periods to study. For this is the time when the Greeks rediscovered the Near East. After the Mycenaean period, beginning in the protogeometric period, there is evidence of contact between several areas of the Near East and Greece.[2] During protogeometric times Greek objects were exported to the Near East, and the flow of trade, or contact, seems to have been entirely in one direction.[3]

It was sometime in the eighth century that Greeks began an intensive borrowing and adapting of Near Eastern motifs, objects, and ideas, the most important of which was a semitic alphabet — or as some would see it, a Phrygian alphabet.[4] What caused this quickening of Greek interest in the Orient need not concern us here: I am only restating an obvious and well-known archaeological fact — a fact historically documented by Herodotus (i.14), who informs us that King Midas of Phrygia sent objects to a Greek sanctuary in the eighth century B.C.[5]

The classical archaeologist whose special interest is the period under discussion must deal with the evidence of Oriental contacts. And as there is no contemporary Greek historical writing, material remains are the major source. When a given object is encountered, one must ask whether it is a purely local product, whether it is an import from the Orient (Oriental), or whether it is of local manufacture but inspired by an Oriental prototype (Orientalizing). If it is concluded that the object is Oriental or Orientalizing, one must establish the area or culture that produced it. For it is of great significance in the history of ideas to etablish which cultures in the Near East played a role in the development of Western culture. A guess or a hasty conclusion about provenience will create a mythology; it will not help to write history.[6]

There is a great deal of disagreement among both classical and Near Eastern archaeologists not only about the origin of objects found in the West but also about the origin of objects found at given sites in the Near East. Part of the difficulty in establishing places of origin is the fact that in antiquity objects traveled great distances by trade, as booty or as gifts: Italy has more Greek vases than Greece; Hammurabi's stele is found at Susa, and so forth; and practically every site has yielded material that according to the excavator was not made locally.[7] Additional confusion is certainly caused by scholars who firmly believe that they must supply a specific place of origin for every object encountered, whether the object be found in the Near East, in the West, in a museum basement, or in a dealer's shop.[8]

Some of the problems of foreign provenience may be illustrated by discussing examples of Near Eastern bronzes found in the West and summarizing the various opinions expressed about their origin. I am primarily concerned with the Greek world.

Griffin Protomes

Most scholars agree that the griffin is a Near Eastern motif borrowed and adapted by the Greeks. Yet a debate continues over the question of whether the protomes found in Greece and Italy were imported or were made in Greece. (I am referring to the earlier hammered types.) To my mind the important historical problem to be solved is not whether the earliest griffin protomes were made by Greeks or by Near Easterners (in

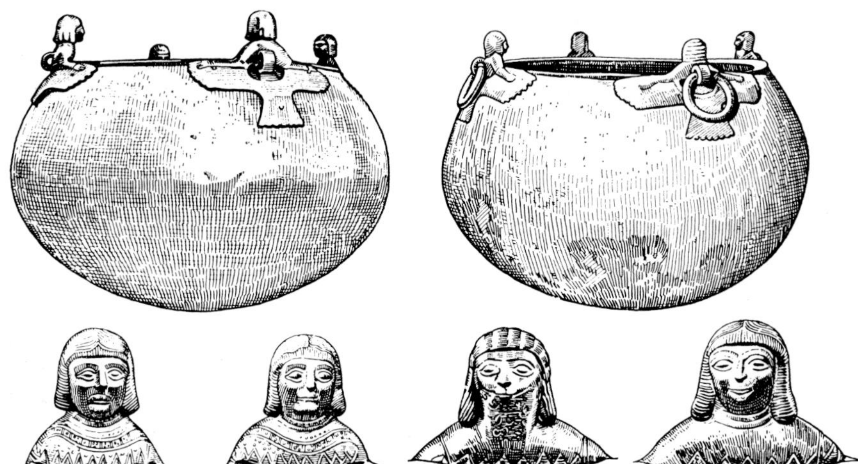

Fig. 1: Cauldrons with siren attachments from Tumulus MM at Gordion.

Greece or in their own homeland),[9] but whether we are able to agree on the Near Eastern source for a product apparently used exclusively in the West.[10] Thus Jantzen, Hanfmann, Benson, Muscarella, Herrmann, etc.[11] describe them as Greek products inspired by contact with North Syrian art; Herzfeld, Barnett, Maxwell-Hyslop, Akurgal, etc.[12] claim them as imports from Urartu; R. S. Young suggests that they were made in North Syria and exported on cauldrons to the West;[13] Amandry thinks that some examples must be imports from somewhere in the East, while others are made locally, and is of the opinion that one cannot tell the imports apart from the copies.[14] Were the griffins Greek-made, or were they made in North Syria or Urartu? This writer still favors the suggestion that they were Greek-made (on Samos?) from the first, based on North Syrian influence. But I do not now think the suggestion that they may have been made first by North Syrians to be an impossibility; and I do not think that Urartu played any role in the creation of the griffin motif or its export to the West.

Siren Attachments

With respect to the siren attachments we note that there is no problem of differentiating Oriental types (Fig. 1) from the Greek copies (Fig. 2). The only problem here is to determine the source (or sources) of the imported pieces. A long list of scholars claims them as Urartian: viz., Lehmann-Haupt, Herzfeld, Piotrovskii, Maxwell-Hyslop, Barnett, Akurgal, Mellink, and recently, Kyrieleis.[15] Lately there has been a rejection of this area as a source, and a major North Syrian center is preferred by Muscarella, van Loon, Herrmann, and Young.[16] At the same time, Herrmann, van Loon, and also Amandry have postulated more than one Near Eastern area as centers of manufacture. Herrmann suggests that two pieces, one in the British Museum, the other in the Danish National Museum in Copenhagen, are Assyrian and served as prototypes for the whole class, especially the *Hauptgruppe* of North Syria; he also sees a possible East Greek center for two examples found in Lindos and at Delphi.[17] Van Loon accepts the British Museum example as Assyrian and would allow only an example in the Vorderasiatisches Museum in Berlin to be an Urartian object;[18] Amandry would accept Urartu as the manufacturing center of at least some attachments.[19] If the theory of multiple centers is acceptable, then the problem of the origin (or origins) of the attachments found in the West and, following upon this, the problem of cultural influences may be even more complex than realized. However, it is important to note here that aside from the Urartian school, which assumes that all the attachments come from that area, the consensus of recent research is that the *Hauptgruppe* is not Urartian but rather North Syrian and that one should look there for the source of the sirens found in the West.

This writer believes that North Syria is the source for the sirens found in the West but does not reject the possibility that the example in the British Museum may have been made in Assyria; whether it was the prototype for the others may never be known. I am not inclined to accept the idea that any sirens were made in Urartu but, of course, cannot categorically reject the possibility.[20]

Winged Bull Attachments

Winged bull attachments for cauldrons and dinoi are found in several parts of the Near East and in Greece and Italy (Figs. 3, 4).[21] A stylistic analysis of the attachments excavated in the Near East enables one to conclude that two groups were manufactured: (1) The examples found in Urartu, at Altintepe and Toprakkale (but not one found at Karmir Blur), and those from northwest Iran, at Guschi and Alishar, form one group which has been called Urartian. The head of the bull is joined at a right angle to a separately made wing and tail, the forelock is rectangular, the horns curve forward, and the ears project out at right angles to the head.

Fig. 2: A Greek siren attachment from Olympia.

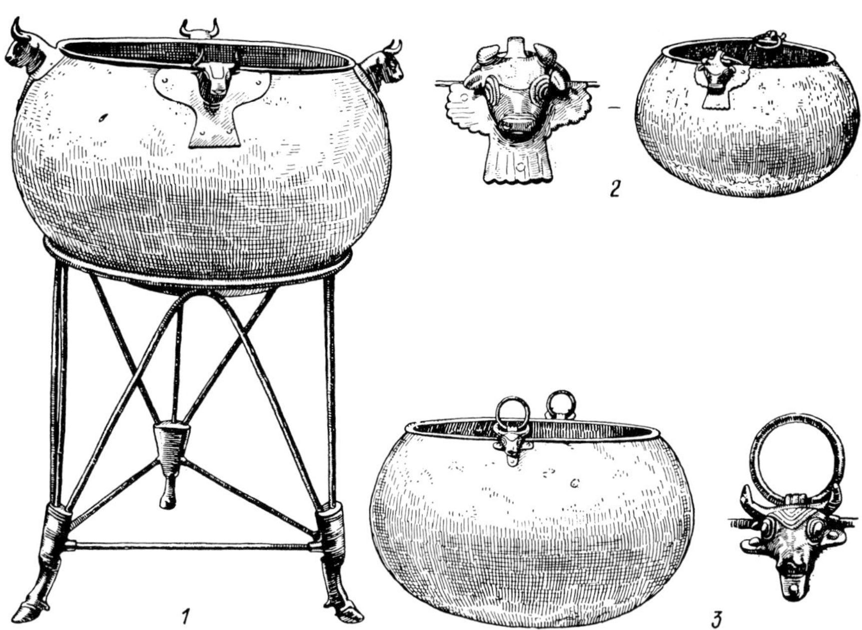

Fig. 3: Bull attachments from Altintepe (no. 1), allegedly from Cumae (no. 2), from Tumulus MM at Gordion (no. 3).

They all face out from the cauldron, and there are usually four bulls to a cauldron. (2) The other group is represented by examples from Gordion, North Syria, and Karmir Blur. The head and the wing and tail, often only a T-shaped plaque, are cast together to form one unit; most examples have a fixed ring at the rear; the forelock is round or triangular. Some face into and others out from the cauldron, and usually there are only two bulls to a cauldron.

No examples or copies of the Urartian group exist in the West to my knowledge, so that we must look to the second group for the source of those found there. Because of differences in style, the attachments of this group cannot easily be classified as having been manufactured in any one particular cultural area. I have suggested elsewhere that there is good evidence for considering a Phrygian and a North Syrian center, or centers, but that when we examine the Near Eastern attachments found in the West, such as those from Cumae, Argos, and Amyclae,[22] it is not at present possible to assign them to one center or the other. Needless to say, attributions have been made, especially for the examples from Cumae. Van Loon suggests these attachments were made in Cyprus; Herrmann thinks they were made in North Syria; and Young says they are "perhaps Phrygian."[23] To my mind they could have been made in Phrygia or North Syria (I do not think Cyprus played a role in this matter), but, as suggested, I do not think that they can be attributed to one particular area; the same situation obtains for the examples from Amyclae and Argos. It is here suggested, therefore, that the general term Near Eastern be employed to describe these attachments at present.[24]

Bird Attachments

An eagle attachment found years ago on the Athenian acropolis is obviously in the tradition of Near Eastern attachments (Fig. 5).[25] The best parallel I know is a griffin — there is a crest and a knob on the head — found somewhere in Iran and now in Tehran (Fig. 6).[26] Both the eagle

Fig. 4: Near Eastern bull attachment from Olympia.

Fig. 5: Bird attachment from Athens, National Museum.

Fig. 6: Griffin attachment from Iran, Tehran Museum.

and griffin faced into the cauldron and have rings at the rear, reminding us of the siren and bull attachments. Both also have plain (unhatched) feathered wings and tails, a feature also occurring on two winged bull attachments allegedly found in Iran.[27] The Tehran griffin has been called Urartian, and the Athenian eagle has been called Assyrian.[28] There is certainly no evidence for the former attribution, and I do not know any attachment in the Near East that has a raised triangular base under the ring as the eagle has.[29]

I would at present avoid attributing the Athenian eagle to any particular area in the Near East. The fact that close parallels occur in Iran must be kept in mind, but it does not follow that one should automatically assume that the eagle was imported from that area. It would be preferable to consider this object simply as Near Eastern and let future research or discovery make a contribution toward solving the problem of its specific provenience.

Griffin Attachments

Another problem concerned with specific Near Eastern provenience is a group of griffin attachments from Olympia (Fig. 7). Two such objects and the head of a third have been found there.[30] The griffin head is cast in one piece with the wings and tail, and there is a ring behind the head, all of which relates it to some of the other objects discussed above. Herrmann suggests that the griffin attachments are related to the sirens and that they also came from North Syria; he raises and then rejects the idea that they may have been the inspiration for the Greek griffin protomes.[31] Akurgal and Demargne think the attachments are Urartian.[32] A griffin-like creature on a handle found in the destruction level at Gordion, and eighth century in date, seems to be the closest parallel (Fig. 8); this handle is in turn related to a bird handle from ninth-century Hasanlu in Iran (Fig. 9).[33] The Olympia attachments are different in form when compared to the Gordion handle, and the heads have different types of horns (or ears) and different incised decoration, but one is nevertheless aware of a certain similarity, especially with regard to the open mouth without teeth or tongue. What then is the Near Eastern source for the Olympia attachments — North Syria, Urartu, or Phrygia? The answer suggested here is Phrygia or perhaps North Syria, but again it seems to me that it is wiser to be cautious and to refer to them as Near Eastern objects.[34]

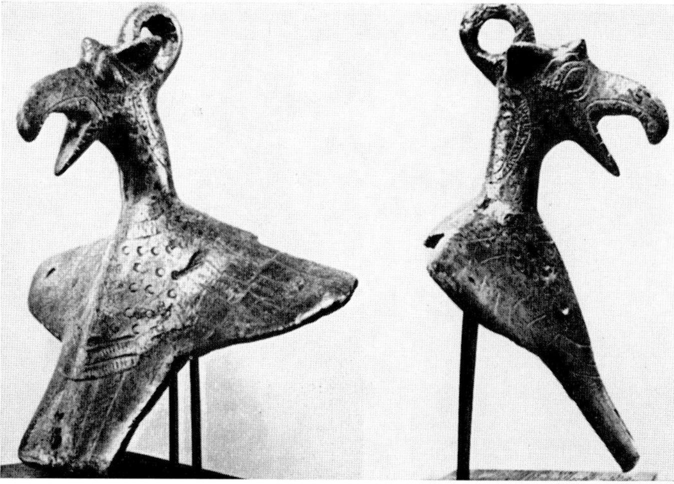

Fig. 7: Griffin attachment from Olympia.

Kesseltiere

In recent years Kunze, Amandry, and Herrmann have discussed a type of attachment that consists of the complete body of an animal whose feet rest on plinths.[35] The plinths were attached to the rim of a vessel with the animals facing inside. Each of these scholars expressed some hesitation about attributing these attachments, excavated examples of which occur only in Greece, to one particular area in the Near East (although Herrmann was inclined toward North Syria). This writer shares their hesitancy.

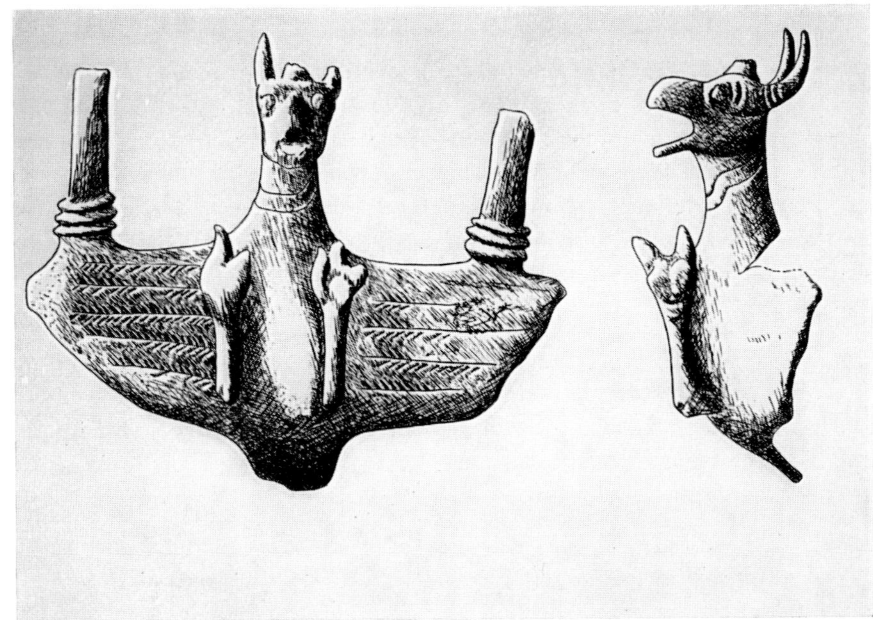

Fig. 8: Griffin (?) handle attachment from Gordion.

Fig. 9: Bird handle attachment from Hasanlu.

Until recently most Near Eastern bronzes found in the West were indiscriminately considered to be of Urartian manufacture. Now scholars are beginning to think that Phrygia and North Syria may have been the sources for many of these objects.[36] Phrygia's role in exporting her manufacture — fibulae, bowls, dinoi, and thrones (Herodotus i.14) — has been recognized, and perhaps as a result of more research and excavation other objects will be attributed to her workshops.[37] North Syria seems at present to have played a larger role than Phrygia in exporting objects and motifs to the West; but we must be on guard against attributing all Near Eastern bronzes to North Syria, as previously they were all attributed to Urartu! Nevertheless, the number of objects and motifs found in the West that may justifiably be attributed to North Syria is rather large; and the number of bronzes from North Syria in private collections is also growing.

I present a list of some of these objects and motifs, which I hope will serve as a convenience for those interested in Oriental relations with the West and at the same time serve as a basis for future discussion. There is no claim to completeness, and no doubt some scholars will add or reject items in the list. First, I shall list the North Syrian bronzes, not including griffins and sirens that have been discussed here:

1. A horse blinker said to have been found in Eretria is in the Athens National Museum (Fig. 10).[38] A man with his face and upper body frontal, his lower body in profile, holds two lions by the tail; a third lion walks at the left, and two rosettes are at the right. The posture and dress of the man, the lions, and the repoussé work are North Syrian: see H. J. Kantor, "A Bronze Plaque in Relief Decoration from Tell Tainat," *JNES*, XXI, No. 2 (1962), 93 ff., pls. XI-XV, with references; W. Andrae, *Die Kleinfunde von Sendschirli*, V (Berlin, 1943), 77, fig. 90, pl. 40, d.
2. H.-V. Herrmann has published and given references to several North Syrian bronzes excavated at Olympia; they are listed here as a convenience (nos. 2-6): a plaque in repoussé of a man walking left: *Die Kessel der orientalisierenden Zeit, Olympische Forschungen*, VI (Berlin, 1966), no. B 1950,

Fig. 10: Horse blinker from Eretria, National Museum, Athens, no. 15020.

p. 177 and n. 2; E. Kunze *et al.*, *V. Bericht über die Ausgrabungen in Olympia* (Berlin, 1956), 81 ff., figs. 37, 38.

3. A repoussé bowl, double-walled with filling. The decoration consists of panther heads and sphinxes, heads frontal, bodies in profile: Herrmann, *Die Kessel*, no. B 1145, p. 178, pl. 76; R. S. Young, "A Bronze Bowl in Philadelphia," *JNES*, XXVI, No. 3 (1967), 146, 151.

4. Fragments of six cauldron stands *(Untersatz)* with various motifs: Herrmann, *Die Kessel*, 161 ff., pls. 65-73, U1 to U6; Young, *JNES*, 1967, 150 f. (Herrmann has suggested three workshops [180 f.]. On a purely subjective basis, working only from the photographs, I would suggest, that the Capena bowl [here, no. 3, p. 118] is a copy, that U5 and U6 are not necessarily from the same workshop, and that the Bernardini bowl, no. 64 [here, no. 2, p. 118], is a copy.)[39]

5. A repoussé plaque with a prancing lion, Athens National Museum Br. 1325: Herrmann, *Die Kessel*, 177 and n. 1, 180; G. Daux, "Chronique des fouilles 1961," *BCH*, LXXXVI, No. 2 (1962), 635, fig. 8.

6. An incompletely published large repoussé panel with many scenes of animals and warriors, placed in several zones: Herrmann, *Die Kessel*, 177 f., n. 3; G. Daux, "Chronique des fouilles 1959," *BCH*, LXXXIV (1960), 716 ff., fig. 6; E. Kunze, "Die Ausgrabungen in Olympia," *Deltion*, XVII (1961-62), 115 f., pls. 129, 130. In the summer of 1966 I was shown this extraordinary panel and wish to thank the German Archaeological Institute for its courtesy.

7. At least two repoussé bowls, double-walled with filling, from the Kerameikos cemetery in Athens. The decoration consists of sphinxes, heads frontal and bodies in profile: K. Gebauer, "Ausgrabungen im Kerameikos," *AA* (1940), cols. 338 ff., figs. 19, 20; K. Kübler, "Ausgrabungen im Kerameikos," *AA* (1943), cols. 341 ff., fig. 4 for a better photograph of one of the bowls; Young, *JNES*, 1967, 146, 151. These bowls are apparently exactly the same as a bowl from the Bernardini Tomb, no. 65 (here no. 11).

8. A horse blinker found in the Heraeum at Samos, decorated in repoussé with a pair of sphinxes (one missing) flanking a tree: H. Payne, "Archaeology in Greece, 1929-30," *JHS*, L (1930), 249 f., fig. 7; Kantor, *JNES*, 1962, 109.

9. A horse frontlet from Samos decorated in repoussé with three nude ladies supported by a fourth; below are two resting lions or panthers: Kantor, *JNES*, 1962, 108 f., fig. 13A.

10. Two horse frontlets from Miletus, both repoussé, one consisting of three standing lions, the other, fragmentary, of three nude ladies, frontal: *ibid.*, 108, fig. 13B; R. D. Barnett, *A Catalogue of the Nimrud Ivories* (London, 1957), 101, figs. 38, 39, also in "North Syrian and Related Harness Decoration," *Vorderasiatische Archaeologie* (Berlin, 1964), pl. 1, nos. 1, 2.

11. A repoussé bowl from the Bernardini Tomb, apparently exactly the same as the two bowls from the Kerameikos cemetery (here no. 7): C. D. Curtis, "The Bernardini Tomb," *MAAR*, III (1919), 68 f., no. 65, pl. 46; Young, *JNES*, 1967, 146, 151; Herrmann, *Die Kessel*, 181.

12. The repoussé cauldron stand from the Bernardini Tomb (cf. H. Kyrieleis, "Zum orientalischen Kesselschmuck," *Marburger Winckelmann-Programm* [1966], 20 ff., where these objects are called *Räucherständer)*; Curtis, *MAAR*, 1919, 77, pls. 58, 59; Herrmann, *Die Kessel*, 180, pl. 75; Young, *JNES*, 1967, 150 f.

13. The repoussé cauldron stand from the Barberini Tomb: C. D. Curtis, "The Barberini Tomb," *MAAR*, V (1925), 44 f., pls. 28, 29; Herrmann, *Die Kessel*, 161 ff., 181 f., pl. 74; Young, *JNES*, 1967, 150 f.

14. In private collections and without provenience are three important North Syrian bronzes (nos. 14-16): a repoussé frontlet in the Bomford collection, consisting of two kilted men standing on seated lions, and a winged siren standing on a nude lady who in turn stands on a panther head: Barnett, *Vorderasiatische Archaeologie*, 22 ff., pl. 2, no. 2, pls. 3, 4, no. 1 and fig. 1.

15. A pair of hammered sphinxes in The Metropolitan Museum of Art: Kantor, *JNES*, 1962, 98, fig. 6; Young, *JNES*, 1967, 148 f., pl. XX; C. Wilkinson, *BMMA*, XVIII, No. 8 (April 1960), 243, fig. 2.

16. A repoussé bowl, double-walled with filling, in the University Museum of the University of Pennsylvania, decorated with facing sphinxes: Young, *JNES*, 1967, 145 ff., pls. XIV-XIX, fig. 1.

17. In addition to the bronzes listed above, a North Syrian steatite lion bowl was found on Samos: H. Walter, "Orientalische Kunstgeräte," *AthMitt*, LXXIV (1959), 69 ff., pls. 115-117; B. Freyer-Schauenberg, *Elfenbeine aus dem samischen Heraion* (Hamburg, 1966), 98 ff., for a bibliography and discussion of the steatite bowl and other bowls of this type. The Samos bowl has inlays preserved in the eye sockets, a feature that also occurs on a bowl from Çatal Hüyük in North Syria, now in the Oriental Institute, Chicago, no. a 1900.

18. In addition to the steatite bowl there is another example in ivory from Samos: Walter, *AthMitt*, 1959, pls. 118, 119; Freyer-Schauenberg, *Elfenbeine*, pl. 28. At present ivory lion bowls are known from Megiddo and Nimrud (and one from Crete, here no. 11, p. 119), so that there may possibly have been a source other than North Syria for the example from Samos.

I add a list of objects that I suggest are Orientalizing, reflecting North Syrian influences, but that are apparently not actual imports. Again the bronzes are presented first:

1. A repoussé bowl, double-walled with filling, from the Kerameikos cemetery; decorated with sphinxes flanking a tree: Kübler, *AA*, 1943, cols. 351 f., figs. 5-8; Herrmann, *Die Kessel*, 171, where it is also called a copy.

2. A repoussé bowl from the Bernardini tomb, double-walled with filling; decorated with sphinxes flanking a tree: Curtis, *MAAR*, 1919, 66 ff., pl. 45, no. 64. The face and hair style seem to be Greek, not Oriental: Herrmann, *Die Kessel*, 181, and Young, *JNES*, 1967, 149, 151, refer to it as an import. They could be correct, but I am not sure.

3. The well-known repoussé bowl, double-walled with filling, from Capena. It is known to me from photographs, but I prefer to think it is a copy: F. Poulsen, *Der Orient und die frühgriechische Kunst* (Leipzig, 1912), 119, claimed it as Orientalizing, copying a Phoenician model; W. L. Brown, *The Etruscan Lion* (Oxford, 1960), 9 ff., 23 f., pl. V, a, "if not an oriental import [it] is very close to oriental work"; Herrmann, *Die Kessel*, 180, and Young, *JNES*, 1967, 151, accept it as a North Syrian product.

4. A repoussé bowl, double-walled with filling, from Castelleto Ticinese, now in Turin: Brown, *Etruscan Lion*, 23, pl. XI, a.

5. A repoussé bowl decorated with two facing lions and two sphinxes,

heads frontal, bodies in profile, from Vetulonia: Brown, *Etruscan Lion*, 23, pl. XI, b.

6. A repoussé vessel supported by three legs, decorated with sirens, from the Barberini Tomb: Curtis, *MAAR*, 1925, 43 ff., pls. 26, 27, 1, no. 79. Poulsen, *Der Orient*, 127, Brown, *Etruscan Lion*, 22 ff., Herrmann, *Die Kessel*, 170, 179, all agree it is a copy; E. Herzfeld, "Khattische und Khaldische Bronzen," *Janus*, I (1921), 153, compares this vessel to a silver tripod bowl from Maikop; he considered the Barberini bowl (as well as the siren attachments, griffin protomes, and cauldron stands) to be Urartian.

7. A bronze quiver found at Fortetsa in Crete, decorated in repoussé with walking sphinxes and a hero confronting two heraldic lions: J. W. Brock, *Fortetsa* (Cambridge, 1957), 135 f., 192 ff., no. 1569. The wings of the sphinxes recall those seen on a silver plaque from Zincirli, Andrae, *Sendschirli*, pl. 55; the hero's helmet is exactly paralleled by those worn by soldiers at Carchemish, and so is the position of the hero with the lions: D. G. Hogarth, *Carchemish*, I (London, 1914), pls. B 1b, B 2, B 3, B 11 b; moreover, the style of the lions' paws is paralleled by many North Syrian lion paws. However, note the strong similarity in dress and posture of the hero with the lions to a scene represented on a silver beaker from Marlik in Iran: E. O. Negahban, "Notes on Some Objects from Marlik," *JNES*, XXIV, No. 4 (1965), 322 f., pl. LXIII, fig. 22. Whether the similarity of the Iranian and North Syrian motif is coincidental (which I doubt) remains to be investigated.[40]

8. In a comparison with ivories found in North Syria and also in Nimrud — but considered to be of North Syrian manufacture — a few ivories found in the West may be discussed here (nos. 8-11). The nude ivory lady found in the Dipylon cemetery at Athens is certainly related to North Syrian ivories: P. Demargne, *Birth of Greek Art* (New York, 1964), 292, figs. 380, 381; Barnett, *Nimrud Ivories*, 44 f., 51, and also "Ancient Oriental Influences on Archaic Greece," *The Aegean and the Near East, Studies Presented to Hetty Goldman*, Saul S. Weinberg, ed. (Locust Valley, 1956), 236, and "Early Greek and Oriental Ivories," *JHS*, LXVIII (1948), 4 f.; T. J. Dunbabin, *The Greeks and their Eastern Neighbors* (London, 1957), 38 f., pl. XIII, 1, 2. See a good parallel in G. Loud, *The Megiddo Ivories* (Chicago, 1939), pl. 39, no. 175.

9. Another group of ivories related to examples from Nimrud are the small couchant calves from Sparta and Perachora: R. M. Dawkins, *The Sanctuary of Artemis Orthia* (London, 1929), pls. CLIII, CXLVIII; T. J. Dunbabin, ed., *Perachora*, II (Oxford, 1962), 407 ff., pl. 174; cf. Barnett, *Nimrud Ivories*, 64 ff., pls. CI, CVI. Three couchant calves, two fragmentary, exactly like the Nimrud examples, have been found in the debris of the ninth-century city of Hasanlu in northwest Iran (unpublished). W. F. Albright, "Northeast-Mediterranean Dark Ages and the Early Iron Age Art of Syria," in *The Aegean and the Near East*, 162, discusses the Spartan ivories. His conclusions support Dawkins' dating (early eighth century), and certainly the Hasanlu evidence suggests a ninth-century date for the Nimrud ivories discussed here.

10. A grazing stag from Crete may be an import from North Syria or it may be a good copy. It is discussed by Barnett, *JHS*, 1948, 3 f., fig. 1.

11. An ivory lion bowl related to the bowls discussed here (nos. 17, 18, p. 118) was found on Crete and is now in the Heraklion Museum (no. 70). Its publisher, E. Kunze, "Orientalische Schnitzereien aus Kreta," *AthMitt*,

LX-LXI (1935-36), 222, mentions that the lion head is missing.
12. Pottery imitations of the North Syrian lion bowls are also found in the West. The best-known example is the one found by D. Levi in Crete, "Arkades," *ASAtene*, X-XII, (1927-29), 240, fig. 281, pl. 19, and *idem*, "Early Hellenic Pottery of Crete," *Hesperia*, XIV, No. 1 (1945), 28, pl. 25; also Barnett in *The Aegean and the Near East*, 236, pl. XXIII: 1. A fragment of the same type of object was found on Ithaca, M. Robertson, "Excavations in Ithaca," *BSA*, XLIII (1948), 91, pl. 41, no 558. Other examples have been collected by J. Boardman, *The Cretan Collection in Oxford* (Oxford, 1961), 62 f.: a fragment in Knossos, another fragment in the Ashmolean Museum, and an example in faience from the Idaean cave; he sees these objects as examples of Egyptian influence; see also *idem*, *Greeks Overseas*, 131.
13. In pottery one also thinks of the sphinxes in relief found on Crete, among other places. These sphinxes have bodies in profile and faces frontal; they reflect the style of the sphinxes found on the bronze bowls discussed above: viz., Levi, *ASAtene*, 1927-29, 67, 73, figs. 46, 50; see also Poulsen, *Der Orient*, 148 f., 184, figs. 173, 174, 197.

A final list will be offered here. It concerns examples of motifs copied from North Syrian art and executed in a local style. As stated before, I make no claim to completeness and am only concerned with North Syria.

1. An often-discussed motif is the hybrid creature consisting of an animal with an additional head, human in form, projecting from the shoulder blades. In North Syria the motif occurs at three sites: Hogarth, *Carchemish*, I, pl. B 14A; A. Moortgat, *Tell Halaf*, III (Berlin, 1955), 86 f., pl. 88a, b; F. von Luschan, *Ausgrabungen in Sendschirli*, I (Berlin, 1893), pl. XLIII : 2. It also occurs at Gordion, R. S. Young, "The 1961 Campaign at Gordion," *AJA*, LXVI, No. 2 (1962), 167, pl. 47, fig. 25; the excavator considers it to be of North Syrian origin.[41] A little-known example is on a stone pyxis purchased by Herzfeld in Baghdad and published in *AMIran*, II (1931), 133, fig. 2, pl. 2, and here Fig. 11; it is surely North Syrian. The motif occurs in the West on Corinthian pottery, H. Payne, *Protokorinthische Vasenmalerei* (Berlin, 1933), pl. 20, no. 1. Young has suggested that it occurs on the Bernardini bowl, no. 64, *JNES*, 1967, 149; a variety of this motif, related to the chimaera, occurs on some animal brooches from the same tomb: Curtis, *MAAR*, III (1919), 31 f., pl. 8, no. 3. A similar motif occurs in Luristan and in Achaemenid art: A. Godard, *Les Bronzes du Luristan* (Paris, 1931), pl. XLI, no. 167; R. Ghirshman, *The Arts of Ancient Iran* (New York, 1964), 266, fig. 326. For second millennium examples see A.

Fig. 11: Drawing of the decoration on a stone pyxis bought in Baghdad: after AMIran, *II (1930), 133, fig. 2.*

Dessene, *Le Sphinx* (Paris, 1957), 94 ff.; H. Kantor, "Syro-Palestinian Ivories," *JNES*, XV, No. 3 (1956), 155 f., n. 8.

2. Fish-men, or Mer-men, have an ancient history in the Near East. They occur in art at Kültepe, N. Özgüç, *The Anatolian Group of Cylinder Seal Impressions from Kultepe* (Ankara, 1965), 72, pls. XV, 44, XX, 60; in the Kassite period, E. Porada, *Corpus of Ancient Near Eastern Seals* (Washington, D.C., 1948), 66, nos. 539, 586; in Assyria of the first millennium B.C., C. H. Ward, *Seal Cylinders of Western Asia* (Washington, D.C., 1910), 216 f., nos. 654, 658, 659, 660, 661. In North Syria they are found at T. Halaf: Moortgat, *Tell Halaf*, III, 91, pl. 74 a. For examples in the West see H. Payne, *Necrocorinthia* (Oxford, 1931), 77, figs. 22A, B; Boardman, *Greeks Overseas*, 97, figs. 25 a, b; note also its occurrence in Greek style on the Vettersfelde fish in Berlin, E. H. Minns, *Scythians and Greeks* (Cambridge, 1913), 238, fig. 146.

3. The *Knielauf* motif and its occurrence in the West has been thoroughly explored by Kantor in *JNES*, 1962, 101 ff.; there is no need to repeat her excellent analysis here.

4. Professor Kantor has also explored the occurrence of the "Humbaba" motif in the article mentioned in no. 3.

5. The North Syrian lion and its occurrence in Greek and Italian art was recognized years ago by Payne in *Necrocorinthia*, 14, 67 ff., and has recently been discussed by Brown, *Etruscan Lion*, 1 ff.

Several items which might have been mentioned in this study have been consciously omitted as I consider them controversial as to origin or source of inspiration. The most obvious omission is the bronze tympanon from Crete which I believe was locally made. It probably, but not certainly, reflects North Syrian art[42]; in any event, it is certainly related in technique and style to the Capena bowl (no. 3, p. 118) and to the Barberini cauldron stand (no. 13, p. 118), as Kunze, Poulsen, and Herrmann have maintained: Herrmann, *Die Kessel*, 179, notes 10, 11.

Also difficult for me to judge is the well-known bowl from the Kerameikos cemetery published by Kubler (here note 4). I have not been able to see good photographs of this bowl and would rather reserve comment; my impression, however, is that it belongs to the "Phoenician" or Cypriote school and is not closely related to North Syrian art.

A small bronze from Sounion published by Hanfmann, "A Syrian from Sounion," *Hesperia*, XXXI, No. 3 (1962), 236 f., pl. 85, may actually have come from a coastal region rather than inland Syria, but of this I am not certain.

The Cretan animal-protome shields are certainly based on Near Eastern prototypes. However, because they occur in Assyria, North Syria, and also at Urartian-controlled Musasir, it is difficult to point to one culture as the source of inspiration. A. Snodgrass, *Early Greek Armour and Weapons* (Edinburgh, 1964), 52, which bibliography, says Urartu was the source. I prefer to leave the question open and talk at present of a general Near Eastern background.

Finally, one should keep in mind the problem of the provenience of the class of seals recently published by E. Porada, "A Lyre Player from Tarsus and his Relations," *The Aegean and the Near East*, 185 ff., and J. Boardman, *Cretan Collection*, 122; the former believes that the seals originally were made in Rhodes, and the latter believes they are North Syrian.

In reviewing the opinions expressed about the proveniences of the Near Eastern bronzes and other objects discussed in this study, it is seen that North Syria, Phrygia, Urartu, Assyria, Phoenicia, and cities of Greece and Italy have been suggested as centers of manufacture by different scholars. Moreover, in some cases objects of a given class will be attributed to three or four different areas by as many scholars, thereby illustrating the confusion that prevails. It has been suggested that whenever there is any doubt about the provenience of an object, nothing more specific than the term Near Eastern should be employed in description. This terminology is professionally more satisfactory than a statement that may create an incorrect attribution. One expects that future excavations will yield material that will enable us to draw more parallels and define places of origin more specifically.

Another conclusion that emerges from this study is that on the basis of present knowledge North Syria and Phrygia seem to have been the most important sources for the Oriental objects and motifs found in the West. Urartu seems, to my mind, to have played no recognizable role at all,[43] and Assyria very little. The role Iran played is just beginning to be understood, and the important work of scholars such as P. Amandry and others is providing the evidence needed to document Iran's role in shaping the art of the West.[44] Caution will be needed here, too, for we will have to investigate whether Iranian influences were direct or were transmitted by other cultures. In any event, controlled excavations in Iran are increasing, and materials will be forthcoming that will enable those interested in this problem to continue their research.

Addendum

During the exhibition of "Art Treasures of Turkey" in Boston and New York (1967-68), I was able to examine the cauldron from Altintepe. It was noticed that on either side of the wings of each bull attachment were the remains of rivets, the ends of which were flush with the walls of the

Fig. 12: Bull attachment on the cauldron from Altintepe showing the rivets on both sides of the wings.

cauldron (Figs. 12, 13).[45] These rivets, and a third set that was placed between and below the others, were also visible on the interior walls of the cauldron (Fig. 14). The tails of the attachments covered the lower rivets on the front of the cauldron.

A check of the original publication[46] and information graciously supplied to me by Prof. Tahsin Özgüç confirmed the fact that the bulls were found *in situ* on the cauldron and were never removed for cleaning after their discovery in 1938. In any event, the span of the bulls' wings does not extend as far as these additional rivets. It is clear, therefore, that the additional set of rivets apparently represents an original plan for a group of attachments. To my mind one may interpret these facts as follows: the cauldron had an original set of attachments which for some unknown reason

Fig. 13: Close-up of one of the rivets (scale 1:1).

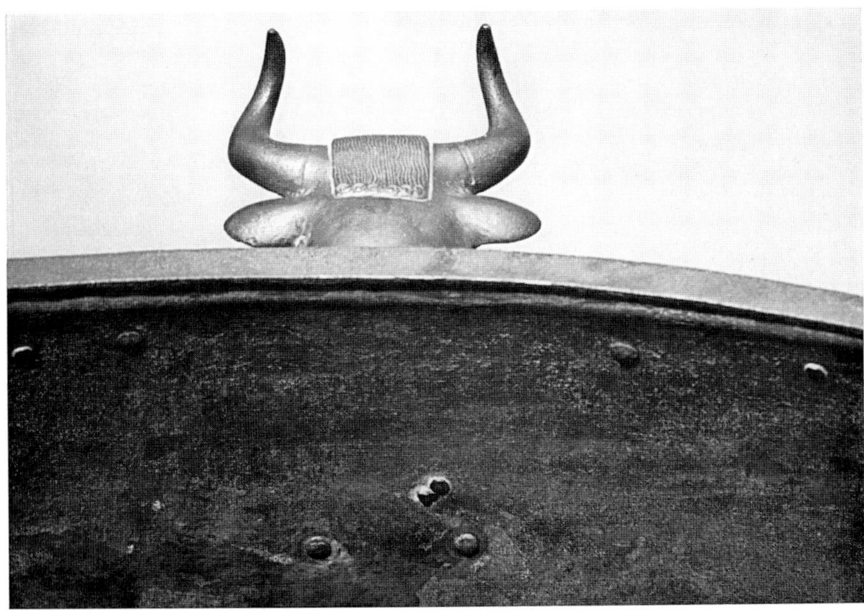

Fig. 14: Interior of the vessel showing the rivets of the present attachment and the extra ones. The latter may be recognized by the reflected light.

were replaced with the present smaller ones; the original rivets were then cut off and filed flush with the outer walls of the cauldron; or less probably, the craftsmen originally planned to apply a certain group of attachments but, after drilling the holes and setting in the rivets, decided to use the present attachments.

I do not wish to speculate further about what type of attachments may have been originally planned or why the change was made. My aim in adding this note here is to bring the matter to the attention of interested students and to present good photographs. I wish to thank Mr. Kemal Uğur and Mr. Lufti Tuğrul for their help and co-operation in discussing this matter and for allowing the photographer of The Metropolitan Museum of Art, Mr. William Pons, to make excellent photographs.

Notes

1 This paper originated in a talk and has been amended to change it from a spoken to a written statement. Therefore I have expanded the discussion on North Syrian objects and motifs found in the West and have reduced the discussion on bull attachments and eliminated the discussion of fibulae, as I deal with these objects elsewhere: "Winged Bull Cauldron Attachments from Iran," *Metropolitan Museum of Art Journal*, I (1968), 7 ff., and *Phrygian Fibulae from Gordion* (London, 1967).

2 V. R. d'A. Desborough, *Protogeometric Pottery* (Oxford, 1952), 218 ff., 74; C. Clairmont, "Greek Pottery from the Near East," *Berytus*, XI, No. 2 (1955), 85 ff., 98 ff.; T. J. Dunbabin, *The Greek and Their Eastern Neighbors* (London, 1957), 28 ff., 72 ff.; J. M. Cook, "Greek Settlement in the Eastern Aegean and Asia Minor," *CAH*, fasc. 7, Vol. II (Cambridge, 1964), Chap. XXXVIII, 13 ff.

3 Problems concerned with the date for the borrowing of literary motifs, such as, for example, the Kumarbi myth, need not detain us inasmuch as there is no easy solution.

4 R. D. Barnett, review of R. Deringer, *Writing, its Origin and History*, in *Antiquity*, XXXVIII, No. 147 (1963), 249; for further discussion see R. S. Young, "Gordion on the Royal Road," *ProcPhilSoc*, CVII, No. 4 (1963), 362 ff. The famous bronze bowl from the Kerameikos cemetery in Athens is said to be ninth century in date. Even if the bowl is that early (it appears to me from the published statements that it could perhaps be early eighth century in date), it does not eliminate the eighth century as the crucial period for the importation of Oriental objects to Greece; K. Kubler "Eine Bronzeschale im Kerameikos," *Studies Presented to D. M. Robinson* (St. Louis, 1953), II, 25 ff. While I was in Athens in 1967, Mrs. E. Smithson showed me the contents of a ninth-century tomb ("late-early geometric in date") found in the Athenian Agora in 1967. Among the finds was a beautiful pair of gold earrings with excellent granulation; it may have been made in the Near East. [Now see E. L. Smithson, "The Tomb of a Rich Athenian Lady," *Hesperia*, XXXVII, No. 1 (1968), 112 pl. 32, Nos. 77 a, b.]

5 See my *Phrygian Fibulae from Gordion*, 59 ff., for a discussion of the King Midas mentioned by Herodotus and for a discussion of Phrygian relationships with the West.

6 I do not intend to get involved in a discussion about how much of a role the Orient played in creating the unique Greek mind and spirit. Too often arguments of this nature reflect not the facts observable but rather the chauvinism of the scholar. Some scholars seem to think that the Greeks need to be defended against the charge that they borrowed heavily and eagerly from the Orient. Indeed they did borrow – in art, literature, science, and philosophy – but, of course, they turned everything into Greek!

7 An example of this may be seen in the problem of the origin of the two bronze situlae found in Tumulus MM at Gordion: R. S. Young, "Bronzes from Gordion's Royal Tomb," *Archaeology*, XI, No. 4 (1958), 228 f. They occur in art on an Assyrian relief at Khorsabad, *ibid.*, figure on p. 227, are made in a technique known for bronzes attributed to North Syria, R. S. Young, "A Bronze Bowl

in Philadelphia," *JNES*, XXVI, No. 3 (1967), 146, and are also allegedly found in Iran, *7000 Years of Iranian Art* (Washington, D.C., 1964-65), 85, 147, no. 424; C. K. Wilkinson, "Two Ram-Headed Vessels from Iran," *Monographien der Abegg-Stiftung Bern*, I (Bern, 1967), figs. 12, 13, pls. VIII-XII; see also his fig. 3, for situlae represented on a bronze receptacle from Ziwiye. Cf. a bronze vessel in Copenhagen, said to come from Palestine, *Guide to the Danish National Museums, Oriental and Classical Antiquity* (Copenhagen, 1950), 31 f., fig. 7a. Who made them?

8 An example of this is the discussion concerned with the origin of the candelabrum in the Erlangen collection: H.-V. Herrmann, *Die Kessel der orientalisierenden Zeit, Olympische Forschungen*, VI (Berlin, 1966), 66, and M. van Loon, *Urartian Art* (Istanbul, 1966), 99, 176, suggest North Syria; H. Kyrieleis, "Zum orientalischen Kesselschmuck," *Marburger Winckelmann-Programm* (1966), 13, n. 68, suggests Assyria; S. Smith, "The Greek Trade at al Mina," *Antiquaries Journal*, XXII (1942), 104, and E. Akurgal, *Die Kunst Anatoliens* (Berlin, 1961), 22, suggest Urartu.

9 It is an academic question when one group of scholars claims that foreign immigrant-craftsmen came west and there made the early Oriental objects recovered, and another group suggests that the Oriental objects were imports: the same historical-archaeological implications result, namely that Western art and ideas were in contact with art and ideas from the East. Moreover, the same implications obtain if one interprets an object to be "Orientalizing," rather than an import. In fact, it would seem to me that the Orientalizing objects are more important for documenting *influence*, whereas an import only informs us that *contact* and exposure occurred. When R. D. Barnett, "Early Greek and Oriental Ivories," *JHS*, LXVIII (1948), 6, W. L. Brown, *The Etruscan Lion* (Oxford, 1960), 2, 5, and J. Boardman, *The Greeks Overseas* (Baltimore, 1964), 87, suggest that Oriental bronzes were made in the West by Orientals, they seem to be begging the question: in fact, are the bronzes Oriental or Orientalizing? After all, we do not know whether a given Oriental object attributed to a particular area was made by the craftsman at home or while on a business trip.

10 I do not think that the griffins and lions allegedly from Ziwiye were meant to be placed on a cauldron; cf. R. Ghirshman, *The Arts of Ancient Iran* (New York, 1964), 315, fig. 381.

11 U. Jantzen, *Griechische Greifenkessel* (Berlin, 1955), 34 f., 50 f., *passim*; see also his discussion on p. 73 of the griffin protome from Susa; G. M. A. Hanfmann, review of Jantzen in *Gnomon*, XXIX (1957), 245; J. L. Benson, review of Jantzen in *AJA*, LXI, No. 4 (1957), 400 ff., and "Unpublished Griffin Protomes in American Collections," *Antike Kunst*, III, Heft 2 (1960), 60 ff.; O. W. Muscarella, "The Oriental Origin of Siren Cauldron Attachments," *Hesperia*, XXXI, No. 4 (1962), 319 ff.; Herrmann, *Die Kessel*, 48, 67 (Herrmann's ideas on the origin of the griffins were misinterpreted in Young, *JNES*, 1967, 151).

12 E. Herzfeld, "Khattische und Khaldische Bronzen," *Janus*, I (1921), 145 ff.; R. D. Barnett, "Ancient Oriental Influences on Archaic Greece," *The Aegean and the Near East* (New York, 1956), 232; K. R. Maxwell-Hyslop, "Urartian Bronzes in Etruscan Tombs," *Iraq*, XVIII, No. 2 (1956), 156; E. Akurgal, *Die Kunst Anatoliens*, 55 ff.; *idem*, "Urartaische Kunst," *Anatolia*, IV (1959), 102, 108, 110 f.

13 Young, *JNES*, 1967, 151, 153.

14 P. Amandry, "Objets orientaux en Grèce et en Italie," *Syria*, XXXV (1958), 95; see also his "Grèce et Orient," *Études d'archéologie classique*, I (1955-56), 7 ff.

15 References may be found in E. Kunze, *Kretische Bronzereliefs* (Stuttgart, 1931), 270, n. 7; Muscarella, *Hesperia*, 1962, 317 f., notes 1-3, 322, n. 24; and Herrmann, *Die Kessel*, 50 f., n. 2; add M. Mellink, "Mita, Mushki and Phrygians," *H. Bossert Festschrift* (Istanbul, 1965), 323; Kyrieleis, *Marburger Winckelmann-Programm*, 1966, 1 ff.; B. B. Piotrovskii, *Vanskoe tsarstvo* (Moscow, 1959), 175 f.

16 Muscarella, *Hesperia*, 1962, 317 ff.; van Loon, *Urartian Art*, 107 ff.; Herrmann, *Die Kessel*, 27 ff., 59 ff.; Young, *JNES*, 1967, 150.

17 Herrmann, *Die Kessel*, 63 f., 70 ff., 82 f., following Kunze, *Kretische Bronzereliefs*, 271, who also called the British Museum siren Assyrian; on pp. 83 f. Herrmann plays with the idea that his "ostgriechische Werkstatt?" may be

Phrygian, but there is no stylistic reason to assume this; and on p. 82 he says of the "Sonderbildungen" group that they "müssen aus provinziellen — anatolischen oder syrischen? — Handwerksbetrieben stammen." On pp. 56 and 186, the map, Herrmann has confused the site of Alishar on the Araxes river with the Anatolian Alishar as the site where Kurds found a siren and bull attachment in 1858. Kyrieleis, *Marburger Winckelmann-Programm*, 1966, 12 f., agrees with Herrmann that the British Museum and the Copenhagen Museum sirens are Assyrian, but he does not accept them as prototypes; van Loon, *Urartian Art*, 110, accepts the British Museum siren as Assyrian, apparently leaving the Copenhagen siren as North Syrian, a position with which I could agree, *Hesperia*, 1962, 327.

18 Van Loon, *Urartian Art*, 110; M. A. Brandes, cited in Herrmann *Die Kessel*, 53 ff., postulates that the sirens found in Italy came from North Syria, those found in Greece came from Urartu; Herrmann rejects this idea with good arguments.

19 Amandry, *Études d'archéologie classique*, 1955-56, 7, 12.

20 Herrmann has done admirable work in his attempt to work out the various workshops, and his study represents the best examination of the sirens yet produced. Nevertheless, he does not mention the fact that some of the arguments he presents to refute an Urartian provenience for the sirens were stated years ago by this writer: *Hesperia*, 1962, 317 ff.; see *Die Kessel*, 51, n. 2, and 54, n. 21. I do not find the recent study of Kyrieleis convincing. He wrote his article to refute Herrmann's thesis that the sirens were North Syrian. To my mind it seems arbitrary to call the bronze statuette from Marash (in North Syria!) Urartian (p. 3) when its Hittite posture and kilt are perfectly at home in North Syria; moreover, its helmet is not really the same as those worn by Urartians as represented on the Balawat Gates, but it is the same as those worn by the twin sirens in the de Vogüé collection. Also, the helmet worn by the sirens on the Vetulonia and on the Olympia (A 5) sirens is known in North Syria: Muscarella, *Hesperia*, 1962, pl. 104, C, F, G. It is also arbitrary to call an ivory head from Nimrud Urartian because of its physiognomy (p. 6), which he says is related to the sirens; apparently there is a circular argument here. I think he is in error also when he says that in North Syria there are not mixed creatures with human faces (pp. 14 f.) and no thick eyebrows (p. 8); and he ignores the problem of beards and lack of mustaches on the bearded sirens, a feature common in North Syria but not reported in Urartu. The best parallel he brings forth is the profile on the Adilcevaz relief (p. 8), which was, of course, already pointed out by Akurgal, *Die Kunst Anatoliens*, 38.

21 A bibliography may be found in Muscarella, *Metropolitan Museum of Art Journal*, 1968, 1 ff.

22 *Ibid.*, for a discussion of these attachments.

23 Van Loon, *Urartian Art*, 106; Herrmann, *Die Kessel*, 122, 128; R. S. Young, "The Gordion Campaign of 1959: Preliminary Report," *AJA*, LXIV, No. 3 (1960), 231.

24 Herrmann discusses some bull attachments found in several areas of Greece which he suggests are North Syrian imports, 121 ff., 128 f., n. 46, pls. 43, 45-52; see n. 20 in *Metropolitan Museum of Art Journal*, 1968, where I suggest that these attachments are actually Greek products. But if my conclusion is rejected and one believes them to be imports, then they would have to be referred to as Near Eastern in general, rather than as North Syrian or Phrygian.

25 Herrmann, *Die Kessel*, pl. 58 for a good photograph.

26 I wish to thank Dr. E. O. Negahban for his kindness in sending me a photograph of this object; no provenience is recorded.

27 Muscarella, *Metropolitan Museum of Art Journal*, 1968, figs. 1-5.

28 Ghirshman, *Arts of Ancient Iran*, 432; Herrmann, *Die Kessel*, 70, 136.

29 An Assyrian lion weight in the Louvre from Khorsabad has a similar base below the rear ring: A. Parrot, *The Arts of Assyria* (New York, 1961), 117, fig. 132.

30 Herrmann, *Die Kessel*, 131 ff., pls. 55, 56.

31 Herrmann, *Die Kessel*, 133 f.; Boardman, *The Greeks Overseas*, 86, fig. 14c, thinks they may have "suggested the motif" for the Greek griffin.

32 Akurgal, *Anatolia*, 1959, 110; P. Demargne, *The Birth of Greek Art* (New York, 1964), 330 f., fig. 424.

33 R. S. Young, "The 1961 Campaign at Gordion," *AJA*, LXVI, No. 2 (1962), 163, pl. 43, fig. 15; R. H. Dyson, "Digging in Iran: Hasanlu, 1958," *Expedition*, I, No. 3 (1959), 13, figure at upper left.

34 Another attachment that should be mentioned here is discussed in *Die Kessel*, 151 f., pl. 61, nos. 1-3: a bearded man with a pointed forward-falling hat or helmet forms a handle. It is unique and may be Greek, although I have no strong feelings on this matter; if Oriental it should be referred to as Near Eastern, although it reflects, apparently, North Syrian inspiration or manufacture.

35 E. Kunze, "Verkannter orientalischer Kesselschmuck aus dem argivischen Heraion," *Reinecke Festschrift zum 75. Geburtstag von Paul Reinecke*, G. Behrens, ed. (Mainz, 1950), 99 f., pls. 16, no. 1, 17, nos. 1-2; Amandry, *Études d'archéologie classique*, 1955-56, 11; Herrmann, *Die Kessel*, 153 ff., pls. 63, 64; for a reference to some of these objects on the antiquities market, see Muscarella, *Metropolitan Museum of Art Journal*, 1968, n. 29.

36 Muscarella, *Hesperia*, 1962, 325; Herrmann, *Die Kessel*, 61, 64, *passim;* Brown, *Etruscan Lion*, 1 ff.; Young, *JNES*, 1967, 153.

37 Muscarella, *Phrygian Fibulae from Gordion*, 59 ff., for a bibliography and discussion concerned with Phrygian exports to the West.

38 To my knowledge this object has not been published before. I am very grateful to the authorities at the Athens National Museum, and especially to Dr. George Dontas, for permission to publish the blinker.

39 Brown, *Etruscan Lion*, 9, puts the Bernardini, the Barberini, and the Olympia (U 2) stands together in "the same circle of works."

40 For examples of artistic parallels between Iran and North Syria in the ninth century B.C. see my "Hasanlu 1964," *BMMA*, XXV, No. 3 (Nov., 1966), 125 ff.

41 Note that at Gordion the shoulder head is in frontal position whereas the North Syrian examples are in profile.

42 For example, a god represented with his foot resting between the horns of a bull occurs in North Syrian art: F. Thureau-Dangin, et al., *Arslan Tash* (Paris, 1931), pl. II : 1, 2; idem, *Til-Barsib* (Paris, 1936), pl. III. Note, however, that the same position of the foot occurs in the art of Urartu: B. B. Piotrovskii, *Iskusstvo Urartu* (Leningrad, 1962), 75, fig. 43; 97, fig. 61; 106, fig. 71.

43 I would modify this strong statement by referring to one possible parallel between an object excavated in Urartu, and inscribed with an inscription of Sarduri II (ca. 764-735 B.C.), and similar but locally made objects found in Italy. I am thinking of the apparent lion protome from Karmir Blur and the lion protomes from the Regolini-Galassi Tomb. It is not impossible to my mind that there may be a connection (indirect?) between the lions: Brown, *Etruscan Lion*, pl. IX; Piotrovskii, *Iskusstvo Urartu*, 65, figs. 36, 37. And, needless to say, those scholars who believe that the siren attachments came to the West from Urartu would modify this statement more drastically!

44 P. Amandry, "Un Motif 'Scythe' en Iran et en Grèce," *JNES*, XXIV, No. 3 (1965), 149 ff.; R. D. Barnett in *The Aegean and the Near East*, 229 f.; B. Segall, "Greece and Luristan," *BMFA*, XLI (1943), 72 ff.; C. Hopkins, "Oriental Evidence for Early Etruscan Chronology," *Berytus*, XI, No. 2 (1955), 75 ff.; T. J. Arne, "Luristan and the West," *ESA*, IX (1934), 277 ff.

I acquired G. Ahlberg's important study, "A Late Geometric Grave-Scene Influenced by North Syrian Art," *Opuscula Atheniensia*, VII (1967), 177 ff., just before receiving the proofs of this paper. His discussion of the relationship between the banquet scenes on late geometric vases in Greece and similar scenes represented in North Syrian art is convincing. In particular, one is impressed by the common use of certain motifs: the "two-sided" banquet (two people facing each other at a table), pomegranates, harps, and birds. A few comments on the banquet-scene motif are necessary here. The "two-sided" banquet scene is rare outside of North Syria. A good example is represented on a situla said to have been found in Iran (Y. Maléki, "Situle à scène de banquet," *Iranica Antiqua*, I [1961], 20 ff.; P. Amandry, "Situles à reliefs des princes de Babylone," *Antike Kunst*, IX:2 [1966], 60, fig. 4; P. Calmeyer, "Eine westiranische Bronzewerkstatt des 10./9. Jahrhunderts v. Chr. zwischen Zalu Ab und dem Gebiet der Kakavand—I," *Berliner Jahrbuch für Vor- und Frühgeschichte*, V [1965], 9, fig. A 1); a harp-player also exists in this scene. Examples from Iran of the same type usually have "one-sided" scenes (one person at a table), sometimes accompanied by a harp-player. "One-sided" scenes are also known — but are rare — in North Syria (e.g., W. Andrae, *Die Kleinfunde von Sendschirli*, V Berlin, [1943], pls. 46, 47 g and d). The same type of scene is also represented along with musicians, including a harp-player, on some bowls found on Cyprus (e.g., MMA 74.51.5700, H. T. Bossert, *Altsyrien* [Tübingen, 1951], 309). The close relationship of the banquet scenes represented on the vessels allegedly from Iran to those represented in North Syrian art is striking and deserves more attention: aside from the basic idea itself, the use of a cross-legged table, a chair whose uprights sometimes end in a bird's head, pomegranates, harp-players, and a man waving a palm branch (or feather?) over the dinner table. Pl. Vb of Ahlberg's paper illustrates the last motif, but note that there is no harp-player represented, as Ahlberg, p. 181. I do not now think that the "two-sided" banquet scene came to Greece from an area east of North Syria, and I am therefore in agreement with Ahlberg. Amandry's dating of the eastern examples to the tenth century B.C. (*Antike Kunst*, 1966, 69) may be 100 years too early, and I would tentatively call them roughly contemporary with the North Syrian examples, i.e., ninth and eighth century B.C. An example of a "one-sided" banquet scene on an object imported to Greece may be seen on a bronze bowl found at Olympia (Bossert, *Altsyrien*, 342). This bowl, clearly not North Syrian in origin but filled with Egyptianizing elements, demonstrates that the Greeks were also aware of another type of banquet scene, perhaps one that had its origin in Cyprus.

45 While going through the bibliography again, I discovered that this feature was mentioned by R. D. Barnett and N. Gökçe in "The Find of Urartian Bronzes at Altin Tepe, Near Erzincan," *AnatSt*, III (1953), 122. I wish to thank the editors of this volume for allowing me to include this addendum. My article on bull attachments in *The Journal of The Metropolitan Museum of Art* was already in press before I was able to assemble all the facts.

46 H. H. von der Osten "Neue Urartaische Bronzen aus Erzincan," *Bericht über den VI. Internationalen Kongress für Archaeologie* (Berlin, 1940), 225 ff., pl. 9a; see also H. T. Bossert, *Altanatolien* (Berlin, 1942), figs. 1188–1190, 1192. None of the photographs of the Altintepe cauldron known to me shows the extra rivets.

Panoplies from Afrati

Herbert Hoffmann

The bronze armor presented in this paper is said to be from Afrati, a village on the southwest slope of the Lasithi mountains in central Crete.[1] Halbherr visited this region in 1898 and conducted trial excavations on the hill known as Prophetis Ilias, which overlooks the village of Afrati.[2] A later excavation, by an Italian mission under the direction of Doro Levi, yielded several fine pithoi, as well as large quantities of ceramic material dating from Late Minoan III C down to the end of the seventh century B.C., and led to the identification of Afrati as ancient Arkades, a settlement marked on the *Tabula Peutingeriana* as lying between Lyttos and Viannos.[3] The imprints of pithoi recovered by Levi can still be seen in places on the upper slopes of Prophetis Ilias, and pithos fragments are strewn over a wide area on the ancient acropolis. Pithoi of recent manufacture, of great interest to the student of ancient traditions, may be observed in the village below, where they are used as storage vessels or, with the bases removed, as chimney pots.[4]

The Afrati armor comprises at least four complete panoplies of canonical Cretan type — helmet, bell corslet, and *mitra*. Many of the pieces are lavishly decorated, and a number of them bear inscriptions. These inscriptions are fairly uniform in form and content, consisting generally of a name (in some instances followed by a father's name), of the verb ἧλε (or, in one case, ἀπήλευσε,[5] and of the demonstrative pronoun τόνδε or τόδε, which seems to refer to the piece of armor on which it is inscribed. In three instances identical inscriptions on different pieces of armor (in two cases a helmet and a *mitra*, in another a *mitra* and a corslet) prove that they belong to one panoply; in other instances the evidence seems to indicate that inscriptions continue from one piece of armor to another. Judging from these inscriptions, the panoplies were captured in battle, distributed to individual warriors, inscribed by them or on their orders, set up as trophies (ἀκροθίνια),[6] and dedicated to a divinity, perhaps Athena.[7]. The inscriptions are written in the alphabet of Lyttos,[8] within the sphere of influence of which Afrati-Arkades may be presumed to have lain.

I

The find is in the Norbert Schimmel Collection, New York, with the exception of a corslet (C 3) and a *mitra* (M 9) in the Heraklion museum, two *mitrai* (M 4, M 10) belonging to Mr. Nikos Metaxas in Heraklion, three *mitrai* in the Museum für Kunst und Gewerbe Hamburg (one of them is M 5), and two corslets (C 1, C 2) and fragments of two helmets (H 4, H 5) presently on loan to the Antikenmuseum, Basel. Four of the finest items of the find (H 1, H 2, M 1, M 2) were lent by Mr. Schimmel to the exhibition "Master Bronzes from the Classical World"; they were illustrated and briefly described in the catalogue of that exhibition, cited in this article as *Master Bronzes*.[9]

To turn first to the *mitrai:* these crescent-shaped abdomen protectors seem to have been a Cretan specialty.[10] They were suspended by rings from a belt worn under the flange of a bell corslet,[11] and A. E. Raubitschek has suggested that they may have belonged to the standard equipment of the Cretan warrior, offering protection for the abdominal organs while leaving the archer free to draw the bow and the hoplite to protect his neck with his shield against arrows.[12]

M 1 (*Master Bronzes*, No. 31) is decorated by a pair of facing horse protomes in relief, supplemented by fine tracing. The heads, necks, and

Fig. 1: Mitra *(M2). Norbert Schimmel Collection.*

chests of the animals occupy nearly the entire height of the *mitra,* the edges of which are decorated with groups of parallel ridges. The vivacious horse heads with eloquently swelling necks, pointed forelocks, and manes rendered as a series of overlapping pointed S-strands are of a type familiar from Attic horse-head amphoras dating from the turn of the seventh century B.C.[13] The horses' eyes are lentoid with drawn-out corners and traced pupils; the ears are spade-shaped, details that can be matched on Attic and Corinthian black-figured vases of the late seventh and early sixth centuries B.C. The inscription reads Συνήνιτος τόδε ὁ Εὐκλώτα; the same inscription is found on a helmet (H 2) that was evidently made by the same armorer. The verb ἧλε, found in inscriptions on other *mitrai* from the find, is here omitted.

M 2 (Fig. 1)[14] figures a pair of confronted winged horse protomes. The strands of the horses' manes are straighter and more schematic than on M 1, and the modeling is in general somewhat cruder. The horses appear to prance; at their shoulders they have sickle-shaped wings. The revolving effect produced by wings, horse heads, and forelegs resembles a *triskelis.* The inscription on this *mitra* is similar in form and content to that on M 1; only the names are different, and the verb is given: Αἰσονίδας τόνδ' ἧλε ὁ Κλοϙιδίο.

M 3 (*Master Bronzes,* No. 32) shows a pair of confronted sphinxes. They stand stiff-legged, one foot advanced. Their hindquarters rest against the steep upcurve of the panel frame; their heads, in higher relief than their bodies, turn out to face the beholder. The sphinxes wear short "Dedalic" perukes, decorated with rows of traced chevrons, and tall poloi supported by ringlike brims. Behind each polos and attached to it by a long curling stem is a delicately engraved "floating" palmette.[15] This *mitra* is uninscribed.

M 4, closely related to M 1 and M 2, is one of the two *mitrai* in the Nikos Metaxas Collection. The relief represents a handsome double-bodied panther. This curious monster, whose next-of-kin are to be found in Early and

Fig. 2: Inscribed mitra *(M6). Norbert Schimmel Collection.*

Fig. 3: Inscribed mitra *(M7). Norbert Schimmel Collection.*

Fig. 4: Inscribed mitra *(M8). Norbert Schimmel Collection.*

Middle Corinthian vase paintings,[16] is represented in a pose recalling that of the sphinxes on M 3: forequarters standing (or walking), hindquarters sitting, a device well suited to accommodate the crescent-shaped space the figure has to fill. This *mitra,* which is now published by Angelika Lembessis [16 bis], is also uninscribed.

A number of undecorated *mitrai* probably belong to the same find. I list only those furnished with inscriptions:

M 5. Museum für Kunst und Gewerbe Hamburg (Fig. 2).[17] Inscribed Καρισθένης ὁ Πειθία τόνδ' ἀπήλευσε.[18]

M 6. Norbert Schimmel Collection (Fig. 2).[19] Inscribed: Εὐωνυμος ἦλε τόδε ὁ 'Ε[ϱ]ασιμένιος.

M 7. Norbert Schimmel Collection (Fig. 3). Inscribed: Fισοκάϱτης τόνδε (verb not given).[20] The same inscription occurs on H 3, showing that M 7 and H 3 belong together.

M 8. Norbert Schimmel Collection (Fig. 4). Inscribed: ἦλε.[21]

M 9. Heraklion Museum, Giamalakis Collection. Inscribed: Οπϱιος ὃς τόνδε ἦλε.[22]

M 10. Nikos Metaxas Collection, Heraklion. Unpublished. Inscribed: Νλὼν τὸν δ'ἦλε [Νέων τόνδ' ἦλε].[22 bis]

Unlike the heavy Corinthian helmets, the Cretan examples are remarkably light.[23] If one supposes that, like the *mitrai,* the helmets were worn by archers rather than hoplites, the light weight could be easily understood. It would also explain the absence of the nose guard, which an archer would not need. The shape is characteristically Cretan — different from that of the standard Corinthian helmet — with a rounded flange decorated with a rosette at the bottom of each cheek piece.[24]

H 1 (*Master Bronzes,* No. 29, here Fig. 5) originally had an applied fixed visor, but of this only the imprint remains. The neck guard is decorated with two rows of traced ornaments, separated by three ridges: hatched dog-tooth pattern above, dotted tongue pattern below. This ornamental border is flanked at each end by a palmette on a curving dotted stem. A traced eight-petal rosette decorates the tonguelike projection of the cheek piece.

The figure decoration of this helmet, executed in a combination of repoussé work and tracing (the latter forming double outlines),[25] shows two identical pairs of winged youths, one on each side of the helmet. The youths, represented approaching each other in the archaic *"Knielauf"* position, hold a pair of large serpents entwined in a double figure eight between them. A seated double-bodied panther of the type encountered on *mitra* 4 is traced in the triangular space formed by the serpents' tails and the base line.

Whereas the heads of the two serpents confront each other heraldically, both youths turn their heads away from the snakes and from each other. Each grasps a serpent at the neck with one hand and steps on a serpent's tail with one foot. The free hand of one youth is raised, with fingers extended as if in greeting; that of the other is lowered. Both figures wear two pairs of wings, a small sickle-shaped pair attached to the sandals and rendered by traced lines only, and a large shoulder pair rendered in relief, curving downward and apparently strapped across the chest and shoulders by a harness. Puzzling details are the two circles on each youth's shoulder (Fig. 6), which do not seem to be part of the harness.

The heads of the young men, with their large eyes, jutting noses, and fleshy lips, are of a type peculiar to early archaic Crete, which will be discussed further. They wear diadems to which scroll-shaped decorations

Fig. 5: Helmet (H 1). Norbert Schimmel Collection.

seem to be attached above the forehead; it is uncertain, however, whether the three scrolls are part of the diadem (as I first thought) or whether they represent curls of hair. Above the diadem the hair is rendered in long parallel curved lines (hatched on the left figure), below the diadem by several banks of short curved lines. It is gathered at the nape by a ring or cord and then divided into two long wavy locks falling nearly to the waist.

The figures have broad shoulders and narrow waists. Although a certain plasticity is achieved by the low relief, there is little anatomical differentiation except in the legs, where the thigh and calf muscles are rendered by long ridges bordered by traced lines, the kneecap as a skeletal ball-and-socket joint. The short belted kilts are edged with a welt and decorated with a pattern of alternately plain and hatched lozenges.

On the front of the helmet, between the figures' raised hands, is an inscription: Νεόπολις (Fig. 6). If one takes this to be a proper name, as Raubitschek proposes, one might relate it to Pollis, the legendary founder of Lyttos,[26] and assume that the person who added the inscription came from that city; this assumption is supported by the fact that the inscriptions are in the Lyttan alphabet.

H 2 (*Master Bronzes*, No. 30) is of the same type as H 1 and also has very similar traced ornament on the neck guard, except that elongated tongues, stacked horizontally, rather than a palmette, abut the dog-tooth pattern on the tonguelike extensions. One end of the visor, with an embossed rosette, is preserved in this example. A horse is shown on each side of the helmet, the relief being supplemented by fine incision as on H 1. The animals' stiff "wooden" legs call to mind the horses of the Prinias lintel. The mane, in overlapping S-shaped locks tapering to points, the large lentoid eyes, the projecting forelocks, and other details connect this helmet closely with the *mitra* M 1. It is therefore not surprising that the inscriptions on the two pieces of armor are identical, suggesting that helmet and *mitra* were once part of the same panoply. The inscription on the helmet (written

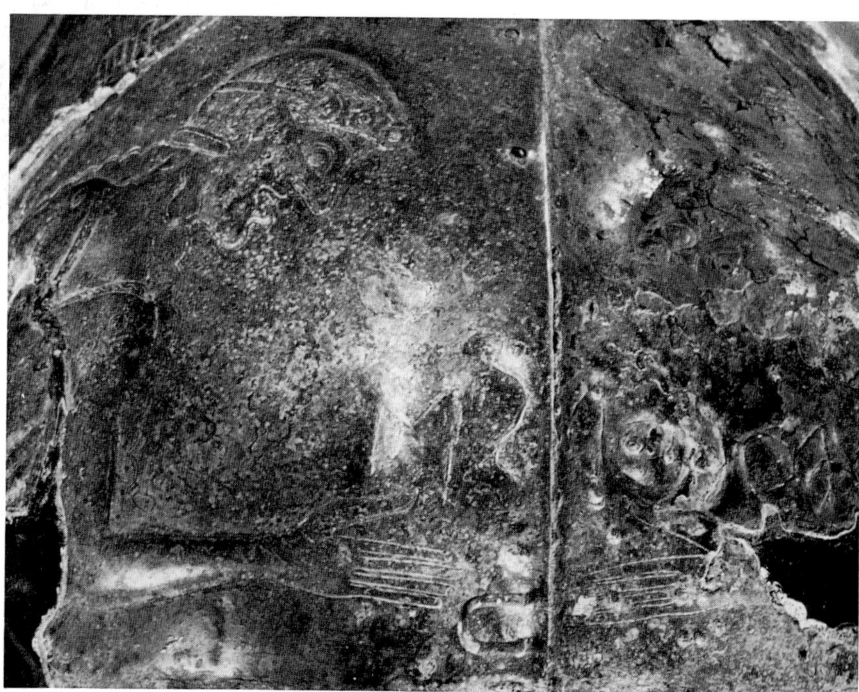

Fig. 6: Detail, Helmet (H1).

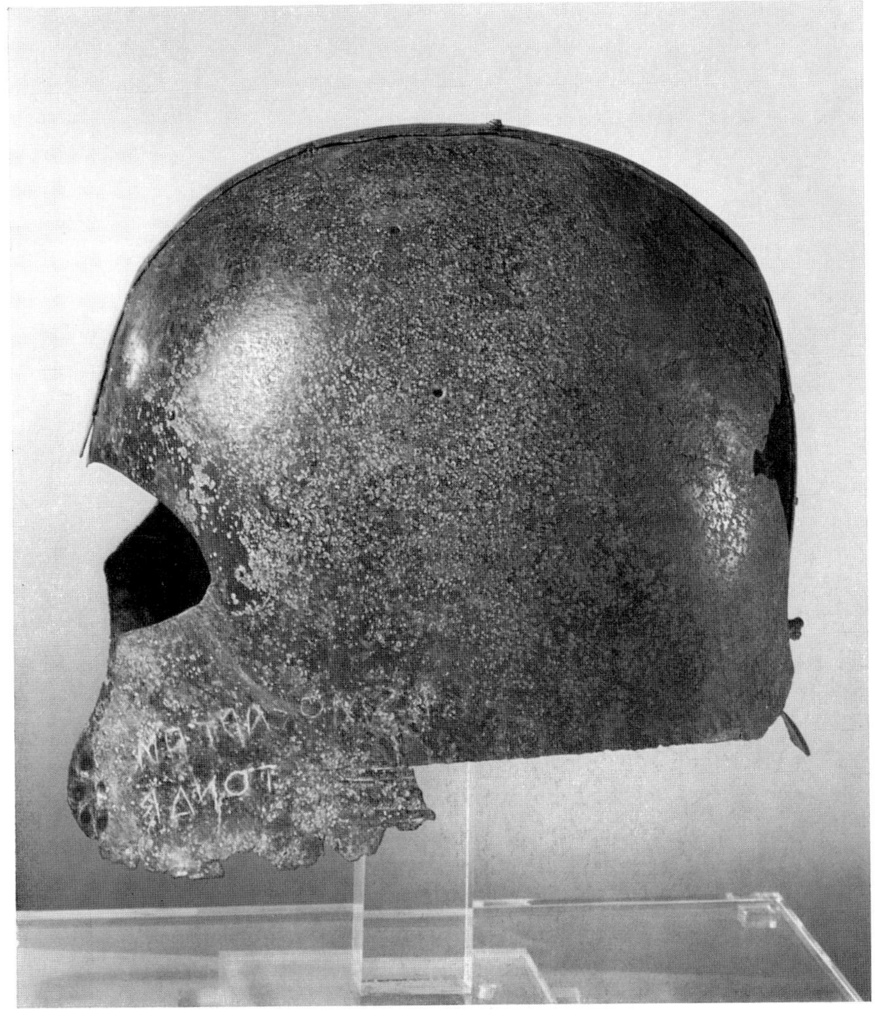

Fig. 7: Helmet (H3). Norbert Schimmel Collection.

vertically in the field between the horse's legs on the side shown in the illustration) reads [Σ]υνήνιτος [τόδε] ὁ Εὐκλώτα.

H 3 (Fig. 7) is preserved unbroken and virtually complete. The helmet has no figural decoration. The ornament of the neck guard is similar to that of H 1 and H 2, except that the petals of the rosette on the extensions of the cheek piece are given in relief. The helmet is inscribed (on the left cheek piece) Fισοκάϱτης τόνδε; the same inscription occurs on M 7, showing that the two pieces once formed part of one panoply.

Finally, there is a fragmentary helmet (H 4) decorated with life-size ears in relief,[27] another (H 5) with a high, toppling crest[28] and a relief figuring a hoplite on the cheek piece.

At least six corslets were found with the helmets and *mitrai* at Afrati; of these all but two (C 2, C 3) are in fragmentary condition.

C 1. Private collection; on loan to the Antikenmuseum, Basel. Figure decoration (traced and in low relief):[29] two rampant lions heraldically disposed on each side of the pectoral. A slender griffin[30] strides upward along each of the two profiled ridges that circumscribe the lower boundary of the thorax, while a hoplite balances on one foot atop a floral tendril that curls from the bottom of these ridges up onto the rib cage. This corslet appears not to have been inscribed.

Fig. 8: Fragments of a corslet (C5). Norbert Schimmel Collection.

C 2. Heraklion Museum (Giamalakis Collection). Preserved intact with backplate. Unpublished. I did not note an inscription, but I was unable to examine the corslet carefully.

C 3. Norbert Schimmel Collection. Undecorated. Inscribed: [. . .]ων τόδ' ῆλε.

C 4. Formerly on the art market; present whereabouts unknown to me. Seen uncleaned and in many fragments but nearly complete and with the neck guard intact. The letters *iota* and *kappa* (the spacing might permit the reading Ϝισοκάρτης as on M 7 and H 3) were noted on the backplate.

C 5. Norbert Schimmel Collection (Fig. 8). Two adjoining fragments only. Decorated with palmettes in relief supplemented by tracing.[31] Inscribed: Οπριος ο[. .]νο. Cf. M 9.

C 6 and C 7 (?). Undecorated and uninscribed fragments.

II

It is evident at a glance that the new find is closely related to the decorated helmet (Fig. 9) and nine *mitrai* (Fig. 10) found in 1899 at Axos;[32] the Afrati and Axos bronzes are, in fact, probably the work of the same atelier. Decorated and undecorated *mitrai* have also been found at other sites in Crete — one at Rethymnon[33] and three at Dreros[34] — as well as on the Greek mainland, at Delphi (two examples)[35] and at Olympia (nine examples).[36] Cretan helmets similar in type to H 1, H 2, H 3, and that of Axos have also been found at Dreros, Palaikastro, Onythe near Rethymnon, and Delphi.[37] The bronze gorgoneion from Dreros, with its finely traced symplegma of serpents in the forehead area, has likewise been compared with the Axos bronzes.[38] None of these pieces of armor except those from Afrati is inscribed.

Scholarly opinion concerning the date of the Axos armor ranges over more than a century. Jenkins favors an early date (early seventh century B.C.),[39] while Levi advocates a date in the mid-seventh century B.C.;[40]

Fig. 9: Helmet from Axos. Courtesy Scuola archeologica italiana di Atene.

Fig. 10: Mitra *from Axos. Courtesy Scuola archeologica italiana di Atene.*

Boardman recently proposed mid-seventh century B.C. dates for the Axos and Dreros *mitrai* and late dates (first half of the sixth century B.C.) for the Axos helmet;[41] and Heinrich Bartels has placed the Axos *mitrai* "well into the sixth century" B.C.[42]

The Afrati panoplies present us with the first instance of inscriptions on archaic works of art from Crete.[43] There is, unfortunately, no epigraphic

Fig. 11: Bronze cut-out plaque. Courtesy Musée du Louvre.

Fig. 12: Bronze cut-out plaque. Courtesy Musée du Louvre.

evidence for an exact chronology. The style of the Afrati bronzes should be described as "post-Dedalic," to use Jenkins' term, or, more generally, as "Dedalic."[44] It would appear to follow immediately on that of the Prinias lintel, the kore from Auxerre, and the bronze *kouriskos* from Delphi.[45]

Comparison of the Cretan armor with Corinthian and Attic vase painting tends to confirm the correctness of this broad dating, which I think can be narrowed down to the last quarter of the century, around 620 B.C. If this tentatively assigned date should turn out to be justified, it will have far-reaching implications for an entire range of monuments imprecisely assigned to the early archaic period in Crete. These include the Dedalic terra cottas,[46] the Cretan relief pithoi,[47] and the so-called "Eteocretan" cut-out appliqués.

A total of six such cut-outs are known: two in the Louvre (Figs. 11-12), two in Heraklion, one in Copenhagen, and one in Oxford.[48] The larger Louvre plaque (Fig. 11) figures two facing hunters, one carrying a small mountain goat, the other a bow, and similar figures are represented in the plaques in Copenhagen (Fig. 13) and Oxford (Fig. 14). In the former the hunter carries the forequarter of an enormous wild mountain goat; in the latter he loads a similar animal onto his back. On one of the two plaques in Heraklion a *kriophoros* is shown, on the other a winged demon (Figs. 15-16). More will be said about the latter in connection with the subject of the Afrati helmet.

All six of these openwork plaques are quite similar in style. They are executed in "pseudo low relief" and show a surprisingly advanced rendering of certain anatomical details. W. Lamb compared them with the Axos and Dreros *mitrai* and coined the apt name "the Cretan Group" for these works, which she recognized as representing the output of a single atelier.[49]

The find of armor from Afrati can certainly be associated with this Cretan Group. A comparison of the figures on H 1 (Fig. 5) with the "hunters" of the cut-out reliefs (Figs. 11-14) speaks for itself. Of the many stylistic features these works have in common, attention might be drawn to the angular lines of the heads with low foreheads, jutting chins, and fleshy lips, to the long wavy tresses that flow over the shoulders and along the upper arms, to the big eyes drawn out at the corners, and especially to the rendering of the hands. The drawing of the leg muscles and kneecaps characteristic of this group has already been mentioned.[50]

Close stylistic analogies among monumental sculptures to the bronzes of the Cretan Group can be found in the poros stelai from Prinias and Eleutherna.[51] These somewhat crude works of art are best understood as enlargements of *Kleinkunst* to a monumental scale. Of better quality is the upper part of the poros statue from Eleutherna, in the Heraklion museum,[52] one of the few monumental sculptures dating from the early archaic period that was actually found on Cretan soil.

Fig. 13: Bronze cut-out plaque. Courtesy National Museum, Copenhagen.

Finally, the question may be posed whether the origin of the ivory statuette of a kneeling youth discovered in Samos[53] should not be reconsidered in the stylistic context of the new find. Comparison with the Eleutherna statue as well as with the winged youths of the Afrati helmet (H 1) would appear to provide strong arguments in favor of assigning the Samos ivory to the Cretan school.[54]

The conception of the human face presented in the youths of the Afrati helmet and again in the Samos ivory is thoroughly Greek, yet not without a trace of Near Eastern style. The influence of the Orient is very marked in the large almond-shaped eyes, in the striking symmetry of the brows, which was emphasized by inlaid grooves, and especially in the rendering of the ear with well-differentiated helix and lobe, which is quite distinct from the ornamental double volute rendering known from the earliest marble kouroi. And yet the difference between the taut and dynamic forms of the Greek work of art and the schematic though technically perfect Oriental products is a difference between two worlds.

Stylistic forerunners of the Afrati bronzes can be found among the Cretan bronze shields, especially the example from Palaikastro.[55] In turn, the artists who left us the splendid bronzes of the Cretan Group may have influenced the development of monumental sculpture on the islands and on the Greek mainland. Not only are the bronzes of this group the products of one workshop, but they reflect the artistic personality of a single master who set the style. The Afrati find inevitably brings to mind the tradition of the "historical" Daidalos.[56] This Cretan master, who first combined Orientalizing art with Greek naturalism, lived, as Miss Richter has suggested, at the end of the seventh century B.C.[57]

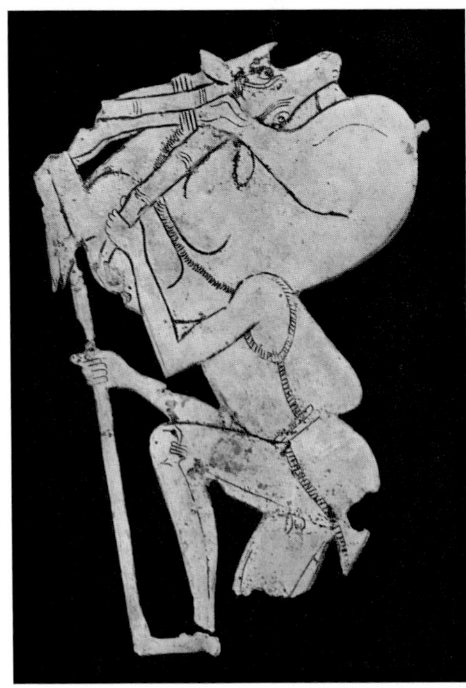

Fig. 14: Bronze cut-out plaque. Courtesy Ashmolean Museum, Oxford.

The representations on the decorated Afrati *mitrai*, as well as that on one of the helmets (H 2), are of a standard Orientalizing type familiar to us from a large number of monuments, but the extraordinary scene depicted on the other helmet (H 1) is not easy to explain.

Who are these winged youths holding serpents? Can they be identified by name, or should they be considered as anonymous demons selected from the repertory of Cretan folk religion?

The fact that the figures have their wings tied to their bodies and feet has been stressed by those who favor a mythological explanation. The heraldic symmetry of the scene, on the other hand, and its repetition on both sides of the helmet, have been held as evidence against too specific an interpretation.

Two other representations of what is probably the same subject are known to me. One is the bronze cut-out relief from Afrati (Figs. 15-16),[58] of which unfortunately less than half is preserved. The extant portion suffices, however, to show that the winged figure is probably part of an antithetical two-figure group. The other probable representation of the subject is a fragment of a terra-cotta pinax in the Heraklion museum,[59] on which a running or kneeling winged figure — obviously belonging to an antithetical pair — and a coil of a serpent's body are preserved.

Levi and Marinatos have suggested Ikaros as the subject of the Afrati cut-out plaque[60] (seeing it as a single figure, on the analogy of the Attic black-figured hydria fragments, Acropolis 601[61]), and this interpretation has recently been supported by Boardman.[62]

If, however, the Afrati cut-out relief can, as I believe, be reconstructed as a two-figure composition, then the scene depicted is almost certainly the same as that on the Schimmel helmet. So far the scenes on other pieces of Cretan armor and on the cut-out bronzes have defied convincing interpretation. A probable explanation of the winged youths — be it mythological, be it daemonological, or even a combination of the two — must take into account the entire body of related material. A fuller iconographic study will be contained in a forthcoming publication.

Fig. 15: Bronze cut-out plaque from Afrati. Heraklion Archaeological Museum. Photograph by the author.

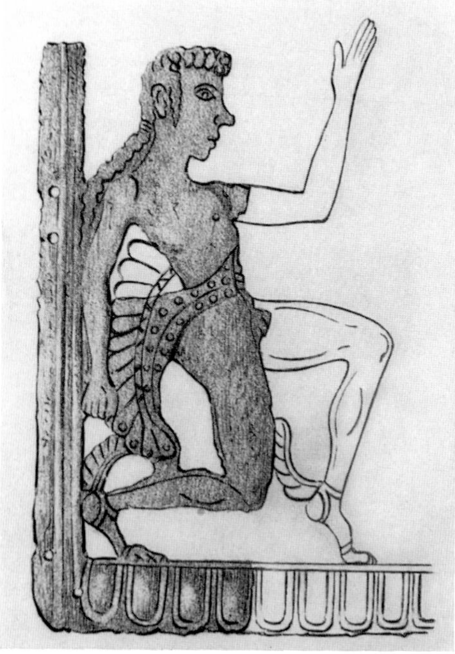

Fig. 16: Reconstruction drawing of plaque in Fig. 15. After Boardman, Cretan Collection.

Notes

1 Two helmets and two *mitrai* selected from the Afrati armor have been illustrated and briefly discussed by the author in David Gordon Mitten, Suzannah F. Doeringer, *Master Bronzes from the Classical World* (Mainz, 1967), the catalogue of the Master Bronzes exhibition, Nos. 29-32. The present paper is the preliminary publication of the entire find. The full publication of the find, by H. Hoffmann with the collaboration of A. E. Raubitschek, is scheduled to appear in book form late in 1970 as a Fogg Museum Monograph in Classical Archaeology.

The epigraphic data and many ideas presented in this paper were contributed by A. E. Raubitschek. I also wish to thank him for his counsel and encouragement, as well as for his kindness in reading and criticizing my manuscript. A grant-in-aid from the American Philosophical Society enabled me to travel to Crete during the summer of 1967 in order to study the material related to this find.

2 F. Halbherr, "Ruins of Unknown Cities at Hagios Ilias and Prinià," *AJA*, V (1901), 393 ff., figs. 1-9; D. Levi, "Arkades," *ASAtene*, X-XII (1927-1929), 15 ff.; *Enciclopedia dell'arte antica*, I (Rome, 1958), 659 ff., s.v. "Arkades" (W. Johannowski).

3 Johannowski, "Arkades" (n. 2).

4 Cf. R. Hampe, A. Winter, *Bei Töpfern und Töpferinnen in Kreta, Messenien und Zypern* (Bonn, 1962), 1 ff., figs. 1-60, pls. 1-50. See especially fig. 19 (pithos chimney in the Mt. Ida region).

5 The aorist of *αἱρέω* = to take. S. Marinatos, *ArchEph* (1966), 105.

6 Actual tropaea have not, to my knowledge, been documented previously by archaeological finds of the archaic period, although they must have existed. Cf. *DS*, V, s.v. "Tropaeum," and E. Kunze "Waffenweihungen," *VIII. Bericht über die Ausgrabungen in Olympia* (Berlin, 1967), 83 ff., figs. 28-37, pls. 30-49. Cf. also F. Poulsen's interpretation of the enigmatic scene represented on the *mitra* from Rethymnon, "Eine kretische Mitra," *AthMitt*, XXXI (1906), 374 ff. On trophies of armor before the Roman period see Z. Gausiniec, *Geneza Tropaionu* (Warsaw, 1955), with French summary.

7 The evidence of an archaic inscription mentioning arrows dedicated to Athena (F. Halbherr, *Inscriptiones Creticae* [Rome, 1935], I.V, 4, copied by Halbherr in the village church at Afrati) must be considered in the context of the new find; see F. Halbherr, *AJA*, 1901 (n. 2), 397 f., fig. 9.

8 The rendering of the *omega* as a circle within a circle, which occurs on the inscriptions from this find, is a feature peculiar to inscriptions found at Lyttos and is documented nowhere else; see now M. Guarducci, *Epigrafia Graeca*, I (Rome, 1967), 183 and 189, no. 5.

9 See n. 1.

10 The term (borrowed from Homer) may be a misnomer, because the Cretan name for this piece of body armor is not known to us; see the literature cited in *Master Bronzes*, 49; C. Rolley, review of A. M. Snodgrass, *Early Greek Armour*, *REG*, LXXIX (1966), 513, and A. M. Snodgrass, review of H. Brandenburg, *Studien zur Mitra*, in *Gnomon*, XXXIX (1967), 426.

11 Cf. A. Hagemann, *Griechische Panzerung* (Leipzig, 1919), 99 ff. and the complete panoply from the fifth-century Thracian tomb at Rüec, L. Ognenova, "Les cuirasses de bronze trouvées en Thrace," *BCH*, LXXXV (1961), 522, fig. 14a. See also the Etruscan examples (?) mentioned by H. Brandenburg, *Studien zur Mitra* (Münster, 1966), and E. Hill, "Etruscan Votive Bronze Warriors in the Walters Art Gallery," *JWalt*, VII-VIII (1944-45), 107, n. 8.

12 Note that there are no shields or any fragments that might be identified as belonging to shields in the Afrati find. *Mitrai* and shields might appear to have been alternatives.

13 Cf. the Attic panel amphora with a pair of facing horse protomes in each panel, Boston, Museum of Fine Arts, acc. no. 63.1611 (Pl. 1 in my forthcoming *CVA* fascicule, Boston I, *The Attic Black-figured Amphoras*), and the representation of the same subject on an amphora in the Agora Museum, H. A. Thompson, "Excavations in the Athenian Agora : 1952," *FA*, VII (1952), 1422, fig. 21. A study of the Attic horse-head amphoras, by Ann Birchall, is in preparation.

14 Height 13.5 cm.; diameter (as reconstructed) 22.4 cm.

15 The Oriental prototypes for this motif are discussed by J. Schäfer, *Studien zu den griechischen Reliefpithoi* (Kallmünz, 1957), 31 ff., notes 76 ff.; cf. esp. pl. 5:2; see the comparable though not identical "lily-caps" worn by the sphinxes on the eighth-century Cretan shields (e.g. E. Kunze, *Kretische Bronzereliefs* [Stuttgart, 1931], pl. 2), for which L. Holland, "Mycenaean Plumes," *AJA*, XXXIII (1929), 173 ff., figs. 1-11, postulated Minoan origin, but which may likewise prove to be Oriental-inspired.

16 On double-bodied creatures cf. H. Payne, *Necrocorinthia* (Oxford, 1931), 51, n. 8, and the literature there given. To this add: A. Roes, "L'histoire d'une bête," *BCH*, LIX (1935), 313 ff. (cited by H. Payne, *Perachora*, II [Oxford, 1962], 142, no. 1521).

16 bis 'Α. Λεμπέση, *Δύο μίτρες τῆς συλλογῆς Μεταξᾶ, Κρητικὰ Χρονικά, Κα'* (21), fasc. 1 (1969), 97 ff., pls. Ε', ΣΤ'.

17 Inv. no. 1967, 50 a. Height 17 cm.; diameter 24 cm. Two other *mitrai* from the find, inv. nos. 1967, 50 b and c, are uninscribed.

18 This is the only inscription in which *ἀπήλευσε* replaces the usual verb *ἦλε*. According to Raubitschek the former is the active aorist of a verb the future of which is documented in the middle voice: *ἐλεύσομαι* = "I shall come" or "I shall bring myself." Raubitschek takes the form in the inscription to mean "he brought it away" (perhaps as his prize or allotment).

19 Height (as reconstructed) 16 cm.; diameter (as reconstructed) 24 cm.

20 Height 15.4 cm.; diameter 23 cm. Raubitschek suggests that the verb on this *mitra* may continue or complement the inscription on the *Mitra* M 8 (in which only the verb is given), i.e., that in some instances the inscriptions continue from one component of a panoply to another.

21 Height (as reconstructed) 16 cm.; diameter (as reconstructed) 24 cm.

22 Marinatos, *ArchEph*, 1966 (n. 5), 104 ff., figs 1-3.

22 bis 'A. Λεμπέση, *op. cit. (infra*, n. 16 bis), 112 ff., pl. Z', figs. 1 - 2.

23 Weight of H 3: 498 grams (as kindly transmitted to me by Suzannah Doeringer); weight of a Corinthian helmet in Hamburg (E. v. Mercklin, *Griechische und römische Altertümer, Führer durch das Hamburgische Museum für Kunst und Gewerbe*, II [Hamburg, 1930], no. 832, pl. 44:1), 1520 grams.

24 On Cretan helmets see E. Kukahn, *Der griechische Helm* (Marburg, 1936), 15 ff.; A. Snodgrass, *Early Greek Armour and Weapons* (Edinburgh, 1964), 28 ff.

25 Double outlines for greater emphasis appear also on Cretan bronzes of the geometric period: cf. J. Boardman, J. Dörig, W. Fuchs, M. Hirmer, *Die griechische Kunst* (Munich, 1966), fig. 129.

26 Plutarch, *Mul. Virt.* 247 D. "New Pollis" on the analogy of *Νεοκρέων*.

27 This helmet type is not, to the writer's knowledge, documented in published Greek armor. For the ornament of the neck guard cf. H 1-3. The ears are represented with a suprisingly naturalistic helix and lobe but with two curious ribbonlike excrescences, presumably the stylized tragus and antitragus, emanating from the concha.

28 This helmet type is documented in several miniature helmets from Praisos, one of which is published. Cf. Snodgrass, *Armour* (n. 25), 28, n. 98.

29 The breast muscles appear to be delineated by two serpents or *ketoi*, whose heads confront each other on each side of the sternum under the clavicle, but this detail could not be verified. For a similar scheme on a corslet from Bulgaria, cf. Kukahn, *Der griechische Helm* (n. 24), n. 252. The heraldic lions of C 1, executed with traced line only, are remarkably similar in style to the lions flanking a tripod on an Axos *mitra* (no. 3, see n. 32).

30 The representation of the griffin's ears as V's appears to be an Oriental device. Cf. most recently H.-V. Herrmann, *Die Kessel der orientalisierenden Zeit, Olympische Forschungen*, VI (Berlin 1966), 131 ff., pls. 55-56. Compare also the griffin protomes on the terra-cotta cauldron from Afrati, D. Levi, "Early Hellenic Pottery of Crete," *Hesperia*, (1945), 22, pl. 11, or Johannowski, "Arkades," (n. 2), 661, fig. 845.

31 The traced palmettes are illustrated in a drawing by Suzanne Chapman, *Master Bronzes*, 48 (bottom).

32 D. Levi, "I bronzi di Axos," *ASAtene*, XIII-XIV (1930-31), 57 ff., figs. 13-20, pls. 10-15; F. Matz, *Geschichte der griechischen Kunst* (Frankfurt, 1950), pls. 271, 272a; Snodgrass, *Armour* (n. 24), fig. 16.

33 F. Poulsen, *AthMitt*, 1906 (n. 6), 373 ff., pl. 23; Levi, *ASAtene*, 1930-31 (n. 32), 78, no. 5, 138 ff., figs. 35a-c; Matz, *Geschichte* (n. 32), 459 and n. 603; Snodgrass, *Armour* (n. 24), 241, n. 56.

34 S. Xanthandides, "*παράρτημα του ἀρχαιολογικοῦ δελτίου του* 1918," *Deltion*, IV (1918), 27, fig. 12; Levi, *ASAtene*, 1930-31 (n. 32), 80, figs. 28a, b; Matz, *Geschichte* (n. 32), 459 and n. 603; Snodgrass, *Armour* (n. 24), 28 ff.

35 P. Perdrizet, *Fouilles de Delphes*, V:1 (Paris, 1908), 102 f., no. 514, fig. 353; J. Marcadé, "Un casque crétois trouvé à Delphes," *BCH*, LXXIII (1949), 421 ff., figs. 1, 3, 4, pl. 21; Matz, *Geschichte* (n. 32), 459 and n. 602; Snodgrass, *Armour*, 28 ff. Cf. E. Kunze, *VII. Bericht über die Ausgrabungen in Olympia* (Berlin, 1956-58), 74, n. 19. An undecorated *mitra* from Delphi will be published by Claude Rolley in a forthcoming fascicule of Delphi bronzes.

36 Now assembled by H. Bartels in E. Kunze, ed., *VIII. Bericht über die Ausgrabungen in Olympia* (Berlin, 1967), 196 ff., pls. 100-105.

37 Snodgrass, *Armour* (n. 24), 28 ff.

38 S. Marinatos, "Le temple géometrique de Dréros," *BCH*, LX (1936), 270 ff., pl. 29; illustrated most recently by W. Schiering, "Masken am Hals kretisch-mykenischer und frühgriechischer Tongefäße," *JdI*, LXXIX (1964), 15, fig. 18. Kunze, *Olympiabericht* VII (n. 35), 104, n. 55, has related the similar inscribed snake designs. Cf. also the design on the fragmentary *prometopidion* from Stam-

nitza in Arcadia, E. Kunze, *Olympiabericht* VIII (n. 36), 184 ff., pl. 98.

39 R. J. H. Jenkins, *Dedalica* (Cambridge, 1936), 59 ff. Cf. also Langlotz in *Corolla Curtius* (Stuttgart, 1937), 61 and Matz, *Geschichte* (n. 32), 459, who places Axos *mitra* no. 2 in the second quarter of the seventh century and Axos *mitra* no. 3 (with the engraved lions) in the last quarter of the century. The three Axos *mitrai* with horse protomes in relief are considered by Matz to be "schon hocharchaisch."

40 Levi, *ASAtene*, 1930-31 (n. 32), 135.

41 J. Boardman, *The Cretan Collection in Oxford. The Dictaean Cave and Iron Age Crete* (Oxford, 1961), 141 ff.

42 Bartels, *Olympiabericht* VIII (n. 36), 205.

43 The letters *ΔΟΦΡ* incised on the back of a "Dedalic" terra-cotta pinax, E. H. Dohan, "Archaic Cretan Terracottas in America," *MMS*, II (1930), fig. 15; L. H. Jeffery, *The Local Scripts of Archaic Greece* (Oxford, 1961), 311 and 316, no. 18, pl. 60 ("seventh century") are the exceptions. The excavator, Halbherr, dated the inscription to ca. 625 B.C., while Buchanan and Dohan assigned the object to the beginning of the seventh century B.C.

44 See E. Homann-Wedeking, *Die Anfänge der griechischen Großplastik* (Berlin, 1950), 155 f., n. 105.

45 G. Lippold, *Die griechische Plastik* (Munich, 1950), 18 ff.

46 Dohan, *MMS*, 1930 (n. 43). A previously unknown "Dedalic" terra-cotta relief from Afrati is now published by G. I. Despinis, *Deltion*, XXI (1966), 35 ff., pls. 20a, b; 21a.

47 J. Schäfer, *Reliefpithoi* (n. 15).

48 A full discussion is given by Boardman, *Cretan Collection* (n. 41), 46 ff., with bibliography on p. 46, n. 2.

49 W. Lamb, *Greek and Roman Bronzes* (New York, 1929), 59 ff.

50 A similar rendering of these elements can also be found in Cretan vase painting of the early archaic period. Compare, for example, the Afrati pitcher with its curiously Minoan air and the painted cinerary urns from the same site, Levi, *Hesperia*, 1945 (n. 30), 21 ff., pls. 9, 10. An excellent summation of this style is that given for the pithoi by Schäfer, *Reliefpithoi* (n. 47), 26 ff.

51 Excavated before World War I by L. Pernier, "Vestigia di una città ellenica arcaica in Creta," *Memorie dell' Istituto Lombardo di Scienza e Lettere*, XXII (1910), fasc. II and VII, pp. 53 ff., 213 ff. (unavailable to me at the time of writing) and recently re-excavated. N. Platon is preparing a full publication. Only the Artemis with bow has been illustrated (Matz, *Geschichte* [n. 32], 489, n. 684, pl. 292a; E. Langlotz, "Ein Votivrelief aus Tarent," in *Antike Plastik, W. Amelung zum 60. Geburtstag* [Berlin and Leipzig, 1928], 116, fig. 6). Most interesting in our context are the stele with a woman holding a wreath (Heraklion) and the series of hoplite stelai (Heraklion and Rethymnon).

52 A. Joubin, "Une statue crétoise archaïque," *RA*, XXI (Jan.-June 1893), I, 10 ff., pls. 3, 4; Jenkins, *Dedalica* (n. 39), 51, 72 ff., pls. 7:8, 8:1, 9:1, 10:2; G. Lippold, *Die Griechische Plastik* (Munich, 1950), 22, n. 2, pl. 2:2; Homann-Wedeking, *Anfänge* (n. 44), 70 ff., 98, 107 f., 114, 122, fig. 56; C. Picard, *Manuel d'archéologie grecque*, I (Paris, 1935), 445, fig. 124; L. Alscher, *Griechische Plastik*, I (Berlin, 1954), 139, n. 50 ("ca. 610 B.C."); Matz, *Geschichte* (n. 32), 198, pls. 125, 126. I am indebted to Brigitte Freyer-Schauenburg for much of the literature contained in this note.

53 H. Walter, "Ein samischer Elfenbeinjüngling," *AthMitt*, LXXIV (1959), 43 ff., pls. 87-89; D. Ohly, "Zur Rekonstruktion des samischen Geräts mit dem Elfenbeinjüngling," *ibid.*, 48 ff.; B. Freyer-Schauenburg, *Elfenbeine aus dem samischen Heraion* (Hamburg, 1966), 3, 19 ff., pl. 2 ("not Samian, perhaps Corinthian").

54 The attribution of the Samos ivory to a Cretan workshop was first proposed to me by A. E. Raubitschek; it is considered very plausible also by B. Freyer-Schauenburg, with whom I recently discussed the question.

55 Kunze, *Kretische Bronzereliefs* (n. 15), 12 ff., no. 8, pls. 21-23.

56 J. Oberbeck, *Die antiken Schriftquellen* (Leipzig, 1868), 11 ff.; Lippold, *Griechische Plastik* (n. 52), 18 ff., n. 9; Homann-Wedeking, *Anfänge* (n. 44), 42 ff.; G. M. A. Richter, *Kouroi*[2] (London, 1960), 28 ff., and notes 28-37. G. Kaulen, *Daidalika* (Munich, 1967), 163 ff.

57 Richter, *Kouroi* (n. 56), 28 ff. and notes 28-37.

58 Levi, *ASAtene*, 1927-29 (n. 2), 28; Marinatos, *ArchEph*, 1966 (n. 5), 277; Boardman, *Cretan Collection* (n. 41), 46 ff., fig. 22, pl. 16; C. Kardara, *Athens Annals of Archaeology* II (1969), 216 ff. figs. 1 - 5.

59 R. Rizza — V. Santa Maria Scrinari, *Il santuario sull'acropoli di Gortina* I (Rome, 1968), no. 163 d (pl. 25), there considered to be a replica of no. 163c, which, however, lacks the scroll and also differs in other details.

60 See n. 58.

61 J. D. Beazley, *Attic Black-Figure Vase-Painters* (Oxford, 1956), 80, no. 1.

62 Boardman, *Cretan Collection* (n. 41), 48.

The Artistic Context and Environment of Some Greek Bronzes in the Master Bronzes Exhibition

Mogens Gjødesen

After a visit to the beautifully arranged Master Bronzes exhibition and after a first perusal of the magnificent catalogue, the meditative symposiast, with whom I would like to identify myself, indulged in various reflections. He may have thought, for instance, that the show, by virtue of its considerate and well-balanced selection of objects, brilliantly serves its first and specific purpose: to be a working exhibition, an instrument of technological, aesthetic, and historical instruction, not, as one might have expected it to be and as in a way it would have been easier to make it, simply a parade of glamorous "collectors' pieces" — although fortunately there are a great many of those as well.

Other more whimsical ideas and questions flash through the observant mind, such as, "Why do the lenders to the exhibition, private and public collectors, dedicate their energies or a large part of them to the acquisition of Greek bronzes — because they are Greek or because they are bronzes? Is a Greek geometric cauldron more closely related to a Roman bronze made a thousand years later than to a roughly contemporary Chinese ritual vessel of the Chou period?"

The exhibition's composition, with small bronzes predominating, recalls a man who might be called the prototype of today's enthusiastic collector of Greek bronzes, Richard Payne Knight,[1] a great connoisseur of the early nineteenth century, a generous donor to the British Museum, and quite a character as well. He is reported to have pronounced the categorical dictum that beauty and magnitude cannot exist together; in other words, if a thing is big, it is *eo ipso* ugly.

Even though a few of the visitors to the exhibition — owners, guardians, and students of small ancient bronzes — may feel inclined at the bottom of their hearts to walk part of the way with Mr. Payne Knight, I have little doubt that all will agree that he was going a bit far. The full acceptance and adoption of Payne Knight's attitude would not only preclude the enjoyment of some great, and large, works of art but also, and above all, would deprive us of the opportunity to observe Greek art in its entirety and inner coherence. It is only fair to add that Payne Knight did occasionally acquire works of art in other sizes and materials, like most of the bronze devotees of our day in whose collections bronze statuettes flourish in the company of other, sometimes humbler, categories of ancient art such as vases, terra cottas, and sculpture.

It might, therefore, be slightly precarious to isolate the bronzes, as has been done in the exhibition and in certain museums, and establish a sort of édition de luxe of classical art — were it not for the equally interesting opportunity thus provided to see and enjoy the bronzes within their own internal context. Regarding the systematic, historical study of ancient bronzes — and I shall confine myself here to Greek bronzes of the early, progressive periods — it is certainly feasible, if not profitable, to study them as a particular category.

Except for the rare cases where inscriptions offer clues, the normal procedure has been a stylistic comparison of comparable pieces combined with a scrutiny of stated and alleged proveniences; in other words, the method has been based on analogy, statistics, and common sense. Since bronzes are comparatively rare finds, replicas are practically nonexistent, and small bronzes are apt to travel a lot, a mere statistical evaluation does not take us far. Classification of widely distributed types of plastically decorated utensils should be helpful, as they vastly increase the quantity of

Fig. 1: Pithos from Crete; Copenhagen, Ny Carlsberg Glyptothek.

available find statistics, which are instrumental in determining the centers of manufacture. Frankly, however, the method has not thus far been satisfactory because the bronzes in question are often simple and are sometimes imitated by distant provincial workshops.

To the historian the fundamental problem that arises whenever a bronze turns up or is reconsidered is, "Where and when was it made?" Only too seldom do we feel prompted to ask, "By whom?" Some scholars stress and give priority to dating, a procedure which is quite legitimate and useful as a working hypothesis. However, although most dating is done by analogy — a sort of mechanical synchronization accordant with the standards of established chronology and based on the assumption, largely justified, that progress is universal and occurs *pari passu* — it is for some mysterious reason frequently thought safer to date a work of art than to locate it regionally or attribute it to a specific workshop. This, in my opinion, is a sad delusion. An arbitrary dating, even if it should happen to be correct, has no point and tells little of a work of art as long as one associates nothing with the date except chronology and development and does not subsequently attempt to localize the object. Our principal endeavors should, I think, be aimed at placing a stray bronze in its environment, against a local background, which is likely to be more constant than a period style.

Afterward one can hope to ascertain a sound relative dating, and at this stage the date takes on some meaning.

Precise or approximate localization and dating of a bronze lend it an additional intellectual quality and add a new dimension to our appreciation of it. To achieve this and to construct the background mentally, one has to extend the visual field and bring together all available clues and parallels in any material and technique, however incommensurable they may appear and regardless of scale.

It is high time to give substance to some of these prejudices. Choosing the splendid bronzes from Afrati as a starting point, I propose to resume the thread spun by Herbert Hoffmann.[2] In describing the subjects and style of the decorated bronze armor, he repeatedly stresses their connection with the reliefs on Cretan pithoi. The urge to make this comparison would have been even stronger, and the justification for making it even more obvious, had he been in a position to know of a clay pithos that was acquired on the art market a few years ago by the Ny Carlsberg Glyptothek and, after protracted restoration, has recently been placed on view (Figs. 1-4). For the present discussion the interest and importance of this most impressive vase,[3] certainly of Cretan make, are further enhanced by the dealer's information that the sherds from which it has been recomposed came from Afrati.[4]

The decoration, limited to the front of the jar, is done in a mixed technique. The two heavily framed reliefs of antithetical sphinxes are moldmade. The alternating rosettes and bosses, repeated to form ornamental friezes, and the tongue pattern on the lip are stamped. Stamps were also used for certain details of the figures such as the eyes of the horses and the scale pattern of their wings; very economically, the same tongue-pattern stamp used for the lip of the vase has been adapted for the feathers.

The principal decoration, a dramatic, fantastic scene dominating the entire façade and representing a winged god or demon between two dragon-like, long-legged horses, is modeled freehand. So is the frieze of grazing

Fig. 2: Pithos from Crete; Copenhagen, Ny Carlsberg Glyptothek.

deer below. In places where the flat relief has fallen off, the sketch lines beneath are exposed. They were incised in the leather-hard surface, and they show that the thin clay sheet of the relief was stuck onto the wheel-made body of the vase.

The bearded, winged creature in the center clearly belongs to the same species as the twin youths on the bronze helmet (No. 29; Hoffmann, Fig. 5). Here, too, the mythological interpretation remains doubtful, but even if no proper name can be assigned to the figure, there is no doubt that he plays the role of a δεσπότης θηρῶν.[5] The male counterpart of the πότνια θηρῶν, though perhaps generically earlier, is certainly much rarer. On a cinerary urn from Afrati a winged, running demon is shown between two sphinxes,[6] and on a clay pinax from Gortyn he is mastering two griffins.[7] A pinax from Lato, preserved in several copies, represents a winged youth standing or walking between two rearing horses.[8] On a fragmentary pinax from Gortyn the central figure grasps the right foreleg of a prancing horse.[9] Here, as in other cases, the horses are normal and of the same breed as those on the Afrati helmet (No. 30), unlike the much later Pegasoi on the well-known helmet from Axos.[10] However, on a pithos fragment from Lyttos[11] two winged horses appear, marching peacefully and a bit stiffly; a more spirited horse on another sherd in Heraklion (Giamalakis collection) was also born winged, according to Dunbabin.[12]

The search for a precise parallel for the composition takes us to another recent find of Greek armor, presumably Cretan — the magnificently engraved bronze corslet from Olympia.[13] Whereas the main scene offers several points of contact with the Afrati helmet (No. 29), the subordinate lower representation calls for a comparison with our pithos relief: a winged πότνια θηρῶν is flanked by two winged monsters. The equine character of these is as unmistakable as that of the pithos horses except that, in spite of being regularly maned, their disproportionately small heads are strongly reminiscent of griffins' heads.[14]

The fiery heads of the Copenhagen horses, growing from supernaturally long serpentine necks, are most closely paralleled by another pithos fragment showing the forepart of a horse,[15] also in the collection of Dr. Giamalakis. Dunbabin dates the sherd as late as the sixth century, and Schäfer agrees.[16] Its connection with our pithos favors an earlier date.

As a comparison with the youths on the helmet (No. 29) the catalogue text points to a cut-out bronze relief in Heraklion, again from Afrati.[17] Its resemblance to our demon is even stronger for, though both are incomplete, it is obvious that each was equipped with only one wing, fastened to the waist.

Fig. 3: Pithos from Crete; Copenhagen, Ny Carlsberg Glyptothek. Profile of head of demon.

Beards do not seem to have been fashionable in seventh-century Cretan art. Our demon has grown a pointed chin beard and whiskers, like the hunter at the right on another well-known cut-out bronze relief.[18] In painting, the man leading a horse on a vase from Afrati also wears a pointed beard.[19] A similar, though not identical, spiral stylization of the bangs is met with on a head vase from Arkhanes,[20] a clay head once attached to a vase from the Little Palace in Knossos,[21] and a protome from Afrati in the Metaxas collection.[22] The full dress of the demon, actually a chiton, differs from the kilt worn by the youths on the helmet. On the other hand, he is dressed in much the same way as the four youths on the *mitra* from Rethymno,[23] the hunters on the Louvre cut-out,[24] and the lion tamer on an eighth-century (?) bronze quiver from Fortetsa.[25]

The principal clue to the dating of the pithos is provided by the head of the demon. Though there is every indication that it was modeled by hand, the head conforms to a well-defined phase of the Cretan Dedalic style, the development of which is most reliably traced in the sequence of mold-made heads. Within the class of relief pithoi the manifest parallel is the head of a sphinx on a fragment from Gonies Pediada, which is characterized by the approximately triangular shape of its face, its broad forehead, its large eyes with marked brow ridges, and its thick-lipped, breathing mouth.[26] Schäfer assigns this fragment to his group III, covering about twenty-five years, and dates it about 660 B.C., or to a transitional stage on the way to Jenkins' Middle Dedalic mid-century phase; this seems likely.[27] Even closer, perhaps because like ours it was made freehand, perhaps because it is slightly earlier, is a head in the Metaxas collection, probably from Afrati,[28] that was also attached to a vase. Definitely earlier, in fact comparable with Cretan heads of Jenkins' Early Dedalic period,[29] is the head of a sphinx in relief, again a pithos fragment, in Oxford.[30]

Turning now to the class of early Cretan bronze armor within which the Schimmel pieces hold a prominent position, the newly found Olympia corslet,[31] the Cretan origin of which can now be considered beyond dispute, is clearly somewhat earlier than the pithos. In harmony with this impression, Schefold dated it 670 to 660 B.C. Among the Schimmel pieces the *mitra* with the full-face sphinxes (No. 32) is the one to which the established Dedalic chronology is most easily adaptable, or should be. According to it the elegant sphinxes would seem to fit well into Jenkins' Middle Dedalic second phase, especially recalling the rather square-jawed sphinx on a fine pithos fragment from Eleutherna.[32] This Jenkins groups with the Auxerre statuette ("645-640 B.C."), and Schäfer (p. 20) agrees in dating it toward 640 B.C. Does the date thus suggested apply to all the Schimmel pieces? Pending the exhaustive first-hand publication of them I shall refrain from discussing this problem and indeed from anticipating any precise date, contenting myself with the provisional conviction that the helmet, No. 29, with which we are particularly concerned here because of the related representations, can be associated with the earliest group of Cretan decorated armor, starting shortly before 650 B.C. Following the Olympia corslet this group includes, in tentative chronological order, a helmet from Delphi,[33] a *mitra* from Olympia,[34] the *mitra* from Rethymno,[35] which was compared with the Copenhagen pithos, and the Schimmel helmet, No. 29.

The intertwining snakes held by the youths on the helmet form a symmetrical structure essentially like the snake belt of the Corfu gorgon[36] or the crowning member of a *kerykeion*.[37] The snakes are crested, and each has two beards under its jaw. Though of unmistakably serpentine description,[38] they are most closely paralleled by a pair of antithetical *kete* that used to command the shoulder of another Cretan pithos (Fig. 5); only this fragment, composed of three sherds, has been preserved. It is now in the Ny Carlsberg Glyptothek.[39] When comparing the *kete* with the snakes of the helmet, one realizes that what the sale catalogue described as a polos is really a tagged comb on top of the head, foreign to the orthodox *ketos*. The tails are gone, but fins on back and belly leave no doubt of the marine character of the monsters. The shape of the head is canine, if anything, and so is the nose, though not unlike that of the Afrati snakes. The elongate flaps running into pointed ears vaguely recall the rendering of the transition from head to body of two snakes on a painted and engraved pinax

Fig. 4: Pithos from Crete; Copenhagen, Ny Carlsberg Glyptothek. Detail of head of demon.

Fig. 5: Fragment of Cretan pithos; Copenhagen, Ny Carlsberg Glyptothek (I.N. 3374).

from Gortyn.[40] The pithos fragment is covered by a cream-colored slip, against which the incised outlines and details of the monsters and ornaments stand out in dark to red-brown paint. The relief is very low. Because of its technique and coloring the fragment approaches Schäfer's group IV.[41] Schäfer dates this "Phaistos Group" in the last quarter of the seventh and beginning of the sixth century B.C. The author of the Lucerne sale catalogue text dated the fragment with *kete,* the provenience of which is unstated, in the first half of the seventh century. Even if this is taken to mean shortly before the middle, which would make the fragment about contemporary with the large Copenhagen pithos from Afrati, the dating seems rather early. For the technical reasons mentioned previously this sprightly fragment should be associated with the much tamer members of the Phaistos group, though I find it hard to remove it too far from the grand mid-century pithoi of Schäfer's group III and to place it later than, say, 625 B.C. This impression is, I think, borne out by another newly acquired pithos fragment in Copenhagen, of the same or a very similar fabric (Figs 6-7),[42] which shows a female figure, a πότνια θηρῶν, in frontal view. Her precisely molded and articulated head fits smoothly into Jenkins' Middle Dedalic third phase ("640-630 B.C.")[43] and offers specific points of resemblance to the noble bronze kouros from Delphi.[44] The inference that the Copenhagen pithos *kete* and the Schimmel helmet snakes are approximately synchronous seems inevitable and recommendable.

Fig. 6: Fragment of Cretan pithos; Copenhagen, Ny Carlsberg Glyptothek (I.N. 3375). Profile of head.

Even if the possibility is granted, on this evidence, that the large pithos with winged horses might be earlier than the bronze helmet, the interval is slight and becomes insignificant for determining whether this kind of relief work originated and developed in metalworking or in pottery. Schäfer (pp. 20, 43) and others argue that the bronze-workers were the inventors and the potters the imitators, whereas Hoffmann[45] leaves the question open. It should probably not be raised at all because the idea of

Fig. 7: Fragment of Cretan pithos; Copenhagen, Ny Carlsberg Glyptothek (I.N. 3375).

an artistic order of precedence according to the material chosen is completely unfounded.[46] In the present case one site has yielded work in both media, formally, spiritually, and in subject matter so very much alike that everything points toward their having also been manufactured within a limited space of time and if not on the same spot, then within a narrow area or at least by people who knew each other or were acquainted with each other's work. Furthermore, one must consider that not only do the artists in both media use the same artistic effects (such as the interplay between the low relief of the body and the protruding frontal head, the vivid linear surface decoration and the calligraphically abstracted formulas for indicating muscles and sinews), but they also to a great extent employ an identical technique (tracing and engraving of outline and detail).

A tangible intermediary between smith and potter, between the low repoussé of the bronzes and the superimposed, sharply outlined "gingerbread" relief of the pithos, is provided by the bronze cut-outs.[47] By virtue of the outstanding quality of the engraving, apart from the exceptionally delicate coloring, the clay pinax from Gortyn already referred to,[48] on which is depicted a group suggestive of that on helmet No. 29, serves pre-eminently as another connecting link between the two media. One can imagine how these artists worked closely together, on a basis of mutual interdependence and the interchange of experience — in fact a kind of cooperation. If the bronze armor is distinguished by the preciousness of the material and the meticulousness of the workmanship, the monumental pithos presented here, animated by the dashing hand of a Titanesque craftsman, excels in spontaneousness, vigor, and imagination.

Concentrating on Crete but turning to cast bronzes, my next choice is the Berlin sphinx (No. 41). With a magic Homeric word it has been called "Eteocretan," or true Cretan,[49] because it is supposed to display reminiscences of Minoan tradition, as opposed to the Doric or Dedalic trend in the

Figs. 8-10: Bronze from the Argive Heraeum; Athens, National Museum. Courtesy of the Museum.

seventh-century art of the island. The riddle of this sphinx is that her separate, streaming locks of hair do recall Minoan female statuettes such as Nos. 4, 5A and B, and notably the Berlin praying woman,[50] while her surface is strikingly different. Demargne and van Effenterre include in the same category, which they prefer to call sub-Minoan and which they think may last beyond 600 B.C., a small male bronze found in Dreros.[51]

More likely than Langlotz's assignment of the sphinx to the late eighth century B.C. is the seventh-century date suggested by D. G. Mitten in the Master Bronzes catalogue. Very appositely, Boardman[52] compared with it the Siren painted on a sherd from Praisos, a notorious "Eteocretan" stronghold. Kunze's Late Minoan definition and dating of the sherd[53] were firmly contested by Levi, who insisted on its Orientalizing status.[54]

Of the two bronzes which, for want of better parallels, Mitten associates with the Berlin sphinx, the Delphi youth[55] is to little avail, since it veritably embodies the canon of the pure Dedalic style; the Berlin *kriophoros* is definitely on the Dedalic side too, though evidently post-Dedalic and datable toward the turn of the century[56] or even later.[57] A kilted youth in New York, a modest work said to be from near Knossos, in which G. M. A. Richter justly recognized touches of Minoan survival,[58] looks sixth century to me and later than the Berlin statuette.

It is frequently maintained that Cretan art, which flourished in the seventh century B.C., declined in the sixth. In our field this impression seems justified by the fact that hardly any bronzes of notable quality have been recorded.[59] Perhaps we could cite one. During the American excavations at the Argive Heraeum from 1892 to 1895 the upper part of a solid-cast female figure, broken at the waist and 9.4 cm. tall, was found (Figs. 8-10). The bronze, which is now in the National Museum in Athens, was clumsily mounted, and carefully described and miserably illustrated by Fletcher DeCou,[60] who interprets it as Aphrodite with an Oriental headdress and dates it in the period of the Apollo by Kanachos. The figurine was probably nude, for the navel is visible just above the break. Fastening upon the small mouth, Payne[61] tentatively compared it with a bronze statuette from Ptoion that he suspected was Peloponnesian,[62] but he did not quite convince himself. Neither did he convince Jenkins, who hesitantly connected the piece with his Argive group of terra cottas ("F," ca. 550 B.C. and later) while admitting that the bronze might not be Argive at all. Indeed, although obviously Greek, its appearance does seem oddly exotic in these surroundings. What at first look like flat, articulated locks of hair curling around the naked breasts on closer inspection are more likely construed as snakes clinging around the woman's neck, as no effort has been made to effect a smooth transition to the remaining mass of hair. May we here confidently assume an echo of the Minoan Snake Goddess?[63] A similar arrangement is found in a fragmentary bronze statuette, possibly a bust, from Lyttos in Crete (Fig. 11), now in the museum at Heraklion.[64] It is not certain whether the convolutions are here meant to represent ringlets or twisting snakes.

The floral headdress balancing on the forehead of the Heraeum statuette consists of a lotus rising from a pair of horizontal double volutes, enclosing two palmettes. Only the stump is left of a tendril or some other connecting link growing from the volute. The predominance of the central calyx recalls the Egyptian lotus and the crown worn by the god Nofertêm.[65] However, the insertion of palmettes points to Greece, where an almost identical ornament is found, e.g., on an Attic cavetto capital in New York, of about 560 B.C.[66] One is also vaguely reminded of a series of bronze attachment busts of unknown purpose from the Acropolis, each surmounted with a plastic, three-dimensional lotus,[67] and, more distinctly, of a complicated bronze attachment, again from the Acropolis.[68] Not infrequently, volutes or tendrils are seen to grow from the heads of sphinxes, as on the Chigi vase,[69] and Laconian vase painters excel in fancy headgear, even for human beings, in which palmette and lotus are combined with a volute;[70] in Crete they occur on a quantity of heraldic sphinxes on relief pithoi, as well as, for example, on an Early Dedalic pinax from Gortyn[71] and a Middle Dedalic one with two sphinxes flanking a lotus that itself shoots from volutes.[72] The frontal rosettes are too common to be conclusive in themselves, though it is worth noting that they are found on a male mirror support from the Acropolis, apparently non-Attic.[73] In Cretan art one might point to the female on a pinax from Gortyn[74] and to a terra-cotta head in Athens.[75]

Jenkins described the nude Argive Heraeum woman as a mirror handle (a mirror support of the well-known Laconian type?); this is not quite satisfactory in view of the unusual and inappropriate asymmetry in the position of her arms and the fact that the raised left hand could not possibly reach the mirror disc. It is more likely that it held an object or made a gesture. The knob, shaped like a vase mouth and placed on the crown of her head, reflects the vaselike protuberance of the sphinx (No. 41), which suggests the base of a column shaft. However that may be, both bronzes seem to have been part of some type of implement standard. The tapering

Fig. 11: Bronze from Lyttos; Heraklion Museum. Courtesy of the Museum.

Fig. 12: Poros head from Axos; Heraklion Museum. After BCH 1952.

Fig. 13: Poros head from Axos; Heraklion Museum. Courtesy of the Museum.

hair at the back is just one point of resemblance to the Cretan bronze kouros in Berlin mentioned in note 59.

What has been adduced so far is hardly sufficient to claim the Heraeum bronze as a Cretan import.[76] Fortunately, a more decisive connection between the enigmatic woman and Crete is offered by a piece of sculpture. While digging in Axos in 1899, Halbherr unearthed a poros head, 16.2 cm. high, of remarkable quality and well preserved (Figs. 12-13). The head remained in the museum in Kanea, from which it was taken to the museum in Heraklion in 1934 along with the bronzes found at the same site. It was briefly described by Levi[77] and led an obscure life until it was published by S. Alexiou in 1952;[78] Alexiou produced strong arguments for identifying it as the head of a sphinx, and no objection can be raised against his date, second quarter of the sixth century B.C. Nor can it be denied, I think, that there is a striking structural and spiritual affinity between the poros head and the bronze head: the identical broad forehead and firm chin, the big, slanting, slightly protuberant eyes, the tiny, almost pouting mouth, and the petaled rosettes over the forehead; in addition one might compare such imponderables as the subtle harmony of the face and its intent, serene expression. Is it sheer coincidence that the slender proportions and the graceful, gently undulating outline of the bronze woman's long hair conjure up the delicate shape of the swimming Herakles (?) on the famous plate from "Eteocretan" Praisos,[79] a figure who is perhaps no ghost but an immediate predecessor or a contemporary?[80]

Passing over altogether some comments on the geometric bronzes in the exhibition and other items in my symposium lecture, I shall single out a few passages dealing with subjects of a fundamental or systematic nature.

The reclining goat lent by Vassar College (No. 63) invites the sometimes rewarding pastime of reuniting pairs or sets of bronze statuettes disconnected from the vessel they used to adorn and separated by mischance; the vessel is usually entirely lost. In the few cases where companion pieces have remained *in situ* or where detached counterparts were found together, e.g., a pair of lions from Perachora,[81] they differ in size by several millimeters. This is a warning that a final decision on questions of matching groups requires not only exact measurements but also minute comparisons or, better still, an actual physical confrontation of the objects in question.[82]

In rarer cases the connection of *disjecta membra* is obvious. An attachment for the handle of an early fifth-century B.C. situla (Figs. 14-15), belonging to the type exemplified in the Master Bronzes exhibition by the fourth-century piece, No. 149, has been in the Louvre since the nineteen-thirties.[83] Its evident counterpart, covered by an identical bluish-green patina, was acquired by the Ny Carlsberg Glyptothek in 1955 (Figs. 16-17).[84] Nonetheless, because of the lost-wax casting technique used by the Greeks and the individual tracing of details, the two are not identical twins.

This touches on the problem of replication, best visualized by the patera from the Royal Ontario Museum, No. 76. A handle of the same class, the same type, and even the same group (Fig. 18) has been in the Fogg Museum since 1960.[85] A third one, in the Pomerance collection,[86] is so similar that when it was exhibited at Queens College in 1958[87] it was confounded with the Fogg piece and has been so repeatedly since then. From these few examples, chosen from among a vast number of recorded specimens, it appears that duplications, replications, and even multiplications — and I am talking only of genuine ones — are less exceptional than is generally thought,

Figs. 14-15: Bronze situla attachment, Paris, Musée du Louvre. Courtesy Musée du Louvre.

Figs. 16-17: Bronze situla attachment; Copenhagen, Ny Carlsberg Glyptothek.

Fig. 17(a): Bronze situla attachment from Perachora; Athens, National Museum.

that is, among utensils of fairly coarse workmanship but still of a certain artistic standard and complexity of form.[88]

Often one is reminded that a bronze, before it was cast and became a bronze, was modeled in a material other than bronze. I do not know whether a model for a bronze has ever been found or whether, if we came across one, it would be possible to identify it as a model. There is no cogent reason for believing that the reverse procedure, the reproduction of terra cottas from bronzes, which certainly occurs, was the normal or exclusive one. It seems natural, however, that artists employed in terra-cotta work-

Fig. 18: Bronze patera handle; Fogg Art Museum (1960. 481).

Fig. 20 (above): Bronze mirror; Munich. Courtesy Staatliche Antikensammlungen.

Fig. 19 (left): Terracotta kore; Reggio, Museo Nazionale.

shops would have been designing for foundries as well or that they would have worked on their own in both materials. Comparing a late archaic terra-cotta kore from Rosarno in Calabria (Fig. 19)[89] and a caryatid mirror from Croton (Fig. 20)[90] seems to illuminate this phenomenon.

Castings did not always turn out successfully. Few casting failures have survived because they were usually melted down for re-use. Perhaps one could point to one even rarer case, where both the failure and the success are preserved: a striding warrior in Copenhagen (Fig. 21),[91] slightly distorted and without surface decoration, and another warrior in Oxford (Fig. 22),[92] beautifully finished. The measurements agree in detail.

My last choice is the "walking girl" in the Walters Art Gallery (No. 57), clumsy and graceful, an old favorite and a much-debated bronze that needs no introduction (Figs. 23-26).[93] The catalogue states that the feet have been restored. Whether the restoration is felicitous can perhaps be questioned in comparing the small feet with the girl's strong and well-shaped, if not exactly feminine, right hand, and in consulting a statuette in Mariemont (Fig. 27), strikingly similar but of slightly reduced scale and notably inferior quality.[94] Renard classifies the Mariemont bronze as Etruscan. I have not seen it and will not dispute the attribution, though the Etruscan parallels he cites are remote and futile. The full-face view given in the first publication[95] certainly testifies in favor of Etruria; so does the fact that the Walters-Mariemont type was imitated in provincial North Etruscan workshops.[96] On the other hand, the "Etruscan boots" worn by the Mariemont girl are scarcely an argument for declaring her, much less the Walters girl, to be Etruscan. Some years ago a late archaic, nearly life-size headless terra-cotta statue wearing unmistakably peaked shoes was found in Paestum.[97] Mrs. Richardson has reminded me that the kerchief on the head of the Walters girl is never found in Etruria but occurs in Campanian bronzes from Capua.[98] I should not call it common, but it is true that the maenad dancing with a silen on the lid of the exceptionally fine London dinos sports a head cloth like that.[99]

The parallels adduced by Müller[100] suffice to place the Baltimore statuette in the context of Magna Graecia (and with greater assurance than he himself concluded with in voting for the alternative, Old Greece), whereas adverse Etruscan comparisons clearly preclude an Etruscan origin. The figure's movement and gestures are controlled; the way she cautiously and almost ostentatiously holds an egg (?) between thumb and forefinger is expressive but devoid of the affectation displayed by Etruscan statuettes of equal rank.[101] The somewhat ambiguous evidence offered by the Mariemont bronze, a component of Italiote rusticity in the prevailingly Ionian attire and style of the Walters girl, and her possibly Campanian head cloth all suggest that she is balancing on the borderline between Greek and Etruscan art. If this is taken literally in a geographical sense, and if we are ready to disregard all traffic by sea, we find ourselves in Campania. The obvious comparanda are the bronzes of the Capuan dinos group already referred to;[102] but even the most "Greek" specimens of the group look more "Etruscan" or non-Greek than the Baltimore girl. If we admit her salient features to be Greek, the inference is that we must move further south and cross the Lucanian frontier.

So much for the theoretical aspect. It is no use pretending that this is a calculation of probability and not merely an afterthought and an attempt at counterverification. The genuine premises of the deduction are some

Fig. 21: Bronze warrior; Copenhagen, National Museum. Courtesy Dept. of Oriental and Classical Antiquities.

Fig. 22: Bronze warrior; Oxford, Ashmolean Museum. Courtesy of the Museum.

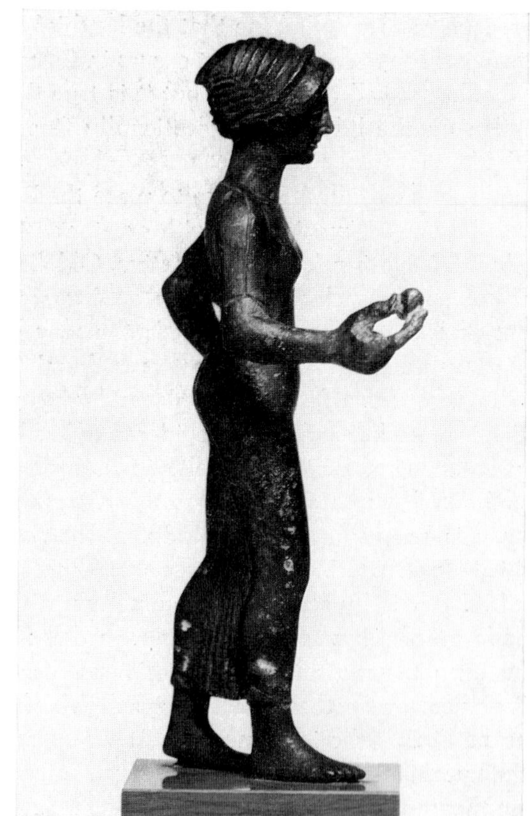

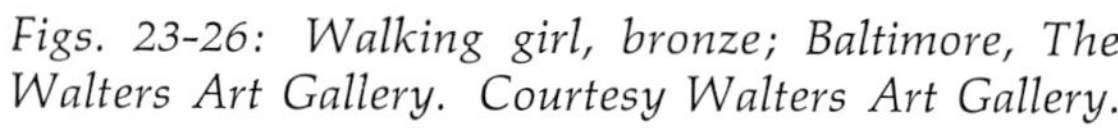

Figs. 23-26: Walking girl, bronze; Baltimore, The Walters Art Gallery. Courtesy Walters Art Gallery.

chance observations made on recent finds at Paestum. A terra-cotta statue has already been mentioned.[103] Others are the fragments of several terra-cotta antefixes in the form of female busts, shaped for the insertion of heads and almost life-size.[104] The most completely preserved of the busts (Figs. 28-29)[105] was found in 1953 north of the altar of the so-called Basilica, to which building, according to Sestieri, the busts may belong, presumably as pedimental decorations. With her right hand the woman clasps the hem of what Sestieri takes to be an *apoptygma,* whereas Neutsch[106] explains it as a jacket (blouse?) of Etruscan cut. In any case, the garment is most peculiar. The sleeves reach below the elbow and are each adorned

Fig. 27: Walking girl, bronze; Musée de Mariemont. Courtesy Domaine de Mariemont.

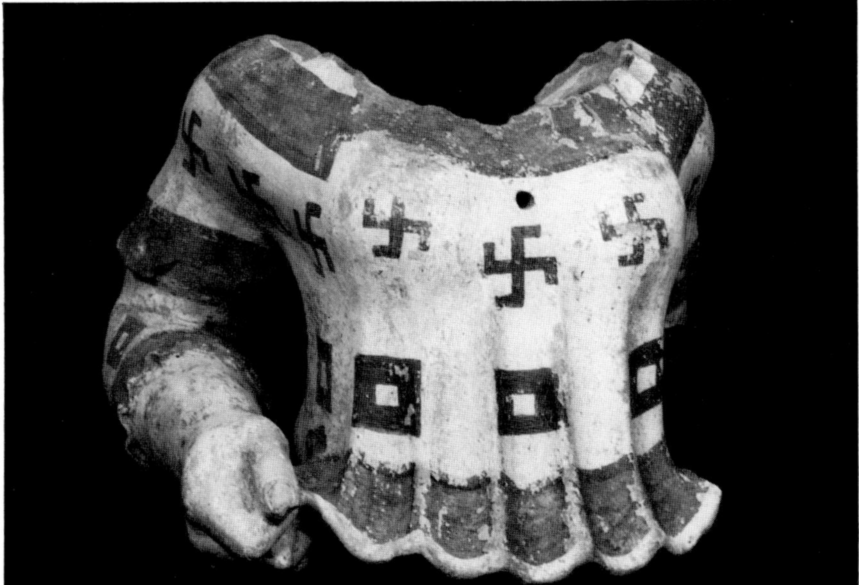

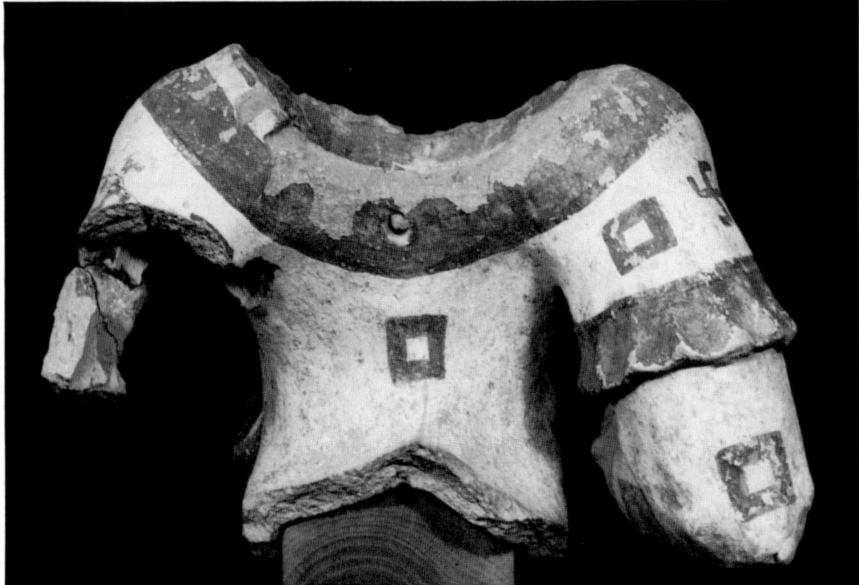

Figs. 28-29: Terracotta bust (antefix); Paestum, Museo Nazionale.

Figs. 30-31: Metope from Temple at Foce del Sele; Paestum, Museo Nazionale.

with two flounces. It is interesting and perhaps significant that the flounced sleeve is worn by the maenad on the London dinos from Capua,[107] already discussed with regard to her head cloth. Whereas the *sakkos*, though not readily found in plastic works, would seem to be widespread around 500 B.C., as it appears from Attic vases by Oltos, Euthymides, and Euphronios, the flounced sleeves are most likely a local Campanian or Lucanian fashion. The terra-cotta bust is of the same sturdy build as the bronze kore, with broad shoulders, slender waist, and enormous fists.

Unfortunately, none of the heads belonging to these busts has been found. What they looked like can be imagined from a marble head in Paestum[108] if the Walters kore is interpolated, for a direct confrontation of the profile views of marble and bronze seems to me most stimulating.

In metopes from the temple of Hera at nearby Foce del Sele, datable, like the works considered thus far, around 500 B.C., vigorously active female figures abound. Within the series representing fleeing girls in pairs, metope no. 5 (Figs. 30-31),[109] despite its mutilated state, invites comparison with the bronze girl. Only part of the foreground figure is preserved, and this in turn eclipses the figure in the background, but as they are complementary they offer together a concentrated image of the motifs, the manners, and the local color of this amazing indigenous tour de force.

With regard to the physical type and the proportions of the body, the small bronze and the monumental sculpture have much in common: the large head, the muscular build, arms of wildly exaggerated length, and huge hands. More precise points of agreement are the facial profiles and the semitransparent, fluid garment solidifying into rigid concertina-like pleats between the legs.[110] The somewhat infelicitous effect of the bronze girl's clutching the thin stuff of her chiton is more nearly approximated in a subsequent metope.[111]

On the basis of this evidence I do not think it too audacious to connect the Baltimore girl with Paestan art. It remains to be stated that she is by no means incompatible with the Berlin *kanephoros,* differently dressed but roughly contemporary, dedicated to Athena by Phillo and found in Paestum (Fig. 32).[112]

The extension of this narrow circle of works[113] and the obvious implications for the art of Sybaris will have to await discussion at a later date.

Fig. 32: Phillo's kore, bronze; Berlin, Staatliche Museen.

Notes

1 H. B. Walters, *Catalogue of the Bronzes, Greek, Roman and Etruscan* (London: The British Museum, 1899), p. XIV f.

2 Here, pp. 129 ff. and the Master Bronzes catalogue, Nos. 29-32.

3 I. N. 3380. Original height ca. 1.50 m; present maximum height 0.87 m. Red clay, no signs of color.

4 I have not been in a position to verify a rumor that the bronze armor was contained in this pithos. Recent additions to the class of Cretan pithoi are noted by J. Schäfer, "Kretische Pithosfragmente," *AA* (1959), 5 ff.; others by E. Berger, "Antikenmuseum Basel, Neuerwerbungen," *Antike Kunst,* X (1967), 68, no. 16; *idem,* Antikenmuseum Basel . . ., Neuerwerbungen und Schenkungen," *ibid.,* 137, pl. 39:1-3. At least five fragments from five different pithoi were on the London art market in 1965. A complete pithos and neck fragment from another one, both from Afrati, are in the Metaxas collection in Heraklion: S. Alexiou, *Δελτίον* XX (1965), 550 f., pl. 694, *α* and *γ*; G. Daux, "Chronique des Fouilles 1967," *BCH,* XCII (1968), 995 f., figs. 6-7. The emblematic sphinxes are possibly from the same mold as ours. Fragments of two more pithoi in the Ny Carlsberg Glyptothek will be mentioned below (notes 39, 42).

5 On this theme see, most recently, H. Jucker, *Bronzehenkel und Bronzehydria in Pesaro (Studia Oliveriana,* XIII-XIV [1966]), 31 ff.

6 D. Levi, "Arkades," *ASAtene,* X-XII (1927-29), 101 f., fig. 76; *idem,* "Early Hellenic Pottery of Crete," *Hesperia,* XIV (1945), 22, pl. 10:1.

7 G. Rizza and V. Santa Maria Scrinari, *Il santuario sull'acropoli di Gortina,* I [Monografie della Scuola Archeologica di Atene e delle Missioni Italiane in Oriente, II] (Rome, 1968), no. 127, pl. 21.

8 P. Demargne, "Terres-cuites archaïques de Lato," *BCH,* LIII (1929), 422 ff., fig. 35, and pl. 30:1 and 3; E. Kunze, *Kretische Bronzereliefs* (Stuttgart, 1931), 202, who reproduces the most complete copy as Beilage 2b, is doubtful as to the sex of the demon, whereas Jucker (n. 5), p. 34, pl. 23:2, takes it to be male.

9 D. Levi, "Gli scavi del 1954 sull' Acropoli di Gortina," *ASAtene,* XVII-XVIII (1955-56), 266, fig. 61; Rizza and Scrinari (n. 7), 186, no. 236, pl. 35.

10 D. Levi, "I bronzi di Axòs," *ASAtene,* XIII-XIV (1930-31), pl. 10; W. Lamb, *Greek and Roman Bronzes* (London, 1929), pl. 42a. Here p. 137.

11 Levi, *ASAtene,* 1927-29 (n. 6), 68, fig. 47b; J. Schäfer, *Studien zu den griechischen Reliefpithoi* (Kallmünz, 1957), 13, no. 10.

12 T. J. Dunbabin, "Cretan Relief Pithoi in Dr. Giamalakes' Collection," *BSA,* XLVII (1952), 153, no. 6, 155, pl. 28:6; Schäfer, *Reliefpithoi* (n. 11), 22, no. 59.

13 K. Schefold, *Frühgriechische Sagenbilder* (Munich, 1964), 39 f., pl. 26; *idem, Propyläen Kunstgeschichte,* n. f. I (Berlin, 1967), fig. 180.

14 Of late geometric date, ca. 700 B.C., according to S. Benton, is a bronze tail-to-tail group of two horse-griffins from Ithaca, S. Benton, "Further Excavations at Aetos," *BSA, XLVIII* (1953), 340, E 198, pl. 66.

15 Dunbabin, *BSA,* 1952 (n. 12), 153, no. 7, 156, pl. 28:7.

16 *Reliefpithoi* (n. 11), 23, no. 60. He includes it in his group V (ca. 590-570 B.C.).

17 D. Levi, "Gleanings from Crete," *AJA*, IL (1945), 282, fig. 12; J. Boardman, *The Cretan Collection in Oxford* (Oxford, 1961), 48, pl. 16 top right. Here p. 140.

18 In the Louvre: A. de Ridder, *Les bronzes antiques*, Musée National du Louvre, I (Paris, 1913), no. 93, pl. 11; Lamb, *Bronzes* (n. 10), pl. 19. Here p. 138.

19 Levi, *Hesperia*, 1945 (n. 6), 22, pl. 10:2. On the Middle Dedalic plastic vase from Arkhanes see R. J. H. Jenkins, *Dedalica* (Cambridge, 1936), pl. 6:1-1a; beard and mustache were indicated in paint.

20 See n. 19.

21 M. Hartley, "Early Greek Vases from Crete," *BSA*, XXXI (1930-31), 106, fig. 31; Jenkins, *Dedalica* (n. 19), pl. 4:5.

22 Alexiou, *Δελτίον*, 1965 (n. 4), 551, pl. 695a; L. von Matt, *Das antike Kreta* (Zurich, 1967), fig. 227.

23 F. Poulsen, "Eine kretische Mitra," *AthMitt*, XXXI (1906), 373 ff., pl. 23 (drawing); Levi, *ASAtene*, 1930-31 (n. 10), 137, fig. 35a-c (photograph).

24 Cf. n. 18.

25 J. K. Brock, *Fortetsa* (Cambridge, 1957), no. 1569, pls. 116, 169; Boardman, *Cretan Coll.* (n. 17), 134 f., fig. 50b.

26 Heraklion. Levi, *Hesperia*, 1945 (n. 6), pl. 31:1; Schäfer, *Reliefpithoi* (n. 11), 16, no. 21, pls. 4:4, 5:2; p. 20.

27 The course of this transition and the initial Middle Dedalic phase are most abundantly illustrated by the series of heads from Gortyn, Rizza and Scrinari (n. 7), pls. 13-17. Cf. also a clay head from the Dictaean Cave, in Oxford, Boardman, *Cretan Coll.* (n. 17), 60 ff., no. 256, pl. 20, with more references.

28 Alexiou, *Δελτίον*, 1965 (n. 4), 551, pl. 694*β*; Daux, *BCH*, 1968 (n. 4), 996, fig. 8.

29 Jenkins, *Dedalica* (n. 19), pl. 2, figs. 5-6.

30 H. W. Catling, "Recent Acquisitions by the Ashmolean Museum, Oxford," *Archaeological Reports 1967-68*, no. 14 (1968), 51 f., fig. 5; sale, Sotheby, May 22, 1965, lot 95.

31 Cf. n. 13.

32 Schäfer, *Reliefpithoi* (n. 11), 15, no. 14, pl. 5:1; Jenkins, *Dedalica* (n. 19), pl. 5:1. Cf. also head from Phaistos (Jenkins, pl. 5:3); pinax with walking sphinx, from Lato (Boardman, *Cretan Coll.* [n. 17], 110, 116, no. 500, pl. 39, "third quarter of the seventh century"); head from Gortyn (Rizza and Scrinari [n. 7], 232, fig. 309, pl. 23:142).

33 J. Marcadé, "Un casque crétois trouvé a Delphes," *BCH*, LXXIII (1949), 421 ff.

34 H. Bartels in E. Kunze, ed., *VIII. Bericht über die Ausgrabungen in Olympia* (Berlin, 1967), 198 ff., pls. 102-105.

35 Cf. n. 23 and Boardman, *Cretan Coll.* (n. 17), 141. With the profiles of the youths (in the photograph) cf. the profile of an early Middle Dedalic head from Gortyn (Rizza and Scrinari [n. 7], 228, fig. 300).

36 G. Rodenwalt, *Korkyra, II, Die Bildwerke des Artemistempels* (Berlin, 1939), 38, fig. 25.

37 J. F. Crome, "Kerykeia," *AthMitt*, LXIII-LXIV (1938-39), 117 ff., pls. 17-20. The earliest known, still archaic, *kerykeion*, with a votive inscription to Hera Argeia, happens to come from Polyrhenion in Crete: K. Schefold, *Meisterwerke griechischer Kunst* (Basel, 1960), 40, 225, no. 184. It is in the Ortiz collection.

38 On the classical distinction between *ketos* and snake see D. E. L. Haynes, "The Portland Vase Again," *JHS*, LXXXVIII (1968), 61 f., fig. 6.

39 I. N. 3374; Ars Antiqua Luzern, auction No. V (November 7, 1964), lot 105, pl. 24.

40 Levi, *ASAtene*, 1955-56 (n. 9), 271 f., pl. I, d (color); Rizza and Scrinari (n. 7), 186, no. 243, pl. 36.

41 Schäfer, *Reliefpithoi* (n. 11), 20 ff., nos. 48-51, pls. 7-9.

42 Ny Carlsberg Glyptothek I. N. 3375.

43 Jenkins, *Dedalica* (n. 19), pl. 6; Rizza and Scrinari (n. 7), 235.

44 P. Perdrizet, *Fouilles de Delphes*, V:1 (Paris, 1908), pl. 3; G. de Miré and P. de La Coste-Messelière, *Delphes* (Paris, 1943), 18 f., fig. 10.

45 *Master Bronzes*, p. 49.

46 Rizza, in Rizza and Scrinari (n. 7), 200, goes so far as to derive the occurrence of incision in Cretan limestone sculpture and architectural ornamentation from the metal technique.

47 Boardman, *Cretan Coll.* (n. 17), 48, considers these, which he is inclined to assign to the third quarter of the seventh century at the earliest, to be inspired by the molded or partly molded cut-out clay reliefs used for the decoration of [pithoi.

48 Cf. n. 40.

49 E. Langlotz, "Eine eteokretische Sphinx," in *Corolla, Ludwig Curtius zum sechzigsten Geburtstag* (Stuttgart, 1937), 60 ff., pl. 5.

50 K. A. Neugebauer, *Katalog der statuarischen Bronzen im Antiquarium*, Staatliche Museen zu Berlin, I (Berlin, 1924), 1, no. 1.

51 P. Demargne and H. van Effenterre, "Recherches à Dréros," *BCH*, LXI (1937), 12 f., pl. 2. Cf. in general P. Demargne, *La Crète dédalique* (Paris, 1947), 259 ff.

52 Boardman, *Cretan Coll.* (n. 17), 146.

53 E. Kunze, "Sirenen," *AthMitt*, LVII (1932), 135 ff., Beilage 32-33.

54 Levi, *AJA*, 1945 (n. 17), 280 ff., fig. 11.

55 Cf. n. 44. Disregarding in this connection the Dreros *sphyrelata* and leaving out the controversial Karlsruhe head, other seventh-century Cretan bronzes are (1) Head in Klagenfurt: C. Praschniker, "Ein bronzenes Köpfchen in Klagenfurt," *WJh* XXXII (1940), 60 ff. (2) Three-quarter statuette of a man with bobbed hair from Phaistos, in Oxford, Ashmolean Museum 1933.1569: Boardman, *Cretan Coll.* (n. 17), 121, no. 527, pl. 45. (3) Upper part of female statuette, New York, Metropolitan Museum, 39.11.12: G. M. A. Richter, "Recent Acquisitions of the Metropolitan Museum of Art," *AJA*, XLIV (1940), 181 f., figs. 1-3; *idem, Handbook of the Greek Collection*, Metropolitan Museum of Art (Cambridge, Mass., 1953), 33, pl. 22i. Its Cretan provenience and Middle Dedalic date are confirmed by a terra-cotta head from Zakro: H. Schmid, "Frühgriechische Terrakotten aus Kreta," in *Gestalt und Geschichte: Festschrift Karl Schefold* (Bern, 1967), 171 f., pl. 58:3, and by another head, from Phaistos: P. Amandry, "Vases, bronzes et terres cuites de Delphes," *BCH*, LXII (1938), 328, fig. 15a.

56 An admirable analysis is given by Jenkins, *Dedalica* (n. 19), 82 ff.

57 Lamb, *Bronzes* (n. 10), 84, pl. 25b.

58 Metropolitan Museum, 47.11.8 G. M. A. Richter, *Archaic Greek Art* (New York, 1949), 34, fig. 57; *idem, Handbook* (n. 55), 33, pl. 22c.

59 (1) Kouros in Berlin: Neugebauer, *Katalog*, I (n. 50), no. 159, pl. 20; Lamb, *Bronzes* (n. 10), pl. 21a. (2) Cuirassed warrior in Paris: de Ridder, *Bronzes* (n. 18), I, no. 106, pl. 12; Lamb, *Bronzes* (n. 10), pl. 25a. (3) Runner (and other figures) from the Idaean Cave, in the museum at Heraklion: Levi, *ASAtene*, 1927-29 (n. 6), 703, fig. 667. (4) A small head of a kore acquired at Onythe, in Heraklion, looks archaic but can hardly be judged from the photograph; briefly mentioned by N. Platon, "*᾿Ανασκαφὴ . ᾿Ονυθὲ Γουλεδιανῶν Ρεθύμνης*", *Πρακτικα*, 1955 (1960), 302 f., pl. 114a.

60 In C. Waldstein, *The Argive Heraeum*, II (Boston and New York, 1905), 196, pl. 70.

61 Quoted by R. J. H. Jenkins, "Archaic Argive Terracotta Figurines to 525 B.C.," *BSA*, XXXII (1931-32), 33, pl. 15:7 (head only). My figures 8-10 are from the same set of photographs, taken years ago by Payne and Young. I am indebted to the British School at Athens for allowing me to have prints made from the negatives in 1949, and to the School and the National Museum for permission to publish them.

62 Lamb, *Bronzes* (n. 10), pl. 35c; H. Payne, "A Bronze Herakles in the British Museum at Athens," *JHS*, LIV (1934), 163, n. 2.

63 Like the diademed goddess between rearing snakes on a proto-Attic (Middle Dedalic) votive plaque in the Agora Museum, from the Areopagos region: D. Burr (Thompson), "A Geometric House and a Proto-Attic Votive Deposit," *Hesperia*, II (1933), 604, no. 277, figs. 72-73; E. Brann, *Late Geometric and Protoattic Pottery . . ., The Athenian Agora*, VIII (Princeton, 1962), no. 493, pl. 30.

64 I. N. 1080. From a museum photograph by E. Androulakes. Height ca. 0.04 m.

65 G. Roeder, *Ägyptische Bronzewerke* (Glückstadt, 1937), 2 ff., nos. 33 and 321, pls. 1d-f and 2g.

66 Metropolitan Museum of Art, 17.230.6; G. M. A. Richter, *The Archaic Gravestones of Attica* (London, 1961), no. 21, figs. 72-76.

67 A. de Ridder, *Catalogue des bronzes trouvés sur l'Acropole d'Athènes* (Paris, 1896), nos. 820-835.

68 *Ibid.*, no. 415, fig. 88. Height 0.11 m.

69 *AntDenk*, II, pl. 45; H. Payne, *Protokorinthische Vasenmalerei* (Berlin, 1933), pl. 27.

70 E. A. Lane, "Lakonian Vase-Painting," *BSA*, XXXIV (1933-34), pls. 44c, 45a-b.

71 Rizza and Scrinari (n. 7), pl. 14, no. 79a.

72 Levi, *ASAtene*, 1955-56 (n. 9), 267, pl. 1b; Rizza and Scrinari (n. 7), pl. 27, no. 171, and figs. 318, 365.

73 De Ridder, *Acropole* (n. 67), no. 704, fig. 221; E. Langlotz, *Frühgriechische Bildhauerschulen* (Nürnberg, 1927), 31, no. 22 ("Sicyon"); M. Gjødesen, "Bronze Paterae with Anthropomorphous Handles," *ActaA*, XV (1944), 157.

74 Rizza and Scrinari (n. 7), pl. 14, no. 82, and fig. 293. These rosettes and those of the Heraeum bronze inevitably evoke the memory of the protogeometric terra-cotta idols from Karphi: J. D. S. Pendlebury, *Archaeology of Crete* (London, 1939), 312, pl. 41:1; von Matt, *Kreta* (n. 22), figs. 208-209, and their Minoan ancestresses.

75 National Museum. S. Karousou, "Documents du Musée National d'Athènes," *BCH*, LXI (1937), 350 ff., pl. 26:3; cf. also the head referred to in n. 28.

76 On Cretan export see Boardman, *Cretan Coll.* (n. 17), 154 ff. H. Goldman takes a terra-cotta mask from Halae to be probably of Cretan make: "The Acropolis of Halae," *Hesperia*, IX (1940), 423 f., fig. 76.

77 Levi, *ASAtene*, 1930-31 (n. 10), 57.

78 S. Alexiou, "Tête archaïque en poros du Musée de Candie," *BCH*, LXXVI (1952), 1 ff., pls. 1-2.

79 J. H. Hopkinson, "Note on the fragment of a painted pinax from Praesos," *BSA*, X (1903-04), pl. 3; Levi, *Hesperia*, 1945 (n. 6), 30, pl. 29; *idem*, *AJA*, 1945, (n. 17), 293; P. Courbin, "Un fragment de cratère protoargien," *BCH*, LXXIX (1955), 33, fig. 19.

80 Boardman, who (*Cretan Coll.* [n. 17], 148) aptly remarks that the Axos head is strongly reminiscent of the seventh century, inclines toward a post-600 B.C. dating of the plate (*ibid.*, 146).

81 H. Payne, *Perachora*, I (Oxford, 1940), 136 f., pl. 43:8-9.

82 An established triad of reclining Sileni in Olympia, of much the same size and build, show a surprising difference in quality: E. Kunze, VIII. *Ol.-Bericht* (n. 34), 236 ff. Though reclining goats are more numerous and as individualized as the Sileni, no set of three has been recognized.

83 Br. 4235, assumed to be from Dodona; height 0.08 m. Museum photograph by G. Franceschi. C. Picard, "Courrier de l'art antique," *GBA*, ser. 6, XVII (1937), 216, 220, fig. 23; H. W. Parke, *The Oracles of Zeus* (Oxford, 1967), 208, 277, pl. 4 (following Picard he misinterprets the ornamental volutes behind the Dionysiac mask as horns of Ammon). A marvelous late archaic specimen representing the mask of a silen comes from Perachora: Payne, *Perachora* (n. 81), I, 139 f., pl. 44:8-9 (fig. 17a).

84 I. N. 3166. Not surprisingly, the provenience was reported to be Dodona. Height 0.08 m.

85 1960.481, bequest of David M. Robinson; Fogg Art Museum *Acquisitions 1959-1962*, ill.; Münzen und Medaillen, *Auktion XIV* (June 19, 1954), lot 24, pl. 8.

86 *The Pomerance Collection of Ancient Art*, catalogue of an exhibition at The Brooklyn Museum (June 14-October 2, 1966), no. 93.

87 *Man in the Ancient World*, catalogue of an exhibition at Queens College (February 10 to March 7, 1958), no. 130, ill. p. 50.

88 Cf. M. Gjødesen, "Greek Bronzes: A Review Article," *AJA*, LXVII (1963), 334.

89 Reggio, Museo Nazionale; height 0.44 m. A. de Franciscis, *Agálmata, Sculture antiche nel Museo Nazionale di Reggio Calabria* (Naples, 1960), pl. 9.

90 Munich, Staatliche Antikensammlungen, Samml. Loeb 5; height of figure 0.175 m. Museum photograph by G. Wehrheim. U. Jantzen *Bronzewerkstätten in Großgriechenland und Sizilien* (Berlin, 1937), 46, no. 2, pl. 18:74.

91 National Museum, Department of Oriental and Classical Antiquities, 12 744; height 0.108 m.

92 Ashmolean Museum, B 9; height 0.117 m. Museum photograph.

93 I regret to say that in *ActaA*, 1944 (n. 73), 147, n. 33, I rashly referred to the kore as "little convincing."

94 [G. Faider-Feytmans], *Les antiquités . . . du Musée de Mariemont* (Brussels, 1952), 121, no. I 2, pl. 45. Height 0.12 m.; bought in Paris, provenience unknown.

95 *Collection Raoul Warocqué, Antiquités égyptiennes, grecques et romaines* (Mariemont, 1903), 31, no. 45.

96 E.g., Cassel: M. Bieber, *Die antiken Skulpturen und Bronzen des Königl. Museum Fridericianum in Cassel* (Marburg, 1915), no. 126, pl. 39.

97 B. Neutsch, "Archäologische Grabungen und Funde in Unteritalien 1949-1955," *AA* (1956), 414 ff., fig. 138; he describes the statue as male; L. von Matt and U. Zanotti-Bianco, *Magna Graecia* (New York, 1962), fig. 62, take it to be female.

98 See p. 168.

99 British Museum 560. P. J. Riis, "Some Campanian Types of Heads," *From the Collections of the Ny Carlsberg Glyptothek*, II (1938), 156 ff., A no. 2, figs. 20a-b.

100 See p. 169, n. 12.

101 Contrast the kore (No. 56) from the J. Paul Getty Museum, which is doubtless Etruscan; very revealingly, the Master Bronzes catalogue illustrates it above the Walters kore.

102 Riis, "Heads" (n. 99), with a supplement, "The Danish Bronze Vessels of Greek, Early Campanian, and Etruscan Manufactures," *ActaA*, XXX (1959), 43 f.

103 Cf. n. 97.

104 P. C. Sestieri, "Terrecotte Posidoniati," *BdA*, XLVIII (1963), 212 ff., and color plate II; A. W. Van Buren, "News Letter from Rome," *AJA*, LVIII (1954), 325, pl. 67, fig. 3; A. D. Trendall, "Archaeology in Sicily and Magna Graecia," *Archaeological Reports 1955*, suppl. to *JHS*, LXXVI (1956), 54; von Matt and Zanotti-Bianco, *Magna Graecia* (n. 97), fig. 60.

105 Phot. Gabinetto Fotografico Nazionale. Height 0.35 m.

106 Neutsch, *AA*, 1956 (n. 97), 413 f., fig. 137.

107 Cf. n. 99. For the details consult the drawing in *MonInst*, V (1849-1853), pl. 25.

108 Neutsch, *AA*, 1956 (n. 97), 423 f., fig. 141 (profile); von Matt and Zanotti-Bianco, *Magna Graecia* (n. 97), fig. 63; E. Langlotz, *Die Kunst der Westgriechen in Sizilien und Unteritalien* (Munich, 1963), fig. 45. Height 0.165 m.; made for insertion.

109 P. Zancani-Montuoro and U. Zanotti-Bianco, *Heraion alla Foce del Sele*, I (Rome, 1951), 157 ff.

110 The same pattern is met with in a running woman in Reggio (*NSc*, 1913, suppl. p. 14, fig. 14) and in another in Berlin (Jantzen, *Bronzewerkstätten* [n. 90], pl. 36:149), both of them rude and sketchy. Jantzen is inclined to assign them to an Etruscan workshop, in spite of the fact that the Reggio piece was found in Locri (*ibid.*, p. 5, note 1,3). Cf. also the Dionysos statuette mentioned in n. 113.

111 P. Zancani-Montuoro, "Altre metope scolpite dallo Heraion alla Foce del Sele," *Atti e memorie della Società Magna Grecia*, n. s. II (1958), 12 ff., pls. 2-4.

112 7429; height 0.132 m. K. A. Neugebauer, *Antike Bronzestatuetten* (Berlin, 1912), 64 ff., fig. 34; Lamb, *Bronzes* (n. 10), 143, pl. 51b; Zancani-Montuoro, *Heraion* (n. 109), I, 133, fig. 37; U. Gehrig, A. Greifenhagen, and N. Kunisch, *Führer durch die Antikenabteilung*, Staatliche Museen, Berlin (Berlin, 1968), 146 f.

113 Candidates are (1) Dionysos in Oxford, Ashmolean Museum: P. Gardner, "Bronzes Recently Acquired for the Ashmolean," *JHS*, XXX (1910), 233 f., pl. 15:2; bought in Italy. (2) Centaur from Rollos, in Madrid, Museo Arqueológico Nacional, 18 536: A. García y Bellido, *Los hallazgos griegos de España* (Madrid, 1936), no. 5, pls. 6-8. (3) Herakles Oppermann, Paris, Bibliothèque Nationale: J. Babelon, *Choix de bronzes et terres cuites des collections Oppermann et de Janzé* (Paris and Brussels, 1929), no. 18, pl. 16.

Discussion Session 2

David Gordon Mitten, *Discussant*

Having examined the Cretan armor discussed by Dr. Hoffmann, Professor Steinberg commented that it was apparently work-hardened in antiquity to make it more impervious to weapons. By hammering and plenishing the bronze in the final stages of fashioning it, the craftsman could harden the metal by a factor of two or three, depending on the tin content and the amount of working done.[1] As Dr. Hoffmann pointed out, although these archaic Cretan helmets weigh only one third as much as the average Corinthian helmet, they are nearly as strong.

Professor David Gordon Mitten, the discussant, asked Dr. Muscarella whether there is any evidence such as workshop debris that might help to localize the places of manufacture of bull protomes or other protomes. Dr. Muscarella replied that there are three possible regional workshops — one in North Syria, possibly at Tel Rifa'at, one at Gordion, and one in Urartu. However, because of stylistic differences among the various groups associated with Gordion, it is difficult to establish a set of characteristics that can be clearly called "Phrygian." The same situation obtains for the North Syrian examples. Hence the term "Near Eastern" is suggested for the North Syrian and Phrygian groups. It is somewhat easier to distinguish between Urartean and Near Eastern works. Finally, one can identify those bull attachments produced by various Greek schools.

Dr. Muscarella added that he had recently seen three unpublished bull protomes allegedly from Eastern Turkey. Although they were found with Urartean objects, they seem to fit stylistically into his Near Eastern series. He outlined the possible alternative conclusions that may be drawn from this: (1) that the distinctions between Near Eastern and Urartean groups he had detected are not valid; (2) that the group of objects does not belong together, but was given to the dealer as such, or (3) that the protomes were imported into Urartu and buried with Urartean objects.

Dr. Hoffmann asked whether one might perhaps also postulate a Cretan group of protomes and whether one of the griffin heads from Olympia (A 35)[2] might not be Cretan. Dr. Muscarella said that he thought the griffin to be from the Greek world but was not prepared to be more precise in localizing it. He mentioned that Rodney Young believes such objects to have been imported from North Syria.[3]

Dr. Muscarella was asked to comment on a recent find of a cauldron with eight griffin protomes and four sphinxes *in situ*,[4] from a royal tomb of the late eighth or early seventh century B.C. at Salamis, on Cyprus. He had only studied a photograph of the piece but thought the griffins to be similar to those he had discussed. He felt that the find will raise further issues about the origin of griffin protomes. But he considers Cyprus to be in the Greek sphere, so that his argument (p. 109 f.) and Jantzen's and Benson's[5] are not to be dismissed because of the find.

Dr. Dietrich von Bothmer of the Metropolitan Museum of Art asked Dr. Hoffmann whether he felt that the armor from the Schimmel collection represents the booty of a battle fought only between archers. Normally, he said, the more extensive armor would belong to hoplites, and the victors would take as spoils not what they already had but rather what they did not have. Dr. Hoffmann pointed out that shields are usually found with hoplite armor but that no shields have yet been located in this find, although three complete panoplies may be distinguished on both epigraphic and stylistic grounds. Dr. von Bothmer then asked whether the booty of the archers of Lyttos, presumably belonging to an opponent army, would not have been made elsewhere. Dr. Hoffmann replied that he had not been able to localize the place of manufacture of the armor any more precisely than to say it was from Crete, although stylistic parallels seem to connect it with finds from both Afrati and Axos.

In the ensuing discussion between Dr. von Bothmer and Dr. Hoffmann it was made clear that epigraphists such as Guarducci[6] and Jeffery[7] have dated inscriptions on Cretan material by the artistic style of the objects on which inscriptions are found. This being the case, the art historian must be wary of in turn establishing a stylistic chronology on the basis of letter forms in inscriptions. Dr. Hoffmann made it clear that Jeffery, Guarducci, and Raubitschek all agree that the inscriptions on the Schimmel armor are among the earliest known Greek inscriptions from Crete.

Professor Mitten asked Dr. Gjødesen whether the gesture of a mirror caryatid figure in the Master Bronzes exhibition (No. 75), with arms akimbo and hands on her hips, has any iconographic significance or can be associated with a regional style. Dr. Gjødesen replied that he did not see any stylistic connection between this piece and the kore from Paestum in Berlin,[8] which also has its hands on its hips, nor with the "Sybarite" mirror stand.[9] He conjectured that the unusual pose might have to do with the figure's use as a support, the position of the arms seeming to make it more steady. It is worth noting, however, that all known examples of this motif come from Italy.[10]

Professor Emeline Richardson of the University of North Carolina agreed with Dr. Gjødesen that the striding woman from the Walters Art Gallery (No. 57) is not Etruscan, but she questioned his attribution of the piece to Paestum because the figure's dress is not Greek. She explained that a sleeved chiton worn unbelted and so short that the ankle bone is left bare was *de rigeur* in late archaic and even classical Etruria but is never found in a Greek figure. On the other hand, the kerchief that the lady wears on her head does not occur in Etruria but is quite common in Campanian bronzes from Capua. The Campanian costume may have been a conflation of Greek and Etruscan dress. In addition, she suggested, the "prettiness" of the lady and the grace of her stride seem Campanian — but Etruscan Campanian rather than Greek Campanian.

Dr. Hoffmann then asked whether there were not other Etruscan influences in Paestum. Mrs. Richardson explained that Etruscan influence on Paestan architecture, for example, was very late and that she still believed the influence on the bronzes to have come from Greece rather than Etruria. Dr. Gjødesen then inquired whether Mrs. Richardson would call the statuette in Mariemont (Gjødesen, Fig. 27) Etruscan or Greek. She replied that she had only seen photographs of the piece, but it seemed that it, too, might be Campanian Etruscan, perhaps Capuan. Dr. Gjødesen did not exclude this possibility. Regarding the Walters Art Gallery statuette, which he considered essentially Greek, and the suggested exchange between Paestum and Etruria via Campania, he referred to the plastic groups of Herakles, Hera, and the sileni on Vulcian tripods. These, as Paola Zancani-Montuoro has shown,[11] reproduce a myth found on the metopes from Foce del Sele, near Paestum.[12]

Notes

1 H. H. Coghlan, *Notes on the Prehistoric Metallurgy of Copper and Bronze in the Old World* (Oxford, 1956), 44.

2 Br. 7400, Athens, National Museum, inv. no. 6147. H.-V. Herrmann, *Die Kessel der orientalisierenden Zeit, Olympische Forschungen*, VI (Berlin, 1966), 130 f., pl. 55.

3 Rodney S. Young, "A Bronze Bowl in Philadelphia," *JNES*, XXVI:3 (1967), 151, 153.

4 Vassos Karageorghis, "Chronique des fouilles et découvertes en Chypre," *BCH*, XCI (1967), 344, fig. 149.

5 See n. 11, p. 25.

6 Margherita Guarducci, ed., *Inscriptiones Creticae* (Rome, 1935); *idem*, *Epigrafia Graeca*, I (Rome, 1967).

7 Lillian H. Jeffery, *The Local Scripts of Archaic Greece* (Oxford, 1961).

8 Ulf Jantzen, *Bronzewerkstätten in Grossgriechenland und Sizilien* (Berlin, 1937), 62, pl. 26.

9 P. E. Arias, "Bronzetti inediti di provenienza italiota," *La Critica d'Arte*, V:1-2, fasc. XXIII-XXIV (1940), 1 ff., pl. 1:1-2, 2:3; H. Fuhrmann, *AA* (1941), cols. 671 ff., fig. 142.

10 See in addition the Etruscan kore from near Populonia in the Schimmel collection (Jucker, Fig. 29a-c, p. 211).

11 P. Zancani-Montuoro, "Un mito italiota in Etruria," *ASAtene*, VIII-X (1946-1948), 85 ff.; P. Zancani-Montuoro and U. Zanotti-Bianco, *Heraion alla Foce del Sele*, II (Rome, 1954), 141 ff.

12 K. A. Neugebauer first drew attention to the Baltimore statuette ("Kohlenbecken aus Clusium und Verwandtes," *RömMitt*, LI [1936], 210). He admitted that his comparing it with Etruscan (Clusine) bronzes was to no avail and did not solve his Etruscan problem. The closest parallel adduced by V. Müller in his publication is a bronze maenad in Amsterdam, similarly dressed and of Italian provenance ("A Greek Bronze Statuette," *JWalt*, I [1938], 36, fig. 7; Jantzen, *Bronzewerkstätten* [n. 8], 3, no. 14, pl. 3:13; Neugebauer, fig. 13, left). This and another maenad from Italy in the same collection (Jantzen, 3, no. 15; Neugebauer, fig. 13, middle) C. W. Lunsingh Scheurleer (Catalogus eener Verzameling [The Hague, 1909], 85) had taken to be Campanian (Capuan), comparing them and a matching male statuette with bronzes of the Campanian dinos group. On the evidence of two very similar maenads in Syracuse, both from Locri (Jantzen, 3, no. 16, pl. 3:14-15, and no. 17; *AA* [1928], 690, fig. 10), Jantzen was no doubt right in claiming that the four maenads should all be assigned to a Locrian workshop. (Gjødesen)

PART 3

Introduction to Part 3

Arthur Steinberg

These three papers deal with votive and decorative Roman and Etruscan bronzes, which raise some complicated aesthetic and technological questions. One is immediately struck by the relatively "second rate" quality of many of these pieces. This is generally taken to mean that they are provincial copies or adaptations of familiar Greek prototypes by which we tend to judge these pieces. Such unfortunate comparisons result in our applying to many Etruscan and Roman small bronzes pejorative adjectives such as "provincial," "degenerate," "decadent," or "poor." In forming such judgments on artistic and technical quality we tend to overlook the functions, markets, and means and place of production of many of these bronzes, which were all quite different from those of their Greek prototypes. We should not simply dismiss them as poor adaptations of those Greek pieces but must look much more closely at who made these small bronzes, why they were made, how they were made, and for whom they were made. Many of these questions cannot be resolved by studying individual pieces but require an extended study of a workshop or a group of similar objects. It is hoped that archaeologists might focus on such contextual and aggregate studies in the near future, as Menzel's paper does.

The *function* of these bronze statuettes is of primary importance for understanding and appreciating them. Whether they were intended as ex-votos, household gods, furniture decorations, or utensils probably influences their appearance, as they may well have been made in workshops specialized according to the type of objects produced. We should certainly not judge an ex-voto and a furniture decoration by the same aesthetic or technical criteria, since the relative values attached to them by either their makers or users were surely different. We do not yet know which of the categories was considered most highly, or rather in what order the various kinds of bronzes were ranked qualitatively, and to determine this will require a much greater knowledge of the social values of antiquity.

Aside from function, the *markets* for these various bronzes also must have influenced their appearance. Jucker, for instance, notes that the exploiters of the rich mineral resources around Populonia were probably the people who demanded the great quantity of small votive bronzes that were produced in that city. What effect this market of a large class of "nouveaux riches" might have had on the quality and quantity of the bronze workshops is not yet clear. But the relatively sketchy objects that Jucker illustrates as products of the Populonia workshop might be the result of such a new, unsophisticated, and rapidly expanding market. Similarly customer-oriented workshops are the legionary ones, mentioned by Menzel, which produced the votives for legions stationed in the various provinces of the Roman Empire. We tend to expect that legionnaires would not require as fine style and execution of a votive as a more sensitive senator back in the capital, and this might account for the relatively "poor" quality of many of the provincial Roman pieces. It is further possible that the introduction of mass-production methods resulted in a reduction in quality but made possible an increase in the quantity of pieces made, making it possible to reach a larger market.

The *means of production* is still another factor to be considered in judging these statuettes. Dorothy Hill has suggested (*Hesperia*, XXVII [1958], 318 ff.) that some Roman statuettes were made by mass-production methods. There is some indication that parts of these statuettes were cast separately and then assembled before the final casting of the object, but it is not clear from the remains whether the parts were first cast in wax and then built into a wax model or whether the parts were cast in bronze and somehow held in place in the wax model that served for the major portion of the casting. In any case it is fairly certain that there were models whose arms and legs could be attached in different postures. On a basic Hercules type, for example, the position of arms and legs, and possibly even the turn of the head, could be altered according to the desire of the customer. On the other hand, the owner of the workshop, or whoever produced the pieces, could decide to turn out a large quantity of several different types of statuettes on the assumption that these types would be readily purchased by his customers. Such a form of mass production, approaching an industrial scale, certainly must have had marked effects on the aesthetic and technical quality of the bronzes.

The technical concerns of the people producing these Roman and Etruscan statuettes were different from those of an "art" founder. The mass producer of statuettes does not lavish the same attention upon the original modeling, mold building (he is, if anything, interested in multiple molds), or cold working of the finished product as the man who is both artist and founder. Rather, the mass producer is concerned with rapid building of model and mold and with a minimum of cold working, since this is surely the most time-consuming part of the production system. Casting the *model* in wax, plaster, or some such material from piece molds would be the fastest and most efficient way for the industrialist to produce his working models. These models might then be touched up slightly before they were invested with molds for the final casting in bronze. Jucker has suggested, in fact, that the hair on some Etruscan bronzes was worked on the wax model. This seems likely, since it is both faster and easier to make adjustments on the wax model prior to casting than on the finished bronze. On the other hand, his suggestion that there is also much cold working on pieces from the Populonia workshop seems less plausible, since time-consuming cold working is in sharp contrast to the efficient mass-production technique of working on the wax models.

How the bronze workshops were organized and who did the different kinds of work is not yet clear. Somewhere in the production there must have been an artist, probably at the making of the original model. From then on mold builders and foundrymen carried on in a repetitive, automatic fashion. Whether the artist or master craftsman was involved in the finishing or mounting of the bronzes is also questionable. This system of mass production for small bronzes could have operated with a minimum of skills and a maximum of routinization.

Whether further distinctions among various categories of bronzes can be made according to *place of production* — distinguishing between the products of large urban centers and smaller rural ones — is still uncertain. Can we distinguish qualitatively between the objects from a local workshop in a small provincial center in Gaul and a workshop producing similar or even identical kinds of objects in Rome itself? Is there, in short, a reasonable distinction on both aesthetic and technical grounds between urban art and rural art serving similar needs but different markets? Is it perhaps such a distinction that is apparent in the exquisite bronzes that both the Romans and Etruscans produced in certain typical genres such as Praenestine cistae and mirrors, Vulcian tripods, extraordinarily large statuary, and some Roman portraits? The Etruscan categories each tend to be connected with a particular bronze-working center. The Vulcian tripods are probably all the products of one or at most two or three workshops in Vulci, and the Praenestine bronzes are probably from a very few workshops localized in a single city. Similarly the materials from some of the great seventh-century Etruscan tombs and from later tombs at Chiusi appear to be the products of particular local workshops centered in the urban areas where the material was found. Whether closer study of much of this kind of material will show that there were urban workshops producing the masterpieces and rural ones making imitations of them for local consumption remains to be seen. This is merely another of the considerations that should be raised in a discussion of Etruscan and Roman statuettes.

I am suggesting here that the Etruscan and Roman bronzes considered in these papers are the products of very particular cultures. They are not necessarily "works of art," nor should we judge them by either classical Greek or modern aesthetic and technical standards, for they fulfilled certain specific requirements in the cultures that produced them. To understand and appreciate them properly we must try to examine the cultural conditions in which these bronzes were produced and realize that they have been expediently adapted to the demands of function and market of a certain culture by explicit means of production.

Etruscan Bronzes in the British Museum: New Acquisitions and Old Possessions

Sybille Haynes

Many years ago my husband found in an antiquarian bookshop the two volumes of George Dennis' *Cities and Cemeteries of Etruria* which had been the author's own. They contained some loose pieces of notepaper with Dennis' handwriting on them. Among these was the draft for a review, destined for the *Dublin University Magazine* of November 1844, of Mrs. Hamilton Gray's book, *Tour of the Sepulchres of Etruria,* which had appeared in London in 1843.

It began with the following sentences: "Antiquity is a dry, severe and cautious study; the female mind is warm, imaginative, indisposed to doubt, eager to conclude. Here are not the elements of consistency or excellence. Any deep and earnest investigation of matters connected with the social institutions of the gentile nations is not properly within the female province. . . ."

Because this chastening indictment of our sex is ever present in my mind, the invitation to participate in this symposium came as a particular surprise and honor.

The purpose of my contribution is twofold: first, to present in detail some unpublished Etruscan bronzes which the British Museum recently acquired from the collection of the late Captain Spencer-Churchill,[1] and second, to draw attention to a number of Etruscan bronze figures which have been in the Greek and Roman Department of the British Museum for a considerable time. Although most of them were published in H. B. Walters' catalogue of 1899, they have hardly received the attention their quality deserves; a reminder of their existence will, I hope, bring them into discussion again.

The earliest of the recently acquired bronzes[2] is the figure of a naked youth which Captain Spencer-Churchill bought at the Fairfax Murray sale at Spink's in March 1920 (Figs. 1, 2). Although the base on which it stands is now fragmentary, it was clearly once circular, and the figure probably comes from the top of a candelabrum.

The youth has put his left foot slightly forward, but the weight of his body rests evenly on both legs so that the hips are level and the torso rigidly frontal; his broad shoulders are pulled well back. He holds in his right hand a wine jug with a trefoil mouth and in his left hand a strainer with a loop handle. The latter is a rare form; the normal strainer has a long, horizontal handle. Both utensils are richly decorated with engraved spirals and have beaded rims and handles.[3] The boy's head is turned a little to the right on its short, strong neck, and the closely cropped hair is treated in rows of concentric circles of small, beadlike curls. The figure must represent one of the young attendants responsible for filling the wine cups at Etruscan banquets.[4] His wide open eyes, the eager expression of his face, and the ready gesture of his bent arms charmingly convey his willingness to serve his feasting masters.

The pose, which is not altogether free of archaic stiffness, and the formal treatment of the hair suggest a date early in the second quarter of the fifth century B.C. Stylistically the piece is closely related to a number of bronzes which were either found at Vulci itself or have been assigned to a Vulcian workshop on the strength of their likeness to bronzes known to have come from that town.

A figure of Herakles decorating the top of one of the rods of a tripod from Vulci in the British Museum[5] has the same beadlike locks of hair framing the forehead as this youth, and the features are similar: strongly

Figs. 1-2: Standing boy with wine jug and strainer, Etruscan, ca. 470 B.C. The British Museum (1966 3-28 14).

arched eyebrows, wide open eyes, a short, straight nose, a small mouth slightly pulled up at the corners, and a firm little chin. The same type of face and hair occurs in a bronze group of a woman and child in the Louvre,[6] which has been listed among Vulcian candelabrum figures by Riis.[7] Finally, we may compare the British Museum piece with the figure of a youth holding a patera from Monteguragazza, now in the Museo Civico in Bologna, which is also considered by Riis to have been made at Vulci.[8] Both share the same physical type, and there is a strong family likeness in the face. Both are of meticulous workmanship with carefully engraved decoration; but the sparkling freshness and charm of the smaller bronze surpasses the slightly earlier and somewhat wooden votive statuette from Monteguragazza. That both were made in a Vulcian workshop seems to me highly probable.

A bronze figure of a reclining young man on a gently curved striplike base[9] (Figs. 3, 4) once belonged to Alessandro Castellani[10] and was acquired by Captain Spencer-Churchill at Sotheby's sale of the Weber Collection on May 23, 1919, for £ 17. As far as one can tell from the not-very-clear drawing in *Notizie degli Scavi* of 1878, it appears to be the bronze excavated together with other bronze figures shortly before 1878 in a tomb at Ancarano, near Norcia.[11] The young man lies on his left side, propping himself up on two cushions under his left elbow and turning his chest and head toward the spectator. His legs, which are entirely wrapped in a smooth cloak, are crossed, and he supports his right elbow on his thigh. His left hand holds a five-stringed lyre close to his body; the hemispherical sound box, decorated with small circles, may be meant to represent a tortoise shell. In his relaxed right hand he holds a plectrum. The cloak, which has a turned-over upper border incised with a decorative row of circles, is draped over the young man's arm and shoulder, leaving most of his chest bare. He has raised his head and turned it slightly to his left as if something had diverted his attention from the instrument. A thick, cross-hatched wreath, composed of two halves which meet in front, encircles the straight, finely grooved hair which falls on his forehead in a short fringe. Level brows, large almond-shaped eyes, a big nose, heavy cheeks, and an unsmiling mouth with full lips impart a serious, almost puzzled expression to the youthful face. The lower border of his cloak and the edges of the two small cushions on which he leans are emphasized by engraved double lines and dots.

The curved shape of the bronze's flat base, which can be compared with other figures of this type,[12] makes it fairly certain that this young man once decorated the rim of a bronze vessel. The companion figures were probably other reclining musicians and banqueters, and the bowl they embellished must have had a considerable diameter, judging from the fairly shallow curve of the base of the piece. Neugebauer, Kunze, Jantzen, and Denys Haynes have discussed such decorative rim figures, both Greek and Etruscan.[13] Numbers 43, 44, 45, 95, and 162 in the Master Bronzes exhibition all belong to this type. We know that vessels so adorned and of sumptuous size were sometimes made as royal presents; more often they were dedicated as votive offerings in sanctuaries,[14] and many of a smaller kind were used as cinerary urns[15] or funerary gifts.[16] Some of these, at least, must have served for a long time as precious tableware before being deposited in the tombs of their former owners. The subject of a lyre player would suit both the profane and the sacred use of such a bronze vessel.

The closest stylistic parallel to the lyre player is provided by a figure of

Hermes (Figs. 5, 6) in the British Museum,[17] said to have been found at Civita Castellana. The two bronzes are strikingly similar in the simplified modeling of the body, in the draping of the cloak — completely devoid of folds — which smoothly follows the spherical planes of the underlying limbs, and in the decoration of their turned-over upper border with small incised circles. There is a likeness, too, in the way the hair frames the forehead in a finely grooved fringe, but the face of the Hermes is more delicate and animated in expression than the somewhat inert features of the heavy-jowled lyre player.

A third bronze figure, from the top of a candelabrum found in 1915 in a richly furnished tomb near Todi, is also characterized by its unusually smoothly draped cloak with the turned-over upper border incised with

Figs. 3-4: Reclining musician, Etruscan, ca. 400-380 B.C. The British Museum (1966 3-28 17).

Figs. 5-6: Standing figure of Hermes, Etruscan, ca. 450-430 B.C. The British Museum (Walters, 641).

circles.[18] Like the cloak of the Hermes, it is decorated all over with groups of three small circles making a trefoil effect.

Riis thought that the Hermes might be Vulcian,[19] which seems to me more probable on stylistic grounds than that it was made in the Faliscan territory in which it was found. But, in default of other evidence, the likeness of the lyre player and the candelabrum figure from Todi to the Hermes is hardly enough to prove conclusively that they were all made in Vulci, particularly since their findspots are all on the periphery of Etruria proper. The date of the lyre player must be later than that of the Hermes. The difference in the face, which we have already mentioned, and the slightly opaque, unlively quality of the whole figure[20] point to the fourth century B.C. rather than the fifth, to which the Hermes must be assigned.

I shall next consider the beautifully engraved and well-preserved bronze mirror (Fig. 7) with a turned bone handle, which Captain Spencer-Churchill acquired in 1927 through Spink's from a Mr. Weightman.[21] There can be little doubt that it is the same mirror as the one published in Perugia by Vermiglioli in 1845,[22] which was subsequently mentioned by Braun[23] and traced to England by Gerhard.[24] It is covered by a fine olive and bluish-green patina which has stained the upper part of the handle the same color. This encourages me to believe that mirror and handle originally belonged together, although the pin fixing the ancient bronze disc and cone to the bottom of the handle, as well as a bronze disc resting on its top, are modern. The handle is not shown in Vermiglioli's drawing of the mirror but does appear in Gerhard's. It may well be that the two parts had become separated when found and were fitted together by a restorer.

The disc is cast, and its reflecting surface is plain except for a beaded border above an egg-and-dart molding and an engraved floral and palmette motif at the point where the circle is extended to form a tang. The incised scene on the back is framed by a wreath of ivy branches. Inside this circle and flanked by a formalized wave pattern, a young man pursues a winged girl. She runs toward the left, arms and wings spread out, her hair flying loose as she turns her head back toward the man, who grasps her by her left wrist and upper arm. Her transparent chiton, buttoned on both shoulders and decorated with a dotted border on the overfold, flutters in swirling folds and reveals her strong, agile body. She wears thonged sandals, drop earrings, and a wide diadem or wreath decorated with lines of dots, made in two parts that meet over her forehead. Her attacker is naked save for a brief cloak held round his shoulders by a brooch; a pointed hat or *pilos* covers his wavy hair. Four letters running from his mouth down toward her arm give his name, Pele = Peleus, and the girl is identified as Thetis by the inscription above her head and left wing.

The scene is a lively representation of the struggle between the two, which ensued when the gods decreed that the Nereid Thetis should be married to the mortal hero Peleus, and the bridegroom had to win an unwilling bride. To escape Peleus, Thetis transformed herself into fire and water and various kinds of wild beasts but was overcome in the end.[25] Her divine nature and powers of transformation are here hinted at by her wings, while her element is indicated by the stylized wave pattern surrounding the pair.

The subject seems to have been a popular one for the decoration of Etruscan mirrors: almost identical representations occur on a number of other engraved mirrors of inferior quality. Nogara gives a list of these in his publication of two examples in the Vatican,[26] and a further specimen is found in the Royal Scottish Museum in Edinburgh.[27] The myth of Peleus and Thetis was also a favorite subject of Greek painted pottery, from which the Etruscan artists no doubt derived their inspiration. A polygnotan hydria from Spina shows Peleus in a brief cloak and a *pilos*-like helmet pursuing Thetis to the left.[28] But the British Museum mirror is later in style and was probably inspired by South Italian vase painting of the fourth century B.C., in which young heroes wear the *pilos* and short cloak fastened at the throat more frequently than they do in Attic vase painting.[29] Thetis is a less obviously Greek figure: her wings,[30] the somewhat exaggerated size of her hands, and the shape of her diadem[31] are characteristically Etruscan. Etruscan, too, is the urge of the artist to fill the available space to the utmost. If we compare it with the economy with which a Greek artist would decorate the interior of a cup, for example, this circular space will strike us as busy and almost overcrowded.[32] But considered on its own merits the engraving is lively, vigorous, and successfully adapted to the shape of the disc.

Fig. 7: Mirror decorated with Peleus pursuing Thetis, Etruscan, ca. 350 B.C. The British Museum (1966 3-28 13).

Figs. 8-9: Incense-burner, Etruscan, ca. 300 B.C. The British Museum (1966 3-28 12).

The fact that several inferior versions of the same scene occur on mirrors which have come to light in Perugia[33] suggests the existence of a local workshop there. Our mirror probably represents the masterpiece of a series of designs taken from a pattern book and executed by engravers of varying ability. The presumption of a Perugian origin for our mirror receives some support if we compare it with another Etruscan mirror, also in the British Museum,[34] which is known to have been found at Perugia. It, too, has a turned bone handle, and the scene on its back — framed by an ivy wreath — shows Perseus, Hermes, and Athena engraved in a similar style and likewise typologically related to South Italian vase painting.[35] Perugia was a flourishing local center from the fourth century B.C. onward,[36] a center where one would expect the existence of a bronze-working industry. I would therefore suggest that the mirror was made there after the middle of the fourth century B.C.

Latest but most important of the figured bronzes is an exquisitely decorated incense burner[37] (Figs. 8, 9). The history of this bronze in England can be traced back to 1857, when it was sent for sale at Sotheby's by F. Böcke and acquired for £ 157.10.0 by W. A. Forman.[38] When the Forman Collection was in turn sold at Sotheby's in June 1899, the bronze was acquired for £ 130[39] by an unrecorded buyer, presumably J. S. Taylor, who was its owner when in 1903 it was shown at the Burlington Fine Arts Club in an exhibition of ancient Greek art.[40] Finally at the sale of the Taylor Collection at Christie's in 1912 it was bought by Captain Spencer-Churchill for £ 150.

The censer is composed of a three-legged foot, a shaft, and a bowl on top of it which served to hold the burning incense. The foot is formed by three lions' hind legs which rest on circular moldings rising from square bases. The upper parts of the legs disappear into the gaping beaks of three griffin heads, whose elongated necks unite to form a raised central platform, their juncture being strengthened by three projecting palmettes of seven petals each. On top of the neck of each griffin lies a tail-less feline facing outward, its head turned to the right, and its left forepaw placed on a dead bird. Above this composite foot a youthful naked satyr stands on a circular base and balances the fluted shaft of the censer on his head. His weight rests on his left leg, while his right foot is set well back; the resulting tilt of the hips gives a pronounced curve to the muscular torso with its masterfully rendered anatomical detail. In his right hand the satyr grasps an object which is broken off at the top and can no longer be identified; in his raised left hand he holds up a fruit, perhaps a bunch of grapes. His pointed horse's ears are the only vestiges of his semibestial nature. His finely striated hair is encircled by a cord which is visible at the back only, but to which the small knob above the forehead is presumably attached; the knob perhaps represents an ivy fruit, frequently associated with satyrs in ancient art. The sullen features with fleshy lips and upward-pointing nose are dominated by the deeply furrowed brows. As a satyr, the figure may have had a small horse's or goat's tail, but this seems to have been broken off and the place of its attachment filed smooth.[41] Halfway up the shaft of the censer a fourth tail-less feline crouches to pounce on a pigeon which turns its head as if to look around at its pursuer. The shaft terminates above in a naked female figure whose twisted legs end in two snakes' heads glaring down at the approaching bird. The body of the girl is well proportioned, her smoothly rounded forms contrasting with the emphatic musculature of the satyr. With both her raised hands she steadies the bowl of the censer which rests on her head. Her calm, regular face is framed by carefully dressed and beribboned hair that hangs down in finely grooved tresses. She wears disc earrings and a bead necklace. The circular bowl above her has a square surround, on each corner of which perches a pigeon, its plumage indicated by hatching and small semicircles. The birds are riveted in position, but only one of the ancient rivets survives.

There appear to be only two passing mentions of this censer in archaeological literature: Ludwig Curtius refers to it in an article[42] in which he suggests that this type of utensil was derived from Assyrian prototypes; and C. F. Lehmann-Haupt lists it among many other examples of ancient censers and candelabra with "zoomorpher Junktur," claiming that feet of this kind were an invention of Chaldean art.[43]

The censer in question is, in fact, a particularly richly decorated example of a small class of Etruscan bronze utensils of which the foot in the form of three lions' hind legs emerging from griffins' beaks is the distinguishing characteristic. Feet of this kind occur most frequently in censers but are also found in bronze candelabra and braziers.[44] Censers with such composite feet vary considerably in the form and decoration of their shafts. Many are plain except for the animals attached to them, like Bronze 781 in the British Museum (Fig. 10); others are supported by single human figures, like the example from the Museo Kircheriano, now in the Villa Giulia at Rome (K 7786), or by pairs of human figures like the censer No. 221 in the Master Bronzes exhibition. When going through the sale catalogue of the Castellani collection, which was auctioned in Rome in 1884, I noted down as belonging to this group No. 284 of the bronzes, "un petit candelabre étrusque," and added "present whereabouts unknown." But since the description and height of the Castellani censer tally perfectly with No. 221 in the Master Bronzes exhibition, which has been part of the R. H. Lowie Museum of Anthropology since 1904, we can be fairly certain that it is the same piece, and I am very grateful to be able to locate it now and add it to the list of such utensils.

Fig. 10: Incense-burner, Etruscan, ca. 300 B.C. The British Museum (Walters, 781).

A very few censer shafts, like that of the newly acquired one in the British Museum, are supported and surmounted by human or semihuman figures. The nearest parallel for this censer is one formerly in the collection of Lucien Bonaparte, Prince of Canino, and presumably found in his excavations at Vulci.[45] Unfortunately the Canino censer is known only from small drawings of poor quality (see Fig. 10a), and a stylistic comparison of the two bronzes would be impossible; nevertheless they seem to me so closely related in their motifs as to suggest a common workshop for both. The Canino bronze had lost its foot and bowl. The shaft was supported by a standing naked satyr with powerfully modeled torso and frowning face; in his left hand he held a staff with which he impaled a snake writhing at his feet, while in his right hand he raised a stone ready to hurl it at the creature. The shaft itself, up which a dog (?) ran, was twisted and ended at the top in a mermaid with intertwined legs and uplifted arms, wearing a brief, belted chiton.[46] Since this lost Canino censer is only one of several utensils with lion-and-griffin feet known to come from Vulci,[47] this was probably the center where such bronzes were produced.

Fig. 10a: Incense-burner, Etruscan, ca. 300 B.C. Formerly Collection Lucien Bonaparte.

The date of the British Museum censer must be late in the fourth century B.C., close to that of the Cista Ficoroni in the Villa Giulia at Rome.[48]

Figs. 11-12: *Standing boy holding a ball, Etruscan, ca. 500-475 B.C. The British Museum (Walters, 500).*

We may compare the satyr with the two satyrs supporting Dionysus on the lid of the cista, whose poise, modeling, and facial expression are equally typical of the late classical phase of Etruscan art. The hair style and face of the girl-monster on the censer point to the same date.[49]

We know too little about the religious and mythological beliefs of the Etruscans to determine the significance of the censer's figures. Much of the Etruscan pantheon was borrowed from the Greeks, but the Greek names and types are often strangely changed; and inexplicable divinities occur whom we cannot even name. The girl-monster is one of these. The Greek *Echidna,* half woman, half snake, and mother of monsters, seems to me too savage and repulsive to have served as the inspiration for our gentle and elegant creature. The snake as such often has a chthonic and funerary significance in ancient art,[50] and it is therefore possible that the girl represents a genius of death, like the stern-faced bronze figure of a winged girl carrying two snakes in the British Museum[51] and the male winged demons with legs ending in writhing snakes who support the cornice in the Hellenistic wall paintings of the Tomba del Tifone in Tarquinia.[52] The satyr, too, may allude to death and the afterlife, since he is a follower of Dionysus, the god of wine and vegetation, whom the Greeks associated with the underworld and life in the beyond.[53] And in Hellenistic and Roman imperial times the Bacchic *thiasos* became a favorite symbol of immortality and a blissful life in the other world.[54] Even the birds on censers like ours have been interpreted as "Seelenvögel" and therefore suitable for incense burners used in the cult of the dead.[55] But that is all conjecture; it may well be that the censer was made for use in everyday life and that the motifs incorporated in it have no funerary significance at all.

Having dealt with these newly acquired and unpublished bronzes in some detail, I shall now discuss more briefly a number of Etruscan figures that belong to the old stock of the British Museum's collection. They are all in their way of excellent quality and deserve to be better known. My suggestions as to their date and provenance, which will be of a provisional nature, are meant to provide no more than a point of departure for critical comment and discussion.

Walters, *Bronzes,* no. 500 (Figs. 11, 12)

The first is a candelabrum figure of a long-haired, naked boy who holds a ball in his right hand. Both the sturdy proportions of his body and his wide-awake features strongly remind me of the young banqueting attendant discussed previously. You will remember that we found the lively face with its large eyes and arched eyebrows, the small, smiling mouth, the short, straight nose, and the firm little chin in other figures of Vulcian provenance or style.[56] In view of the similarities of these bronzes I think we are justified in assuming that this ball player, too, was made at Vulci. The date of the figure must be slightly earlier than that of the banqueting attendant. The body is still rigidly frontal and lacks even the slight inclination of the head toward the right and the more differentiated posture of the arms that characterize the later figure. His long hair, too, is an indication that the ball player still belongs firmly to the late archaic tradition. A date in the first quarter of the fifth century B.C. would probably not be wide of the mark.

Bronze 1907 10-20 2 (Figs. 13, 14)

The next figure likewise comes from the top of a candelabrum and is an athlete — this time a youth scraping his right thigh with a strigil. Again a kind of family relationship in the face and in the treatment of the body is noticeable between this bronze and those just discussed.[57] But as he is a youth rather than a boy, his proportions are slimmer. There is also a greater freedom in his posture: the young man has raised his right heel off the ground to push his thigh up and slightly forward, thus facilitating the use of the strigil, and this movement results in a slight loosening of the late archaic stiffness in the torso. The softer, more naturalistic modeling of the short hair with fine, wavy strands also points to a more advanced date. I would like to suggest that the youth was made at Vulci about the middle of the second quarter of the fifth century B.C.

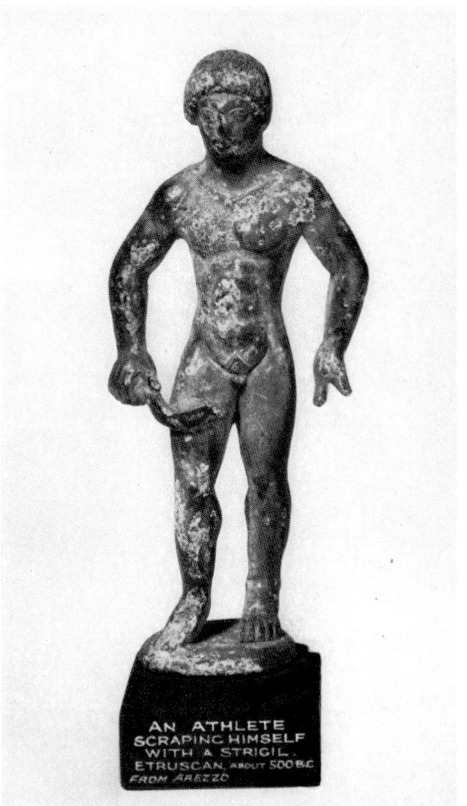

Walters, *Bronzes*, no. 526 (Figs. 15, 16)

Next is a figure of a boxer who stands on a cross-shaped support, the four vertical tangs of which may have served to fix the bronze in a stone or wood base. The tough, slightly stunted figure exhibits proportions not unlike those of the bronzes at which we have just been looking. And the face, although fittingly more brutal in expression, has the features with which we have now become so familiar — the characteristic eyes, eyebrows, and mouth. The pugilist's closely cropped hair underlines the lowness of the ignoble forehead and hangs down at the back as far as the nape; it is rendered with small circles. His only garment is a cloth belt tied in front. Like the strigil-holding youth's, the boxer's stance, with most of the weight resting on one leg, imparts some slight movement to the torso; his left hip is, in fact, just a little higher than his right. The vigorous and threatening gesture of his arms also suggests the same advanced date to which we have assigned the scraper. Such a date in the second quarter of the fifth century B.C. is confirmed by comparing this boxer with the similarly dressed and proportioned pugilists represented in the frescoes of the Tomba della Scimmia at Chiusi, which have been assigned to that period.[58]

Figs. 13-14: Standing athlete scraping himself, Etruscan, ca. 465 B.C. The British Museum (1907 10-20 2).

Walters, *Bronzes*, no. 680 (Figs. 17, 18)

This bronze represents the draped figure of a young man who stands with his feet slightly apart, his right hand pulling at the stuff of his cloak on his hip and his left arm and hand completely hidden by the elaborate folds of the garment. The face, which is unfortunately slightly damaged by corrosion, again shows the characteristic features that we have associated with the late archaic school of Vulci. And what we can see of the body — the short neck, the broad shoulders and the strong buttocks, molded by the tightly pulled mantle — is not incompatible with the physical type of the Vulcian bronzes so far discussed. The curious draping of the cloak, with the point of a turned-over pleated end hanging down from the chest, and the somewhat formalized treatment of the slim ridges[59] that indicate the folds suggest a date for this candelabrum figure at the beginning of the second quarter of the fifth century B.C.[60]

Fig. 15

Fig. 16

Fig. 17

Fig. 18

Fig. 19

Fig. 20

Figs. 15-16: Standing boxer, Etruscan, ca. 465 B.C. The British Museum (Walters, 526).

Figs. 17-18: Standing youth wrapped in cloak, Etruscan, ca. 475 B.C. The British Museum (Walters, 680).

Figs. 19-20: Boy in cloak adjusting his sandal, Etruscan, ca. 450-425 B.C. The British Museum (Walters, 449).

Walters, *Bronzes*, no. 449

Figures 19 and 20 show a figure also presumably from the top of a candelabrum, representing a young boy wrapped in a cloak who balances on his left foot and adjusts his right sandal while supporting himself on a stout stick with his left arm. Walters boldly describes him as an Aphrodite, but I don't think he can have looked very closely. The action of fixing one sandal, which is often found in statuettes of Aphrodite, must have blinded him to the fact that the uncovered chest of the boy exhibits no female characteristics at all. The stick disappearing under the cloak does not suit the goddess either, nor do the proportions of the figure, which has the large head of a child and a boy's thin but muscular arms. His face shows the familiar Vulcian features, but owing to the later date of the figure they seem somewhat veiled and have lost in liveliness of expression and crispness of definition. The drapery, too, points to a more advanced date than that of the previously shown figure, although the characteristic arrangement of the pleated triangle of cloth that hangs down in front of the body clearly harks back to the same late archaic formula. But the softly flowing, almost naturalistic folds, which both outline and conceal the shape of the limbs, particularly at the back, already belong to the classical phase. I would therefore suggest a date for this bronze after the middle of the fifth century B.C.

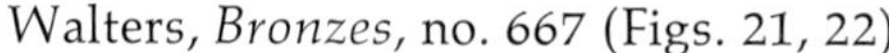

Walters, *Bronzes*, no. 667 (Figs. 21, 22)

Next comes a bronze group representing Peleus wrestling with Thetis, which belongs to the top of a candelabrum. The Nereid stands calmly with her left foot forward and her head turned slightly to the right. With her left hand she is attempting to detach Peleus' arm from her waist, but she does not try very hard; for the time being she seems to rely on frightening Peleus by her power of transformation, indicated by the snake in her right hand which she is thrusting toward the hero's face. She is dressed in a simple chiton with buttoned sleeves, which falls to her ankles in heavy folds. Over each shoulder hangs one of the curious and still unexplained ribbons which occasionally appear as part of the costume of Etruscan ladies in the later fifth and fourth centuries B.C. Mrs. Richardson has suggested that they may be a sign of rank.[61] Peleus is naked, and his muscular body, straining to clasp Thetis round the waist, is modeled with great skill and anatomical understanding. The faces of both exhibit the gloomy features so characteristic of Etruscan figures of the late classical phase: full-lipped mouths with corners pulled down and heavy cheeks and chins. The bronze comes from the Canino collection, which indicates Vulci as a provenance.

The faces of the pair and the heavy, simple treatment of the folds of Thetis' chiton are close in style to the patera figure (Walters, *Bronzes*, no. 659) which came to the British Museum from the same collection. In my booklet on Etruscan bronze utensils I have ascribed the patera to a Vulcian school of the later fourth century B.C.,[62] and I feel tempted to do the same with this candelabrum group. This suggestion may perhaps be strengthened by comparing the hair style and diadem of Thetis with those of the lady on the lid of a Vulcian sarcophagus in the Museum of Fine Arts, Boston (A 1281). The panels of the sarcophagus also show the character-

Figs. 21-22: Peleus wrestling with Thetis, Etruscan, late fourth century B.C. The British Museum (Walters, 667).

istic repetitive treatment of the heavy, rather doughlike folds that we found in the bronzes, and the central figure of the wife on the long side is particularly close to Thetis in every respect.[63]

Walters, *Bronzes*, no. 748 (Figs. 23, 24)

This so-called group of Peleus and Atalanta wrestling formed the handle of a cista lid. The figures stand on a base plate which has rounded ends and undulating sides. This feature, as well as the subject of the group and its style, closely connect the bronze with No. 205 in the Master Bronzes exhibition.[64] The bulging, muscular body of the man, the simple treatment of the girl's short chiton, and the hair style of both figures — strongly

Figs. 23-24: Man and girl wrestling; cista handle, Etruscan, late fourth century B.C. The British Museum (Walters, 748).

separated strands waving down radially from the crown of the head — also recall the candelabrum group of Peleus and Thetis just discussed. Since we have had reason to assume that the candelabrum group came from Vulci, I would like to suggest that this cista handle, too, was made there at about the same time.[65] Praeneste was not the only place where cistae and their handles and feet were manufactured, and it is worth pointing out that the base plates of Praenestine handles tend to be plain strips with straight, pointed, or palmette-shaped ends, rather than of rounded form as on this bronze and on No. 205 in the exhibition. Nor does the physical type of the figures correspond closely to that which we know as Praenestine of the late fourth century B.C., which is characterized by a smoothly faceted modeling of bodies and straight, striated hair.

Walters, *Bronzes*, no. 771 (Figs. 25, 26)

The last of the bronzes to be discussed was found at Orvieto and is the top of a stand from which household or toilet utensils could be hung. Two superimposed rows of bud-shaped suspension hooks are topped by a triangular base inlaid with a silver meander. On it a maenad and a satyr walk along, he with his arm around her waist, she with her arm around his neck. The girl wears a clinging sleeveless chiton, belted at the waist, and soft leather shoes, while her companion is naked. Though the bronze is somewhat damaged by corrosion, we can, I think, recognize that the style of the body and the face with its pointed animal's ears are close to those of the satyr supporting the censer from the Spencer-Churchill Collection (Fig. 8). The easy and graceful movement of the group and the subtly flowing thin folds of the girl's chiton also suggest the same early Hellenistic date. Her attractive coiffure — all the hair swept up and forward to be tied into a kind of crobylus above the forehead — is unusual and occurs, as far as I know, on only one other Etruscan bronze of this period, the patera handle in the form of a Lasa in the Metropolitan Museum of Art.[66] The triangular stand inlaid with a silver meander recurs on a patera handle from Todi in the form of a youth, now in the Villa Giulia in Rome.[67] The piece closely resembles the Lasa in the figure's attitude and in the draping of the cloak, as well as in the details of the attachment for the patera, decorated with two rosettes. To my knowledge, the majority of Etruscan bronzes that show silver inlay or appliqué — and there are not many — either come from Vulci or can be assigned to that city on stylistic grounds. At the risk of being accused of having a Vulcian bee in my bonnet, I would like to suggest that, for stylistic reasons as well as for the rare feature of silver embellishment, the stand from Orvieto and the related patera handles from Todi and in the Metropolitan Museum were originally made at Vulci toward the end of the fourth century or early in the third century B.C.

I realize that I have ventured far into unmapped territory, and perhaps I have undertaken the journey with too few landmarks to go by. But if we want to learn more about Etruscan local schools of the late classical and early Hellenistic period, some such tentative exploration of this *terra incognita* is necessary.

Figs. 25-26: Satyr and maenad; top of stand for the suspension of utensils, Etruscan, late fourth or early third century B.C. The British Museum (Walters, 771).

Notes

1 These four bronzes have since been published, *BMQ*, XXXII: 3-4 (Spring 1968), 112-122, pls. xxxiv-xxxix.

2 1966 3-28 14. Height 9.3 cm. Figs. 1, 2.

3 For the shape of the jug cf. an engraved bronze oinochoe in the Metropolitan Museum of Art, G. M. A. Richter, *Greek, Etruscan and Roman Bronzes* (New York, 1915), no. 492.

4 Cf. the wall painting in the Tomba dei Leopardi at Tarquinia, M. Pallottino, *Etruscan Painting* (Geneva, 1952), 67.

5 H. B. Walters, *Catalogue of the Bronzes, Greek, Roman and Etruscan*, Department of Greek and Roman Antiquities, British Museum (London, 1899), no. 587. This volume is hereinafter abbreviated as Walters, *Bronzes.*

6 A. de Ridder, *Les bronzes antiques,* Musée National du Louvre, Départment des antiquités grecques et romains, I (Paris, 1915), 245.

7 P. J. Riis, *Tyrrhenika* (Copenhagen, 1941), 82, no. 8.

8 *Ibid.*, 90, pl. 18:2.

9 1966 3-28 17. Length 7.8 cm.; height 4.8 cm. Figs. 3, 4.

10 *Collection Alessandro Castellani, Catalogue des objets d'art . . .*, sale, Rome, March 17-April 10, 1884, I, p. 51, no. 323.

11 *NSc* (1878), 22, pl. II, no. 5.

12 Cf. a reclining girl with castanets in the Museo del Teatro Romano at Verona, O.-W. von Vacano, *Die Etrusker* (Stuttgart, 1955), pl. 73b, and a similar girl with a five-string lyre, in the British Museum, Walters, *Bronzes,* no. 609, pl. xiii.

13 K. A. Neugebauer, "Kohlenbecken aus Clusium und Verwandtes," *RömMitt*, LI (1936), 181, pls. 23-24; E. Kunze, *et al., VII. Bericht über die Ausgrabungen in Olympia* (Berlin, 1961), 173; VIII. (Berlin, 1967), 241; U. Jantzen, *Griechische Greifenkessel* (Berlin, 1955), n. 146; D. E. L. Haynes, "A Bronze Banqueter," *BMQ*, XX (1955), 36-37.

14 Herodotus, i. 70. The bowl sent by the Spartans to Croesus was intercepted at sea by the Samians, who made an offering of it to Hera.

15 Cf. the Capuan urns in the British Museum, Walters, *Bronzes,* nos. 558-561.

16 For example, the so-called Loeb tripod and cauldron, A. Minto, "Dove e quando furono scoperti i famosi tripodi Loeb," *StEtr*, IX (1935), 401 ff.; M. Pallottino, H. Jucker, M. Hürlimann, *Art of the Etruscans* (London, 1955), nos. 48-49.

17 Walters, *Bronzes*, no. 641; figs. 5, 6.

18 G. Bendinelli, "Tomba con vasi e bronzi . . .," *MonAnt,* XXIV (1916), 865-866, figs. 20-22.

19 *Ibid.*, 168.

20 The liveliness in movement and expression of the late archaic bronze figure of a reclining girl with a lyre, Walters, *Bronzes,* no. 609, provides an illuminating contrast; it underlines the lack of vigor and inventive power of much of Etruscan art of the later fifth and part of the fourth century B.C., which frequently copies earlier prototypes without capturing their spiritedness.

21 1966 3-28 13. Width across disc 17 cm.; total height 30.8 cm., excluding the protruding modern pin at the bottom of the handle. Fig. 7.

22 "La favola di Peleo e Tetide" (Perugia, 1846), 12, p. 8, Articolo estratto dal Giornale scientifico-letterario di Perugia, 1845 (inaccessible to the author).

23 "Archäologische Gesellschaften," *AZ*, IV (1846), col. 260.

24 E. Gerhard, *Etruskische Spiegel*, IV (Berlin, 1867), pl. ccclxxxvi, p. 35. The engraving, of course, reverses the scene.

25 W. H. Roscher, *Lexikon der griechischen und römischen Mythologie,* Vol. III, Abt. II, col. 1833. Pauly-Wissowa, *RE*, Vol. XIX, s. v. "Peleus." Cf. D. E. L. Haynes, *The Portland Vase* (London: British Museum, 1964), 16 ff.

26 B. Nogara, "Di alcuni specchi del Museo Vaticano-Etrusco," *StEtr*, VIII (1934), 131 f., pl. xxxiii. Nogara seems to have assumed that the mirror published by Vermiglioli and that which de Witte found in London in 1844 were two different ones, but Gerhard (*Spiegel* [n. 24], IV, 35, n. 89) clearly states that he thinks the Perugia mirror must be the same as the London one.

27 M. A. Johnstone, "Etruscan Collections in the Royal Scottish Museum, Edinburgh . . .," *StEtr*, XI (1937), 393, pl. L:1.

28 S. Aurigemma, *La Necropoli di Spina in Valle Trebba,* I (Rome, 1960), pls. 183-186.

29 Cf. H. Sichtermann, *Griechische Vasen in Unteritalien aus der Sammlung Jatta in Ruvo.* Bilderhefte des Deutschen Archäologischen Instituts in Rom, Heft

3-4, no. K 70, p. 118; no. K 40, p. 63; no. K 11, p. 18; A. D. Trendall *South Italian Vase Painting* (London: The British Museum, 1966), pls. 2, 3b, 12a, pl. B and *idem, Frühitaliotische Vasen, Bilder griechischer Vasen* (Leipzig, 1938), 12, pl. 16; B. Neutsch, *Herakleia Studien*, 11. Ergänzungsheft der Mitteilungen des Deutschen Archäologischen Instituts in Rom (1967), pl. 65:1; A. D. Trendall, *Paestan Pottery* (London, 1936), pl. Va, XVIc, XXVIIIb, c; A. D. Trendall - M. Cambitoglou, *Apulian Red-figure Vase-Painters of the Plain Style* (New York, 1961), pl. X. Professor Trendall in recent conversation has kindly confirmed my supposition about the probable South Italian source of inspiration for the figure of Peleus.

30 Cf. I. Mayer-Prokop, *Die gravierten etruskischen Griffspiegel archaischen Stils*, 13. Ergänzungsheft der Mitteilungen des Deutschen Archäologischen Instituts in Rom (1967), 59, n. 143.

31 Cf. the diadems of the bronze figures from Spina in the Museo Archeologico in Ferrara, M. Santangelo, *Musei e monumenti etruschi* (Agostini, 1960), 61; on a cup from Vulci in the Vatican, L. Banti, *Il mondo degli Etruschi* (Rome, 1960), pl. 87b; and the actual gold wreaths in the British Museum, F. H. Marshall, *Catalogue of the Jewellery, Greek, Etruscan and Roman* (London: The British Museum, 1911), pl. 48, nos. 2294, 2292, 2302, pl. 49, nos. 2296, 2293.

32 Cf. S. Haynes, "Ein neuer etruskischer Spiegel," *Mitteilungen des Deutschen Archäologischen Instituts*, VI (1953), 41 ff.

33 Cf. B. Nogara, *StEtr*, VIII (1934), 132.

34 Walters, *Bronzes*, no. 620.

35 Cf. K. Schauenburg, *Perseus in der Kunst des Altertums* (Bonn, 1960), 77 ff.

36 Cf. Banti, *Mondo degli Etruschi* (n. 31), 118.

37 1966 3-28 12. Total height 51.4 cm.; height of satyr 12.6 cm. Figs. 8, 9.

38 Sale, Sotheby, June 12, 1857, p. 6, no. 51.

39 C. H. Smith, *The Forman Collection*, sale, Sotheby, June 19-22, 1899, 25, no. 143, pl. V.

40 Burlington Fine Arts Club, *Exhibition of Ancient Greek Art* (London, 1903), 43, no. 28, and pl. XLIX; Burlington Fine Arts Club, *Exhibition of Ancient Greek Art* (London, 1904), no. A 28.

41 Smith, *Forman Collection* (n. 39), 25, no. 143, text.

42 L. Curtius, "Assyrischer Dreifuß in Erlangen," *MJb*, VIII (1913), 19 ff. fig. 14.

43 C. F. Lehmann-Haupt in *Kulturgeschichtliche Studien und Skizzen aus Vergangenheit und Gegenwart, Festschrift zur 400-Jahrfeier der Gelehrtenschule des Johanneum zu Hamburg* (Hamburg, 1929), 226 f., pl. VII; *idem, Armenien einst und jetzt*, II, Heft 2 (Berlin, 1910-1931), 514 f.

44 To a list of such utensils given by F. Magi in *La raccolta B. Guglielmi nel Museo Gregoriano Etrusco*, II, *Bronzi e oggetti vari* (Vatican, 1939), 210, we may add

(A) A censer in the Museo Nazionale, Naples, the shaft balanced by a boy holding a cloak, a cock halfway up the shaft, and four birds on the corners of the framed bowl on top. Inv. No. 72196. A. Ruesch, *Guida illustrata del Museo Nazionale di Napoli* (Naples, 1908), no. 1689; Coll. Borgia, *Real Museo Borbonico* (Naples, 1843), XIII, pl. XIV.

(B) A censer in the Bibliothèque Nationale in Paris, E. Babelon - J. A. Blanchet, *Catalogue des bronzes antiques de la Bibliothèque Nationale* (Paris, 1895), no. 1482.

(C) A censer in the Antiquario of the Villa Giulia in Rome, K. 7786, from the Museo Kircheriano Buono, no. 388.

(D) The lower part of a censer in the Greek and Roman Department of the British Museum (marked K), which has the usual plinths, bases, lions' legs and griffins' heads; instead of the more customary palmette or floral motif at their juncture, the necks of the griffins are elongated to form rippling leaflike excrescences meeting at an angle.

(E) A candelabrum in the Metropolitan Museum of Art, Richter, *Bronzes* (n. 3), no. 1299.

(F) A set of three feet of the composite lion-griffin type, from an Etruscan brazier in an English private collection. *Antiquities from the Bomford Collection*, exhibition, Ashmolean Museum, Dept. of Antiquities (Oct. 10-30, 1966), 366 bis.

45 S. Reinach, *Répertoire de la statuaire grecque et romaine*, II:1 (Paris, 1897), 140:9, and F. Wieseler - C. O. Müller, *Denkmäler der alten Kunst*, I (Göttingen, 1854), 61, pl. LIX, fig. 295.

46 A mermaid in the same position, supporting an incense bowl in a square frame with four frogs at its corners, appears on a censer with three horse's legs surmounted by a girl with a mirror in her hand, who balances the shaft; it came from Telamone and is now in the Museo Archeologico, Florence, inv. no. 70825.

47 Others are: in the British Museum, Walters, *Bronzes*, no. 781; Vatican, Museo Gregoriano Etrusco: G. Q. Giglioli, *L'Arte etrusca* (Milan, 1935), pl. CCLXXXII:2, and Magi, *Racc. Guglielmi* (n. 44), 62, no. 18; Berlin: C. Friedrichs, *Kleinere Kunst und Industrie* (Düsseldorf, 1871), 761.

48 Cf. *Enciclopedia dell'arte antica*, III (Rome, 1960), 647, s. v. "Ficoroni."

49 Cf. Walters, *Bronzes*, nos. 659 and 650, illustrated in S. Haynes, *Etruscan Bronze Utensils* (London: British Museum, 1965), pls. 10, 11; also the figure of a Lasa from Perugia in the Museo Archeologico, Florence, R. Herbig, *Götter und Dämonen der Etrusker* (Mainz, 1965), pl. 43.

50 It occurs, for example, on Greek hero reliefs: cf. C. Blümel, *Die archaisch griechischen Skulpturen der Staatlichen Museen zu Berlin* (Berlin, 1963), 22, no. 16, pl. 42, and 25, no. 17, pl. 45; it also occurs on Etruscan sarcophagi: R. Herbig, *Die jüngeretruskischen Steinsarkophage* (Berlin, 1952), 24, 25, figs. 2-4, pl. 42b.

51 Walters, *Bronzes*, no. 1449.

52 Giglioli, *Arte etr.* (n. 47), pl. CCCLXXXIX.

53 Cf. S. Haynes, *Burlington Magazine*, CVIII (December, 1966), 600, n. 15, for the relevant literature.

54 Cf. E. Strong, *Apotheosis and Afterlife* (New York, 1915), 197 ff.; F. Cumont, *Les religions orientales dans le paganisme romain* (Paris, 1929), appendix; K. Lehmann-Hartleben and E. C. Olsen, *Dionysiac Sarcophagi in Baltimore* (Baltimore, 1942), 23 ff.; M. P. Nilson, *The Dionysiac Mysteries of the Hellenistic and Roman Age* (Lund, 1957); R. Turcan, *Les sarcophages romaines à représentations dionysiaques* (Paris, 1966).

55 K. Wiegand, "Thymiateria," *BonnJbb*, CXXII (1912), 36.

56 Cf. *supra*, notes 5-8; cf. also statuettes of two warriors from a candelabrum in the Metropolitan Museum of Art, 1947.47.11.3, in R. S. Teitz, *Masterpieces of Etruscan Art*, catalogue of an exhibition at the Worcester Art Museum, April 21-June 4, 1967, 57 f., no. 46, ill. p. 153, and the figure of an archer from a candelabrum in the Nelson Gallery — Atkins Museum, Kansas City, 47.94, *ibid.*, 72, no. 60, ill. p. 167.

57 Cf. also the handles in the form of youths, on the bronze amphora from Vulci in the British Museum, Walters, *Bronzes*, no. 557.

58 L. Banti, *Mondo degli Etruschi* (n. 31), pl. 68, and R. Bianchi-Bandinelli, ed., *Monumenti della pittura antica scoperti in Italia*, Sez. I, *Pittura etrusca*, Clusium, fasc. I, *Le pitture delle tombe archaiche* (Rome, 1939), 26, pl. I b.

59 Cf. the same treatment on the slightly later candelabrum figure in the British Museum, Walter, *Bronzes*, no. 593, and on a censer figure from Orvieto in Copenhagen which Riis ascribes to Vulci, *Tyrrhenika* (n. 7), 79, no. B 4, pl. 15:3.

60 An almost identical figure in the Metropolitan Museum is dated by G. M. A. Richter to the early 5th century. *BMMA*, XXIII (1928), 78, fig. 3.

61 E. Richardson, *The Etruscans* (Chicago, 1964), 134.

62 Haynes, *Utensils* (n. 49), 22, pl. 10.

63 C. C. Vermeule and G. H. Chase, *Greek, Etruscan, and Roman Art; The Classical Collections of the Museum of Fine Arts* (Boston, 1963), 202, 203, figs. 185 a-c, 186.

64 D. G. Mitten - S. F. Doeringer, *Master Bronzes from the Classical World* (Mainz, 1967), 202, No. 205. A cista handle in Munich, Staatliche Antikensammlungen und Glyptothek, Inv. No. 3025, K. A. Neugebauer, *Antike Bronzestatuetten* (Berlin, 1921), 105, fig. 56, represents another variant of this group.

65 Cf. also the earlier cista handle in the Vatican, Museo Gregoriano Etrusco, Falcioni Collection, inv. no. 76: W. L. Brown, *The Etruscan Lion* (Oxford, 1960), pl. LI, b. 1, b. 2. Brown thinks it a Vulcian work of the second half of the fifth century B.C. (p. 142). The physical type of the Herakles strangling the lion is very close to that of the "Peleus."

66 1919.19.192.65. Teitz, *Masterpieces* (n. 56), 93 f., no. 84, ill. p. 202.

67 Giglioli, *Arte etr.* (n. 47), pl. CCCXIII:2.

68 The bronze amphora from Vulci in the British Museum, Walters, *Bronzes,* no. 557, and the mirror from Atri (?), *ibid.*, no. 542; also a helmet from Vulci in the Bibliothèque Nationale in Paris, Babelon-Blanchet, *Catalogue* (n. 44), no. 2013, and a mirror from Vulci in the Vatican Museum, Giglioli, *Arte etr.* (n. 47), pl. CXXXIV:1.

Etruscan Votive Bronzes of Populonia*

Hans Jucker

Five Mycenaean potsherds were discovered during the Swedish excavations in 1960-1963 at the Late Bronze Age settlement of Luni sul Mignone, about fifteen kilometers east of Tarquinia. These northernmost of Aegean finds discovered so far in Italy span the periods LH III A 2 to LH III C. Although Cyprus was the primary supplier of copper to the Mycenaean civilization, it was quite probably the search for this metal that brought daring Mycenaean sailors to the Tyrrhenian coast.[1]

In the eighth century B.C. colonists from Eretria and Chalcis, the ore city of Euboea, followed the route taken by their Mycenaean forefathers. They undoubtedly first took over the straits of Cumae and Messina with the intention of securing access to the copper and iron resources of northern Latium and southern Tuscany. These mineral-rich areas were at that time already in the unimpeachable possession of the Etruscans.[2]

Copper mining was also carried on in Fufluna-Populonia, according to Pseudo-Aristoteles, περὶ θαυμασίων ἀκουσμάτων, 93.[3] The importance of its harbor to the shipping of ore may go back to Villanovan times.[4] It was probably in the fourth century B.C. that Populonia increased the exploitation of the iron resources on Elba, which belonged to her.[5] Diodorus reports the first operations that took place on the island; the whole refining operation was apparently later moved to Populonia.[6] Impressive witness to this industry are the slag heaps, which have been successfully worked again since World War I. In the process whole necropolises have been uncovered; their stately edifices, partly novel in form, bear witness to the wealth attained by the leading citizens of the city in the seventh and sixth centuries B.C.[7] As proof of the early importance of Fufluna as a trade center, Minto points out that the oldest coins of Asia Minor are supposed to have been uncovered here. Unfortunately, evidence from finds is not sufficient to support such a conclusion.[8] However, if the three small gold coins with lion's head facing right and notation of value on the obverse, and smooth reverse sides (Fig. 1)[9] are to be attributed to Fufluna, as Gammurini attempted to do about a hundred years ago, then this city was ahead of the other Etruscan cities in coinage. Of course, the pieces can hardly have been issued before the first West Greek gold coins and thus at the earliest around 400 B.C.[10] A comparison with a tetradrachm of Leontinoi (Fig. 2),[11] struck around 450 B.C., shows even more clearly how individualistic the forms of the North Etruscan die cutter are. Certain details, such as the representation of the eye or the ear set over the outline,[12] are not to be found among Greek representations of lions; but the ear position is that of the protome (Fig. 4) to be considered later.

The two chariots unearthed by Minto in 1913 in a tumulus of the Cerbone necropolis were probably made in the middle of the seventh century B.C.[13] The metal revetment of one of them is decorated with a peculiar technique: figurative cut-out iron ornaments are attached to or inlaid into the bronze backing (Fig. 3a-b).[14] This apparently Caucasian technique of iron intarsia appears on only one other example in Italy, a lion protome from Praeneste (Fig. 4a-b).[15] Like the griffin protomes with the same type of rectangular sockets, which are known only in Etruria,[16] it was nailed onto the end of a member of a piece of furniture. Only sparse traces

Fig. 1a-d: Gold coins with lion heads; b-d are shown actual size.

Fig. 2: Tetradrachm from Leontinoi (2:1).

* I wish to thank Peter Ludwig of the Information Gathering Service, Harvard Student Agencies, and the editors of this volume for their help in preparing the translation.

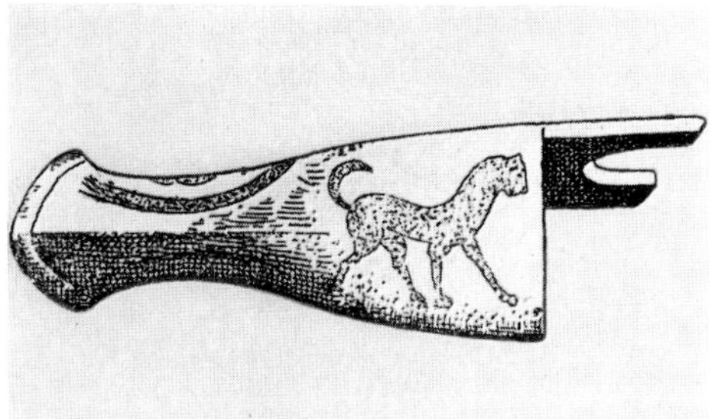

Fig. 3a-b: Revetment of a chariot from Cerbone, bronze with iron inlay.

of the iron inlays have remained preserved in the chiseled-out grooves. One band is drawn over the nose to the jaw, a second band across the forehead. On the neck and breast we can recognize a warrior with lance and shield; between them, a rampant goat. The warrior appears again at the nape of the neck, and the rampant animal, here more likely a horse, below and on both sides of him. Behind the stunted foreleg of the protome stands a griffin, whose beak shows the Etruscan tonglike stylization.[17] The dog-tooth pattern on the edge of the socket appears again on the hub of the wheel[18] of one of the chariots and on the rims of the wheels of the other, so that Brown's conjecture[19] that the protome could have been made in Populonia seems to be supported. It is not necessary to posit an immigrant craftsman from the Caucasus as Brown does. But the technique, which appears to be limited to Populonia, indicates the presence of some direct contact with the sources of Orientalizing art, perhaps via a port on the Black Sea. I have been informed that it is easier to inlay hard metal into softer metal than vice versa. Thus, although one may not reach a conclusion about the relative value of these two metals from this use of iron for decorating bronze, the unusual technique does perhaps tell something about the satisfaction and pleasure in technical experimentation which is so characteristic of Etruscan craftsmanship.

A massive, heavily corroded cast lion's head, now in a private collection (Fig. 5), is supposed to have been found in Serre di Rapolano, between Siena and Chiusi. The protome, 4.5 cm. high, rests on a 4.5 cm. square slab, 2.2 cm. thick, which was attached to iron.[20] The eyes were inlaid in another material,[21] though it is no longer possible to determine whether it was iron

Fig. 4a-b: Lion protome from Praeneste, bronze with iron inlay.

as well. This ornament for some unidentified utensil is typologically no less isolated than the head from Praeneste (Fig. 4), and, were it not for its provenience, one would assume it to have come from the Near East rather than Italy. But even there nothing is closer to the protome than are the lion heads on the gold coins discussed previously (Fig. 1). Not only do the similar contours and the applied ornamental details make them seem related, but the small heart-shaped ears also reappear, although in a different place. One might perhaps venture to classify this highly unusual animal head as a descendant of the Orientalizing piece from Praeneste, chronologically between the latter and the gold coins.

Bronze utensils and vessels from the necropolis of Poggio della Porcareccia[22] are numerous; but he who searches in the excavation publications for figurative bronzes from that rich industrial city is disappointed. The archaistic Apollo from Piombino, in the Louvre, has had to endure many interpretations, and recently someone has even called it Etruscan.[23] And the Ajax falling on his sword, in Florence, which comes from Populonia, is by no means North Etruscan.[24] In his fundamental examination of the stylistic groups of Etruscan small sculpture, P. J. Riis attributes North Etruscan characteristics to only three bronze statuettes, two of which are companion pieces (Fig. 24). Riis judges that the man from Elba (Fig. 8) has no true counterpart, aside from one statuette of unknown origin now in Florence; even in this case, the relationship does not go beyond a similarity of motif.[25] Thus, Luisa Banti had to concede in her book *Die Welt der Etrusker*, "There are no miniature bronzes which can be attributed to the city [Populonia]."[26]

Are we to assume, then, that the pious religiosity for which the Etruscans have always been known found a different form of expression in Fufluna than in more isolated Volterra, where quite a number of votive bronzes of local origin exist?[27] Or did the "slag" of profitable business so deeply bury the soul of the population that they forgot to offer thanks for rich blessings to their patron Fufluns and to the other gods, in spite of their surplus of metal? I hope it will be possible to free them of this suspicion.

Pliny the Elder claims to have seen a statue of Jupiter of vine wood in Populonia, "still well preserved after so many years." The material gives rise to the conjecture that he named the piece incorrectly or that the god Dionysos-Fufluns had attributes similar to those of Jupiter.[28] We are more concerned here with the fact that early, and quite probably native, wooden sculpture is likely to have existed in Populonia. But we turn now to a few bronze figures, half of which have appeared in the last two or three decades. Two have certainly been found in or near Populonia; three others, on which reliable sources agree, are to be connected with them. If with these as a basis we look for further related pieces, it appears after rigorous selection that three others exhibit such a resemblance that we may consider them as belonging to the same family.

A figure only 8 cm. tall, now in Florence (Fig. 6a-c), was found in the slag heaps of Populonia in 1923[29] — somewhat poorly characterized and such a simple creation that it is difficult to determine whether it represents a boy or a girl. Minto considers it undoubtedly feminine, probably because of its dress; but the "bare-knee" sleeved "mini-chiton" is probably too short for an Etruscan woman. A fisherman in the Tomba della Caccia e Pesca and the biga driver on the Monteleone chariot[30] wear such chitons with belts, and the coiffure, combed upward from the forehead, is best

Fig. 5: Lion's head protome, said to have been found in Serre di Rapolano.

Fig. 6a-c: Statuette from Populonia, Museo Archeologico Nazionale, Florence.

Fig. 7a-c: Statuette of a woman from Campiglia Marittima, Norbert Schimmel collection.

known from the Ionian kouroi of the third quarter of the sixth century, as, for example, the one from Samos whose head is now in Istanbul.[31] Further, the exaggerated back of the head, the roundish, full face, and the elongated, narrow eyes point to a distant East Greek model.[32] In spite of its static, rigid posture, this little figure may not be dated before 530 B.C. The two nude male statuettes pointed out by Riis show certain similarities in facial structure and in their rigidity, but here there is no more than a very distant geographical relationship.[33] Riis places them in Northwest Etruria, in which he includes Fiesole. The sharply bent nose-forehead line and the fleshy ears set over the hairline appear to be more individual. The brows and the lower garment hem are vigorously hatched. The sculptor also seems to have subsequently chiseled the fingers in cold work.

The statuette of a woman with lead base preserved, in the Schimmel Collection in New York, is only one centimeter larger (Fig. 7a-c). The findspot is given as Campiglia Marittima, ten kilometers north of Populonia.[34] The figure's feet are stuck into much-too-long, pointed shoes, *calcei repandi*.[35] The customary turban-like head covering, which one could most probably call a *tutulus*,[36] hides the circularly styled hair. Both hands lift gently at the chiton at hip level. A single band with punched dots ornaments the neckline. The figure is certainly somewhat more substantially built than the youth just considered, but it, too, appears quite stiff and awkward. Particularly obvious are the massive legs, the angularly cut hands with long fingers, again done in cold work, and the overly large head. The small, smiling mouth is placed directly under the nose. The almond eyes, in particular, outlined similarly to those of the statuette already discussed but placed more obliquely, evince an Ionian ideal of beauty. Again, the ears are superimposed over the hair and even over the tutulus. There is no closer connection with Vulci, to which the bronze was attributed at first, but much more probably with Populonia. This should be clearer after comparison with the following figure.

We have already mentioned this piece briefly. It is the stately male figure, 26.2 cm. tall, found in 1764 by a certain Domenico Agarini on his property on Elba and immediately turned over to the King of Naples (Fig. 8a-f), who was just in the process of building up his museum. This statuette, still on a rectangular base, was made public in 1771 in the *Antichità di Ercolano* (Fig. 8a-b) and was said to represent a god. Vulcan, the lord of the iron island,[37] was thought particularly likely. In a surprisingly progressive manner the Accademici Ercolanesi attempted a metallurgical analysis. With the aid of the "fire test" they concluded that the bronze contained silver.[38] If that conclusion is correct, then the admixture of the precious metal could have had the same purpose as in some modern forgeries: it is supposed to make casting easier and to result in an especially fine surface. The figure is completely free of flaws in any case and is covered with a uniformly thin patina, which was praised by Giglioli when he rescued the bronze from 145 years of oblivion thirty years ago.[39] He was correct in interpreting it as a votive statue of a mortal. The tangs under the feet are evidence that it was not made for the decoration of some utensil, as are most of the Etruscan bronze figures; these tangs were used for fastening the statuette into a stone base. The Accademici concluded simply on the evidence of the findspot that a citizen of Populonia gave this votive offering.

The extended right hand grasps a stafflike object which is generally interpreted as a spear, or as a *lituus* or some similar symbol of office —

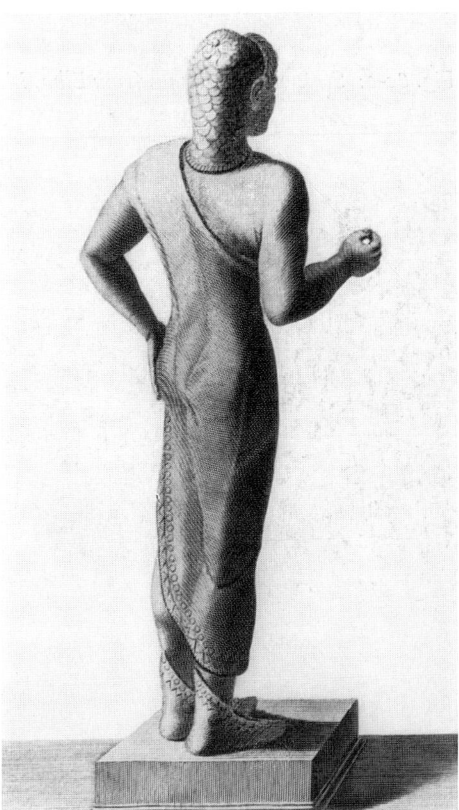

Fig. 8a-b: Statuette of a man, from Elba, Museo Nazionale, Naples; after Antichità di Ercolano *(1771).*

Fig. 8c-e: Statuette of a man, from Elba, Museo Nazionale, Naples.

Fig. 8f: Detail of head.

analogous to the sharply delineated Central Etruscan statuette from Isola di Fano, now in Florence,[40] and the man on the cippus from Fiesole, now in East Berlin (Fig. 9).[41] The relief has the larger-planed, more swollen, yet less accented rendering typical of that end of the Northwest Etruscan region opposite Populonia. Both figures also correspond to the one from Elba in that they rest their left hands on their hips. One finds this position of one hand remarkably often among archaic and late archaic Etruscan statuettes (before about 450 B.C.), in both utensil and votive bronzes. Some tentative remarks will have to suffice here. A few archaic Greek bronze statuettes place both hands on the hips. The earliest example may be the small woman from Paestum,[42] whose back was once attached to something. A projection on her head shows that she once carried some burden, thus resembling the stylistically related, although more slender and erect, somewhat later winged mirror-caryatid in the Master Bronzes exhibition (No. 75). At any rate, both are from Magna Graecia. The powerfully rendered youth, now in Boston, was found in Campania or at least was certainly produced there; it was attached to some utensil by the back of its head and its supporting plinth, apparently as a handle (Fig. 10a-b).[43] Even if it is not as immediately obvious here, as with the mirror support, the stance is certainly also functionally determined by the tectonic connection. The only Etruscan figure

Fig. 9: Cippus from Fiesole, Staatliche Museen zu Berlin.

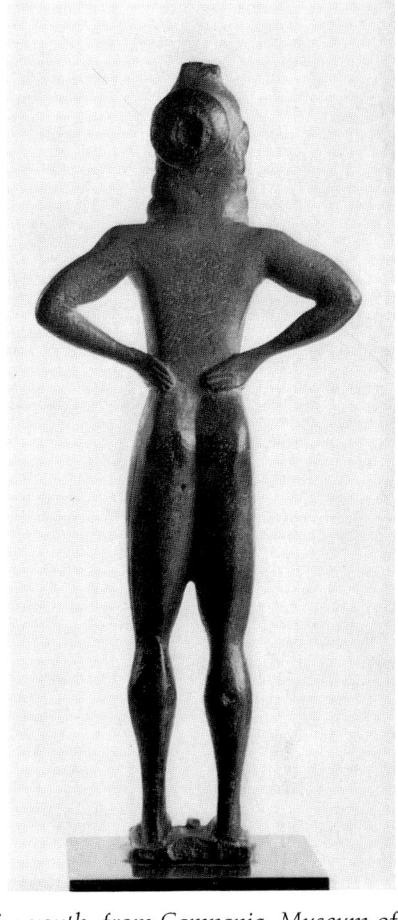

Fig. 10a-b: Utensil attachment in form of a youth, from Campania, Museum of Fine Arts, Boston.

Fig. 11a-c: Utensil attachment in form of a girl, Römisch-Germanisches Zentralmuseum, Mainz.

Fig. 12: Standing male figure, Musées royaux d'Art et d'Histoire, Brussels.

Fig. 13 (left): Standing male figure, Louvre.
Fig. 14 (right): Standing male figure, Musées royaux d'Art et d'Histoire, Brussels.

Fig. 15: Standing male figure, Musées royaux d'Art et d'Histoire, Brussels.

Fig. 16: Syrian statuette, Louvre.

known to me with both hands on its hips, however, appears to have raised itself freely from the knees (Fig. 11a-c).[44]

The placing of only one hand on the hip does not occur at all in Greek art before the beginning of the fifth century B.C., with one exception, timorously veiled, on the "trainer" on the calyx krater of the Kleophrades painter in Tarquinia.[45] It appears about ten years later in free-standing sculpture with the Athena of Euenor,[46] followed by the Oinomaos on the east pediment of the Temple of Zeus at Olympia.[47] In every case the other hand, contrappostally opposed, grasps a staff or a spear. Such a pose is suited to the expression of self-assuredness, somewhat imperious.

The man from Elba, then, anticipates this motif of Greek art. As J. C. Balty has shown, the motif already had a long history in Etruria. He has collected more than 40 male statuettes, all clothed in loincloths, almost all approximately 9 cm. high; almost every one stands in a severe pose on a plinth pierced in the middle, the left hand on the hip and the pierced right hand stretched forward (Figs. 12-15).[48] The examples in Brussels (Figs. 14-15) have the whole spear preserved, whereas on the others only a piece of the shaft still remains in the hole in the hand. The weapon is usually made of iron, which calls attention to its importance and reminds one of the iron intarsias of Populonia. Balty's explanation, that the figures are offering their spears to some god and that the figures themselves are votive offerings, makes sense. Furthermore, setting the date of the beginning of this series in the third quarter of the seventh century and the end of the series toward the middle of the sixth century is well founded. North Etruria is clearly the center of its distribution area, which stretches out over the Po Valley, into the Danube region, and into Provence; the starting point here might well be in Volterra, which had political and economic ties with Populonia. The type no longer appears south of Chiusi.[49] A few unpublished figures from the late sixth century, which have gotten rid of their loincloths under Greek influence,[50] constitute a transition to the votive figure from Elba, which far excells its predecessors in size and artistic expression.

Fig. 17a-b: Male figurine from the Menelaion, Sparta.

The interpretation of the spear-holding figures previously discussed leads to the question of whether some particular significance might not also be attributed to the stereotyped pose of the left arm. The most reasonable conjecture is that touching the loins seems to emphasize virility, to intensify the prayer for its strengthening. This would correspond to the female "pudicitia" gesture, which the Etruscans adopted from the Near East.[51] Actually, the left hand resting on the hip occurs in a few Syrian figures which are, however, some 500 years older and usually belong to a pair (Fig. 16).[52] Again, they hold weapons in their outstretched right hands.[53]

The technique of iron intarsia could have come directly to Populonia from the Near East. The type of female figure with bent forearms, and the male costume which occurs in bronzes that on the evidence of form and distribution belong among the "Schurzkouroi" are both derived from Eastern models. The finds from the tumuli in Florence show that Orientalizing culture pushed deep into the interior of North Etruria without perceptible interruption.[54] We can consider the motif of the hand on the hip, appearing first in the heyday of Oriental influence, to be of the same origin. Its single exceptional appearance in Greece before the "Severe Style" period is also evidence for this. The 6.5 cm. tall statuettes from the Menelaion at Sparta (Figs. 17a-18b) are dated by pottery found in context with them to the Laconian II period, at the end of the seventh century or the beginning

Fig. 18a-b: Male figurine from the Menelaion, Sparta.

Fig. 19: Back of the head of an Attic kouros, Glyptothek, Munich.

of the sixth century B.C. Wace[55] presented them 60 years ago with the remark that "the two small men, from the close similarity between them in size and style and from the curved shape of the feet, obviously stood facing one another on the handles of a bowl." It is evident that they belong together. In the same manner as the related North Etruscan statuettes, both forearms of the statuette in Fig. 18 are bent forward, while its pendant repeats the scheme with which we are now familiar; here, however, his loincloth is missing, and the right hand is extended horizontally before him. Since this unique pair cannot be directly related to the North Etruscan votive figures, the typological agreement can only be explained by the assumption that they have a common Eastern origin.

We have seen that "Schurzkouros" type spread its influence far beyond the old North Etruscan borders in late archaic times. At times the spear was replaced by some sign of office, which, by the way, could also have been a spear that had lost its original meaning.[56] After 500 B.C. the motif of the hand on the hip must also have made a transition from Greek art to Etruscan. However, it appears in Etruria far more often than in Greece; in sculpture at least, one may ascribe it to the old connections and in part to its retaining some remnants of its original meaning; yet also it must surely reflect the fact that from the front view a distinct projection of the unengaged arm satisfied the Etruscan impulse toward movement and decorative elaboration. Both of these form an intrinsic part of Etruscan art.

Let us turn again to the figure from Elba (Fig. 8). Its feet are in the customary *calcei repandi* with high flaps over the heels. The garment, thrown across the left shoulder, appears to have been cut round, so that when the piece was first published it was called a toga worn *sine tunica.*[57] A zigzag-and-circle pattern ornaments the shoes and the hem of the gown in the same way. The hair is cut somewhat shorter than that of the little boy in Florence (Fig. 6), but it still falls onto the shoulders, and the bangs combed upward from the forehead are also repeated. The bangs are only incised, whereas the hair that falls downward is decorated in an unusual pattern. The bottom edge is hatched, and the master has decorated the rest with small half circles that were applied with a punch after casting, as were the little circles on the shoes, toga border, and for the pupils of the eyes. In the inventory of the Naples Museum a helmet is mentioned, which is supposed to have been worn by the youth. Giglioli believed that he recognized "una specie di rete o cuffia," a sort of net or cap.[58] But the scaled pattern to which he must refer is nothing more than a simplified version of short locks covering the back of the head. Since they are arranged concentrically to the crown, a coiffure resembling parallel strings of beads — such as the one worn by the Ionian kouroi mentioned previously — cannot have been intended; rather, the "voluted locks coiffure" is meant, which we recognize particularly from the Attic boy in Munich (about 540-530 B.C.) (Fig. 19).[59] A nude Etruscan spear-thrower of unknown provenience, now in the Cabinet des Médailles in Paris (Fig. 20a-b),[60] shows this spiral curl coiffure in a plastic rendering. In this case the coiffure has not been done later in cold work, but was worked on the clay model prior to casting. Although the spirals in the hair of the trim and accurately modeled boy from Chiusi, now in the British Museum (Fig. 21),[61] are deeply sunken into the hair cap, the roundness of the spirals reveals that they were previously impressed into the clay model, apparently with some special tool. The locks on the graceful Etruscan boy of unknown origin, now in Dresden (Fig. 22a-c),[62] as on a few

Fig. 20a: Spear-thrower, Cabinet des Médailles, Paris.

Fig. 20b (left): Detail of head, spear-thrower, Cabinet des Médailles, Paris.
Fig. 21 (right): Detail of head, nude youth, from Chiusi, British Museum.

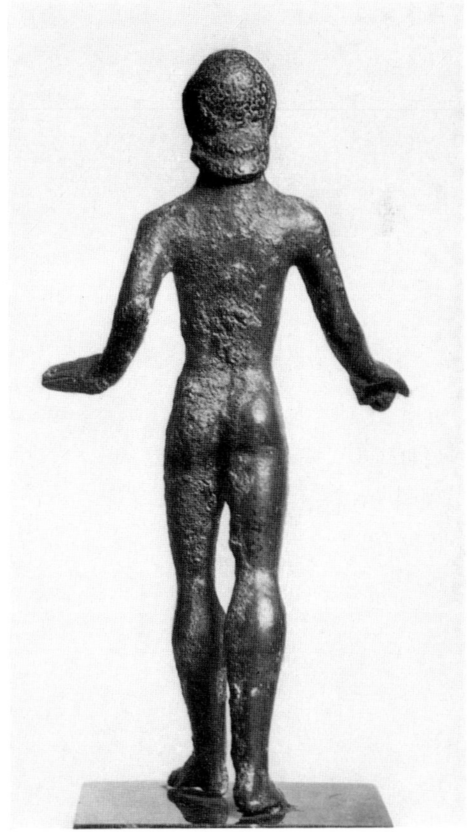

Fig. 22a-c: Standing youth, Skulpturensammlung, Dresden.

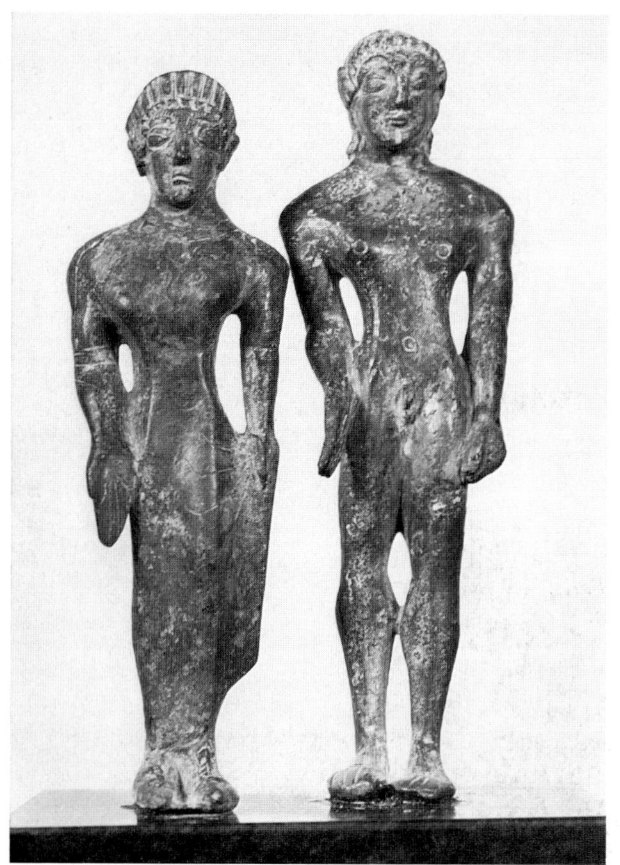

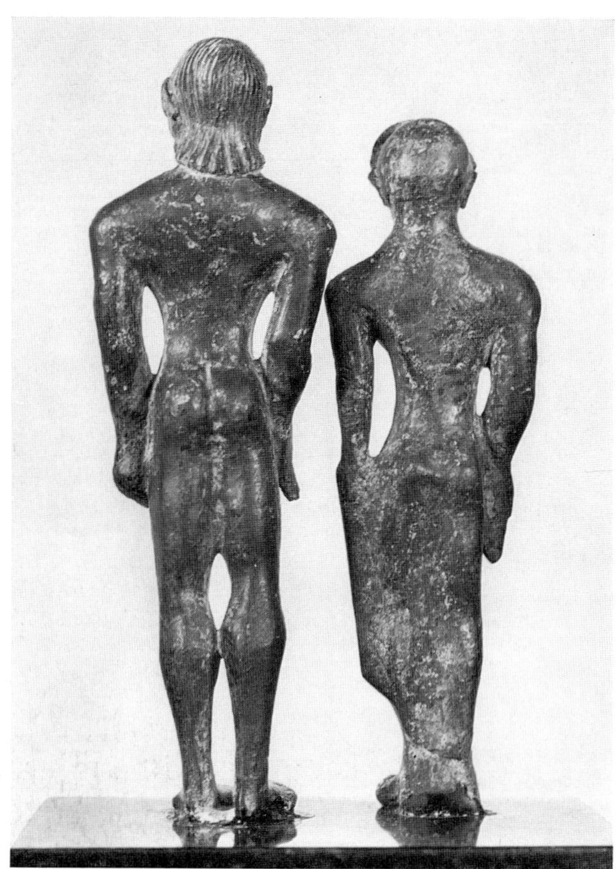

Fig. 23a-d: Standing male and female figures, Emil G. Bührle collection, Zurich.

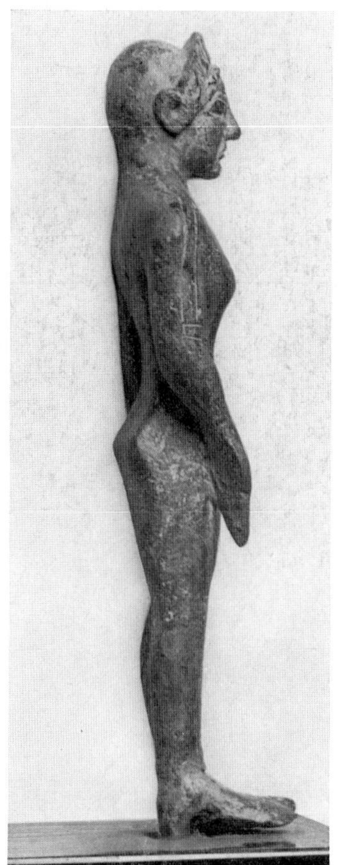

small Vulcian candelabrum figures,[63] close to a circle and are no longer spirals. They are the latest members of this series, which began in about the last quarter of the sixth century. No artist of Greece or Magna Graecia is known to have patterned the head of a miniature bronze with this mechanical, mass-production technique.[63a]

Type, clothing, and technique of the bronze from Elba are in the local Etruscan tradition; the Greek influence prevails only in details such as the stylish coiffure and becomes evident in the more powerful, more voluminous, almost monumental modeling of the body — as compared with the older figures. But even in this respect the fundamental simplicity of the forms remains native, even provincial. In contrast the spear-thrower from nearby Chiusi (Fig. 21) seems so much more effective and gentleman-like, so to speak. The "primitivismo della visione" led Giglioli to date the Populonian figure at the beginning of the sixth century. But we see from the Greek style that it can hardly have been made before 520 B.C.[64] and that its rustic nature is not a matter of its date but of the place where it was made.

A similar profile relates the man from Elba to the little figure from Populonia discussed first (Fig. 6b) and to the kore in the Schimmel Collection, allegedly discovered ten kilometers north of Populonia (Fig. 7b). We find the characteristic indentation between the receding forehead and the nose, the perpendicular hatching used on the brows of the former statuette, the ears superimposed over the hair cap, the generally ample proportions, and the heavy legs. The pursed lips, high above the heavy chin and close under the nose, are not found in the Vulcian bronzes; they are too pronouncedly individual to be called characteristic of the general style of the period. Granted, the characteristics described thus far would not suffice for assigning the three bronzes to a common place of origin, were it not that they were all found in the territory of Populonia. I hope, however, to be able to outline and define here even more clearly the stylistic individuality of the archaic bronzes of that city.

More than ten years ago a pair of bronzes, obviously belonging together and reported to have been found at Piombino, entered the collection of Emil Bührle in Zurich (Fig. 23a-g).[65] Their heights, not including the tangs inserted into the stands under their feet, were 16.1 cm. for the boy and 14.8 cm. for the girl. The strongest imaginable family resemblance not only connects these two figures, which are undoubtedly by the same hand, but also associates them with the man from Elba (Fig. 8). Their most obvious common trait is the general form of the bodies, characterized by rhythmic swellings and curvaceous contours, particularly evident in the broadly expansive contour of the chest of all three figures — boy, girl, and man. Their shoulders and heads are asymmetrically placed — those of the boy to the viewer's left, those of the girl to the right. The figure from Elba has been carefully tooled after casting. The incised lines on the girl are limited to representing garment folds, the border of an unpatterned hem, and the shoelaces. Her eyebrows are also incised, however (Fig. 23g). Her hair flows down her back into the gown without demarcation, while the boy's hair has been tooled after casting, this time, however, without the use of a punch. The nipples and navel have been made with a punch. We notice again the indented forehead-to-nose line (Fig. 23f), the receding chin, and the unusually high skull of Ionian type, probably represented most distinctly in Etruscan art on the Caeretan hydrias.[66] Again, the ears are superim-

Fig. 23e-g: Details of heads.

posed on the hair cap. The stephane of the girl is an adornment we know from Greek korai.[67]

The question of the significance of the gesture of the pair is more difficult to answer. It does not seem as demonstrative as that which Neumann calls the gesture of greeting in Greek art; yet it would hardly seem to be a gesture of prayer, even though we are concerned with votive statuettes.[68] In some figures when the right hand grasps a gift the surface of the left hand is stretched obliquely downward, as here. We will apparently have to be satisfied with the general interpretation that the gesture expresses turning toward and addressing the god.

Fig. 24: Pair of votive figures from Populonia.

While I know no male-female pairs of votive statuettes in Greek art,[69] this is by no means the only Etruscan example. An older find from Populonia should be mentioned first (Fig. 24).[70] In size, style, and provenience the girl and boy belong together. The Greek prototype has already imposed itself upon these two figures, now in Florence, to a much greater extent than is the case with their counterparts in Zurich. For this reason they may be dated in the second quarter of the fifth century. The less articulated, flowing forms, however, are still clearly in the local tradition, the beginnings of which concern us here. Among the best-known Etruscan bronzes is the pair of about the same date, from Monteguragazza in Bologna; it has also served as a model for several forgeries. Riis has attributed the pair to Vulci, although a real stylistic parallel has not yet been established and we know the bronze work of Vulci exclusively in the form of vessel and utensil decoration.[71] Two statuettes from a votive deposit in Brolio agree in stance (Fig. 25)[72] with the later pair from Populonia (Fig. 24). Others have already concluded that both are by the same hand, and they were probably offered at the same time. They were produced just about 500 B.C. in a North Etruscan workshop. A still more archaic pair, although perhaps not older, comes from the new excavation at Marzabotto (Fig. 26);[73] it is also undoubtedly of local origin. Now, after a first tentative look around, there are five examples. It is not mere chance that they all originated in North Etruria, just as, as demonstrated here, the migration of the "Schurzkouros"

Fig. 25 (left): Pair of votive figures from Brolio.
Fig. 26 (right): Pair of votive figures from Marzabotto.

Fig. 27a

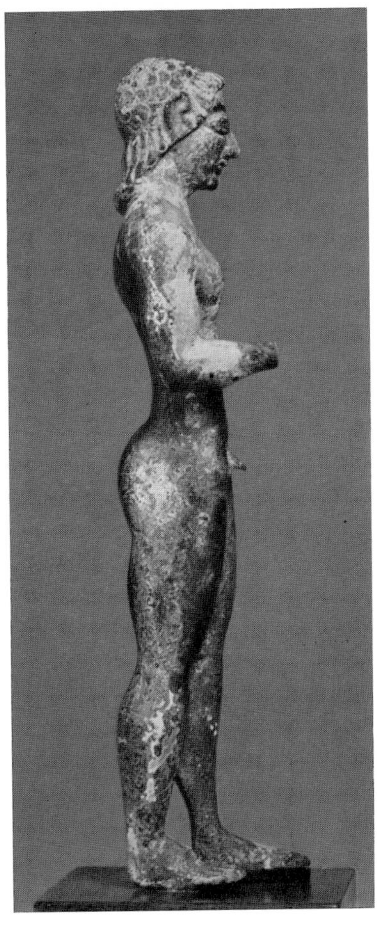

Fig. 27b

Fig. 27c

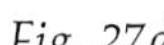

Fig. 27d

Fig. 27e

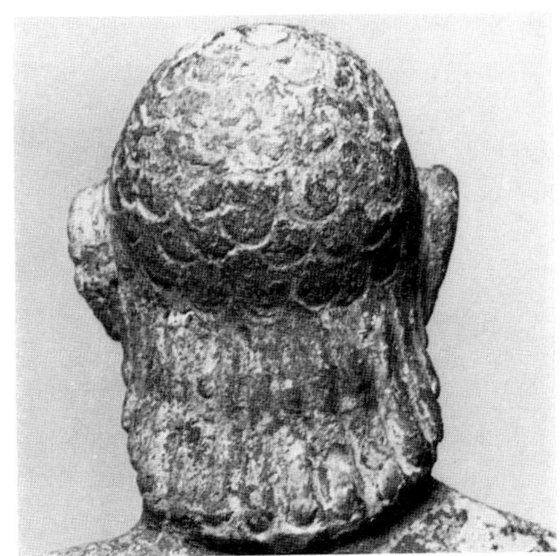

Fig. 27f

Fig. 27a-f: Nude youth, Antikenmuseum, Basel.

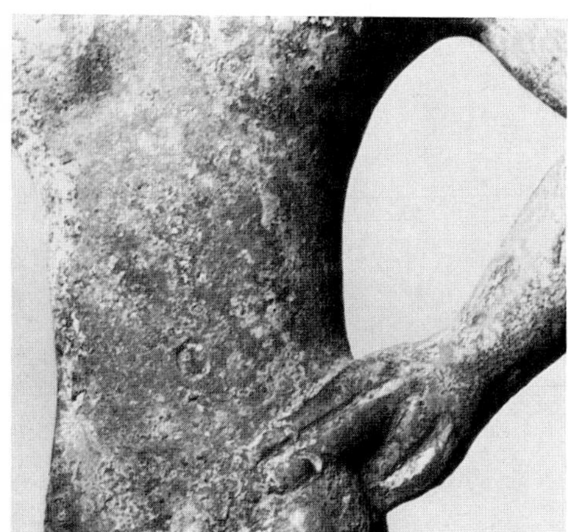

Fig. 27g: Detail of hand, nude youth, Antikenmuseum, Basel.

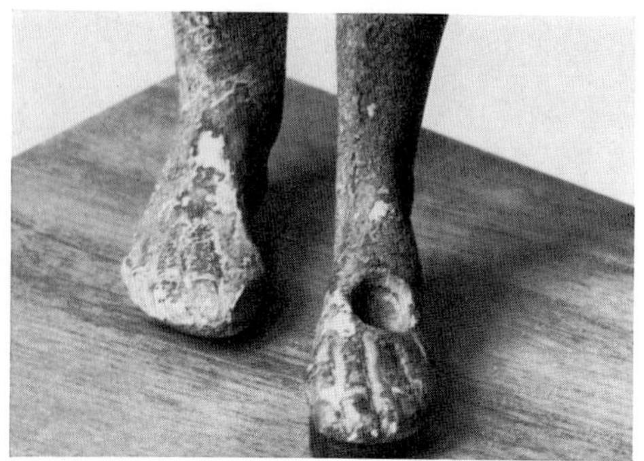

Fig. 27h: Detail of feet, nude youth, Antikenmuseum, Basel.

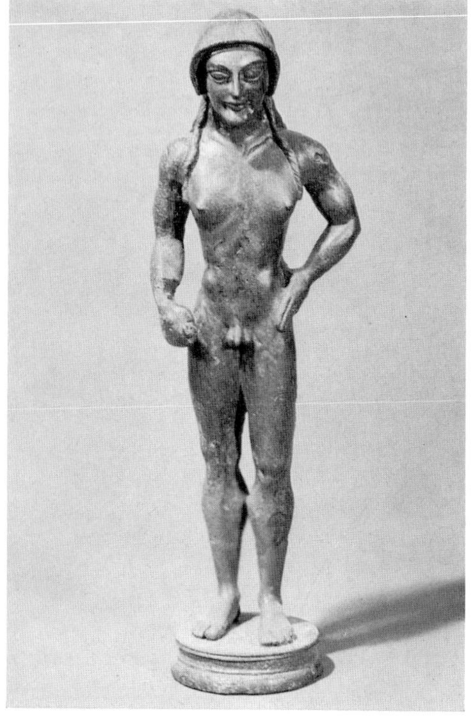

Fig. 28: Youth, from Falterona, Louvre.

type did not overstep the same southern boundary. These groups probably represent bridal pairs or married couples presenting themselves thus to the god. The special position of the woman in Etruscan society and family — as we know it from the literary tradition, from pictures of banquets, and from tomb paintings[74] — is also reflected in these votive couples.

In assigning the following figures to the school of Populonia, we shall have to depend completely on stylistic criteria. It is said of the boy in the Käppeli Collection in the Antikenmuseum in Basel (Fig. 27a-h)[75] that he was found near Bracciano; this is highly improbable. I do not know of any similar finds made in that area. Stylistically this statuette, 20.4 cm. tall, forms the link between the man from Elba (Fig. 8) and the boy in Zurich (Fig. 23). In all three figures the slender-hipped body build is employed especially to create an animated and elegant contour. The broad chest this time occurs in a somewhat angular form. Again, the head rests eccentrically on the shoulders. The motif of the left hand on the hip and the extended right hand appears again, as in the piece from Elba; however, this time the left hand is not laid flat on the hip, but the fingers grasp around it in a late archaic-mannerist fashion, just as in the boy from Falterona in the Louvre (Fig. 28).[76] The position of the right hand can no longer be determined; perhaps it was simply extended in an "addressing" manner. The legs are set somewhat more broadly and freely than in the two related figures; holes in the feet suggest that the piece was attached with some special dowels to a base, which here also might have been made of lead. The same hatchings border the hair as on the boy in Zurich, but the main portion of the hair is covered with the scale pattern which we saw on the Naples figure (Figs. 27e, f; 8a, d, e). When we place the faces next to each other, we see that all three little men have inherited the dimple on the chin, the family characteristic. Some Greek kouroi, such as the Milani one in Florence (from about the middle of the sixth century) or the head in Catania (about 500 B.C.),[77] show a faint trace of this trait, although always only immediately below the lower lip and without cleaving the chin. The cleft appears deeper, on the other hand, on the Lydian ivory head in Istanbul.[78] The high brows and the low forehead, the short lower lip, and the outer ear superimposed over the hair cap are characteristics familiar to us.

The 16.5 cm. tall nude spear thrower, which has been transferred from the Simkhovitch collection to that of Norbert Schimmel (No. 159; Fig. 29a-c),[79] is unfortunately without information as to its provenience. Nevertheless, and even though the piece appears to have been less carefully worked, I should like to include it in our series. It has the angular, very extended chest contour of the boy in Basel and shares with him and the Zurich bridegroom the same form and treatment of the edge of the hair cap, over which the ears are superimposed. The relationship is more convincing when one compares the rear view of the bronzes of the Bührle collection (Fig. 23b) with that of the Schimmel collection piece (Fig. 29c). I should like to point out only the shoulders, displaced toward the right, the extremely slender hips, and the powerful calves. The main surface of the hair is smooth, as is that of the girl in Zurich.

The Zurich girl actually has two sisters. In 1960, Matossian, in Lucerne, acquired the 15 cm. tall female figure, who holds a bud in the tips of the fingers of her extended right hand (Fig. 30a-c).[80] The vigorously curved, flowing contours, the prominent shoulders, the relative lack of depth dimension, and the left hand webbed to the gown appear again. Only the

Fig. 29a-c: Spear-thrower, Norbert Schimmel collection.

Fig. 30a-c: Standing female figure, Matossian collection.

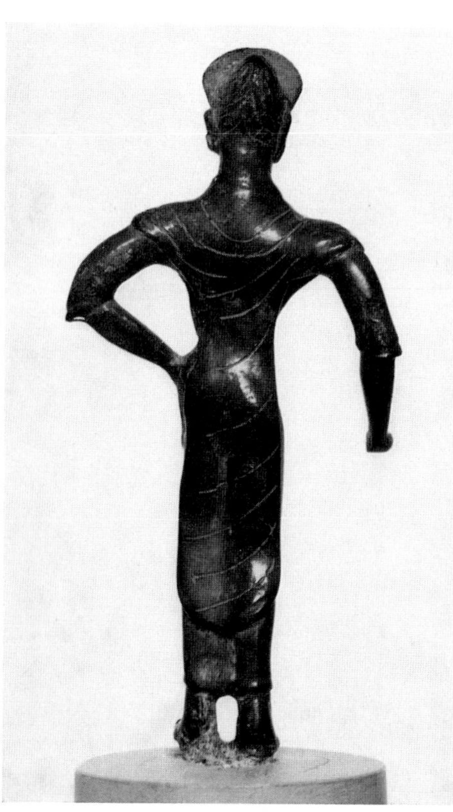

Fig. 31a-b: Standing female figure, Archäologisches Institut, Göttingen.

folds above the legs are tooled. Here, too, the stephane consists of a cord-and-tongue pattern. This time the hair falling onto the shoulder blades has been incised after casting. Little circles and zigzags make up the pattern of the gown's border at the neck, as on the man from Elba (Fig. 8), though the circles on the girl perhaps represent a necklace. Again, the ears are superimposed over the hair. The skull arches out high over the stephane. The profile of the large face is a more pure rendition of the Ionian type than is the head of the girl in Fig. 23c. But the traits which they have in common — which differentiate these two bronzes from any others known — stand out strongly indeed. We may without hesitation include this little work among the bronze figures of Populonia's leading atelier. It must have been produced there about 520 or 510 B.C. The large lead cone under the feet can be noted as a regional characteristic, at least until the possibility of using isotope analysis as an aid in determining the source of the material, and thereby of the statuettes themselves, can be realized.[81]

I should like to introduce a 14 cm. high statuette of unknown provenience, now in Göttingen, as the second sister of the bride in Zurich (Fig. 31a-c).[82] Let us now simply allow the illustrations to speak for themselves and be satisfied with a few key words: contours — wide, drawn out shoulders — folds merely incised, as in Fig. 23a — hem of the little coat ornamented with the circle punch, the same punch used for patterning the stephane and the pupils and also for the gown hem and eyes of the man from Elba (Fig. 8). And as with the latter, the hand, turned downward, is laid flat on the hip, although otherwise the Etruscan female dressed figures of this time lift up at the dress in the manner of the Greek korai.[83] It seems reasonable to presume that the Greek scheme has here been assimilated into that of the North Etruscan spear-throwers, especially if one considers the votive couples, where the Etruscan urge toward symmetrical order and plasticity[84] is most apparent. The disc-shaped earrings, which by the way are also worn by the girl from Campiglia (Fig. 7 b), could have been taken over from the Greek korai.[85] The profile does not recede as much as that of the man in Fig. 8e. In place of the scale pattern, which is only appropriate for representing the male lock coiffure, there is an equally rigid schematic net pattern used over the head. The little crosses in the fields of the net make it clear that a hood is intended.[86] This figure, too, was set into lead.[87] W. Schiering has interpreted this charming figure from his museum with meticulous care, even though he does not attempt a precise determination of its provenience; he believes that "the displacement of the buttocks and shoulders already shows the influence of Greek models of the Severe Style."[88] Nevertheless, we have recognized the displacement of the shoulders to the side as a characteristic of our Populonian family and should therefore prefer not to attribute so much importance to such a subtle stylistic criterion as the slightly asymmetrical formation of the gluteals. Dating the piece at the end of the sixth century, therefore, appears most reasonable in this case, too.

According to dealers two very significant pieces, Nos. 164 and 168 in the Master Bronzes exhibition, are also supposed to have come from Populonia.[89] A still larger male figure now in the Hirshhorn collection[90] previously traveled with these two pieces along the tortuous paths of the art market. I ran across them about thirteen years ago in Zurich. Reliable indications lead to a place northwest of Siena, which, as far as I know, otherwise has little role in the art trade. The triad was apparently put up for sale there for the first time. If — as was reported, and is unlikely to have been invented — a stone plinth with traces of the attachment of feet was shown with them, we may conjecture that the quite weighty complex was not transported over very great distances. Populonia-Piombio, a name which sounds much more likely than that of the village with which we are concerned, would have lain about one hundred kilometers away. In spite of not insignificant differences in style, one might identify the North Etruscan characteristics of the three figures, especially of the girl and the Hirshhorn kouros; we are forced to postpone such an examination until another opportunity is offered, however.

A figure in Basel is associated with the youth in the Hirshhorn collection; E. Berger says that in quality and style it stands alone in Etruscan art.[91] R. Käppeli had acquired it with the same hardly credible designation of provenience that was given for the figure in Fig. 27. Because of the usual secretive methods in such affairs, it was impossible to find out if it was on the market at the same time and came from the same source. This addition to the group of three does not really contribute much of significance to establishing a connection with the series of works assembled above; and the later pair in Florence (Fig. 24) appears to frustrate any attempt to rescue for Populonia — by assuming a break in the local tradition — these richer creations so much nearer to Greek art.

Thus, for now we must be satisfied with the present results. The seven statuettes (nine, including the somewhat later pair in Florence) still suffice for absolving the rich Fufluna from a reputation for complete lack of art or pious nature.

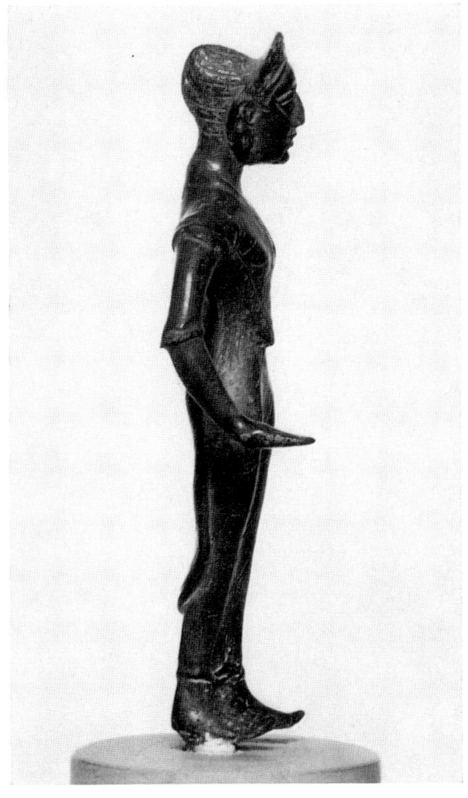

Fig. 31c: Standing female figure, Archäologisches Institut, Göttingen.

Notes

The following abbreviations are used, in addition to those outlined on p. xiv:

Balty I	J. C. Balty, "Un centre de production de bronzes figurés de l'Étrurie septentrionale, Volterra ou Arezzo?" *Bulletin de l'Institut Belge de Rome,* XXXIII (1961), 5 ff.
Balty II	J. C. Balty, "Un centre de production de bronzes figurés de l'Étrurie septentrionale. Note additionnelle," *Bulletin de l'Institut Belge de Rome,* XXXVII (1965), 137 ff.
Banti, *Welt*	L. Banti, *Die Welt der Etrusker* (Zurich, 1960).
EAA	*Enciclopedia dell'arte antica classica e orientale,* I-VII (Rome, 1958-1966).
Giglioli, *AE*	G. Q. Giglioli, *Arte etrusca* (Milan, 1935).
Kat. Köln	I. and H. Jucker *et al., Kunst und Leben der Etrusker,* exhibition catalogue (Cologne, 1956).
Minto, *Necropoli*	A. Minto, *Populonia. La Necropoli arcaica* (Florence, 1922).
Minto, *Populonia*	A. Minto, *Populonia* (Florence, 1943).
Mostra	N. Alfieri *et al.,* "La Mostra dell'Etruria Padana e della città di Spina," exhibition catalogue (Bologna, 1960).
Riis, *Tyrrhenika*	P. J. Riis, *Tyrrhenika* (Copenhagen, 1941).

1 A. W. van Buren, "News Letter from Rome," *AJA,* LXVIII (1964), 375; C. E. Ostenberg, "Luni sul Mignone e problemi della preistoria d'Italia," *Skrifter Svenska Inst. Rom, Acta,* XXV (1967), 245 ff. The Aegean "colonies" in southern Spain and Portugal were already established for the metal trade at the beginning of the Bronze Age. On the following see H. Jucker, *AA* (1967), 619 ff.

2 J. Boardman, *The Greeks Overseas* (Baltimore, 1964), 180 ff.; G. Buchner, "Pithekussai, Oldest Greek Colony in the West," *Expedition,* VIII, No. 4 (1966), 15 ff.; A. D. Trendall, "Archaeology in South Italy and Sicily, 1964-66," *Archae-*

ological Reports for 1966-67 (1967), 30; cf. H. Jucker in K. Schefold, *Die Griechen und ihre Nachbarn*, Propyläen-Kunstgeschichte, I (Berlin, 1967), 310.

3 *Aristoteles*, ed. by I. Bekker (2nd ed.; Berlin, 1960), II, 837; Minto, *Populonia*, 30 ff.; Balty I, 29 f.; *EAA*, VI (1965), 378 ff. (P. Bocci).

4 Minto, *Populonia*, 56 ff.; *RE*, XXII (1953), 97 ff. (G. Radke).

5 Minto, *Populonia*, 33.

6 Diodorus i. 13. 1 f.; Minto, *Populonia*, 34.

7 Minto, *Necropoli*; Minto, *Populonia*, 36 ff., 76 ff., 160 ff., pl. 21:1; Å. Åkerström, *Studien über die etruskischen Gräber* (Uppsala, 1934), 139 ff.; M. Demus-Quatember, *Etruskische Grabarchitektur* (Baden-Baden, 1958), 17 ff., figs. 1 f.

8 G. F. Gammurini, "Notizie di ripostigli," *Periodico di numismatica e sfragistica per la storia d'Italia*, IV (1872), 209; Minto, *Populonia*, 220; S. P. Noe, "A Bibliography of Greek Coin Hoards," *Numismatic Notes and Monographs*, LXXVIII (New York: American Numismatic Society, 1937), no. 226 (Cecina).

9 Bern, Bernisches Historisches Museum, 213.25 Litra. Diameter 11.7 cm., weight 1.40 gm. All three denominations Ad. Hess, AG, Lucerne, and Bank Leu and Co., Zurich, *Auktion*, XXXI (1966), nos. 10-12, pl. 1.

10 G. F. Gammurini, "Le monete d'oro etrusche," *Periodico di numismatica e sfragistica*, VI (1874), 58 ff.; Minto, *Populonia*, 220 ff. (not aware of L. Cesano, *Tipi monetali etruschi* [Rome, 1926]). G. K. Jenkins, "Greek Coins Recently Acquired by the British Museum," *NC*, 6th ser., XV (1955), 131 f.; Banti, *Welt*, 90. As F. Panvini Rosati has been kind enough to inform me, no stratigraphically dated finds exist to date.

11 Collection H. Krähenbühl, Steffisburg. From Münzen und Medaillen AG, Basel, *Auktion*, XXVIII (1964), no. 46; *Antike Kunst*, catalogue of an exhibition in Solothurn (Bern, 1967), no. 457, pl. 52.

12 The tetradrachm in Fig. 2 has a flaw at the very same place; I can hardly venture to conjecture that a coin of Leontinoi of this die served as a model.

13 A. Minto, *NSc* (1914), 453 ff.; Minto, *Necropoli*, 131 ff.; Minto, *Populonia*, 118 ff.; Banti, *Welt*, 88 f.

14 Museo Archeologico Nazionale, Florence, photo N. 17524. Figure 3b after Minto, *Populonia*, fig. 42b. F. Nicosia, "Radiografie di bronzi antichi," *StEtr*, XXXV (1967), 248 f., figs. 4-5, pl. 43. In spite of the flood catastrophe G. Maetzke sent me photographs, for which I sincerely thank him once again.

15 Munich, Antikensammlungen, Inv. 1; height 12.8 cm. H. Mühlestein, *Die Kunst der Etrusker* (Berlin, 1929), figs. 114 f.; W. L. Brown, *The Etruscan Lion* (Oxford, 1960), 21 f., pl. 10 a 1-2. I thank D. Ohly for photographs and permission to illustrate the piece.

16 D. G. Mitten, "Two Griffin Protomes," *Fogg Art Museum Acquisitions* (Cambridge, Mass., 1964), 11 ff.

17 U. Jantzen, *Griechische Greifenkessel* (Berlin, 1955), 80 ff., pl. 59; C. D. Curtis, "The Bernardini Tomb," *MAAR*, III (1919), pl. 38.

18 Minto, *Necropoli*, pl. 10; Minto, *Populonia*, 121, fig. 39b, pl. 26. The closest parallel is a Near Eastern club from Teheran: J. M. Birmingham, "The Overland Route across Anatolia in the Eighth and Seventh Centuries B.C.," *AnatSt*, XI (1961), 192, fig. 10 (erroneously quoted as no. 7).

19 Brown, *Etruscan Lion* (n. 15), 21 f.

20 In the collection of H. Vollmöller, Zurich, whom I thank for permission to study and publish the piece. The handwritten note was read by its owner as "Serre di Popolano," which, as far as I know, does not exist.

21 Cf. Jantzen, *Greifenkessel* (n. 17) for griffin heads in various techniques.

22 Minto, *NSc* (1940), 376 ff.; Minto, *Populonia*, 137 ff.

23 G. M. A. Richter, *Archaic Greek Kouroi* (London, 1960), no. 181, figs. 533-540. B. Ridgway, "The Bronze Apollo from Piombino in the Louvre," *Antike Plastik*, VII (Berlin, 1968), 43 ff. After renewed study of the original in June 1969, I am now inclined to believe that the work is Western Greek.

24 L. A. Milani, *NSc* (1908), 207 f., fig. 12; *idem*, "L'Aiace suicida di Populonia," *BdA*, II (1908), 361 ff.; Giglioli, *AE*, pl. 217:1-2; Minto, *Populonia*, 186, pl. 50; Riis, *Tyrrhenika*, 91, with n. 3.

25 Riis, *Tyrrhenika*, 143; G. Q. Giglioli, "Un bronzo etrusco arcaico dell' Elba . . .," *StEtr*, II (1928), pl. 4:6.

26 Banti, *Welt*, 89. Cf. *EAA*, VI (1965), 380 (P. Bocci).

27 Riis, *Tyrrhenika*, 141 f.; Balty I and II; E. Fiumi, "La facies arcaica del territorio volterrano," *StEtr*, XXIX (1961), 253 ff., esp. 272 ff., 284 f.; *EAA*, VII (1966), 1198 f. (E. Fiumi).

28 Pliny *N.H.* xiv. 7; *RE*, VII (1910), 210 f. (Thulin); *RE*, XXII (1953), 94 f. (G. Radke); *EAA*, III (1960), 750 (A. Comotti); G. Radke, *Die Götter Altitaliens* (Münster, 1965), 135 f.

29 Florence, Museo Archeologico Nazionale, 88927. A. Minto, *NSc* (1924), 29, fig. 15 (sketch); Minto, *Populonia*, 178 f., pl. 46:1a-b; Riis, *Tyrrhenika*, 143. I thank G. Caputo for photographs and permission for reproduction.

30 M. Pallottino, *La peinture étrusque* (Geneva, 1953), 51; Jucker (n. 2), pl. XXIX and 401. Perhaps also the seated official on the Campanian plaques: F. Roncalli, *Le lastre dipinte da Cerveteri* (Florence, 1965), pl. 6. The flute-player on the Chigi vase: P. E. Arias and B. B. Shefton, *A History of Greek Vase Painting* (London, 1962), pls. 16, IV.

31 F. Eckstein, "Archaischer Jünglingskopf in Istanbul," *Antike Plastik*, I (Berlin, 1962), 47 ff., pls. 45 ff.; *Art Treasures of Turkey*, exhibition catalogue (Washington, D.C.: Smithsonian Institution, 1967), no. 125; B. Ashmole, "An Archaic Fragment from Halicarnassos," *Festschrift Andreas Rumpf . . .* (Cologne, 1952), 8.

32 E. Langlotz, *Die kulturelle und künstlerische Hellenisierung der Küsten des Mittelmeeres durch die Stadt Phokaia* (Cologne, 1966), pls. 57 f.

33 Riis, *Tyrrhenika*, 143, pl. 23:1-3.

34 I am thankful for the helpfulness and liberality of the owner and to D. G. Mitten for photographs and the opportunity to study the figure. The Queens College Art Collection, *An Exhibition of Pre-Christian Objects from the Regions of the Near East, Egypt and the Mediterranean* (Flushing, N.Y., 1958), no. 135; H. Hoffmann, *The Beauty of Ancient Art: The Norbert Schimmel Collection*, catalogue of an exhibition at the Fogg Art Museum (Mainz, 1964), no. 41. On Campiglia see L. A. Stella, *La civiltà micenea nei documenti contemporanei* (Rome, 1965), 193 ff. and 196, n. 8 on procuring metal in Mycenaean times.

35 *DarSag*, I:2, 819 f. (E. Saglio). Cf. O. Lau, *Schuster und Schusterhandwerk in der griechisch-römischen Literatur und Kunst* (Bonn, 1967), 115, 147.

36 *RE*, 2nd series, VII (1948), 1627 f. (R. Kreis-von Schaewen). A. Rumpf has objected to the name.

37 Naples, Museo Nazionale, 5534. Photos were placed at our disposal by A. De Franciscis. *Delle antichità di Ercolano*, VI (Naples, 1771), III ff.; Giglioli, *StEtr*, 1928 (n. 25), 49 ff., pl. 4:1-4; Mühlestein, *Kunst* (n. 15), figs. 190 f.; A. Solari, *Vita pubblica e privata degli Etruschi* (Florence, 1931), 93; Giglioli, *AE*, pl. 83; Riis, *Tyrrhenika*, 143, pl. 23:4; E. H. Richardson, "The Etruscan Origins of Early Roman Sculpture," *MAAR*, XXI (1953), 116 with n. 162 and fig. 35; M. Pallottino, I. and H. Jucker, *Etruskische Kunst* (Zurich, 1955), fig. 65; Kat. Köln, no. 280; Balty I, 37, n. 2; E. H. Richardson, "An Archaic Etruscan Libation Bearer," *The Art Quarterly*, XIX (1956), 125 ff., figs. 10-12. The author sees the relationship between the bronze in Toledo and that in Naples, but she has concluded that the latter was dependent upon the former. The autopsy, however, has strengthened my conviction that the kouros in Toledo is a modern forgery which was surely made in imitation of the statuette from Elba, not before Giglioli's publication in 1928. Considering the nonantique, characterless style of the whole figure and especially of the head, as well as the bad patina and the casting flaws, I should expect it to be from one of the very productive forgers' workshops in Orvieto or Rome, from which a series of large bronzes have come, for example, H. Mühlestein, *Die verhüllten Götter* (Basel, 1957), second pl. following p. 216. The ivory figure, third pl. following p. 216, which also exists in bronze, comes from the same source. The Diana in St. Louis (*ibid.*, p. 280) is supposed to have been sold through the same circle of dealers, although it originated in another workshop. In 1955 I attempted in vain to convince R. Herbig not to make it public. Metapontum, given as the findspot of the kouros in Toledo, was also given for a large ivory mask, a "pasticcio" containing elements of the Acropolis korai.

38 *Ercolano* (n. 37), VI f.: "è notabile in questo bronzo la mistura dell'argento, che col saggio fattone vi si è ritrovata." See n. 21: "Nel primo saggio fatto su questo bronzo colla pietra paragone si credè, che vi fosse dell'oro, ma colla prova

del fuoco [what this consists of is unknown to me] non vi si ritrovò, che la solita mistura di rame, e stagno, e qualche porzione di argento; con essersi dalle replicate esperienze rilevato, che in ogni libra di questo bronzo (che pesa intutto libre sette, e mezzo) vi erano nove once di rame, e tre di stagno, e in queste tre once di stagno vi erano tre acini di argento." For the natural proportion of silver in Central Italian bronze objects (for example, 0.4 to 1.36 per cent) see L. Cambi, "Ricerche chimico metallurgiche in leghe cupriche di oggetti ornamentali preistorici e protostorici dell'Italia centrale e settentrionale," *StEtr*, XXVII (1959), 91 ff.; S. Junghans, E. Sangmeister, and M. Schröder, *Metallanalysen kupferzeitlicher und frühbronzezeitlicher Bodenfunde aus Europa* (Berlin, 1960), 106 ff., 125 ff., nos. 544 ff. Silanion is said to have alloyed bronze with silver in order to produce certain naturalistic color effects; see Plutarch *Quaestiones convivales* v. 1, 2 (J. Overbeck, *Die antiken Schriftquellen* [Leipzig, 1868], no. 1354).

39 Giglioli, *StEtr*, 1928 (n. 25), 51. Cf. Balty I, 37, n. 2.

40 G. Fiorelli, *NSc* (1884), 270 ff., pl. 3, lead base still visible; Giglioli, *AE*, pl. 85:4; Riis *Tyrrhenika*, 89, with n. 2 (Vulci); L. Goldscheider, *Etruscan Sculpture* (London, 1941), 108; E. H. Richardson, *MAAR*, 1953 (n. 37), 120, fig. 36.

41 Staatliche Museen zu Berlin (East); height 93 cm. I thank Frau Dr. E. Rohde for the photograph and permission to reproduce the piece. A. Rumpf, *Katalog der etruskischen Skulpturen* (Berlin, 1928), E 10, pl. 6.

42 U. Jantzen, *Bronzewerkstätten in Grossgriechenland und Sizilien* (Berlin, 1937), 7, pl. 26:107-109.

43 Boston, Museum of Fine Arts, 98.653; height 21.3 cm. I thank C. C. Vermeule for photographs and permission to reproduce the piece. Jantzen, *Bronzewerkstätten* (n. 42), 3, no. 1, pl. 1:1; P. J. Riis, *An Introduction to Etruscan Art* (Copenhagen, 1953), 41 f., pl. 16:24. R. S. Teitz, *Masterpieces of Etruscan Art*, exhibition catalogue (Worcester, 1967), 27 ff., no. 13.

44 Römisch-Germanisches Zentralmuseum, Mainz, 0.31068; height 10 cm., width 7.5 cm., from the Munich art market. I am indebted to H. Klumbach and H. Menzel for photographs, information, and permission for reproduction. G. Behrens, "Jahresbericht des Zentralmuseums für Deutsche Vor- und Frühgeschichte . . .," *MZ*, XXXVII-XXXVIII (1942-43), 2, pl. 1. For the style cf. Giglioli, *AE*, pl. 85:6. The rather flat representation of the breast and the engraved neckband with two or three lockets allow an interpretation of the figure as female, according to H. Klumbach and H. Menzel. Menzel believes that the small depression on the head does not represent a former point of attachment. It remains a question as to whether the figure was kneeling; cf. also E. Babelon and J.-A. Blanchet, *Catalogue des bronzes antiques de la Bibliothèque Nationale* (Paris, 1895), no. 1828 f., "bras de siège"; and Vatican inv. no. 12058, photo N. XXXII.122.17 A/B, which will be referred to in another context.

45 Arias and Shefton, *Vase Painting* (n. 30), pl. 102. Also, Hermonax stamnos in Munich: E. Buschor, *Griechische Vasen* (Munich, 1940), 181, fig. 202; *ibid.*, Niobid krater, fig. 220, and other works of the Niobid painter. R. Lullies, *Griechische Plastik* (1st ed.; Munich, 1956), pl. 137. H. Sichtermann, "Zu einer Knabenstatue im Prado," Deutsches Archäologisches Institut, *Madrider Mitteilungen*, I (1960), 159 f.; *idem*, "Das Motiv des Meleager," *RömMitt*, LXIX (1962), 47. G. Lippold, *Die griechische Plastik* (Munich, 1950), 95, with n. 6.

46 H. Schrader and E. Langlotz, *Die archaischen Marmorbildwerke der Akropolis* (Frankfurt, 1939), 48 f., no. 5, pls. 9-11, ca. 480 B.C., also the oldest Attic peplos statue; *EAA*, III (1960), 519 (G. Fagolari); E. Simon, "Boreas und Oreithyia auf dem silbernen Rhython in Triest," *Antike und Abendland*, XIII (1967), 104, with n. 15.

47 Lullies, *Plastik* (n. 45), pl. 108. B. Ashmole and N. Yalouris, *Olympia* (London, 1967), figs. 18, 20.

48 Figure 12: Brussels, Musées royaux d'Art et d'Histoire, R. 938.2; Balty I, 42, no. 9, pls. 9:1-12:1. Fig. 13: Paris, Louvre, formerly Effraim collection; Münzen und Medaillen AG, Basel, *Auktion*, XVI (1956), no. 158 (height 9.3 cm.); Balty I, 40, no. 6; II, 16. Fig. 14: Brussels, R 938.1; Balty I, 50, no. 4, pl. 6:1-2. Fig. 15: Brussels, R 937; Balty I, 49, no. 3, pl. 10:1. I thank J. C. Balty and H. A. Cahn for photographs and permission for reproduction. In a mimeographed supplement to Balty I and II the author pointed out H. Rolland, *Bronzes antiques de Haute Provence, Gallia*, suppl. XVIII, nos. 153-158, 199. Also R. Fleischer, *Die*

römischen Bronzen aus Österreich (Mainz, 1967), no. 216a, pl. 112. Some other examples are on the art market.

49 Balty I, 19, fig. 1; 35, fig. 3.

50 *Ibid.*, 37 f., 55 f.

51 Cf. C. Blinkenberg, *Knidia* (Copenhagen, 1933), 209, figs. 88-90. A. Andrén, "Marmora Etruriae," *Antike Plastik*, VII (Berlin, 1967), 7 ff., pls. 1-8 ("Venus" of Orvieto). Giglioli, *AE*, pl. 85:1, 6. G. M. A. Hanfmann, *Altetruskische Plastik*, I (Würzburg, 1936), 54 ff. Balty I, pl. 8:2a.

52 Paris, Louvre, AO 2740; height 9.2 cm. Provenience unknown; purchased from the antiquarian Durighello. Photo Chuzeville, with the kind permission of P. Amiet, to whom I am also grateful for information. R. Stucky called my attention to this unpublished piece.

53 Cf. A. Parrot, "Couples divins," *Syria*, XLI (1964), 219 ff., pl. 12, figs. 7 ff. T. Bossert, *Altsyrien* (Tübingen, 1951), no. 597, pl. 183. In the right hand is a club; a divine couple is doubtless intended. In addition cf. A. Hus, "Quelques cas de rapports diverts entre Étrurie, Cappadoce et Syrie du Nord vers 600 av. J.-C., *MélRome*, LXXI (1959), 9 ff. Balty I, 21; II, 12 ff., literature 13, n. 1.

54 G. Caputo, "Gli Athyrmata orientali della Montagnola e la via dell' Arno e transappenninica," *Arte antica e moderna*, XVII (1962), 58 ff.

55 A. J. B. Wace, "Excavations at Sparta, 1909: The Menelaion, Bronzes,' *BSA*, XV (1908-09), 147, pl. 9:1, 5. W. Lamb, *Greek and Roman Bronzes* (London, 1929), 77, pl. 23a. After a photo of the Deutsches Archäologisches Institut, Athens (Sparta 312/3). I thank U. Jantzen and R. Tölle for reproduction permission.

56 See notes 40 f. A. Alföldi, "Hasta — Summa imperii," *AJA*, LXIII (1959), 1 ff., especially 3, pl. 3:1.

57 *Ercolano* (n. 37), IV, n. 4. Richardson, *MAAR*, 1953 (n. 37), 117; *idem*, *Art Quarterly*, 1956 (n. 37), 125.

58 Giglioli, *StEtr*, 1928 (n. 25), 50 f. Also O. Brendel, according to E. Richardson, *Art Quarterly*, 1956 (n. 37), 131, n. 24. As I have subsequently seen, the author (Richardson) has already given the correct explanation here.

59 Munich, Glyptothek. After E. Buschor, *Frühgriechische Jünglinge* (Munich, 1950), 99 ff., fig. 116. Richter, *Kouroi* (n. 23), no. 135, figs. 391-394, 399.

60 Bibliothèque Nationale, Paris, Cabinet des Médailles, B 517; height 11.2 cm. Babelon — Blanchet, *Bronzes* (n. 44), no. 517. I am grateful to J. Babelon for photographs and permission to reproduce the piece.

61 London, British Museum, B 513; height 21 cm. H. B. Walters, *Catalogue of the Bronzes, Greek, Roman and Etruscan* (London, 1899), no. 513, without provenience. Its relationship with 512 and the copy in Micali, *Monumenti inediti* (Florence, 1844), pl. 2:2, points to Chiusi. Cf. Jucker, *AA*, 1967 (n. 1). I am grateful for the untiring aid of D. and S. Haynes in obtaining photographs and permission for publication.

62 Skulpturensammlungen, Dresden, Z.V. 491; height 12.45 cm. An egg is in the right hand. *Catalogue des objets d'art . . ., collection Alessandro Castellani*, sale, Rome, 1884 (Paris, 1884), 43, no. 360. G. Treu, *AA* (1889), 103, ill. I am again thankful to M. Raumschüssel for photographs, information, and permission for reproduction.

63 R. Zandrini, "Il discobolo del Museo Poldi Pezzoli di Milano," *JdI*, LVIII (1943), 199 ff., figs. 1 f. A stylistically related small candelabrum figure formerly in a private collection in Solothurn. Teitz, *Masterpieces*, no. 68. E. Kohler "Ultimatum to Terracotta-Forgers," *Expedition*, IX, No. 2 (1967), 20, lower right. D. Kaspar in *Antike Kunst* (n. 11), no. 270.

63a But cf. the Silenus from Apollonia, Illyria, in the Louvre, C. Rolley, *Die Bronzen*, in *Monumenta Graeca et Romana*, ed. H. F. Mussche, vol. V, 1, n. 74. Common among Cypriote terra cottas, see G. Schmidt, *Kyprische Bildwerke aus dem Heraion von Samos*, Samos VII (Bonn, 1968), pls. 26 f., 38, 56, 106.

64 Richardson, *Art Quarterly*, 1956 (n. 37), 131, corrected Giglioli's overly early dating to ca. 515 to 485, which, of course, could be too late but probably was meant to point out the necessary difference from the Toledo figure (see n. 37).

65 Zurich, Bührle collection. I am indebted to Mrs. C. Bührle for permission to photograph and publish the figures. H. Jucker in *Sammlung Emil G. Bührle* (Zurich: Kunsthaus, 1958), 36, no. 5. The patina is greenish with rust-red speckles. The piece is mounted on its base by means of tangs.

66 *EAA*, II (1959), 511 ff. (M. Santangelo).

67 H. Payne, *Archaic Marble Sculpture from the Acropolis* (2nd ed.; London, 1950), pls. 39-78. *DarSag*, IV:2, 1508, s.v. stephane (E. Saglio). On Etruscan bronzes the band around the back of the head is usually missing.

68 G. Neumann, *Gesten und Gebärden in der griechischen Kunst* (Berlin, 1965), 41 ff., 78 ff. C. Picard, "Le geste de la prière funéraire en Grèce et en Étrurie," *RHR*, CXIV (1936), 137 ff. Balty I, 31 f.

69 K. Schefold has drawn my attention to his *Basler Antiken im Bild* (Basel, 1958), 28, with n. 71, where he refers to N. Breitenstein, *Danish National Museum, Catalogue of Terracottas* (Copenhagen, 1941), 29, nos. 268 and 269, pl. 28, but I think that the "nude male (?)," no. 268, is also female.

70 Florence, Museo Archeologico Nazionale, 80880.1. I thank G. Caputo for the photograph and permission to reproduce the figure. Riis, *Tyrrhenika*, 143, with n. 5.

71 *Ibid.*, 90, with n. 5, 164, pl. 18:2; Kat. Köln, nos. 291, 292; Mostra, nos. 762-763, pl. 52. In the discussion following the symposium presentation by S. Haynes, E. Richardson expressed reservations regarding attributing this to Vulci. She is of the opinion that utensil bronzes and votive bronzes were not produced in the same workshops. See p. 236.

72 Arezzo; height 10 cm. After Mostra, nos. 840-841, pl. 54.

73 Male figure, height 11.5 cm. Mostra, no. 731, pl. 51.

74 J. Heurgon, *La vie quotidienne chez les Étrusques* (Paris, 1961), 95 ff., 237 ff. A. J. Pfiffig, "Zur Sittengeschichte der Etrusker," *Gymnasium*, LXXI (1964), 17 ff.

75 Basel, Antikenmuseum. E. Berger, *Kunstwerke der Antike*, exhibition catalogue (Lucerne, 1963), no. 14. Balty II, 16, n. 2. K. Schefold *Führer durch das Antikenmuseum Basel* (Basel, 1966), 120, no. 173.2. I. Rácz, *Antikes Erbe* (Zurich, 1965), 38.

76 Paris, Louvre, 66. I thank P. Devambez for the photograph and for permission to reproduce the piece. Giglioli, *AE*, pl. 123:2; Kat. Köln, no. 281.

77 Richter, *Kouroi* (n. 23), no. 70, fig. 243 f.; no. 184, fig. 558; G. de Luca, "Kouroi in italienischen Museen," *Antike Plastik*, III (Berlin, 1964), 33 ff., pl. 42 f.

78 H. C. Butler, *Sardis, The Excavations*, vol. I, part 1, 1910-1914 (Leiden, 1922), 141, fig. 156; A. Akurgal, *Die Kunst Anatoliens* (Berlin, 1961), 156, pl. VII a-b; *Art Treasures* (n. 31), no. 115.

79 N. Schimmel collection, New York. I am indebted to the owner for photographs and permission to publish the piece. Hoffmann, *Schimmel* (n. 34), no. 40; Teitz, *Masterpieces* (n. 43), no. 9; D. G. Mitten, "Capolavori d'arte antica," *Antichità viva*, No. 3 (1965), fig. 19.

80 Paris or Lisbon. Ars Antiqua, Lucerne, *Auktion*, II (1960), no. 85. H. Rosenberg has given me permission to study and reproduce the photographs that E. Berger kindly sent me. I consider the orally expressed questioning of the authenticity to be completely unfounded.

81 N. Gröger, J. Geiss, M. Grünfelder, and F. G. Houtermans, "Isotopenuntersuchungen zur Bestimmung der Herkunft römischer Bleirohre und Bleibarren," *Zeitschrift für Naturforschung*, 21a, Heft 7 (1966), 1167 ff.

82 Göttingen, collection of the Archaeological Institute; height 14 cm., with lead base 17.2 cm. G. Körte, "Göttinger Bronzen," *AbhGöttingen*, XVI:4 (1917), 35 f., pl. 9; W. Schiering, "Etruskische Bronzestatuette in Göttingen," *AA* (1966), cols. 367 ff., figs. 1-4. I thank W. Schiering for photographs and permission to reproduce the piece.

83 Schiering, *AA*, 1966 (n. 82), col. 371.

84 *Ibid.*, col. 370. The analogy about flame and electricity is still unclear to me.

85 Payne, *Archaic Sculpture* (n. 67), no. 669, pl. 28; no. 660, pl. 39; no. 682, pl. 40, etc.; K. Hadaczek, "Der Ohrschmuck der Griechen und Etrusker," *Abh. archäolog.-epigr. Seminar, Wien*, Heft 14 (N.F., Heft 1) (1903), 10 f.; R. A. Higgins, *Greek and Roman Jewellery* (London, 1961), 99, pl. 13E. All the women in the Tomba dei Giocolieri in Tarquinia (no. 2437) wear disc earrings (M. Moretti, *Nuovi monumenti della pittura etrusca* [Milan, 1966], 20-29).

86 Cf. E. Langlotz, "Beobachtungen zu einem Kopf in Kyrene," *AthMitt*, LXXVII (1962), 111 ff., 113 ff.

87 Schiering, *AA*, 1966 (n. 82), col. 379 with n. 2.

88 *Ibid.*, col. 377.

89 *Master Bronzes*, Nos. 164, 168.

90 Teitz, *Masterpieces* (n. 43), no. 47; compare nos. 44 and 59.

91 Berger, *Kunstwerke* (n. 75), no. 15; Schefold, *Führer* (n. 75), 121, no. 173:1; Rácz, *Erbe* (n. 75), 43. The bronzes named here in notes 89-91 have also been doubted occasionally, but without conclusive arguments being adduced.

Observations on Selected Roman Bronzes in the Master Bronzes Exhibition

Heinz Menzel

Roman bronzes have come into a sharper focus of interest only in recent years. They raise a number of questions, of which the most important concern the chronological sequence and workshops. The question of chronological sequence is not easy to solve at the moment; a large number of extant bronzes still remain completely unclassified. Unfortunately, there are very few fixed points for dating, or, more correctly, these must still be established as an aid to setting forth a chronological system.[1] We shall turn first, then, to the other question, that of workshops. Here, too, scholarship has reached only the initial stages, but for a reason different from that which was and is the case with Greek bronzes. Roman monumental sculpture — by this we mean idealized sculpture — is, generally speaking, so dependent on Greek sculpture that one must always seek the Greek original and the name of the Greek artist. The same may be said for smaller sculpture, especially bronze statuettes, which are very dependent on monumental sculpture.

If we were to reconstruct the ideal manner in which a bronze-worker operated, we might imagine the same bronze-caster pouring several statuettes from a single model he had chosen. These would probably differ in size and details of modeling but would have so many basic features in common that one could recognize that the individual pieces belonged to a group. Unfortunately, however, the actual situation was quite different.

If we assume, a priori, that only a certain rather small percentage of bronze statuettes is extant today, this percentage becomes even smaller when one considers how many of these are unpublished and therefore unknown. Of course, the large holdings in Paris, London, New York, and Baltimore have been published,[2] and Salomon Reinach has also tried to make unknown material available in drawings in his oft-derided, but nevertheless widely used *Répertoire*.[3] But the very lack of uniformity of the large collections, whose distinctive composition was often determined by the interests of their collectors, forms the greatest obstacle to a true evaluation of Roman bronzes. Furthermore, with the exception of outstanding individual pieces that almost require separate treatment in a monograph, the greater number of Roman bronze statuettes is of inferior quality and often, in comparison with Greek works, represents that utilitarian mass product that even in ancient times was manufactured for trade. If one adds that the term "Roman bronzes" does not refer only to material from metropolitan Rome or even Italy but also includes the cultural legacy of the provinces, it becomes apparent that a treatment that attempts to answer all unanswered questions will be possible only when the material of a number of neighboring provinces is available in its entirety. Beginnings have been made in this direction, and further studies can be expected in the coming years.[4]

The introduction to the Roman section of the Master Bronzes catalogue briefly outlines the questions that need to be answered. These concern both the artistic aspect and the commercial side. They touch on the value assigned to individual gods and the search for cult centers whose shrines contained cult images that provided the models for small bronzes. It would be folly to compound the questions while at the same time admitting that a solution is not forthcoming at the moment. Thus it seems permissible to introduce several bronzes from the Master Bronzes exhibition in order to show the process to be followed in answering the most important questions.

In recent years three important statues of half and full life-size have

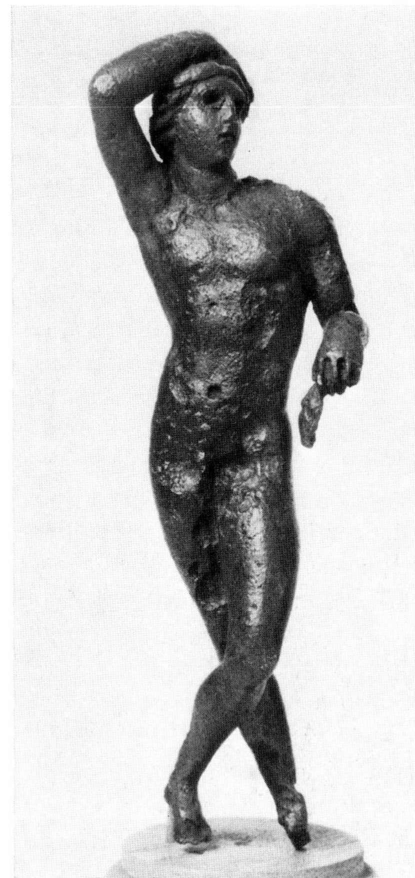

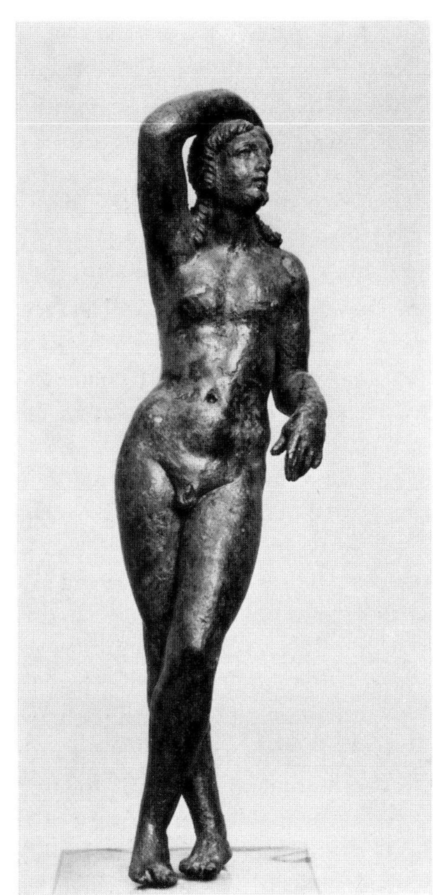

Fig. 1 (left): Apollo from Almenum. *Fig. 2 (right): Apollo from Reims.*

been found: in 1963, a statue of a seated youth[5] was found on the beach at Pinedo in the area near Valencia, Spain; in September 1964, the so-called Youth from Agde[6] was discovered in the Hérault River near Agde, France; and finally, in August 1965, a statuette of Bacchus[7] was found in Avenches, Switzerland. When the youth from Pinedo had just been made known, García y Bellido interpreted it as a seated Apollo and traced it back to a work by Praxiteles; similarly, the Youth from Agde now awaits an interpretation, and the Bacchus from Avenches awaits publication. Without wishing to anticipate the publication of the latter statuette by its discoverer, it should be mentioned that a study of the piece has led to several observations which should be of special interest in connection with the question of defining workshops.

In the first volume of the publication of Roman bronzes of the Netherlands a statuette of Apollo (Fig. 1) from Almenum, in Friesland, previously only unsatisfactorially known, is introduced again with several good illustrations, and thus, properly speaking, is adequately published for the first time.[8] Apollo is represented here with crossed legs and with his right arm held up over his head, a pose also adopted by the Bacchus from Avenches. A related piece (Fig. 2),[9] from Reims, may be connected with the Friesland statuette. In spite of the differences in condition between the two and also the difference in handling, which cannot be overlooked, the over-all structure of the figures and their execution are so similar that we can probably conclude that they both come from a single workshop, probably located in the area around Reims.

Fig. 3 (left): Apollo from Volesvres.

Fig. 4 (right): Apollo from the Jardin du Luxembourg, Paris.

If these two Apollo statuettes, one in the Louvre and the other in the museum in Leeuwarden, are ascribed to a single workshop, and if it may be assumed, further, that the findspot of the former, Reims, might indicate their place of production, we should also consider another pair of Apollo statuettes which could also be assigned to one workshop in spite of their distinct differences and peculiarities. These are the Apollo of Volesvres (Fig. 3),[10] now in the museum in Autun, France, and an Apollo from the Jardin du Luxembourg, Paris (Fig. 4). The latter can be shown here only in a drawing that appeared in a publication of 1807,[11] as the original has apparently now been lost. The differences are clear: a different hair style, a different turn of the head, and even a different position of the arms; yet these differences are outweighed by the similarity in over-all appearance. This similarity, then, is probably the criterion for the assumption of a common workshop. The differences are attributable to differences in the commissions or to other factors.

If one accepts this consideration as a working basis, and only for this reason were these two pairs of statuettes introduced as examples, then one could arrange a whole series of similar statuettes into groups, a procedure by which a first ordering would be created. Only when groups have been formed in this manner will it be possible to place individual pieces within these groups in such a relationship to each other that one can treat the question of workshops with some hope of success.

In seeking further examples a small group of Mars statuettes might be presented that is characterized by the fact that the nude god is depicted

Fig. 5: Alexander, Roman copy, Louvre.

Fig. 6: Roman general, Geneva.

with a high Corinthian helmet on his head, usually carrying a sword in his left arm, the hilt grasped in his hand, the blade resting on his arm or shoulder. It is perhaps not incorrect to assume a monumental sculpture as a prototype for this well-defined type. This model, probably a work of the fourth century B.C., has not yet been found, but one should consider whether it might be sought in an Alexander statue by Lysippos or his school, of which a Roman copy might give us some idea (Fig. 5). A statue of Alexander of Magnesia,[12] now in Constantinople, of the late second century B.C. should be mentioned here as a connecting link, while the bronze statuette from Grado[13] is possibly a Roman copy after a Hellenistic variant. The motif of holding the sword is repeated on a carnelian in Leningrad[14] representing Alexander as Zeus, and may be explained by comparing a coin of Lepidus[15] of 38 B.C. which shows Mars in this position with his sword on his left arm and his right hand on the lance. The representation of Mars on the coin must doubtless have been preceded by an older one, for the transferal of the pose associated with a god to representations of men — the other way around would have been unthinkable for the Romans — had already begun earlier. From the period between 100 and 60 B.C. comes a statue of a Republican general, most recently published by G. M. A. Hanfmann,[16] which must have carried its sword on its left arm, as do the Roman general from the early first century A.D. in the museum in Geneva (Fig. 6) and the Dioskouros in the Louvre (Fig. 7). Thus it is only natural that a ruler should occasionally allow himself to be portrayed in this fashion (Fig. 8). The association of the pose with the ever-victorious Mars evokes the mortal ruler's desire for victory and thus victory itself.

The taking up of this motif in the minor arts, above all in bronze statuettes, is explained by the general concept of victory and its representations. It is not necessary to emphasize that here the portrayal of the god Mars has a special significance. The group of Mars statuettes rendered in this fashion is not particularly large. Its distribution is extremely interesting, although we must remember that only those works actually published and accessible can be mentioned. The main region where they occur is Gallia Belgica; they extend into the interior of Gaul and into purely Germanic regions this side of and beyond the Limes. Because of this relative density of occurrence an attempt can be made to distinguish one or several workshops and to establish their characteristics.

A bronze statuette of Mars (Fig. 9), formerly in the Gréau collection and now in the Louvre,[17] came from Reims. The piece is of excellent quality; it could be termed the work of a master. To this bronze another could be added (Fig. 10),[18] found at Tzum in the Netherlands, which shows all the characteristics of the bronze from Reims. Although it is of lower quality and lacks the classical elegance of the Mars from Reims, one can say, in spite of obvious differences, that the workshop that produced this bronze cannot have been far from the one that created the Reims statuette; indeed, it may have been made in the same workshop but not by the master himself. The same may be said of the Mars from Neumagen (Fig. 11).[19] The deviations are stronger: the stance is changed, the helmet crest is supported by a sphinx, and the position of the arms is different. And yet the over-all appearance, the slender but muscular body with the head turned to the left, is the same.

The Mars (Fig. 12)[20] found in August 1965 at Blicquy near Tournai, Belgium, is different, however. The type is the same, but the concept and

Fig. 7: Dioskouros, Louvre.

Fig. 8: Ruler, so-called Claudius, Louvre.

Fig. 9: Mars from Reims.

Fig. 10: Mars from Tzum.

Fig. 11: Mars from Neumagen.

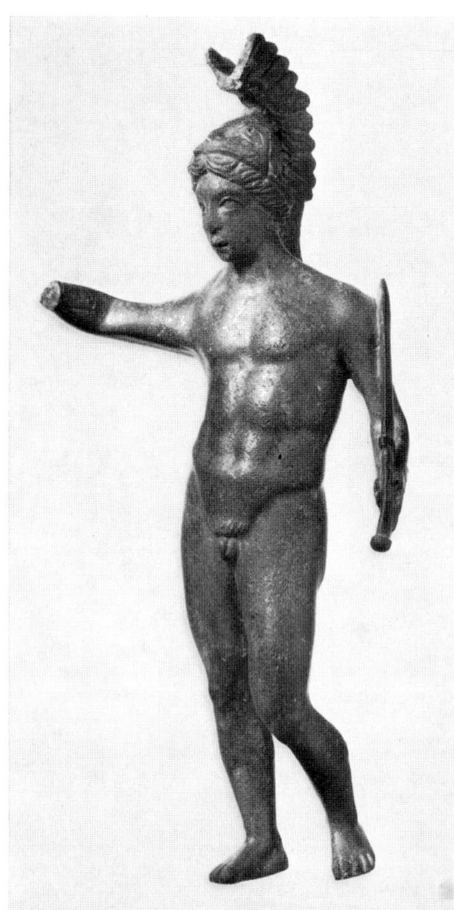

Fig. 12: Mars from Blicquy.

Fig. 13: Mars from Dronrijp.

execution are different. The turn of the head to the right, upward and outward toward the right arm, is perhaps more decisive than the more provincial work, which gives itself away above all in the naïve and dull facial expression. The Mars of Dronrijp (Fig. 13)[21] must have come from the same workshop; it shows almost the same characteristics as does the Blicquy figure. Finally, the Mars of Mandeure (Fig. 14),[22] in the museum in Mariemont, which despite all its differences is still indebted to the same prototype, shows what provincialisms are possible.

Similarly, corresponding examples may be grouped together from among the great number of Mercury statuettes that have come down to us. In 1966, in Schwarzenacker, a small way station on the Roman road from Metz to Worms, the cellar of a Roman house that had collapsed in a fire during the tumults of the third century A.D. was discovered. The most important finds there were a group of statuettes, which were first introduced to the public in an exhibition entitled "Romans on the Rhine" in Cologne in the summer of 1967.[23] In addition to a superbly worked Genius, an enthroned Neptune, a Victory, an Apollo who despite his crossed legs does not belong to the series of Apollo bronzes which must be taken into consideration in connection with the Bacchus of Avenches, and a standing Mercury, the most interesting statuette is a seated Mercury (Fig. 15) with an over-all height of 20 cm. Mercury sits on a rock, leaning far back, holding his staff with his right hand while he supports himself on the rock with his left hand, in which he holds a money bag. The body is slender and muscular; the face has a somewhat simple-minded expression; the hair is arranged in flat curls. At his feet are a wild boar, a goat, and a rooster. His *petasos* and *kerykeion* are of silver; everything else is bronze and is cast separately in some instances. The heavy cloak around the shoulders, held by a brooch, is especially striking. We doubtless have here a work which was produced not long before the destruction of the house, that is, in the first or second third of the third century A.D.

This Mercury group reminds us at once of one from Montorio Veronese in the Kunsthistorisches Museum in Vienna (Fig. 16). In that group Mercury sits somewhat more upright on the rock, but otherwise he is in the same position, and the structure of the body corresponds to that of the Mercury from Schwarzenacker. He, too, wears a heavy cloak around his shoulders, fastened by a brooch. This group is also dated in the third, perhaps even the second, century A.D. Luigi Beschi, in his detailed publication of the entire find from Montorio Veronese,[24] dealt in some detail with the seated Mercury figures known to him. But in this connection it is important to ask whether among extant bronzes of the seated Mercury some can be associated so closely that we may speak of them as products of a single workshop.

In 1924, J. Sieveking published the bronze statuette of a seated Mercury (Fig. 17) which at that time still belonged to the Loeb collection but which is now a valuable part of the Antikensammlungen in Munich.[25] As early as 1899, S. Reinach had published a cast of this statuette[26] and remarked that the original came from Feurs, the Roman *Forum Segusianorum*, located in southern France not far from Lyon. Mercury is represented with his upper body bent back slightly; the head, with a band in the hair, is turned to the right and slightly bowed. The left hand rests on a support and the right is half opened, with the index and middle fingers extended.

It was once and is still sometimes thought that the seated Hermes by

Fig. 14: Mars from Mandeure.

Fig. 15: Seated Mercury from Schwarzenacker.

Fig. 16: Seated Mercury from Montorio Veronese.

Fig. 17: Seated Mercury from Feurs.

Fig. 18: Seated Mercury from Wawern.

Fig. 19: Seated Mercury, Lyon.

Lysippos in the museum in Naples was the prototype for this seated Mercury. It doubtless was the model for the seated Mercury in the collection of Professor and Mrs. George H. Forsyth,[27] whose bearing has a springlike tension. A counterpart without *chlamys*, in the museum at Montbéliard, has been published by P. Lebel.[28] Sieveking, however, had rejected this connection of the Feurs Mercury with Lysippos and wanted to relate it more closely to the Ares Ludovisi. Phyllis Williams Lehmann[29] contributed significantly to this discussion by pointing to coin representations of Himera with the youthful Herakles in repose, dating from the early fourth century B.C., whose model must have been a slightly older original reflected in the marble copy of a seated Herakles in Leningrad. This original is probably the model we seek.

Two old casts of the Mercury from Feurs are preserved,[30] which are relevant to the question of the identification of this bronze. The cast in Roanne that S. Reinach published shows a rocky base covered with a lion skin, and the one in Leipzig shows that the right hand grasped a club. Phyllis Lehmann concluded from this that the statuette was not Mercury but Herakles. Sieveking, who, as Lippold before him,[31] had already pointed to a pre-Lysippan Herakles as a possible prototype, considered the club an impossible attribute and felt that this statuette was a typical example of the fusion of different types in Roman times. One tends to agree with Sieveking when it is ascertained that almost all Mercury statuettes of this type that are unequivocally recognizable through their attributes have the same half-opened hand with two long, outstretched fingers. This has already been seen in the Mercury statuettes from Schwarzenacker and Montorio Veronese and can also be remarked in the Mercury from Augst[32] and others.

At first glance the statuette of a seated Mercury (Fig. 18)[33] from Wawern, Prüm County, in the museum in Trier, seems to represent a different type. The position of the legs is changed, that of the arms is different, the bulkier upper body does not lean back as far but is rendered in a more upright position, and consequently the position of the head is different. But as his distinguishing attribute he holds the money bag in his right hand, with the same long, outstretched fingers. Thus this Mercury is very strongly indebted to the one from Feurs.

In addition the museum in Lyon has another unpublished statuette of a seated Mercury (Fig. 19), unfortunately without data as to findspot but undoubtedly from Lyon or the surrounding area. It falls between the two statuettes just mentioned. The position of the legs agrees more with the piece from Feurs, as does the position of the arms. Again, one's attention is drawn to the half-opened right hand. The more upright position of the upper body connects the piece more with the bronze from Wawern, and the turned, raised head is more reminiscent of the Wawern Mercury than the one from Feurs. Despite these clearly recognizable differences, these three pieces are so closely connected that we may perhaps assume that the two latter works originated in one workshop, which took as a model the work of the master who created the statuette from Feurs. A small, nine-centimeter-tall statuette from Decize (Fig. 20), in the museum in Nevers, France, which is a faithful copy of the Mercury from Feurs,[34] also argues for localizing the workshop of this master craftsman in Lyon.[35]

The number of standing Mercury statuettes is much greater, however. They will be represented here by a single example, a statuette belonging to the Royal Ontario Museum, Toronto.[36] This Mercury, with a garment thrown over his shoulder that falls in rich folds over his bent left arm, holds a caduceus in his left hand and a money bag in his right. The work undoubtedly has as a model the Doryphoros of Polykleitos, as the statues in the Naples museum and the Vatican and the reconstruction in Munich show. The heavier body and somewhat more rounded head, however, recall another work that is indebted to the Diskophoros of Naukydes, the younger brother of Polykleitos, namely the bronze athlete in the Louvre.[37] If this attribution is correct, then in the statuette in Toronto we are again dealing with a Roman fusion of several types. The over-all bearing would come from the Doryphoros of Polykleitos, and the body structure comes from the athlete of Naukydes, which was much favored for representations of Hellenistic rulers, insofar as they do not go back to works of Lysippos.

Many Roman Mercury statuettes are indebted to Polykleitos himself, to his school, and to his successors. The most outstanding example of an immediate derivation from a work by Polykleitos is a magnificent statuette from Fins d'Annecy,[38] which reproduces the Hermes of Polykleitos. The great majority of Mercury statuettes, however, which were dedicated as votive offerings in temples or placed in homes, do not reveal much about their models because of their simple, often crude, workmanship. Often they have only the outlines of body structure and the position of the arms in common with their prototypes.

Fig. 20: Seated Mercury from Decize.

Fig. 21 (left): Mercury from Limoges.

Fig. 22 (right): Mercury from Narbonne.

Fig. 23: Mercury from Chalon-sur-Saône.

Fig. 24: Mercury from Naix-aux-Forges, Bar-le-Duc.

Fig. 25: Mercury from Mollans, Vaison.

Fig. 26: Mercury from Sens.

Fig. 27: Mercury, Walters Art Gallery, Baltimore.

Fig. 28: Mercury from Chalon-sur-Saône.

Probably the most beautiful copy of the Doryphoros among small bronzes is the Mercury statuette from Limoges (Fig. 21) in the Cabinet des Médailles of the Bibliothèque Nationale, Paris.[39] The slender elegance of the Polykleitan body structure is preserved up to the badly damaged head. In spite of the more angular right arm, with the hand grasping the money bag quite energetically, a statuette from Narbonne (Fig. 22) is also indebted to a considerable degree to the Doryphoros of Polykleitos. This very well-proportioned statuette stands at the beginning of a long series of Mercury bronzes that have the following in common: slender body structure, which in the less well-executed pieces can become very flat; a more or less angular right arm, with the hand holding the money bag in such a way that it hangs down; and finally, a garment laid over the left shoulder and falling down over the bent left arm in rich folds. The unfortunate lack of a common prototype for the Gallic bronzes makes it impossible to draw further conclusions, such as, in this case, where the workshops were. The type is widespread but occurs most extensively in southern France, to judge from publications and collections of material thus far available.[40] A few examples may illustrate what modifications of the original model took place. Although the Mercury from Chalon-sur-Saône (Fig. 23) has a powerfully modeled body, in the statuettes from Bar-le-Duc (Fig. 24) and Vaison (Fig. 25) it becomes flatter, and is flattest of all in the statuette from Sens (Fig. 26).[41]

Fig. 29: Mercury from Clermont-Ferrand.

A further variant of the Doryphoros type is the Mercury fully clad in a chlamys, which may be represented here by a statuette of unknown provenience in the Walters Art Gallery, Baltimore (Fig. 27).[42] It can be compared with a few statuettes found in southern France, such as one from Chalon-sur-Saône (Fig. 28) and another from Clermont-Ferrand (Fig. 29). These examples could be multiplied, but they only show that the largest number has been found in this area.[43]

The influence of Polykleitos on the statuettes just discussed has been emphasized, but it was not his work alone that served as a model for the creation of Roman images of the gods. The influence of Lysippos was equally great. To supplement the Mercury statuettes indebted to Polykleitos with a bronze clearly influenced by Lysippos, a Mercury statuette (Fig. 30) may be cited which comes from Logras, Departement Ain, France, and is now in the museum in Geneva.[44]

The same may be said for representations of Jupiter. In a recently published work[45] José Dörig has brought together a few Jupiter statuettes which can give us some idea of Lysippos' bronze Zeus in Tarentum. Dörig also mentions a small Jupiter statuette from Evreux (Fig. 31) without discussing the famous, nearly half life-size Jupiter statuette from the same complex of finds in Vieil-Evreux (Fig. 32).[46] A close relationship between this piece and Lysippos' work has never been established, such as was the case, for instance, with the Frankfurt statuette from Furtwängler's collection, and no such attempt shall be made here either. But, in conclusion, this statuette can serve as a means of pointing out the manifold questions raised by the study of Roman bronzes. Just as the Jupiter of Brée[47] is the work of a bronze-caster who, in true Roman fashion, borrows freely from various centuries and from different masters, so the Jupiter of Evreux is unthinkable without Lysippos, even though the powerful, sharply separated forms of the body express a classicism that is far removed from Lysippos' Zeus.[48]

Fig. 30: Mercury from Logras.

From the few examples given here it has probably become clear that

Fig. 31: *Jupiter from Vieil-Evreux.*

Fig. 32: *Jupiter from Vieil-Evreux.*

Roman bronzes present quite different problems from Greek or Etruscan bronzes. The question of a model or models has to be posed, as must the question of connecting links that have led to the particular form assumed by the statuette in question at any given time. But with the majority of the statuettes it is not this question that is most important but rather the attempt to go beyond the formation of groups, that is, of works similar in type, and to understand the workshops, to localize them, and finally to place them chronologically.

Notes

1 A detailed statement would go beyond the bounds of this general survey; only a sample may be given here to show where and how the task has been begun. The treasure from Detzem, Trier County, in the museum in Trier (see H. Menzel, *Die Römischen Bronzen aus Deutschland*, II, *Trier* [Mainz, 1966], 17 f.) belongs to a complex of finds which are closely related to the events of war in the middle of the third century A.D. This has already been demonstrated for the depots of bronze utensils, which in some cases also contained statuettes; see J. Werner, "Die römischen Bronzegeschirrdepots des 3. Jahrhunderts . . .," *Marburger Studien*, (1938), 259 ff. Besides Detzem, the find at Seltz should be mentioned in particular; cf. F. A. Schaeffer, *Un dépôt d'outils et un trésor de bronzes de l'époque Gallo-Romaine découverts à Seltz* (Hagenau, 1927). The same goes for parade weapons as well, which in some instances were picked up without a proper association with other datable finds; H. Klumbach has enumerated several examples, see "Römischer Gesichtshelm aus Stuttgart Bad Cannstatt," *Fundberichte aus Schwaben*, N. F. XVI (1962), 163 ff., particularly the chart in fig. 2 that notes the finds. The shield boss from Schwarzenacker is named there as representing the westernmost findspot. Because of the treasure of bronze statuettes recovered at Schwarzenacker in 1965, the site has taken on a special significance; see A. Kolling, "Die Bronzestatuetten aus dem Säulenkeller," *14. Bericht der Staatlichen Denkmalpflege im Saarland* (1967), 7 ff. If we can date a series of finds in this way through political events, and if reference can also be made in this regard to the general interpretation of coin finds of the third century A.D., as H. Koethe has already attempted to do ("Zur Geschichte Galliens im dritten Viertel des 3. Jahrhunderts," *RGKomm*, XXXII, 1942 [1950], 199 ff.), there is also the other, unfortunately all too rare, possibility of dating by looking for finds whose date of burial can be firmly placed by coins found in context. As an example I might mention the find from la Comelle-sous-Beuvray, which contained a coin of Commodus as the *terminus ante quem*; see H. de Fontenay, "Notice des bronzes antiques trouvés à la Comelle-sous-Beuvray," *Mémoires de la Société Éduenne*, IX (1880), 275 ff.

2 Paris, Louvre: A. de Ridder, *Les bronzes antiques du Louvre*, 2 vols. (Paris, 1913-1915). London, British Museum: H. B. Walters, *Catalogue of the Bronzes, Greek, Roman and Etruscan* (London, 1899). New York, Metropolitan Museum of Art: G. M. A. Richter, *Greek, Etruscan and Roman Bronzes* (New York, 1915). Baltimore, The Walters Art Gallery: D. K. Hill, *Catalogue of Classical Bronze Sculpture in The Walters Art Gallery* (Baltimore, 1949).

3 S. Reinach, *Répertoire de la statuaire grecque et romaine*, 6 vols. (Paris, 1908-1930).

4 Reference should be made to the works already cited in the Master Bronzes catalogue.

5 A. García y Bellido, "Estatua de bronce descubierta en la playa de Pinedo, Valencia," *ArchEspArq*, XXXVIII (1965), 3 ff. The Mellephebos of Antequera should also be mentioned, although the date of its discovery is not precisely ascertainable; see *idem*, "El melléphebos en bronce de Antequera," *ArchEspArq*, XXXVII (1964), 22 ff.

6 H. Gallet de Santerre, "Informations archéologiques," *Gallia*, XXIV (1966), 464, pl. 1-3; J. Charbonneaux, "Une statue de bronze découverte à Agde," *La revue du Louvre*, XVI, No. 1 (1966) 1 ff.

7 *Illustrated London News* (August 6, 1966), 10; *Master Bronzes*, 256, No. 246. A comprehensive publication by Dr. H. Bögli of Avenches is in preparation.

8 P. C. J. A. Boeles, *Friesland tot de elfde eeuw* (2nd ed.; The Hague, 1951), 162, pl. 19b; A. N. Zadoks-Josephus Jitta, W. J. T. Peters, and W. A. van Es, *Roman Bronze Statuettes from the Netherlands*, I (Groningen, 1967), 4 f., no. 2.

9 De Ridder, *Bronzes* (n. 2), I, 18, no. 1057, pl. 62. Formerly in the Gréau collection, see W. Froehner, *Collection Julien Gréau, les bronzes antiques* (Paris, 1885), 186, no. 914, pl. 21.

10 R. Lantier, "Une nouvelle statuette de bronze polyclétéenne découverte en Gaule," *RA*, ser. 6, XXXI-XXXII (1949), 554 ff., figs. 3, 4.

11 C. M. Grivaud, *Antiquités gauloises et romaines, recueillies dans les jardins du palais du sénat* (Paris, 1807), 98, pl. 1:2.

12 T. Reinach, "Apollon, statue trouvée à Magnésie du Sipyle," *MonPiot*, III (1896), 155 ff., pl. 16. M. Schede, *Meisterwerke der Türkischen Museen zu Konstantinopel*, I, *Griechische und römische Skulpturen des Antikenmuseums* (Berlin and Leipzig, 1928), 11 ff., pl. 19. F. v. Lorentz, "Eine Bronzestatuette Alexanders des Großen," *RömMitt*, L (1935), 333, n. 1.

13 Lorentz, *RömMitt*, 1935 (n. 12), 333 ff., pl. 63.

14 A. Furtwängler, *Die antiken Gemmen*, I (Berlin, 1900), pl. 32:11.

15 H. A. Grueber, *Coins of the Roman Republic in the British Museum*, I (London, 1910), 584 f., nos. 2478-2480; III (London, 1910), pl. 57:20-22.

16 G. M. A. Hanfmann, *Roman Art* (Greenwich, n. d.), 81, no. 47. For further literature see R. Brilliant, *Gesture and Rank in Roman Art* (New Haven, 1963), 47, fig. 1, 80.

17 De Ridder, *Bronzes* (n. 2), I, 127 f., no. 1045; II, pl. 61.

18 Zadoks *et al.*, *Netherlands* (n. 8), I, 44 ff., no. 18; *Master Bronzes*, 276, No. 268.

19 Menzel, *Trier* (n. 1), 7, no. 12, pls. 6-8; *Master Bronzes*, 275, No. 267.

20 M. Amand, "Une statuette de Mars, trouvée à Blicquy (Hainaut)" *Latomus*, XXVI (1967), 82 ff.; H. Menzel, "Bemerkungen zum Mars von Blicquy," *Latomus*, XXVI (1967), 92 ff.; *Master Bronzes*, 277, No. 269.

21 Zadoks *et al.*, *Netherlands* (n. 8), I, 54 ff., no. 23.

22 *Les antiquités ... du Musée de Mariemont* (Brussels, 1952), 168 f., pl. 60.

23 See n. 1. It has appeared also as a special publication: *Forschungen im Römischen Schwarzenacker*, I, A. Kolling, *Die Bronzestatuetten aus dem Säulenkeller* (Saarbrücken, 1967).

24 L. Beschi, *I bronzetti romani di Montorio Veronese* (Venice, 1962), 53 ff.

25 J. Sieveking, "Römische Kleinbronze," *MJb*, N. F. I (1924), 1 ff.; se also *Master Bronzes*, 258, No. 248.

26 S. Reinach, "Quelques statuettes de bronze inédites," *RA*, ser. 3, XXXV (1899), 58.

27 *Master Bronzes*, 260, No. 250.

28 P. Lebel, *Catalogue des collections archéologiques de Montbéliard, III, Les bronzes figurés* (Paris, 1962), pl. 22, no. 17.

29 Phyllis W. Lehmann, *Statues on Coins* (New York, 1946), 49 ff.

30 *Ibid.*, 50, fig. 10a and b.

31 G. Lippold, *Kopien und Umbildungen griechischer Statuen* (Munich, 1923), [129.

32 *Master Bronzes*, 259, No. 249.

33 Menzel, *Trier* (n. 1), 19 f., no. 38, pls. 18, 19; *Master Bronzes*, 272, No. 263.

34 F. Braemer, *L'art dans l'occident romain*, catalogue of an exhibition at the Louvre (Paris, 1963), no. 315.

35 A. Audin has also postulated such a bronze-casting workshop, *Lyon, miroir de Rome dans les Gaules* (Paris, 1965), 156 f. The reference to A. Héron de Villefosse, *BAC* (1917), 101, cited by P. Wuilleumier, *Lyon, métropole des Gaules* (Paris, 1953), 55, n. 58, deals only with the fabrication of bronze utensils.

36 *Master Bronzes*, 257, No. 247.

37 J. Charbonneaux, "Statuette d'athlète au Musée du Louvre," *MonPiot*, XXXVIII (1941), 40 f., pl. 4.

38 A. Héron de Villefosse, "Le Mercure d'Annecy," *GazArch*, II (1876), 55 ff., pl. 18. *Collection Auguste Dutuit, bronzes antiques*, I (Paris, 1897), pl. 1. G. Lippold, *Handbuch der Archäologie*, III, *Die griechische Plastik* (Munich, 1950), 166, pl. 59:4.

39 E. Babelon and J.-A. Blanchet, *Catalogue des bronzes antiques de la Bibliothèque Nationale* (Paris, 1895), 141 f., no. 315.

40 P. Lebel, *Catalogue des collections archéologiques de Besançon.* V, *Les bronzes figurés, Annales Littéraires de l'Université de Besançon,* ser. 2, XXVI (1959), pl. 16:1, 2; 17:1; 23:1, 2. H. Rolland, *Bronzes antiques de Haute Provence* (Paris 1965), nos. 39, 44, 46, 47, 48.

41 Babelon-Blanchet, *Bronzes* (n. 39), 150, no. 388, statuette from Chalon-sur-Saône; Braemer, *L'occident romain* (n. 35), 441, statuette from Bar-le-Duc; *ibid.,* no. 210, from Vaison and no. 375, from Sens.

42 Hill, *Catalogue* (n. 2), 19, no. 32, pl. 6.

43 Naturally, the type of Mercury discussed here also exists in Italy, as is demonstrated by H. Roux and L. Barré, *Herculanum und Pompeji,* V (Hamburg, 1841), pl. 51, with a table of corresponding types. In this connection, however, it should be remembered that the provinces, but especially Gaul, practiced an intensive worship of Mercury, and for this reason the production of statuettes of Mercury there was naturally extremely well-patronized. In Gaul not only was a Roman deity worshipped, but an indigenous god as well, as the many and different epithets make clear. See J. Toutain, *Les cultes païens dans l'Empire romain,* III (Paris, 1917), 205 ff.; F. Benoit, *Mars et Mercure* (Gap, 1959), 103 ff., and E. Thevenot, *Divinités et sanctuaires de la Gaule* (Paris, 1968), 72 ff. A few examples from Gaul might be enumerated here: S. Reinach, *Antiquités nationales, Description raisonnée du Musée de Saint-Germain-en-Laye,* II, *Bronze figurés de la Gaule romaine* (Paris, 1894), 74, no. 58, from Grozon, Jura; Babelon—Blanchet, *Bronzes* (n. 39), 151, no. 340, from Chalon-sur-Saône; Rolland, *Provence* (n. 40), no. 53, from Apt, nos. 54 and 55, findspots unknown but undoubtedly from Provence.

44 W. Deonna, "Catalogue des bronzes figurés antiques du Musée d'Art et d'Histoire de Genève," *AnzSchweiz,* N. F. XVII (1915), 207, no. 27, pl. 15.

45 J. Dörig, "Lysipps Zeuskoloss von Tarent," *JdI,* LXXIX (1964), 257 ff.

46 Reinach, *Gaule romaine* (n. 43), 29, with plate.

47 *Master Bronzes,* 264, No. 255.

48 K. A. Neugebauer, "Eine Bronzestatuette im Berliner Antiquarium," *Antike Plastik, W. Amelung zum 60. Geburtstag* (Berlin and Leipzig, 1928), 160 with note 1.

Discussion Session 3

Cornelius C. Vermeule, III
Discussant

Professor George M. A. Hanfmann asked Mr. Jucker whether there are bronzes from Populonia superior in quality to those that he had discussed. He suggested that a number of objects of high quality, stylistically not attributable to Vulci or Chiusi, should be localized in Populonia or the vicinity. Mr. Jucker replied that he had intentionally limited himself to the objects he had discussed because he felt that they formed a cohesive group, they could be dated in a single period, and they could be localized in the Populonia region by either alleged provenances or more certainly documented findspots. The earlier objects, from the late seventh and early sixth century B.C., such as the lion head (Jucker, Fig. 4) and the decorated metal plates from the Cerbone chariot (Jucker, Fig. 3), are unusual, peripheral art, Mr. Jucker explained. One can, however, trace a development and ripening of the style of Populonia from the late seventh century through the sixth, culminating perhaps in an early fifth-century group that consists of the Hirshhorn[1] and Käppeli[2] kouroi, the Fogg Turan (No. 168), and the Zeus in the Getty Museum (No. 164). [See also pp. 212-213.]

Professor Hanfmann then asked whether any investigations had been made of the Etruscan use of iron inlays in bronze. Mr. Jucker mentioned that a number of bronzes from the Caucasus, shown in an exhibition of Russian art in 1966-1967,[3] had iron inlays. A club head from Iran, perhaps from the Resht region (Fig. 1), another one from Lindos, and a third from Samos[4] are very similar to the wheel ornament from Populonia (Jucker, Fig. 3).

Mr. George Ortiz suggested that a dancing kore in the Museum of Fine Arts, Boston,[5] is a pendant to the kouros in the Schimmel collection (No. 159), because of their similar patinas and because both had probably been in the Joseph Brummer collection in the early 1930's. Professor Emeline Richardson of the University of North Carolina pointed out, however, that the Boston kore has a very unusual treatment of the eye — a "raised flat oval plaque in which the eyeball is deeply incised." She cited a running figure on a jug handle in Providence[6] as having the same sort of eye, but said that in the Schimmel kouros and the pieces attributed by Mr. Jucker to Populonia the eye was formed differently. She thought Mr. Jucker's grouping valid.

Professor Hanfmann then asked Dr. Haynes whether there is any relationship between the candelabrum figure of a woman with snake legs (Haynes, Figs. 8, 9) and the bronze Lasa with a sea monster (No. 184) belonging to the Fogg Art Museum. Dr. Haynes emphasized that there are two different types of ladies — those with snakelike legs ending in snakes' heads and those with twisted legs ending in fish tails. The latter are more frequent and can be identified as representing a kind of sea monster, but the snake-legged figures are quite rare and difficult to identify. She suggested that they might be death demons or other figures associated with the underworld.

Mr. Jucker mentioned that research is underway in Bern on the identification of various lead isotopes as a means of localizing bronze figurines mounted with lead[7] and asked whether similar research was going on in the United States. This technique would be particularly useful in the case of the objects he had attributed to Populonia because so many of them have lead bases preserved (see Jucker, Figs. 7, 30). Professor Cyril Stanley Smith replied that Dr. Robert Brill at the Corning Museum of Glass is the only one doing such work in the United States.[8]

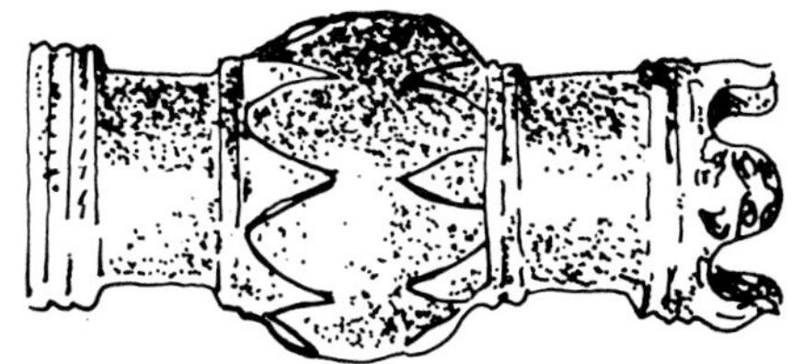

Fig. 1: Club head from Iran, perhaps from the Resht region, with iron inlay.

Professor Richardson took issue with some of Dr. Haynes's attributions to Vulci because, she said, to her knowledge the Etruscan schools that produce decorative bronzes — for candelabra, utensils, and so forth — do not also produce ex-votos. She objected, therefore, to Dr. Haynes's attributing to Vulci both the group of small decorative classical athletes and the standing male votive figure from Monteguragazza;[9] she suggested instead that only decorative bronzes were produced at Vulci. On the other hand, she pointed out, there was a school of the mid-sixth century B.C. in Arezzo that produced a distinctive group of votive statuettes but no decorative bronzes.[10] "The school of Vulci belongs to a period when the Etruscan *koine* is everywhere, and I think that Mr. Riis[11] was mistaken when he attributed everything to the school of Vulci," she continued. Neugebauer has identified a series of decorative bronzes which he attributed to Chiusi,[12] but which Mrs. Richardson feels are connected with the school of Capua. She suggested that yet another decorative school existed, in the Po Valley. Its candelabrum figures have different subject matter from those of Etruria proper — often mythological scenes. By studying subject matter and possibly also the moldings on which the candelabrum figures stand, one might be able to distinguish a group of centers, she added, rather than credit Vulci with everything.

Dr. Cornelius C. Vermeule, the discussant, asked whether a statue such as the one in Philadelphia of Dionysus with the lion[13] might be a prototype for the reclining, seated figures with a hand on a lion skin — be they Dionysus, Herakles, or Hermes. Dr. Menzel replied that he did not know the Philadelphia piece but that from the statues and statuettes he knew it appeared to him that the Herakles type was the earliest and served as a prototype for the later Hermes and Dionysus representations.

Professor Hanfmann asked Dr. Menzel whether he considered the Bacchus from Avenches (No. 246) to be a local product made in Aventicum or an import from Italy. Dr. Menzel replied that it would be necessary to examine a far greater number of half-life-size statuettes before coming to a definite answer, as the evidence from the few such objects already studied is insufficient. Only when a quantity of both Italian and non-Italian pieces has been investigated will scholars be able to define "provincial" work and thence perhaps to recognize distinctions among various workshops, in both Italy and the provinces.

Dr. Herbert A. Cahn suggested that Professor Steinberg had observed that the joins on the Bacchus from Avenches were made in a provincial fashion, so that even though the surface was well-finished, the object was apparently provincial in origin. Miss Heather Lechtman explained that Professor Steinberg had said, rather, that the type of join on the Avenches statue is very close to the type on the Agde figure[14] and on the drapery fragment in Boston (No. 237; see pp. 22-32). She suggested that careful study of the technological idiosyncrasies of various ancient bronzes might afford a new means of classing them into schools or workshops.

Notes

1 See n. 90, p. 219.

2 See n. 91, p. 219.

3 *Historische Schätze aus der Sowjetunion,* exhibition at the Kunsthaus, Zurich, December 17, 1966-February 26, 1967; A. Rieth, "Anfänge und Entwicklung der Tauschiertechnik," *Eurasia Septentrionalis Antiqua,* X (1936), 189, fig. 3.

4 J. M. Birmingham, "The Overland Route across Anatolia in the Eighth and Seventh Centuries B.C.," *AnatSt*, XI (1961), 192, figs. 7 ,9, 10. Figure 1 here is after Birmingham's fig. 10; the object is in his possession.

5 Accession no. 01.7482; G. H. Chase, *Greek, Etruscan and Roman Art, The Classical Collection of the Museum of Fine Arts, Boston*, revised by C. C. Vermeule (Boston, 1963), fig. 190.

6 Accession no. 29.089; M. A. Banks, "The Bronze Jug," *Bulletin of the Rhode Island School of Design*, XXII:1 (1934), 4-5, ill.

7 N. Grögler *et al.*, "Isotopenuntersuchungen zur Bestimmung der Herkunft römischer Bleirohre und Bleibarren," *Zeitschrift für Naturforschung*, XXIa (1966), 1167-1172.

8 R. H. Brill and J. M. Wampler, "Isotope Studies of Ancient Lead," *AJA*, LXIX (1965), 165.

9 As both Dr. Haynes and Professor Richardson pointed out, this attribution was first made by P. J. Riis, *Tyrrhenika* (Copenhagen, 1941), 90.

10 Emeline H. Richardson, "A Series of Votive Bronzes from Arezzo," *AJA*, LXXII (1968), 171, summary of a paper presented at the Archaeological Institute of America meetings in Boston December 29, 1967.

11 Riis, *Tyrrhenika* (n. 9), 72-96.

12 K. A. Neugebauer, "Kohlenbecken aus Clusium und Verwandtes," *RömMitt*, LI (1936), 181 ff.

13 E. H. Hall, "A Seated Dionysos," *The Museum Journal*, University of Pennsylvania, IV:4 (1913), 164 ff., ill.

PART 4

Introduction to Part 4

Arthur Steinberg

Many questions and still unanswerable problems are raised by the provocative paper by Hanfmann and Gazda. Two areas in particular suggest technological problems that need some amplification. The first of these deals with the reintroduction of ancient subjects and motifs in the Renaissance and the degree to which these are coupled with ancient techniques. The second area has to do with the development of the bronze-casting industry during the Renaissance, when apparently a considerable degree of specialization was practiced and had important effects on the products of that period.

In considering the technological impetus for the Renaissance we are concerned again with the cross-cultural diffusion or transmission of certain motifs and techniques, as in the case of the Orientalizing motifs and techniques that were introduced into Greece during the eighth century B.C. (see pp. 103-106). Before the Renaissance, however, there was a period of about 800 years during which motifs and possibly techniques seem to have lain dormant, before their rather sudden rebirth in the fourteenth century. How are we to understand such delayed transmission? The bronze-casting, or rather mold-building, techniques that were used in the Renaissance (prior to the introduction of sand casting, which is a marked innovation) were all known in antiquity and employed by Roman founders. The various methods of building molds described by Biringuccio in 1450 are all evidenced on large Roman statuary. They are also used on large art castings of the fourteenth and fifteenth centuries but are little in evidence in the intervening period. During the Middle Ages direct and indirect lost-wax castings are apparently known only in nonstatuary bronzes or small objects. Are we to assume, then, that the techniques were carried through the Middle Ages on smaller and more utilitarian objects and were then suddenly "reborn" in the fourteenth century with the reintroduction of classical subjects? In short, are technique and subject to be divorced over this long period and then re-wed in the course of the early Renaissance or is there simply a large missing link, possibly in Byzantium, for the intervening period? As we saw before, the Orientalizing Greek griffin protomes are an example of subject and technique imported together and then separated by local craftsmen. Is there in the Renaissance a different kind of transmission whereby technique and subject are separated in the Middle Ages, carried along independently, and then reunited by craftsmen in the early Renaissance; or is this contrary to what we might expect of technological development?

The procedures for building large direct lost-wax casting *statuary* molds are all present in the mold-building techniques of bells and church doors. Therefore, as Hanfmann and Gazda have intimated, it is likely that the technical know-how for casting large statues was continued from Late Antiquity through the Middle Ages (in the West, at any rate) in the making of large bells and doors but was not transferred back to the making of large statues until some time in the thirteenth or fourteenth century. By the fifteenth century some sculptors were sending their models to bell founders rather than casting them themselves, but on other occasions the same sculptors (notable among them Donatello) did their own mold building and casting. The result was a complex and fluid interrelationship between artist and founder. It would be valuable to know to what extent this Renaissance distribution of labor mirrors the practices of antiquity and how it relates to the complicated transmission of large and complex mold-building and casting techniques.

The second area that raises interesting problems about technological development is that of the progress made during the Renaissance in the refinement of mold-building and casting techniques. Because in the Renaissance, for the first time, there are many literary sources and documents to illustrate the story of bronze casting, far too few technical studies have been made of the actual objects to determine how they were modeled, molded, and made. Clearly the "documents" exist for a study of the progress made by sculptors and founders in the refinement of their art; it only remains for us to examine them properly. Such technical examinations not only will reveal the progress made by these craftsmen but also should shed some light on the complex question of how specialization effects technological development.

Hanfmann and Gazda cite Aitchison's *History of Metals,* which states that during the course of the early Renaissance there was a great degree of specialization among bronze-casters by craft — according to the kinds of objects they made. (See pp. 173 ff., where it is suggested that this was probably true in antiquity as well.) The question arises whether such specialization leads to the refinement of techniques within each narrow craft and thence to the invention of new methods, or whether invention and innovation come from outside a specialized craft and are brought by people who are accustomed to viewing a problem in a different way.

The following schemes are suggested by this problem. First, specialization might lead to refinement, which in turn might bring innovation along with it, leading to a technically improved and more efficient practice of the craft. Or alternatively, specialization might lead to technical stagnation, so that only the introduction of new workers or new materials will bring innovation into the craft, leading to improvements in technique and efficiency. A third variant includes improvements from both within and outside the craft. Specialization by craft leads to internal refinements and then has introduced to it an invention from another area which helps to improve the particular craft. Clearly this is a highly theoretical structure to explain technological development, but I should add that to elucidate the general forms of technological development is in itself important, and the Renaissance offers us one set of data upon which to base theories.

In addition to the purely technical elements of technological development noted, important cultural factors are at work in this process. Cultural factors condition the introduction of new methods into a specialized craft and their adaptation. It is the interplay of society and technology that makes technological development so complex and hence difficult to analyze.

One such cultural factor of great importance during the Renaissance is the craft guild and its use of recipe books and the like. Such highly structured institutions as the guild probably canonized traditional techniques and a whole craft to the extent that they became rigidly formalized, incapable of variation and inflexible to innovation. Thus a member of some bronze-making guild, working in the traditional fashion prescribed by his organization, probably went on making bronzes in precisely the same fashion that had been practiced for many years. A new technique that might have permitted greater efficiency, such as sand casting, could only have been introduced with the greatest of difficulty unless economic or social pressures were placed upon the guild to reform its ways. Another strong cultural influence on the development of bronze working might have been the Church and the kind of market that it created for bronzes. Most commissions were for the adornment of churches, which certainly put strong constraints on the subjects depicted. Whether there were also religious sanctions on techniques, either explicit or implicit in the subjects, is still a moot point. We cannot know how the sculptor might have felt about trying a new technique or some variant of an old one on an important church bronze, but we might expect that he was influenced in what he did by the nature of the commission and the immense influence of the Church on his life and livelihood. Similarly, we cannot yet measure the effect that a wealthy patron's demands of quality, speed of execution, and so forth might have had on the technical performance of a bronze worker, be he sculptor, armorer, or bell maker.

These are examples of the kinds of variables involved in the development of technology during a period like the Renaissance. But then the Renaissance situation is much more complex still because of the superimposing of traditional subjects and techniques from antiquity on the contemporary working-out of artistic and technical problems.

Ancient Bronzes: Decline, Survival, Revival

Elaine K. Gazda
George M. A. Hanfmann

Although this paper was originally to deal with the survival of ancient bronzes, the nature of the subject matter, viewed historically, soon led to a consideration of its tangential aspects — decline and revival. Within this extended framework numerous possibilities suggested themselves. We should have liked to consider three comprehensive problems: (1) the condition of the bronze industry in Greece and Rome based on statistical data; (2) the subsequent decline and rebuilding of bronze-working as an industry, the development of its facilities and its technological progress from the early Middle Ages through the sixteenth century, particularly as they affected the production of statues and figurines — in this connection the question of the relationship between the sculptor-designer and the bronze-casting master craftsman would have been of special interest; and (3) the conditions of survival of ancient figurative bronzes, from both the conservationist's point of view and the standpoint of the impact of these classical bronzes on European, Byzantine, and Islamic art.

Filling out the ambitiously sketched contours of such an outline would require the co-operation of experts from many disciplines — economists, metallurgists, archaeologists, and art historians, not to mention cultural historians of all kinds. The following remarks are offered in the hope that they might stimulate such co-operation.[1]

Decline

The decline of ancient bronzes encompasses more than the dramatic falling-off of bronze production at the end of the Roman period. It also includes the demolition of those bronze sculptures that had been so abundant and highly prized in the classical world. This aspect raises many questions. When did the wholesale destruction take place that left so few bronzes extant by the fifteenth century? To what extent, how, where, and by whom were these bronzes melted down and re-used? To what extent were they wasted? A few examples will illustrate the means and types of destruction suffered by the industry and its products.

One is tempted to say that many ancient bronzes were destroyed soon after they were made. We know from the recipe for statuary bronze given by Pliny (*N. H.* XXXIV. xx. 97, 98) that old copper and bronze made up about one third of the alloy.[2] Although some of this was undoubtedly foundry waste, discarded statues and figurines probably furnished part of this scrap requirement. Hundreds of archaic bronzes were lost to posterity when they were buried in the embankment of the classical stadium at Olympia.[3] The Delphic bronze snake tripod was first damaged when the golden bowl that topped it was stolen in 353 B.C.[4]

Natural catastrophes caused the destruction of many ancient bronzes. The Charioteer of Delphi probably fell victim to an earthquake in 373 B.C.[5] Also the victim of an earthquake was the illustrious Colossus of Rhodes, designed by Chares of Lindos around 280 B.C. It is said to have been over seventy cubits high, and though sensibly provided with extra strength at the ankles, it stood only half a century before it was overthrown ca. 224 B.C.[6] Since an oracle supposedly forbade the people of Rhodes to set it up again,[7] it must have lain on the ground for centuries until the Arabs (Saracens) took Rhodes in 653 A.D., dismantled the fallen statue, and sold the bronze to a Jewish merchant from Edessa in Mesopotamia.[8] Although the sources do not inform us of the ultimate fate of the bronze from the

Colossus, we do know that while European metallurgy was going downhill in the seventh century, Arab technology was on the rise, and the Arabs needed bronze.[9]

While destruction by natural disasters occurred repeatedly, man was really the worst enemy of ancient bronzes. Barbarians invading the classical lands are commonly credited with most of the devastation. One of their earliest victims, perhaps, was the head of the Emperor Claudius found in the River Alde at Rendham, Suffolk, and now in the British Museum (Fig. 1).[10] It was violently hacked from its body, probably at the time of the uprising of the British Queen Boudicca in 61 A.D., only eighteen years after the Roman conquest of Britain.[11] Sir George Macdonald conjectured that pieces of the statue were distributed as scrap among the spoilers. Other bronze statues in England may have met their end similarly, though at a much later date.[12] Ideally, a thorough investigation would follow such bronze fragments on their wanderings to barbarian settlements and show how they were melted down and what sorts of British objects were made from them.

Such instances of barbarian destruction were not uncommon throughout the continent under Roman rule. In his fine introduction to the Roman bronzes in the *Master Bronzes* catalogue Heinz Menzel recalls another famous case, related to the German invasion of Gaul in 275 A.D. The statue in question is thought to have been the cult image of Mars in the Temple of Aire, high up in the mountains of the Jura (Fig. 2). When the barbarians invaded, the statue was smashed completely. The fleeing priests picked up the pieces and "buried them when they themselves were endangered." In 1897 a farmer near Coligny discovered the fragments, and the recomposed statue is now in the museum at Lyon.[13]

Alaric the Goth's demand for gold and silver caused the Romans to melt down the statues and ornaments of those metals. Procopius' account of Genseric the Vandal's capture of Rome in 455 A.D. makes it clear that bronzes were among the statues that were taken away:

> . . . placing an exceedingly great amount of gold and other imperial treasure in his ships [Genseric] sailed to Carthage, having spared neither bronze nor anything else whatsoever in the palace. He plundered also the temple of Jupiter Capitolinus, and tore off half of the roof. Now this roof was of bronze of the finest quality, and . . . gold was laid over it exceedingly thick . . . .[14]

But Genseric's ship, bound for Carthage, sank before reaching its destination.

While reports of barbarian demolition of bronzes are far from scarce, it is by no means clear whether the barbarians or the Roman citizens themselves destroyed more bronze statues. We are aware that in the northern provinces the early Christians shared the responsibility for the devastation of classical images;[15] St. Martin was among the most active of the idol smashers.[16] For the city of Rome the over-all picture of despoliation is clear. The Regionary Catalogues of the fourth century, listing extant statues area by area, recorded 3785 bronze statues;[17] by the early fifteenth century only half a dozen were known.[18] The militant writings of SS. Augustine and Jerome suggest that the early Christians had overthrown many pagan images in Rome long before the invasions of the Goths.[19] Imperial edicts beginning in 399 A.D., calling for the removal of cult images from the

Fig. 1: Bronze head of Claudius, The British Museum (photo no. 1763).

sanctuaries, were originally intended to put a halt to pagan cult practices.[20] In some cases they distinguished between statues to be preserved as works of art and those which were to be considered idols and destroyed,[21] but in practice indiscriminate destruction often resulted.

Perhaps as many as several hundred "brazen statues of the most exquisite workmanship"[22] were brought together in Constantinople from 324 to 450 A.D. by Constantine and his successors.[23] Most of the eighty statues collected in the Baths of Zeuxippus and later destroyed were of bronze.[24] In a very illuminating article Cyril Mango has shown how the statues of Constantinople were decimated from the fifth century on by fires, riots, and natural catastrophes.[25] He has illustrated, too, that while there is no record of wholesale suppression of these pagan monuments by the Byzantine government, individual reprisals were taken against certain statues.[26] By the time Constantinople fell in 1453, only the famous serpent column from Delphi and an equestrian statue of Justinian remained.

The greatest single blow against ancient bronze statues in Constantinople was struck by the Latin conquerors of the Fourth Crusade during their infamous looting of the city (April 13-16, 1204). The Byzantine author, Nicetas Choniates, has left a pamphlet on the destruction of the statues. "The need for money," says Choniates, "caused the conquerors to have recourse to the bronze statues, which they threw into the fire. The first to be melted down was the colossal Hera which adorned the Forum of Constantine . . .;" and he proceeds to describe eighteen other famous bronze masterpieces that perished.[27] One of these was the great Athena in front of the Senate, perhaps the Promachos by Phidias.[28] Choniates' claim that the statues were melted down "for coins of the most mediocre sort"[29] has been repeated time and again by modern commentators, yet numismatists have been unable to identify such coins minted in Constantinople during the period. The most recent examination of this troublesome passage does, however, indicate that new evidence may prove Choniates trustworthy. If so, it would provide a rare instance of history's recording exactly how destroyed ancient bronzes were re-used.[30]

For gaining insight into the decline of bronze production, a survey of sites where the mass production of bronze statues and figurines had been carried on would be more important than studying individual cases of destruction, to determine when and how such production ceased. First, a study of known workshop sites throughout the Roman Empire would be necessary and then an examination of the sanctuaries where votive bronzes were concentrated and, as Menzel suggests, perhaps also were made.[31] We can show, for instance, that a flourishing bronze industry at Sardis was brought to a sudden end by the Persian invasion in 616 A.D. Similar data can be gathered for sites in a number of provinces; the exemplary work of R. F. Tylecote and others in Britain has shown the possibilities for advance.[32] Real potential for technological research and analysis is present at sites where armor and implements were manufactured, as, for instance, in the workshops that supplied the military legions.[33] Much preparatory work is needed for such a study of bronzes in the eastern part of the Empire, including the remarkable profusion of bronzes from Coptic Egypt. The first prerequisite is to collect, group, and date the relevant material, especially as it bears on the question of where and how long workshops were active during the transition to the Dark Ages.[34]

Fig. 2: Mars from Coligny, Musée de Lyon. Photo after MonPiot, *X (1903), 74, fig. 5.*

Fig. 3: Colossus of Barletta, Church of San Sepolcro. Alinari photo no. 35200.

Survival[35]

When we turn to the survival of technical competence in bronze-working in the centuries between late antiquity and the Renaissance, it becomes necessary to distinguish the survival of ancient statues and figurines from the survival of the techniques for working bronze. In the Byzantine East the dramatic decline in the number of statues in Constantinople did not signal a corresponding decline in the ability to work bronze. Although in some ways the material is less well explored and organized, evidence from the Byzantine East certainly bears out the thought that Byzantine bronze-casters were capable of making, and did make, some great monuments throughout the many centuries of the Byzantine Empire. In Constantinople they occupied their own quarter of the city and were apparently organized into professional guilds.[36]

Literary notices offer scattered evidence of the continuing manufacture of bronze statues in Byzantium at least until the eighth century.[37] Some information about the early Byzantine making of statues might be secured from the so-called Colossus of Barletta (Fig. 3), which is the only ancient colossal bronze statue of which most of the body is preserved.[38] According to a poem of the late fifteenth or early sixteenth century, the Venetians had shipped the Colossus from Constantinople to Venice, but the ship was wrecked near Barletta. The Colossus was first mentioned as lying on the Customs beach at Barletta in 1309. In 1481, it was erected in front of San Sepolcro; arms, legs, and attributes were restored by the bronze *faber*, Fabius Albanus (Fabio Alfano).[39] From 1348 on, the Colossus was called Heraklios (610-641), a tradition which, if correct, would imply a most impressive state of Byzantine casting of free-standing statuary as late as the seventh century. Modern identifications, which have ranged from Valentinian I (364-367) to Anastasius I (491-518), cast doubt on the late dating.[40] Yet, it may well be that the Colossus was an earlier statue re-used by Heraklios.[41]

The bronze equestrian statue of Justinian, perhaps represented in a fifteenth-century drawing in Budapest (Fig. 4),[42] is considered by some scholars to have been a re-used statue of the Theodosian era. The metal of the column on which the statue stood offers an interesting comment on the composition of Byzantine bronzes. Procopius describes it as ". . . of extraordinary size, not a monolith, however, but composed of large stones in circular courses . . . and finest brass [*chalkos*] cast in panels and garlands covers the stones on every side . . . This brass in its colour, is softer than pure gold, and its value is not much less than that of an equal weight of silver."[43] Roman *aurichalcum,* meaning "golden copper," was used for imitation gold jewelry and ornaments as well as for coins.[44] The Byzantines may have begun to employ a more brassy alloy, perhaps related to this Roman *aurichalcum.*[45] A lion lamp found at Sardis (Fig. 5) also took on a brassy appearance after cleaning. It was found in the Shop of the Lion with coins ranging in date from the reign of Arcadius and Honorius (395-408) to the early seventh century. Presumably it was still in use when the shop was destroyed by the Persians in 616 A.D.[46]

While the iconoclastic period in Byzantium (726-843) probably effectively ended any large-scale use of bronze statues and figurines, the prowess of Byzantine metalworkers continued undiminished in the production, in the Roman tradition, of such objects as magnificent doors.[47] Bronze doors such as those of Hagia Sophia, various parts of which have been dated to the late fourth, the sixth, and the ninth centuries,[48] were paralleled in the West in the cast doors of Mainz (ca. 1009), Hildesheim (1015), and Augsburg (1050-1065). Those doors that are to be found in Italy, dating from the later eleventh century onward, were probably either of Byzantine workmanship or done after Byzantine models.[49] These two series of bronze doors confront us with the survival and continuity of bronze technology in the West.

Historians of metalwork agree that Western bronze-working declined between the fifth and the eleventh centuries. Aitchison's chapter is characteristically entitled "Eclipse in the West," and R. J. Forbes observes that "the paucity of information on copper and bronze suggests that the political troubles hastened the displacement of those metals by iron."[50] The making of bronze weapons, armor, and jewelry spans this nadir of metallurgy, although the disintegration of the state-controlled system of Roman metallurgical enterprises (mines, smelteries, refineries, and factories) dealt the craft a nearly fatal blow.[51] While fine metalwork is known in the early Middle Ages, it has been thought that there are no surviving bronze statues or figurines undoubtedly of this period. Even the Carolingian date of the famous horseman, the so-called Charlemagne, in the Musée Carnavalet has been called into question.[52]

Fig. 4: Imperial rider, University Library, Budapest, ms. 35, f. 44v. Photo after P. Lehmann, ArtB, *XLI (1959), 37 ff., fig. 1.*

Now, however, in the face of concrete evidence for the founding of bronze on a significant scale — although not with certainty for statuary in the round — doubts about Carolingian bronze-workers' ability to deal with complex castings should probably be put aside. Mines in the eastern part of Charlemagne's empire — the regions that are now Saxony, Silesia, and Czechoslovakia — were opened for extracting copper, gold, and silver,[53] and available materials were put to use in numerous royal commissions.

Crucial evidence for the technological attainments of Carolingian bronze-casters was discovered in the workshop at Aix-la-Chapelle, found in 1911 together with parts of the casting furnace and fragments of the molds for the bronze doors.[54] The report of Schmidt-Wöppke is unpublished, but Duard Laging, after examining the mold fragments, affirms with Goldschmidt that the lost-wax process was used in casting the Carolingian doors.[55] Herman Luer finds in the same doors evidence of the fact that the methods of lost-wax casting were never forgotten in the West.[56] Not all scholars, however, are convinced of the technological talents of Charlemagne's subjects; some would still credit Greek workmen, or at least supervisors from Byzantium, with the lion's share of the bronze work at Aix-la-Chapelle.[57]

As an interesting sidelight it might be added that Charlemagne's commissions sometimes drew their inspiration directly from the monuments of the ancient Romans. The bronze Wolf's Door at Aix-la-Chapelle (Fig. 6), for example, was surely modeled after doors in Rome.[58] It has even been conjectured that the lion heads on these doors were inspired by the head of the Roman bronze wolf (or bear) that Charlemagne had brought back from Italy.[59]

Fig. 5: Lion lamp, Sardis, M 67.4 (7291), Byzantine shops 67.96.8.

A further tie to the antique past is suggested by the metal analyses of the doors. Those at Aix-la-Chapelle contain a normal amount of tin (9.6 per cent) and a low quantity of lead (3.5 per cent) and iron (0.6 per cent), compared to later doors. For example, the doors at Hildesheim (ca. 1015) contain 11.25 per cent lead, and those at Augsburg (ca. 1050-1065), 20.1 per

Fig. 6: Wolf's door, Aix-la-Chapelle. Photo Bildarchiv, Marburg no. 5020.

Fig. 7: Fontana Maggiore, Perugia, upper portion. Alinari photo no. 21438.

cent.[60] It has been suggested that the Carolingian doors might have been made in large part from old melted-down bronzes,[61] an ingredient familiar to the users of Pliny's recipe. The high lead content of the later doors is more common in the Middle Ages, probably due to the scarcity of tin.[62]

The progress of bronze metallurgy after the eleventh century is well illustrated by the third book of the so-called Theophilus, written probably in the twelfth century in Germany.[63] Theophilus is especially important for our knowledge of medieval metalworking, as C. S. Smith and J. G. Hawthorne have observed, because "though the processes he described had their roots deep in the past, the information had been transmitted as the living, growing practical tradition in the workshops themselves, not as words passing perilously through scriptoria."[64] In chapter 61, Theophilus gives instructions for making a fearfully complicated censer representing the Heavenly Jerusalem and including "full figures of angels with shields and spears . . ." As far as one can see, the production of such figures owes nothing to direct contact with classical bronzes, but it does show medieval bronze-workers to be technologically capable of casting complex figures in the round.[65]

Beginning in the eighth century much progress in metalwork was made by the bell-casting industry,[66] the lessons of which were later applied to the production of statuary. With large-scale bell-casting the use of direct lost-wax casting (where a core is made, the model is built over it in wax, and the mold is built over the wax model) became popular again. The bronze effigy of Eleanor of Castile in Westminster Abbey, made by William Torel in 1291-1292, has walls four inches thick, typical of the bell-founding method.[67] In Italy in the late thirteenth century rather large and complicated statuary bronzes were made. The Fontana Maggiore in Perugia (Fig. 7), designed by Nicola and Giovanni Pisano and completed in 1278, is a particularly interesting example of the combination of the direct lost-wax casting method used by bell-founders and the indirect lost-wax method of piece-mold casting (in which piece molds are made from a model, then coated with wax and cored, see p. 107 f.). G. N. Fasola, writing after the restoration of the fountain in 1948-1949, points out that the large bronze basin was probably cast by bell-founding methods (by one Rubeus, according to the inscription), while piece molds may have been used for the casting of the caryatids.[68] The group of lions and griffins that rests on top of the caryatids was cast by the direct lost-wax method, and the thinness of the bronze perhaps argues for a much later date. Fasola does, in fact, compare the technique to that employed in the fifteenth century by Ghiberti and Donatello.[69] In any case, on the evidence of the Fontana Maggiore alone — and there are other important bronzes of the period still to be examined — it would appear that several traditions of mold-making had survived the Middle Ages and were being revitalized as the interest in producing bronze statuary increased.

In the fourteenth century foundries turned to casting cannon, and by the fifteenth century the profession had become quite specialized.

> Some, the "potters," were producers of brass pots, small cauldrons, and household articles and utensils while "latoners" or "latteners" worked up the alloy into many domestic forms. Alongside these groups were the bell-casters, the gun-casters, and those founders who, working in cooperation with artists and architects, produced statues and memorial figures in either bronze or brass, some of which were very large indeed.[70]

Between 1200 and 1500 great strides were made in the use of water power and of heating devices such as reverberatory furnaces, but these probably did not improve the quality of casting so much as they increased the founder's capability of working in larger quantities of metal.[71]

For the casting of bronze works of art it is necessary to consider the role played in the fifteenth century by the sculptors, to whom the development of bronze technology posed a great challenge. In their feats of bronze-casting the Renaissance sculptors felt they were rivaling the ancients. The intellectual and aesthetic revival of the classical world was thus being integrated with the technological workshop tradition of the Middle Ages. The new factor was that sculptors like Ghiberti and Donatello experimented with metal-casting and metal-decorating techniques themselves rather than entrust their work entirely to professional casters.

When Ghiberti tried to run his own foundry for casting his St. John the Baptist (ca. 1414), the guild that commissioned the statue, the Arte di Calimala, stipulated that he finance all of the procedures of the casting and assume the costs if he failed.[72] In casting the large St. John in a single piece Ghiberti attempted a tour de force, and he succeeded, but his work did not always go this well. In July 1421, he had to report that parts of the St. Matthew would have to be recast.[73] Donatello perhaps exercised good judgment in turning to the bell-caster Andrea dalle Caldiere of Padua for casting the figures and reliefs of the altar of San Antonio and the Gattamelata.[74] But he did not always rely on bell-founders. In fact, his methods of making molds were at times quite experimental and daring. Not only was the piece-mold system used for the statue of St. Louis of Toulouse, for example, but the statue had to be cast in several pieces so that fire gilding could be used. Even now, although the fit of the parts is not perfect, the seams deftly concealed in folds can be detected only on close inspection.[75]

It is a further sign of the interest in technology among artists that Pomponius Gauricus, a scholar, poet, and in his youth an amateur sculptor, felt obliged in his *De Sculptura* to give exact data on bell-alloy and alloy for statues and wrote a useful chapter on the technology of bronze statuary.[76] It is characteristic of the confident attitude of the Renaissance (he wrote the book as a twenty-one-year-old in 1503) that, following the pattern of the Elder Pliny and enumerating famous bronze sculptors, Gauricus begins with over fifty of those from classical antiquity and lists, immediately following these, nine moderns of the fourteenth and fifteenth centuries.[77] His view is that bronze sculptors of antiquity and the Renaissance constitute one continuous and, in a way, equal phalanx of artistic achievement, to which technology and the study of materials belong as much as do the studies of symmetry, perspective, physiognomics, mathematics, music, geometry, classical antiquity, and horseback riding! Gauricus' polemic is directed against those who would consider the sculptor a mere craftsman and deny that he needs to educate himself as a humanist. He rejects the idea that high or low birth have any bearing on a sculptor's success and would raise sculpture to the rank of the seven traditional *artes liberales*.[78]

Fig. 8: Perseus and Medusa by Benvenuto Cellini, Loggia dei Lanzi, Florence. Alinari photo no. 2489.

The height of enthusiasm among sculptors for bronze technology is reached in Benvenuto Cellini's dramatic account of the casting of his Perseus (1545-1553) (Fig. 8). Cellini could find no foundry in Florence that was able to accommodate his complex plan, so he had to design and build one of his own. He takes the reader step by step through accidents, trials,

Fig. 9: Idolino, Museo Archeologico, Florence. Alinari photo no. 31137.

Fig. 10: Atys-Amor by Donatello, Museo Nazionale, Florence. Alinari photo no. 2648.

and tribulations to the final triumph in which he gloats over his technical omniscience, proved by the fact that the toes of one foot of Perseus had not quite filled out in the casting, precisely as he had predicted to his patron, the Duke Cosimo de' Medici.[79]

During the Mannerist and Baroque periods the casting of sculpture became ever bolder, but, perhaps because of the greater skill and proficiency shown in the technique, it ceased to be a focal subject of concern to the sculptors themselves. Likewise, the founders seemed less concerned with the problem of casting sculpture than with the production of artillery. The new attitude is evidenced in Vannoccio Biringuccio's *Pyrotechnica* of 1539 and in Georgius Agricola's *De Re Metallica*, which was completed, though not published, in 1550.[80] In Biringuccio's book, the "Making of Molds for Bronze Statues" (Chapter VI:4) is sandwiched in between "Guns and Their Sizes" (VI:3) and "Molds for Guns" (VI:5).

Revival

We may ask at this point what role was played by those rare ancient bronzes that managed to survive the centuries; what was their effect on later generations? In his instructive inaugural lecture at Utrecht W. S. Heckscher suggested that a display of several ancient bronzes was put up in the papal palace of the Lateran in the eighth century with a moralizing didactic intent. The Capitoline Wolf, called "Mother of Romans," was a symbol of papal judicial power and presided over executions; the horseman, Marcus Aurelius, was thought to be Constantine, defender of the Christian faith; the colossal head of Constantius II (337-361) — according to some recent scholars, that of Constantine — was interpreted as *Sol Iustitiae;* and the Spinario served as an example of a pagan idol to be abhorred.[81] This is the same collection the humanist Poggio Bracciolini saw around 1430 and described as an example of the changeability of fortune.[82]

Other ancient bronzes wandered farther afield. For these, often, the time of their reappearance was important. Thus Carolingian art could have profited from the equestrian statue of Theodoric which Charlemagne brought from Ravenna to Aix-la-Chapelle — perhaps in emulation of the Lateran display — and also from the wolf (or bear) alluded to earlier. We know that in 1495 Pomponius Gauricus had an opportunity to observe the Colossus of Barletta, although its technological features seem not to have impressed him at that time.[83]

The horses of San Marco, thought Lysippan by many scholars, Roman by others, were probably taken from Chios to Constantinople, where they may have stood in the Hippodrome until the Venetians shipped them to Venice after the sack of Constantinople in 1204.[84] Set up over the portal of San Marco, they may well have inspired Paolo Uccello, who had worked on the San Marco mosaics, when he painted Sir John Hawkwood in the Duomo in Florence (1436). They were studied by Donatello, and as late as 1616 the sculptor Francesco Mocchi made a special trip to Venice to observe them and Verrocchio's statue of Colleoni when working on his equestrian monuments of Ranuccio and Alessandro Farnese.[85]

In examining the revival of interest in bronze sculpture which some of these ancient statues helped to launch, one should consider the study and imitation as well as the creative assimilation of ancient bronzes. The bronze statuette is perhaps one of the most interesting of the ancient art forms

Fig. 11: Weeping Eros, engraving by Sandrart. Photo after L. Curtius, "Poenitentia," Festschrift für James Loeb, *53, fig. 1.*

that reappeared during the Renaissance. Certainly the artists of the fifteenth century knew of Statius' enthusiastic appraisal of a statuette of Hercules, ". . . small to the eye, a giant to the mind . . .," and of Pliny's respect for bronze as a noble material.[86] Historians of Renaissance sculpture claim that both Ghiberti and Donatello must have studied ancient bronze figurines, although pinning down actual models for their work is difficult. It is thought that Donatello studied classical *bronzetti* in the 1420's when he created the charming *putti* on the crozier of Saint Louis of Toulouse (1423-1425) and the Siena Font (1423-1434), and later when he made the Atys-Amor (ca. 1440).[87]

To add a hypothesis to the search for ancient models that *might* have been known to Donatello and have influenced his formal conception of this last figure, we can compare the Atys-Amor (Fig. 10) to the type of weeping Amor that was known at least by the seventeenth century, when Sandrart interpreted it charmingly as an allegory of penitence (Fig. 11).[88] There is some resemblance in the peculiar position of the belt and in the pudgy body, raised arm, and projecting hip. The stumbling block is, of course, the question of whether any statues of the weeping Amor or similar ancient representations of children were known to Donatello. The classical model used in Sandrart's engraving is now in the Palazzo Pitti but was in Rome when he portrayed it.[89] Other ancient examples of the weeping Eros such as the bronze statuette in the collection of Edwin L. Weisl, Jr. (No. 127; Fig. 12)[90] indicate that the type was not uncommon, at least in antiquity.

Renaissance bronze statuettes frequently imitated on a small scale the bronze and marble monuments of antique sculpture, especially those in Rome. The first certain, datable object of this sort, which imitates an antique bronze, is a statuette of Marcus Aurelius on horseback by Filarete (height 49.2 cm., length 37.5 cm., Fig. 13). The inscription on its base states that Filarete sent the statuette to Piero de' Medici in 1465, but also indicates

Fig. 12: Weeping Eros, collection of Edwin L. Weisl, Jr. Photo courtesy of Dumbarton Oaks.

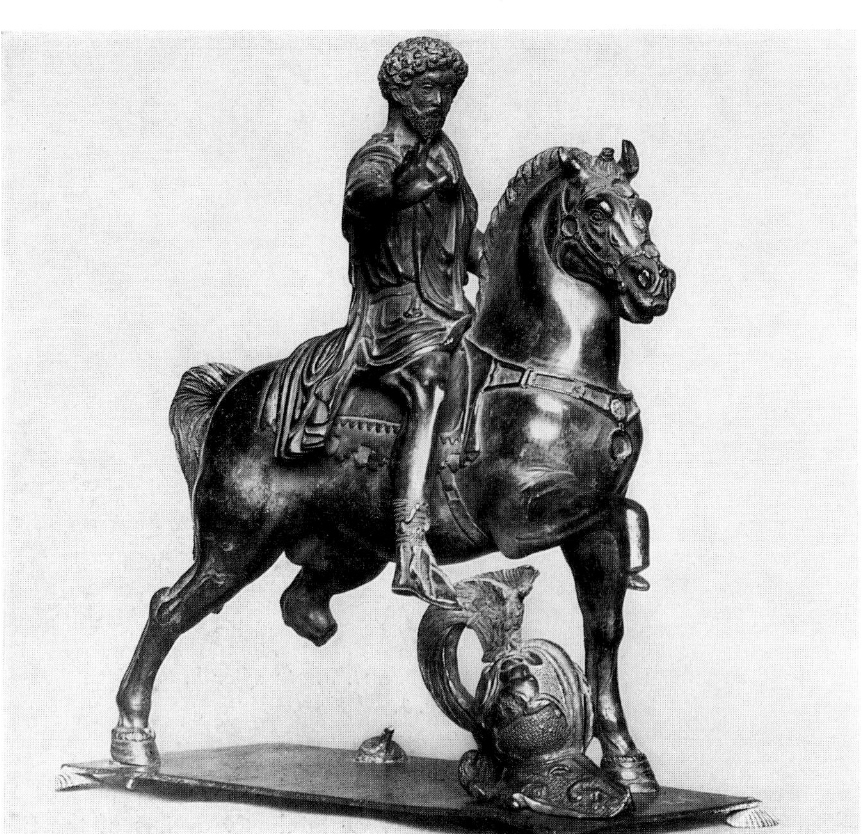

Fig. 13: Marcus Aurelius by Filarete, Skulpturensammlungen, Dresden (photo no. 10517).

that the piece was cast in Rome while Filarete was working on his famous bronze door for St. Peter's between 1433 and 1445.[91] The bronzes seen by Poggio Bracciolini in 1430 were sometimes copied while they were still at the Lateran but apparently much more frequently after they were moved to the Capitoline Hill by Pope Sixtus IV.[92] The she-wolf in the Samuel H. Kress Collection in Washington (Fig. 14)[93] is a reduction to exactly half height of the famous archaic Etruscan original of 500 B.C., now in the Palazzo dei Conservatori (Fig. 15).[94] Pope-Hennessy attributes the piece, known since 1730 when in the collection of August the Strong of Poland, to a late fifteenth-century, possibly Roman, bronze sculptor. Renaissance sculptors were keenly interested in the proportional enlargement and reduction of statues; Pomponius Gauricus prescribes methods for achieving the proper results. By the late fifteenth century artists like Pier Iacopo Bonacolsi, nicknamed Antico (ca. 1460-1528), were being sent out by their patrons to make reduced versions of the most famous antique originals of both marble and bronze. Antico was sent to Rome in 1497 by the Gonzagas of Mantua and later worked for Isabella d'Este.[95] Not only statues but also small ornamental items were imitated. An example is the dolphin appliqué in the Kress Collection (Fig. 16); it may be compared to a Roman dolphin handle in the collection of Norbert Schimmel (No. 288, Fig. 17).[96]

The passion for copying antique pieces in the Renaissance and later periods raises the related question of forgery. Frequently modern scholars find it difficult to distinguish, for example, a Renaissance forged copy from a genuine antique. The fact is that we do not have foolproof scientific data for separating Renaissance techniques from those of antiquity. In the case of a winged Eros with a torch in the Kress collection, black lacquer has been

Fig. 14: She-wolf with Romulus and Remus, National Gallery of Art, Washington, D.C., Samuel H. Kress collection, A-155.

Fig. 15: Etruscan wolf with Romulus and Remus, Palazzo dei Conservatori, Rome. Anderson photo no. 1720.

Fig. 16: Appliqué of paired dolphins, National Gallery of Art, Washington, D.C., Samuel H. Kress collection, A-276.120 C.

rubbed over the reddish-brown bronze surface (Fig. 18).[97] Black lacquer was a popular finish for bronzes in the Renaissance, but it cannot be claimed uniquely characteristic of that epoch.[98] Pliny speaks of "preserving" bronzes by rubbing them with vegetable pitch and states, too, that the ancients applied bitumen to bronzes to tinge them.[99] Lacking the results of scientific analyses, the art historian is left to his own devices for dating problem pieces. Pope-Hennessy, who considers the Kress Eros either a Renaissance forgery after the antique or a Roman bronze, decides that "the perished condition of the surface is most readily compatible" with its being Roman.

Another baffling situation has turned up in the Master Bronzes exhibition. The small lion from the Seattle Art Museum appears to be a perfectly genuine Roman work (Fig. 19),[100] that is, until one's suspicions are aroused by its extraordinary resemblance to a lion of exactly the same size, claimed to be of Renaissance date, in the collection of John P. Coolidge (Fig. 20).[101] The surface condition of the two pieces is entirely different, as is readily apparent, the Seattle piece having a crusty green patina while the Coolidge lion is completely uncorroded. Also, the treatment of certain details differs, for instance, the position of the tail, the texture of the mane, and the feeling for musculature. Yet without the support of scientific analyses, it is difficult to come to a positive conclusion about the date of either piece. It is the merit of Léon Pressouyre to have initiated a study of forgeries among bronzes from the French public collections,[102] but what is still needed is a thorough, amply documented examination of Renaissance bronzes which would include metal analyses and would explain the techniques peculiar to the production of bronzes in the Renaissance.

Fig. 17: Dolphin handle, Nobert Schimmel collection. Photo by Dietrich Widmer, Basel.

Returning for a moment to the Kress she-wolf (Fig. 14), we should observe that the composition includes the twins, Romulus and Remus. They were added to the original Etruscan piece sometime after 1471 by Antonio Pollaiuolo (1431-1498).[103] Here we observe an interesting form of combined survival and revival — the restoration of ancient bronze statuary.[104] The practice was not at all uncommon. We have already pointed out that the legs, arms, and attributes of the Colossus of Barletta were restored by Fabio Alfano, a sculptor otherwise unknown, but several famous sculptors seem also to have repaired ancient bronzes. The tail of the Chimera of Arezzo, for instance, was restored by Benvenuto Cellini.[105] A most intriguing case of eighteenth-century restoration involves the horse from Herculaneum in the Naples National Museum (Fig. 21).[106] The engineer Rocco Giacchino de Alcubierre found numerous fragments of a mighty horse in the theater of Herculaneum. Joseph Canart, the sculptor who was to restore the horse, melted down a number of the pieces and made chandeliers and a statue of a Madonna from them! The remainder was later made into a horse.[107]

Although ancient bronze figurines are frequently mentioned as transmitters of classical influence in the Middle Ages and Renaissance, there seems to be little specific information about their survival and fate. Benvenuto Cellini writes, in reference to a find made at Arezzo in 1553 together with the celebrated Etruscan Chimera, "a quantity of statuettes were found: they were also made of bronze, covered with earth and rust, and

Fig. 18: Winged child carrying a torch, National Gallery of Art, Washington, D.C., Samuel H. Kress collection, A-204.42 C.

Fig. 19: Bronze lion, Seattle Art Museum. Photo courtesy of the Seattle Art Museum.

Fig. 20: Bronze lion, collection of John P. Coolidge. Photo by the Fogg Art Museum.

Fig. 21: Horse from Herculaneum, Museo Nazionale, Naples. Alinari photo no. 11213.

Fig. 22: Perseus, Museum für Kunst und Gewerbe, Hamburg (photo no. 14584).

all missing a head or the hands or the feet."[108] He and Duke Cosimo spent some time cleaning these *bronzetti* with jewelers' chisels — an early essay in mechanical cleaning. This account has given rise to the most tantalizing possibility of an ancient bronze figurine's having served as the possible inspiration of a major sixteenth-century sculpture. The posture of the little Etruscan Perseus from Hamburg (Fig. 22) obviously resembles the wax model, "about a cubit high . . . and beautifully made with great care and skill," (Fig. 23) with which Cellini in 1545 secured the order for his famous Perseus.[109] The Hamburg Perseus is five inches in height. He wears the winged cap which made him invisible to his foe; in his right hand he holds the curved sickle sword, and with his left he raises aloft the head of Medusa which he has just cut off. His feet are missing. Were the Hamburg Perseus to be numbered among the Arezzo figurines, it might be a wonderfully persuasive example of a known find being used for a truly creative revival by a major artist of the Mannerist era.

Unfortunately, the Hamburg bronze cannot be traced beyond the Forman Collection of the nineteenth century.[110] Even more fatal for this lovely hypothesis is that the bronzes which Cellini and the Duke cleaned were found at Arezzo in November of 1553, by which time the Perseus was in its final stages and about to be cast.[111] It had been designed eight years earlier. Still, art historians can and do take refuge in the evasion that if it was not this particular bronze, Cellini might have known one just like it, or he might have known a marble statue of the same type. Tobias Dohrn has, indeed, shown that an Etruscan candelabrum in the Vatican reflects the same Perseus type,[112] and Langlotz has argued that a marble torso known to have been in the Medici collection was a Perseus of a similar design.[113]

Among the drawings made around 1620 for Cassiano Dal Pozzo (1589-1657), C. C. Vermeule has discovered several that depict Etruscan bronzes.[114] One of the two warriors represented on drawing no. 8613 is said to be in the Vatican Library. Another warrior (no. 8612), rather like No. 173 and No. 174 of the Master Bronzes exhibition, and an Etruscan mirror (no. 8388) were also drawn.[115] These drawings are characteristic of the increasingly scholarly nature of the preoccupation with ancient bronzes.

With the formation of large collections of bronzes in the seventeenth century and their publication in the seventeenth and eighteenth centuries, the survival of bronze figurines entered upon a different, more museological, stage. Again, precedents can be found in antiquity, for regular collections of bronzes have been found in the houses and villas of Pompeii and Herculaneum.[116] The excavation of these two cities revealed for the first time the extraordinary extent to which bronze furnishings entered the daily life of the Romans.

Fig. 23: Perseus with head of Medusa, wax model by Benvenuto Cellini, Museo Nazionale, Florence. Brogi photo no. 18084.

Fig. 24: Head of Augustus, Soldani, Vaduz, Liechtenstein. Photo Dita Herein.

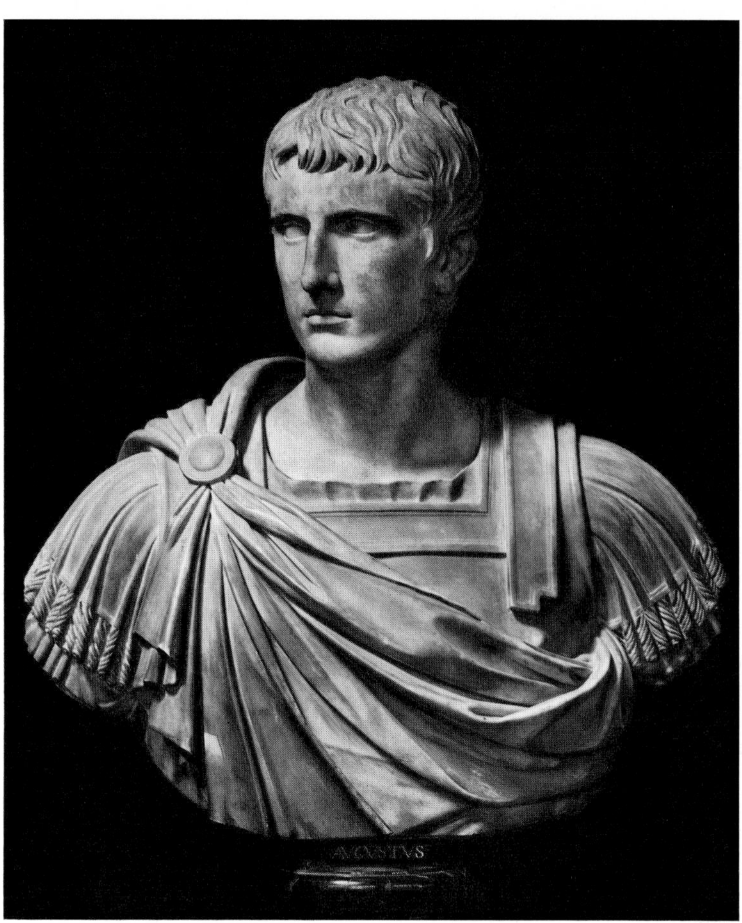

Fig. 25: Bust with head of Augustus, Uffizi, Florence. Alinari photo no. 1183.

Although becoming ever more a separate branch of noncreative sculpture, the copying of ancient bronzes and of ancient marbles in bronze continued. Well into the eighteenth century such copies were considered works of art in themselves. Kurt Lankheit has published very informative material on Massimiliano Soldani (1658-1740), whose workshop around 1700 was famous for the production both of original sculptures and of life-size and reduced copies of antiques.[117] The bronze bust of Augustus in the collection of the Prince of Liechtenstein (Fig. 24) is copied from the Roman bust in the Uffizi (Fig. 25). It reminds us of the popularity of the sets of the twelve Caesars.[118] Sometimes as many as six copies of Soldani's reduced versions of antiquities are known. We know, too, that he vigorously encouraged their sale. Here we approach commercial mass production, such as became the rule in the nineteenth century.

The divergence of copies from creative works continued to grow until the copying of ancient bronzes became a matter for commercial foundries. The history of the reproducion of ancient bronzes in the nineteenth and twentieth centuries remains to be written. It would have to distinguish the "souvenir bronzes," which catered to the taste of a period that considered such objects suitable for interior decoration, from the copies made for didactic purposes and from the forgeries made with the intent to deceive. In the first category, reproductions of ancient bronzes in the Museo Nazionale in Naples are still obtainable.[119] Products of a high-quality didactic enterprise are the reconstructions of famous classical originals in bronze, such as the

Doryphoros of Polykleitos made by Georg Römer, now at the University in Munich.[120] Much rarer is the display of copies of large ancient bronzes as memorial monuments, yet in 1908 a life-size bronze reproduction of the equestrian statue of Marcus Aurelius was given to Brown University by Moses I. B. Goddard and set up behind Sayles Hall on the campus[121] — an imposing testimonial to the survival and revival of Roman bronze statuary in the early twentieth century (Fig. 26).

Fig. 26: Marcus Aurelius on horseback, Providence, R.I. Photo courtesy of Brown University.

Notes

1 We want to thank Cyril Stanley Smith, chairman of the symposium, as well as H. Bloch, H. W. Janson, E. Kitzinger, B. Rowland, J. L. Teall, L. V. Seidel, and Mrs. W. M. Aiken for their help.

2 Professor Earle Caley, in his paper for this symposium (see pp. 37 ff.), refers to Pliny's formula for bronze alloy (*N. H.*, ed. and trans. by H. Rackham [Cambridge, Mass. and London: Loeb Classical Library, 1952], IX. 199):

The proper blend for making statues is as follows, and the same for tablets: at the outset the ore is melted, and then there is added to the melted metal a third part of scrap copper, that is copper or bronze that has been bought up after use. This contains a peculiar seasoned quality of brilliance that has been subdued by friction and so to speak tamed by habitual use. Silver-lead is also mixed with it in the proportion of twelve and a half pounds to every hundred pounds of the fused metal.

In the discussion (see p. 55) Dr. Herbert Cahn pointed out that a scrap heap comprised of parts of statues has been found in Augst: A. Mutz, "Über den Metallmassenfund von Augusta Raurica," *Ur-Schweiz*, XXVI:1 (1962), 18-24. For Samothrace J. R. McCredie has published a large quantity of fragments of bronze statues, chiefly eyelashes and architectural ornaments, "presumably taken off either before the earthquake [of ca. 100 A.D.] or as scrap metal after the earthquake . . ." ("Samothrace: Preliminary Report on the Campaigns of 1965-67," *Hesperia*, XXXVII:2 (1968), 233, pl. 72a-b.

Ulrich Hiesinger calls our attention to Juvenal x, lines 56 ff., where the satirist describes the wrecking and melting down of statues to make "pipkins, pitchers, frying-pans and slop-pails." (*Juvenal and Persius*, trans. G. G. Ramsey [London and Cambridge, Mass.: Loeb Classical Library, 1930], 197.)

3 E. Kunze *et al.*, "III. Bericht über die Ausgrabungen in Olympia," (1938-39), 12 ff., published in *JdI*, LVI (1941).

4 M. F. Courby, "La Terrace du Temple," in École française d'Athènes, *Fouilles de Delphes* II:3 (Paris, 1927), 252-254; Pausanias *Description of Greece* X. xiii. 9-10.

5 F. Chamoux, "L'Aurige," in École française d'Athènes, *Fouilles de Delphes*, IV:5 (Paris, 1955), 33, with earlier bibliography.

6 Pliny *N. H.* XXXIV. xviii. 41.

7 Strabo XIV. chap. 2.5 [C 652].

8 Herbert Maryon, "The Colossus of Rhodes," *JHS*, LXXVI (1956), 68-86. Maryon argues that the statue was about 120 feet high and that it was not cast bronze but made of thin bronze plates beaten into shape and fastened over an elaborate iron and stone armature. After analyzing the various literary sources on the Colossus he estimates that the amount of bronze used for its construction is most correctly given in *De septem orbis spectaculis* (attributed to Philon Byzantinos, ca. 146 B.C.), chap. 4, as twelve and a half tons. This amount, Maryon calculates, could have been carried away by the Arabs with fifty or sixty camels. Some other sources on the Colossus are Constantine VII, Porphyrogennetos (905-959 A.D.), *De Administrando Imperio*, 20-21, who exaggerates the number of camels needed to 900, and Michael the Syrian, Patriarch of Antioch (1166-1199 A.D.). See *Chronique de Michel le Syrien . . .*, ed. J.-B. Chabot, II (Paris, 1904), fasc. III, xi, chap. 10.

9 It is interesting to ponder Leslie Aitchison's remark (*A History of Metals*, I [New York, 1960], 241) that "the first revival of European metallurgy may be dated to about 750; and . . . it came through Arab inspiration." The Arab home-

lands had few sources of metal other than alluvial gold. They opened old Roman workings in Spain.

10 J. W. Brailsford, "The Saxmundham Claudius," *Burlington Magazine*, CVIII (1966), 85-86, fig. 36.

11 Sir George Macdonald, "Notes on Some Fragments of Imperial Statues and a Statuette of Victory," *JRS*, XVI (1926), 5-6, suggests that the head was probably from the cult statue of the temple of Claudius at the Roman fort of Camulodunum (Colchester), destroyed by Boudicca in 61 A.D. J. M. C. Toynbee, *Art in Roman Britain* (London, 1962), Cat. 1, 123, however, thinks the head too small for a colossal cult image; rather, because of its tilt, she suggests that it might be from an equestrian statue.

12 Macdonald, *JRS*, 1926 (n. 11), 7 ff., cites other bronzes destroyed by barbarians in the later years of the Roman occupation of Britain. He proposes that a bronze leg and a bronze sphere found in 1820 on the farm of Milsington in Roxburghshire were carried off by barbarians from the great fortress of Eboracum (York). Macdonald thought the date of the destruction to be either about 158 A.D., when a rebellion was supressed by Julius Verus, or 196, "when southern Scotland was finally lost," i.e., when Clodius Albinus left Britain without Roman soldiers to fight Severus in Gaul. Sheppard Frere suggests, however, a much later date, 367 A.D., when the Roman defenses were broken down. See Frere, *Britannia* (Cambridge, Mass., 1967), 353, n. 1. For the destruction of temples and images in Britain and other northern provinces see M. J. T. Lewis, *Temples in Roman Britain* (Cambridge, 1966), particularly his "Epilogue," 144-146.

13 H. Menzel, "Roman Bronzes," in D. G. Mitten and S. F. Doeringer, *Master Bronzes from the Classical World* (Mainz, 1967), 228. An early publication of the statue by J. Buche, "Le Mars de Coligny," *MonPiot*, X (1903), 61-90, identified the barbarian invasion as that of the Germans (Crocus) in 275-276 A.D. Some bronzes recovered from the rubble of the Alamanni invasion of Augusta Raurica (ca. 260 A.D.) under the emperor Gallienus have been published by Ruth Steiger, "Victoria- und Merkurstatuette aus Augusta Raurica," *Basler Stadtbuch* (1964), 232-246. For the Victory statuette see R. Laur-Belart, "Keltische Elemente in der Kunst der römischen Schweiz," *8ème Congrès international d'archéologie classique, Le rayonnement des civilisations grecque et romaine sur les cultures périphériques*, Paris, 1963 (Paris, 1965), 173, n. 36, pl. 15.

14 Procopius *History of the Wars* III. v, trans. H. B. Dewing (London and New York: Loeb Classical Library, 1916), 47-49.

15 Lewis, *Temples* (n. 12).

16 *Ibid.* Also Sulpicius Severus, *De Vita Beati Martini*, in J.-P. Migne (ed.), *Patrologiae cursus completus* (Paris, 1845), XX, col. 172; E. Mâle, *La fin du paganisme en Gaule* (Paris, 1950), 34 ff.; A. Momigliano, *The Conflict between Paganism and Christianity in the Fourth Century* (Oxford, 1963), 193 ff.

17 The first catalogue, known as the *Notitia regionum urbis Romae cum breviariis suis*, dates from 334 A.D. The second, *Curiosum urbis Romae regionum*, must date in or after 357 since it mentions the obelisk raised in the Circus Maximus in that year.

18 The number 3785 is that calculated by Zacharias in *Narratio de ornatu Romae*, based on summaries of the Regionary Catalogues and other ancient sources. See Ferdinand Gregorovius, *History of the City of Rome in the Middle Ages*, trans. from the fourth German edition by Annie Hamilton, I (London, 1894), 79, n. 1.

19 Gregorovius, *History* (n. 18), 57-59, where St. Augustine is cited on the destruction of pagan idols before the Goths under Rhadagaisus arrived in Rome. *Sermon cv. de verb. evang. Luc* xi. n. 13 (t. v. 1, 546); also St. Jerome, *Ep.* cvii, *Ad laetam de institutione filiae*, t. i. 624. R. Lanciani, *The Destruction of Ancient Rome* (London, 1899), 65, puts less emphasis on the effects of early Christian destruction, favoring the notion that Rome's treasures were plentiful enough to withstand the plunderings of many people over the centuries. Such plundering is described by Cassiodorus, whose images of the "brazen theft" of monumental statues from Rome, the actions of those who "mar the beauty of the ancients with amputation of limbs," and of statues "falling into ruins" from neglect are particularly vivid. The proposals for offering rewards for the arrest of thieves,

posting watchmen, and appointing an Architect of the City of Rome to repair the statues reflect a substantial appreciation for the aesthetic and historical value of these works of art. (Cassiodorus, *Epistolae variae,* trans. Thomas Hodgkin [London, 1886], ii, letters 35-36; vii, formulae 13, 15; X, letter 30.) We are grateful to U. Hiesinger for calling attention to these passages. See also Tilmann Buddensieg, "Gregory the Great, the Destroyer of Pagan Idols; The History of a Medieval Legend Concerning the Decline of Ancient Art and Literature," *Journal of the Warburg and Courtauld Institutes,* XVIII (1965), 44-65.

20 See A. Blanchet and F. Martroye in *Bulletin de la Société Nationale des Antiquaires de France* (1921), 151-154, for a collection of a number of these laws.

21 *The Theodosian Code and Novels and the Sirmondian Constitutions,* trans. and ed. Clyde Pharr *et al.* (Princeton, 1952), 473, Novella 16.10.8. Also of interest is Novella 16.10.19 (*Sirm.* 12): ". . . Simulacra, si quae etiamnunc in templis fanisque consistunt, et quae alicubi ritum vel acceperunt, vel accipiunt, paganorum suis edibus evellantur, cum hoc repetita sciamus saepius sanctione decretum." (J. Adhémar, *Influences antiques dans l'art du Moyen Âge français* [London: Warburg Institute, 1937], 81, n. 1.) As translated by Pharr (p. 483), "If any images stand even now in the temples and shrines, and if they have received, or now receive, any worship of the pagans, they shall be torn from their foundations, since We recognize that this regulation has been very often decreed by repeated sanctions."

22 *Vita Constantini* III. 54. See *A Select Library of Nicene and Post-Nicene Fathers of the Christian Church,* trans. and ed. P. Schaff and H. Wace, I, *Eusebius . . .* (New York, 1890), 534.

23 Prof. John L. Teall has observed that the author of *Vita Constantini* (III, 54) "distinguishes carefully between the fate of the precious statues and those of base metals; the former were melted down — probably as a source of gold and silver for the coinage — while the latter were hauled off to adorn the city of Constantinople." (Personal communication, December 28, 1967.)

24 Cyril Mango, "Antique Statuary and the Byzantine Beholder," *DOPapers,* No. 17 (1963), 57. The literary source for these statues is a poem by Christodorus of Thebes, written in 532 A.D., shortly before the Baths were destroyed. See *The Greek Anthology,* Book II, trans. W. R. Paton, I (London and New York: Loeb Classical Library, 1916), 58-91.

25 Mango, *DOPapers* (n. 24), 55-75.

26 A typical example of individual reprisal, cited by Mango, *ibid.,* 61 and n. 41, is the case of the three-headed statue of Hekate in the Hippodrome. She was thought to be connected by a kind of sympathetic magic to three barbarian chieftains, possibly Russian, who were then assaulting Constantinople. While the learned patriarch, John the Grammarian, recited incantations, three men struck the heads of the statue with hammers. Two heads fell down; one did not. Two barbarian chieftains were killed; one was only wounded. The incident, portrayed in a manuscript in Madrid (Madrid, MS of Skylitzes, Bibl. Nac. M. S. 5-3, N-2. fol. 65r), took place between 825 and 850 A.D.

27 Anthony Cutler, "The *De Signis* of Nicetas Choniates. A Reappraisal," *AJA,* LXXII (1968), 113-118; *Corpus Scriptorum Historiae Byzantinae,* B. G. Niebuhr and I. Bekker (ed.), XXII, *Nicetas Choniata* (Bonn, 1835), 855 ff.; see also W. Treue, *Art Plunder,* trans. Basil Creighton (London, 1960), chap. III, "The Looting of Constantinople by the Crusaders," for a lively account.

28 The opinion is held by Romilly J. H. Jenkins, "The Bronze Athena at Byzantium," *JHS,* LXVII (1947), 31. He cites Nicetas Choniates, "her body humid even in bronze," and Arethas, bishop of Caesareia, who equates her with the Phidian Athena of bronze.

29 Chonites, Bonn ed. (n. 27), 800-861.

30 Cutler, *AJA,* 1968 (n. 27), 116 and notes 38-43. From Mango's interpretation of the average Byzantine's attitude toward the bronze statues in his city — which was one of superstitious suspicion of their magical powers — one might agree with J. L. Teall that the bronze statues were probably not tampered with, at least in the Middle Byzantine period, and therefore not melted down for re-use. Teall suspects that the Byzantines depended upon mined ore for the bulk of their needs. See Speros Vryonis, Jr., "The Question of Byzantine Mines," *Speculum,* XXXVII (1962), 1-17.

31 Menzel, "Roman Bronzes" (n. 13), 231. K. A. Neugebauer, "Über einen gallo-römischen Typus des Mars," *BonnJbb*, CXLVII (1942), 233, on Mars figurines from one provincial workshop.

32 R. F. Tylecote, *Metallurgy in Archaeology* (London, 1962).

33 Ramsay MacMullen, *Soldier and Civilian in the Later Roman Empire* (Cambridge, Mass., 1963), chap. 11, cites Vegetius 2.11. MacMullen (pp. 25-26) points out that perhaps forty large state arms factories — one of which, found at Corstopitum, was capable of employing 100 to 150 men — were active during the reign of Diocletian. See G. S. Keeney, "Corstopitum as a Civil Center," *Archaeologia Aeliana*, 4th ser., XI (1934), 164 ff., where evidence of metalworking enterprises is reviewed. Also A. H. M. Jones, *The Later Roman Empire, 284-602*, III (Oxford, 1964), 280, no. 26.

34 Comparable tasks have been advanced in prehistoric archaeology by such organizations as the International Committee for Spectral Analysis of Metals, sponsored by the Congresses on Prehistoric and Protohistoric Sciences in Hamburg and Rome. See also C. F. C. Hawkes on the work of groups in England, Italy, France, Germany, Austria, Czechoslovakia, and Russia, "Analysis by Optical Spectrometry . . .," *Atti del VI congresso internazionale delle scienze preistoriche e protoistoriche* (Rome, 1962), 33-54. M. Picon, S. Boucher, and J. Condamin, "Recherches techniques sur des bronzes de Gaule romaine," *Gallia*, XXIV (1966), fasc. 1, 189-215, have begun analyses of Gallo-Roman material. One of their preliminary conclusions is that the composition of the bronzes of a certain category of objects — for example, mirrors, vases, and pateras — is generally determined by the technical necessities of fabricating that kind of object (pp. 209 ff.). Such research needs to go hand in hand with archaeological and art historical attempts to build up workshop connections, exemplified by Heinz Menzel's paper for this symposium.

35 It is unfortunate that Hans R. Weihrauch's thorough study, *Europäische Bronzestatuetten, 15.-18. Jahrhundert* (Braunschweig, 1967), appeared too late to be used in the preparation of this article. Many of the issues that the present paper touches on have been dealt with in much greater detail by Weihrauch. His first chapters include a survey of the techniques of bronze-working from antiquity to the eighteenth century and a brief discussion of the situation of bronze statuary in the Middle Ages.

36 See Marvin Ross, "Byzantine Bronzes," in *Byzantine Art and European Art*, ninth exhibition under the auspices of the Council of Europe (2nd ed.; Athens, 1964), 440. Evidence of a bronze-workers' guild comes from the section on the *argyropratai* in the *Book of the Prefect*, where it is forbidden that silversmiths or jewelers buy bronze and linen for retail sale since these products are controlled by other guilds. (Reference from J. L. Teall, n. 23).

37 Mango, *DOPapers* (n. 24), 71, n. 96 after J. Ebersolt, *Les arts somptuaires de Byzance* (Paris, 1923), 130, notes the manufacture of statues of emperors and empresses in the reign of Philippicus (711-713 A.D.) and revivals of the practice in the eighth and twelfth centuries. O. M. Dalton, *Byzantine Art and Archaeology* (Oxford, 1911), 122-123, gives a good summary of statues that are referred to as having existed during the first five centuries after the founding of Constantinople. He specifically notes that bronze animal sculptures are frequently mentioned. These — boars, elephants, hippopotami, hyenas, oxen, and wolves among others — were apparently set up in the Hippodrome. "As late as the time of Basil I, we learn from Constantine Porphyrogenitos and Photius that in the atrium of the new church of that emperor there were marble dragons and bronze rams, goats, and cocks upon two splendid fountains there" (p. 123). Statues of sacred persons were also made during these years. He cites the bronze statue of the archangel Michael in the Church of All Saints which was damaged in the earthquake of 1296 (Pachymeres, *Andronicus Palaeologus*, iii, 15).

38 Present height 3.55 m.; original height 5.11 m.

39 Dalton, *Byzantine Art* (n. 37), 125; Herbert Koch, *AntDenk*, III (Berlin, 1913), 20-27, pls. 20-21. The statue was first mentioned in a rescript of Charles II of Anjou, 1309. The poem mentioned is cited by G. P. Grimaldi, *Vita S. Ruggiero Vescono, Patrone di Barletta* (1607), 119 and Annotazione XVIII, 129 f.

40 Giovanni Villani (d. 1348), *Historie Fiorentine*, II, chap. 11, speaks of this statue as having to do with Heraclius' campaign against the Persians (610-

641) but assigns the image to the Lombard Duke Archicis. Koch, *AntDenk* (n. 39), after careful discussion of coin comparisons, very cautiously identifies the statue as Valentinian I (364-375).

41 A technological investigation was made by the German bronze sculptor, Kurt Kluge. See Kurt Kluge and Karl Lehmann-Hartleben, *Die antiken Großbronzen*, II (Berlin and Leipzig, 1927), 67-71. Kluge's description states that the statue was cast in at least nine large pieces.

42 Cutler, *AJA*, 1968 (no. 27), 114-115, and references.

43 Procopius *Buildings* I. ii. 5-12, trans. H. B. Dewing with the collaboration of G. Downey (London and Cambridge, Mass.: Loeb Classical Library, 1940).

44 Aitchison, *History of Metals* (n. 9), 154-156, fig. 79. He also mentions the brass industry in Stolberg, 150-300 A.D., which specialized in cauldrons and buckets. On Roman brass see also Lenore O. Keene Congdon, "The Mantua Apollo of the Fogg Art Museum," *AJA*, LXVII (1963), 8-9.

45 An eighth-century book of recipes, *Compositiones ad tigenda musiva*, ed. H. Hedfors, Diss. Uppsala, 1932, which contains recipes for artists and craftsmen mostly from earlier Greek and Byzantine books, describes the manufacture of brass (aurichalcum) as well as of bronze (pp. 56-57, 193). See R. J. Forbes, "Metallurgy," in *A History of Technology*, ed. Charles Singer *et al.*, II (Oxford, 1956), 63. Compare also John M. Burnam, *A Classical Technology edited from Codex Lucensis, 490* (Boston, 1920), 69-70 and 131.

46 When the lion lamp was found, it looked like green patinated bronze. It was covered with earth, a deposit of ash and lime, and granulated malachite and cuprite but acquired a markedly brassy yellowish appearance when cleaned by James L. Greaves of the Conservation Center, New York University. Greaves first used dilute formic acid (ash), then alkaline Rochelle salts and sulphuric acid.

47 Ross, "Byzantine Bronzes" (n. 36), conjectures that figurative bronze relief plaques may also have existed in the Middle Byzantine period but were melted down. The Byzantine output of ecclesiastical and domestic bronzes was impressive, at least in bulk, during the early period and seems to have been substantial in the Middle Byzantine era.

48 E. H. Swift, "The Bronze Doors of the Gate of the Horologium at Hagia Sophia," *ArtB*, XIX (1937), 137 ff.

49 Duard W. Laging's recent study, "The Methods Used in Making the Bronze Doors of Augsburg Cathedral," *ArtB*, XLIX (1967), 129-136, discusses the Augsburg doors in relation to other known doors from the East and West, in both terms of style and casting procedures.

50 Forbes, "Metallurgy" (n. 45), 62; Aitchison, *History of Metals* (n. 9), chap. VII. See also John U. Nef, "Mining and Metallurgy in Medieval Civilization," in *The Cambridge Economic History of Europe*, II, chap. VII (Cambridge, 1952), 434, and Tylecote, *Metallurgy* (n. 32), for Britain.

51 Aitchison, *History of Metals* (n. 9), 229 ff., mentions the melting-down of jewelry, coins, etc.; p. 231 deals with the Sutton Hoo find, which yielded a Coptic bronze bowl of ca. 650 A.D. The production of bronze hanging bowls continued well into the early Middle Ages. Their origin is a matter for debate. See R. G. Collingwood, "Roman Britain," in *An Economic Survey of Ancient Rome*, ed. Tenney Frank, III (Patterson, 1959), 96; D. ès L. Françoise Henry, "Hanging Bowls," *The Journal of the Royal Society of Antiquaries of Ireland*, LXVI (1936), 209-246, where an Irish origin is claimed. Collingwood, pp. 94-96, traces strands of evidence in Britain that show a "slender continuity" of the native metalworking traditions which were never totally displaced by the Romans. C. F. C. Hawkes, "Bronze-workers, Cauldrons, and Bucket-Animals in Iron Age and Roman Britain," in *Aspects of Archaeology in Britain . . ., Essays in Honor of O. G. S. Crawford*, ed. W. F. Grimes (London, 1951), 172 ff., states that bronze-working was revived in fifth-century Britain, where "native bronze smiths had kept alive the techniques of their craft." Toynbee, *Roman Britain* (n. 11), 17, suggests that there was a gap between 450 and 600 A.D., and that "the direct artistic legacy of the Roman province to the new English kingdoms was . . . very slight."

52 W. Braunfels, "Charlemagne vu par ses contemporains," in *L'Exposition Charlemagne; oeuvre, rayonnements et survivances*, tenth exhibition under the auspices of the Council of Europe (Aix-la-Chapelle, 1965), 39-40, cat. nos. 29a

and 29b, gives a good summary of the various opinions on the dating of the piece.

53 Aitchison, *History of Metals* (n. 9), 243-244.

54 W. Braunfels, "Karls des Großen Bronzewerkstatt," in *Karl der Große, Lebenswerk und Nachleben*, III, *Karolingische Kunst*, ed. H. Schnitzler and W. Braunfels (Düsseldorf, 1965), 168.

55 Laging, *ArtB*, 1967 (n. 49), 131; A. Goldschmidt, *Die deutschen Bronzetüren des frühen Mittelalters* (Marburg, 1926), 9, n. 3.

56 Herman Luer, *Bronzeplastik* (Leipzig: Monographien des Kunstgewerbes, IV, n. d.), 24.

57 John Beckwith, "Byzantine Influence on Art at the Court of Charlemagne," in *Karl der Große* (n. 54), 299.

58 Braunfels, "La cour d'Aix-la-Chapelle et sa culture," in *L'Exposition Charlemagne* (n. 52), 26, cat. no. 4.

59 Braunfels, "Bronzewerkstatt" (n. 54), 192.

60 *Ibid.*, 193, for Aix-la-Chapelle doors; Laging, *ArtB*, 1967 (n. 49), 131, for Augsburg and Hildesheim.

61 Braunfels, "Bronzewerkstatt" (n. 54), 193. See also Arthur Pelzer, "Geschichte der Messingindustrie und künstlerischen Arbeiten in Messing (Dinanderies) in Aachen und den Ländern zwischen Maas und Rhein von der Römerzeit bis zur Gegenwart," *Zeitschrift des Aachener Geschichtsvereins*, XXX (1908), 235 ff.

62 Tylecote, *Metallurgy* (n. 32), 57-59, attributes the rise in lead content in medieval copper alloys to the fact that the cost of tin "militated against the 90/10 Cu-Sn alloy for castings." Forbes, "Metallurgy" (n. 45), 63, mentions that the text *Mappae clavicula de efficiendo auro* includes a recipe for bronze that is high in lead content. The texts edited by Hedfors and Burnam (n. 45) both give a recipe for bronze with a high lead content.

63 *On Divers Arts: The Treatise of Theophilus*, trans. and ed. J. G. Hawthorne and C. S. Smith (Chicago, 1963), Book III. A brief sketch of the state of bronze metallurgy and the production of bronze objects during the Middle Ages is given by Aitchison, *History of Metals* (n. 9), 320-332.

64 Hawthorne and Smith, *Theophilus* (n. 63), xxx. Laging, *ArtB*, 1967 (n. 49), points out that the lead content of the Augsburg doors (20.1 per cent) agrees with Theophilus' recipe for coarse brass (*aes*).

65 The Gloucester Candlestick, in the Victoria and Albert Museum, is an extraordinary example of the state of lost-wax casting in the North in the early twelfth century. See Herbert Maryon, "Fine Metal Work," in *A History of Technology*, ed. Charles Singer *et al.*, II (Oxford, 1956), 480, and C. C. Oman, *The Gloucester Candlestick*, Victoria and Albert Monograph no. 11 (London, 1958). Another example of twelfth-century bronze-casting in the North is the life-size lion in the cathedral square, Brunswick, made for Duke Henry of Saxony in 1166.

66 Forbes, "Metallurgy" (n. 45), 64. A high degree of organization was required for bell-casting, both in the distribution of labor and in the technological processes. Hawthorne and Smith, *Theophilus* (n. 63), xxxiii.

67 Maryon, "Fine Metal Work" (n. 65), 478-479; Aitchison, *History of Metals* (n. 9), 331-333, fig. 137. He gives a brief survey of other gisant images, also of bell foundries in England in the eleventh century and the transition to cannon casting in the early fourteenth century.

68 G. N. Fasola, *La Fontana di Perugia* (Rome, 1951), 39-41. Fasola depends somewhat upon Bruno Bearzi's article, "Le fusione artistiche in bronzo nell' antichità," *La metallurgia italiana* (1949), 2, not available to the authors. For medieval bell-casting methods see Hawthorne and Smith, *Theophilus* (n. 63), chap. 85. For the observation on the use of a piece mold for casting the caryatids we are indebted to Arthur Steinberg. The caryatids of the Fontana Maggiore were examined during the restoration activities of 1948-1949 and found to be rather crudely cast and largely unchased. Facts concerning the founder and the date of the casting of the baptistry door are reported in several chronicles, notably that of Giovanni Villani (ed. Giunti, 1587, Lib. X, C. 178, p. 641). John Pope-Hennessy, *Italian Gothic Sculpture* (London, 1955), 193, describes the reliefs as having been cast separately — not by lost-wax — and later inserted into the frame.

69 Fasola, *Fontana* (n. 68). Much work needs to be done on thirteenth- and

fourteenth-century bronzes before it will be possible to define with certainty the various techniques employed and to track down the sources and development of those techniques. Some of the outstanding works of the period are the statue of Saint Peter in the Vatican, first attributed to Arnolfo di Cambio by A. Venturi (*Storia dell'arte italiana*, IV, *La scultura del trecento* [Milan, 1906], 119-122); the bronze angels from the central doorway of the Orvieto Cathedral, attributed to Lorenzo Maitani (ca. 1293) (Pope-Hennessy, *Italian Gothic Sculpture* [n. 68], 7 and 178); the lion and griffin of the Palazzo dei Priori in Perugia. Fasola, *Fontana* (n. 68), 39, calls for a thorough analysis of these works. The statue of Saint Peter, according to a superficial examination made by Bearzi, seems to be cast by the same method as the caryatid figures of the Perugia Fountain.

70 Aitchison, *History of Metals* (n. 9), 326-327.

71 *Ibid.*, 326.

72 F. Baldinucci, *Notizie dei professori del disegno* . . . (Florence, 1845), I, 354 (first published in 1681), as quoted by Richard Krautheimer, *Lorenzo Ghiberti* (Princeton, 1956), 73: "December 1, 1414 — In the following I shall record all the expenses I shall have for casting the figure of Saint John the Baptist. I undertook to cast it at my own expense; in case of failure I was to forfeit my expenses; in case of success . . . the consuls and *operai* . . . were to use toward me the same discretion that they would use toward another master whom they sent for to do the casting."

73 Krautheimer, *Ghiberti* (n. 72), 88, and Digest of Documents no. 86, 407 (Doc. 16, July 1421: ASF, Arti, Cambio, vol. 18, Libro del Pilastro, c. 14v.).

74 For the documents see H. W. Janson, *The Sculpture of Donatello* (2nd ed.; Princeton, 1963), 164-166 (for S. Antonio) and 152 (for Gattamelata).

75 Bruno Bearzi, "Considerazione di tecnica sul S. Ludovico e la Giuditta di Donatello," *BdA*, 4th ser., XXXVI (1951), 121 ff.

76 *De Sculptura von Pomponius Gauricus*, trans. and ed. H. Brockhaus (Leipzig, 1886). In the introduction to the *Burlington Fine Arts Club: Catalogue of a Collection of Italian Renaissance Sculpture and Other Plastic Art of the Renaissance*, by E. R. D. Maclagan, G. F. Hill, and C. F. Bell (London, 1913), Maclagan gives an English translation of the sections of Gauricus' treatise which apply to the casting and finishing of bronze statues, pp. 10-17.

77 The "moderns" include Ghiberti, Andrea Pisano, Pisanello, Desiderio da Settignano, Donatello, Verrocchio, Leonardo, Bartholommeo, Bellano, and Andrea Briosco (Riccio).

78 Apparently Alberti also wrote a treatise, *Ars Aeraria*, which has been lost. Another, by Porcello de'Pandoni, *De Arte Fusoria*, is mentioned by Brockhaus. The publication now in preparation of the manuscripts of Leonardo found in Madrid will add to our knowledge of Renaissance casting methods. We are grateful to Mrs. William Aiken for information on the manuscripts contained in an unpublished typewritten preview by Carlo Pedretti, *The Madrid Manuscripts of Leonardo da Vinci*, 15 pp. Pedretti's summary indicates that the Madrid pages contain a good deal of detailed information on Leonardo's project for casting the Sforza horse. It was to be sent to the foundry, but war disturbances prevented its completion. The bronze that had been ordered for the casting was sent to Ferrara to be made into cannon (Pedretti ms., 6). Other sources for Renaissance bronze technique are the introduction prefaced to Vasari's *Lives* (1550 and 1568 editions), Benvenuto Cellini's *Trattati dell' oreficeria e della scultura* (first published in 1568), and Cellini's *Autobiography*.

79 *The Autobiography of Benvenuto Cellini*, trans. George Bull (London, 1966), 290. As a test project for the casting of the Perseus and Medusa, Cellini modeled the portrait of Duke Cosimo. In casting the bust he "made use of the furnace belonging to Zanobi di Panzo, the bell-founder."

80 *The Pirotechnia of Vannoccio Biringuccio*, trans. and ed. M. T. Gnudi and C. S. Smith (2nd ed.; New York, 1959); Georgius Agricola, *De Re Metallica*, trans. and ed. Herbert and Lou Hoover (2nd ed.; New York, 1950).

81 W. S. Heckscher, *Sixtus IIII Aeneas insignes statuas Romano populo restituendas censuit* (The Hague, 1955), 46.

82 Poggio Bracciolini, . . . *Historiae De Varietate Fortunae Libri*, ed. D. Georgius (Paris, 1723), 20 ff., quoted by Krautheimer, *Ghiberti* (n. 72), 277.

83 Gauricus writes: "There is still extant in Barletta, which is a town of Apu-

lia near Cannae, the colossus of Heraklios — to me forever part of a saddest memory of the bitter loss of my father whom five years ago we buried nearby there . . ." (Brockhaus edition [n. 76], 142, lines 16-20. This mention of the Colossus is the only instance where Gauricus names an actual ancient statue; elsewhere his work is haunted by literary allusions to lost antique works.

The tendency of the Renaissance to provide literary interpretations for ancient statues is exemplified in the inscription on the base made by Vittorio Ghiberti for the ancient (Greek?) statue found in Pesaro in 1530 and nicknamed the "Idolino" by Renaissance poets (Fig. 9): *Ut potui huc veni Delphis et fratre relicto,* "I have come here [to Medicean Florence] as fast as I could, leaving behind Delphi and my brother [Apollo]." The inscription thus implies an interpretation of the figure as Hermes, messenger of the gods and brother of Apollo. Georg Lippold, *Die griechische Plastik* (Munich, 1950), 165, calls the Idolino's head Polykleitan, its body classicistic. See also H. Bulle, *Der schöne Mensch im Altertum* (Munich and Leipzig, 1912), 34 f., pls. 52 f.; C. Picard, *Manuel d'archéologie grecque,* II:1, *La sculpture* (Paris, 1939), 270 f., calls it original but Italiote; H. K. Süsserott, *Griechische Plastik des 4. Jahrhunderts vor Christus* (Frankfurt, 1938), 137 f., pl. 27:4, thought of the fourth century for the body.

84 D. W. S. Hunt, "An Archaeological Survey of the Island of Chios," *BSA,* XLI (1940-1945), Appendix B, 47.

85 On Donatello see Charles Seymour, *Sculpture in Italy, 1400-1500* (Harmondsworth: Pelican History of Art, 1966), 124. For Mocchi, J. Pope-Hennessy, *Italian High Renaissance and Baroque Sculpture,* I (London, 1963), 105.

86 J. Pope-Hennessy, *Italian Renaissance Sculpture* (London, 1958), 99-100; Statius *Silvae* IV. vi; Seymour, *Sculpture* (n. 85), 201. Weihrauch, *Bronzestatuetten* (n. 35), 49 ff. and figs. 46-48, illustrates three small bronze horses inspired by those at San Marco.

87 Pope-Hennessy, *Sculpture* (n. 86), 100; Janson, *Donatello* (n. 74), 144-145, attributes and dates the figure. There are no documents. See also the iconographical study by Maurice L. Shapiro, "Donatello's *Genietto,*" *ArtB,* XLV (1963), 135-142. Marvin Trachtenberg, "An Antique Model for Donatello's Marble David," *ArtB,* L:3 (1958), 268-269, figs. 1-9, derives or at least assumes the inspiration of Donatello's David from a headless Etruscan female figurine which belonged to the Medici.

88 Ludwig Curtius, "Poenitentia," *Festschrift für James Loeb* (Munich, 1930), 53 ff.

89 *Ibid.,* 54.

90 *Master Bronzes* (n. 13), No. 127. For another example see the bronze *putto* in the Museo d'Antichità in Turin (Inv. 905), *Arte e civiltà romana nell'Italia settentrionale dalla repubblica alla tetrarchia,* VI Mostra biennale d'arte antica, Città di Bologna (Bologna, 1964), I, pl. 112, no. 227.

91 Wolfgang von Oettingen, *Über das Leben und die Werke des Antonio Averlino gennant Filarete,* Beiträge zur Kunstgeschichte, N. F. VI (Leipzig, 1888), 13-14; Leo Planiscig, *Piccoli bronzi italiani del rinascimento* (Milan, 1930), 2-3, pl. 1.

92 See n. 81.

93 J. Pope-Hennessy, *Renaissance Bronzes from the Samuel H. Kress Collection* (London, 1965), 145, no. 531, fig. 533.

94 Height 38 cm. vs. 75 cm.; length 64.2 cm. vs. 114 cm.

95 Seymour, *Sculpture* (n. 85), 203; W. Bode, *Italian Bronze Statuettes of the Renaissance,* I (London, 1907), 33-35. The great enthusiasm for bronze as a medium is most strikingly illustrated by Primaticcio's offer to Francis I, and his subsequent expedition to Rome in 1540, to take molds of the most famous statues of antiquity, most of which were marbles, and to have them cast in bronze. In the case of the Apollo Belvedere the casting was done by Guillaume Durant and the finishing by Pierre Bontemps. Casts of this kind continued to be made for the various royal houses of Europe well into the eighteenth century. See Rudolf Hallo, "Bronzeabgüsse antiker Statuen," *JdI,* XLII (1927), 193-220.

96 Pope-Hennessy, *Kress Collection* (n. 93), 136, no. 497, fig. 470; *Master Bronzes* (n. 13), No. 288.

97 Pope-Hennessy, *Kress Collection* (n. 93), 124, no. 460, fig. 469.

98 This method of coloring the surface of the bronze is only one of several

"artificial patinas" described by P. Gauricus. See E. Maclagan, *Burlington Fine Arts Club* (n. 76), 16. John D. Cooney, in his article, *ZAeS*, XCIII (1966), 43-47, discusses a process for darkening bronze with a sulphide introduced, probably from Syria early in Dynasty XVIII.

99 Pliny *N.H.* XXXIV. xxi. 99, XXXIV. ix. 15, and XXXV. li. 182.

100 *Master Bronzes* (n. 13), 290, No. 284 (Seattle Art Museum, Eugene Fuller Memorial Collection, Csll. 37).

101 Purchased from Matthias Komor, New York, as sixteenth-century Italian.

102 Léon Pressouyre, "Quelques types de faux bronzes romains dans les collections publiques françaises," *MélRome*, LXXVIII (1966), 251-265. See also *idem*, "À propos d'une statuette en bronze provenant du Mas-d'Agenais," *Revue de l'Agenais*, suppl. to vol. LXXXVIII:2 (1962), 51-61. For information on ancient patination see Bruno Bearzi, "Considerazione sulla formazione delle patine e delle corrosioni sui bronzi antichi," *StEtr*, XXI (1950-51), 261-266; R. M. Organ, "Aspects of Bronze Patina and its Treatment," *Studies in Conservation*, VIII:1 (1963), 1-9. For the detection of forgeries and of Renaissance bronzes by spectopographic analysis and metallographic examination see Germaine Faider-Feytmans, "Examen en laboratoire de statuettes de bronze provenant de Bavai," *Recueil des bronzes de Bavai*, 8th suppl. to *Gallia* (Paris, 1957), 133-136.

103 The attribution to Pollaiuolo was first made by A. Venturi, "Romolo e Remo di Antonio Pollaiuolo nella Lupa Capitolina," *L'Arte*, XXII (1919), 133-135. For recent discussion of the Capitoline Wolf see K. Schauenburg, "Die Lupa Romana als sepulkrales Motiv," *JdI*, LXXXI (1966), 261, n. 1; also P. J. Riis, "Art in Etruria and Latium during the First Half of the Fifth Century B.C.," *Les origines de la République romaine*, III, *Entretiens sur l'antiquité classique*, XIII (Geneva: Fondation Hardt, 1967), 93-94.

104 Michelangelo Cagiano de Azevedo, *Il gusto nel restauro delle opere d'arte antiche* (Rome, 1948).

105 Luigi A. Milani, *Il R. Museo Archeologico di Firenze, storia e guida ragionata*, I (Florence, 1912), 135.

106 Museo Nazionale, Naples, No. 4904; see Kluge and Lehmann-Hartleben, *Großbronzen* (n. 41), 79-82.

107 C. W. Ceram, *The March of Archaeology*, trans. Richard and Clara Winston (New York, 1958), 11-12.

108 Cellini, *Autobiography* (n. 79), 319.

109 *Ibid.*, 278. Cf. Herbert Hoffmann, *Kunst des Altertums in Hamburg*, Museum für Kunst und Gewerbe (Mainz, 1961), no. 43, 14-15, with earlier bibliography, 38; *Master Bronzes* (n. 13), Nos. 181, 178.

110 Eugen von Merklin, "Neuerwerbungen Hamburg," *AA* (1935), cols. 98-99, fig. 27 (before the restored feet were removed).

111 Milani, *Guida* (n. 105), 136, cites the notice of the find in the deliberations of the Commune di Arezzo of November 15, 1553. The hypothesis was originally stated by W. Braunfels, *Benvenuto Cellini, Perseus und Medusa* (2nd ed.; Stuttgart, 1961), 8 ff.

112 T. Dohrn, "Zwei etruskische Kandelaber," *RömMitt*, LXVI (1959), 45-64.

113 E. Langlotz, "Der triumphierende Perseus," *Arbeitsgemeinschaft für Forschung des Landes Nordrhein-Westfalen, Geisteswissenschaft*, LXIX (1960), 18 and 25, where he claims that Cellini was inspired by the type.

114 C. C. Vermeule, "The Dal Pozzo-Albani Drawings of Classical Antiquities in the Royal Library at Windsor Castle," *Transactions of the American Philosophical Society*, n. s. LVI:2 (1966), 25 and 41. No. 8388 is from Vol. III (A 42:157) Fol. 60; nos. 8612 and 8613 are from Vol. VI (A 45:160) Fols. 58 and 59 respectively.

115 At least as early as 1466, Etruscan tombs were being explored and very likely even earlier, according to John R. Spencer, "Volterra 1466," *ArtB*, XLVII (1966), 95-96.

116 Domenico Comparetti and Giulio de Petra, *La Villa ercolanese dei Pisoni e suoi monumenti e la sua biblioteca* (Turin, 1883), 262-263; Gisela M. A. Richter, *Portraits of the Greeks*, I (London, 1965), 22-28, and for individual pieces from the Villa dei Pisoni, 118, no. 2; 196, no. 8; 204, no. 10; 217, nos. 12 and 13.

117 Kurt Lankheit, "Eine Serie barocker Antiken — Nachbildungen aus der Werkstatt des Massimiliano Soldani," *RömMitt*, LXV (1958), 186-198; also *idem*,

Florentinische Barockplastik; die Kunst am Hofe der letzten Medici, 1670-1743 (Munich, 1962).

118 Howard Hibbard, "Palazzo Borghese Studies — II: The Galleria," *Burlington Magazine*, CIV (1962), 10-11 discusses briefly the increasing popularity of the twelve Caesars.

119 F. B. Tarbell, "Catalogue of Bronzes, etc., in Field Museum of Natural History (reproduced from originals in the National Museum of Naples)," *Field Museum of Natural History, Publication 130*, Anthropological Series, VII, No. 3, 93 ff.; Salvatore Chiurazzi, *Riproduzione di opere classiche in bronzo e marmo* (Naples, 1929) is a catalogue of the copies made by the Chiurazzi firm, formerly the firm of Chiurazzi and De Angelis. Other firms were similarly engaged: see G. Sommer (Palazzo Vittoria — Palazzo Sommer, Naples), *Catalogue illustré, Bronzes — Marbres* (Naples, n. d.), which includes a price list for 1914 and many photographs. All reproductions could be ordered either in marble or in bronze, and the latter in any of three different patinas. D. von Bothmer drew our attention to these catalogues.

120 Paul Wolters, "Polyklets Doryphoros in der Ehrenhalle der Münchner Universität," *MJb*, N. F. XI (1934), Heft 1, 4025.

121 Bronson, *History of Brown University* (Providence, 1914), 473. Another gift of M. B. I. Goddard was a bronze cast of the Augustus of Prima Porta which was set up in front of Rhode Island Hall in 1906. It has since been moved to Hughes Court in the Wriston Quadrangle. In the *Brown Alumni Monthly* (January, 1908), 125, it is stated that Goddard ordered the statue of Marcus Aurelius in Italy, but its exact provenance is thus far unknown. Mr. Chesley Worthington of the Brown University Alumni Office has suggested that the casts of both statues might have been made in the foundry operated by G. Michelucci and Son in Pistoia, from whom the Goddard family ordered some gates in 1910 which were also given to the University (personal communication, December, 1967).

Some Thoughts on the Collecting of Bronzes

Herbert A. Cahn

One of the largest private collections of ancient bronzes in central Europe is located today in the old castle of the Dukes of Württemberg in Stuttgart. It formerly belonged to a paper tycoon (money from paper sources has often been fruitful to archaeology), Dr. Heinrich Scheufelen, in Oberlenningen, who in turn had bought the collection in 1928 from the Prince of Waldeck-Pyrmont. The old Prince Friedrich had housed the collection in two small rooms in his magnificent palace of Arolsen. He was in need of money for the political activities of his son Josias.

The man who had assembled these bronzes, Prince Christian zu Waldeck, lived from 1744 to 1798. Brother of the reigning prince, he ended his life as Portuguese Generalissimo in Sintra Castle near Lisbon. He spent most of his life, however, in Vienna, Rome, and Naples. In Rome he belonged to an international circle of philhellenes and artists who continued the heritage of the great Winckelmann, a circle centered around the painters Angelica Kauffmann and Tischbein. Prince Christian was known as an eager collector of bronzes and coins, and as a traveler too. Goethe reports in his *Italian Travels* that the prince invited him on a Hellenic cruise.[1] Unfortunately, he declined the invitation.

To come back to the collection, it is still practically unknown, even though it is now part of the Württembergische Landesmuseum. A description of the collection in Arolsen by Rudolph Gaedechens was printed in 1862.[2] Paul Arndt[3] and Ulf Jantzen[4] illustrated a few bronzes, and German Hafner published a summary catalogue in 1958,[5] with little illustration. Before it entered the Stuttgart Museum, the collection was offered for sale, and I remember the spring day in 1950 when I rode over the Autobahn toward the paper mills of Oberlenningen near Kirchheim-unter-Teck, intensely curious about the treasures and splendors I hoped to see. Great was the delusion. The collection excelled in number — over 700 bronzes — but not in quality. The figures were uniformly mounted on black marble bases. They were all covered with a dark green lacquer hiding the original patina. I counted about five fine Greek originals; the majority was second- to third-rate Etruscan, Roman, or doubtful. Over 100 Etruscan "Ercolini," perhaps the largest series in the world, brandished their clubs at me. In fact, the interest of the princely collection consisted mainly in its date. There one could study how bronzes were treated before 1800; what an early forgery looks like; how a good bronze acquires a fake appearance through irreverent handling — adjusting, restoring, repatinating. With modern collectors the prince shared only his passion for the material but not our love for the work of art; he probably preferred to assemble a large number of objects, regardless of their artistic quality. His collection of Greek and Roman coins numbered over 10,000; in numismatics, however, he showed better taste or had a better expert at hand.

I recount all this to outline the portrait of a bronze collector of the past. We will all agree that it differs much from our ideal. But I find it very hard to describe our ideal with precision. Certainly a bronze collector of today does not go after a series of pieces of a given type; he purchases single, more or less outstanding bronzes, according to his spending capacities. Few modern collectors possess more than a hundred; many have less than ten. The bronze object on his table, in front of him, is a single work of art which transforms its surroundings and which enables him to transcend our modern world and enter the ancient one. If it is a work of high artistic quality, it will tell him more of this ancient world than any textbook. It is this mute, intimate dialogue with the objects that provides the collector with the highest joy and satisfaction, an intimacy that he misses when confronted with objects in museum showcases.

A friend of mine, a distinguished archaeologist and collector, answered the question as to why he collected bronzes by saying, "I cannot afford marble sculptures, and I don't have the space to display them." I found the reply unsatisfactory — good bronzes are sometimes more expensive than good marble sculptures — and urged him to define his position better. In the course of the conversation we found out that most marble sculptures defy intimacy: you cannot move them or play with them; they need a shrine, a temple, a sanctuary, all three embodied in our time in the museum. In addition, bronzes are available from many more periods and cultures than are sculptures, and the range of representations is much larger: bronzes represent the hieratic and the comic, the myth and the scene from daily life.

We then tried to plunge deeper into the psyche of the collector. "What has brought you the greatest delight in your career as a collector?" I asked. The answer came without hesitation. "The acquisition of this athlete, some thirty years ago. When I first saw him I knew that he was to become mine, although I was not well off then. He had such a superbly smooth patina, and the seller did not realize it was Greek." I found out that the owner seldom had the pleasure of the company of his preferred bronze, the piece being stowed away in a vault most of the time. It was the act of acquisition, therefore, that really caused the collector's joy — the falling in love, the liberation from the clutches of the previous owner. Is collecting just a form of gratifying lust, appetite, hunting instincts? Basically, yes. And as someone who is a collector himself (not really of bronzes, but of other tangible, movable remnants of the ancient world) and has had some experience with collectors, I can affirm that this substratum appears more often than we would like to admit. I am even inclined to think that without this emotional impulse a person will never be a real collector. He might collect Impressionist paintings because in a certain social sphere you cannot do without them, or Louis XV furniture or Hard Edge paintings because it is "chic." Will he collect ancient bronzes? I doubt it.

Collecting classical antiquities needs even more than emotional impulse, I think. To achieve a collection, the collector must know how to sublimate this impulse. In the process of sublimation he will perhaps specialize; he will learn about the civilizations that produced his bronzes, about the myths and gods they represent, about the techniques of their manufacture, their styles and workshops; in the end he will become a connoisseur and even a scholar. Arthur Evans and Edward Newell were such collectors.

I have been asked by the organizers of this symposium to present some reflections on forgeries. You will perhaps allow me to make some very personal remarks. Once in his career, many a collector will experience a disappointment. He will have purchased, let us say, a geometric bronze horse, trusting his own judgment or that of the dealer or of other experts. It happens that another expert or scholar whispers in his ear, "There are many fakes in this field" or, "Your piece may cause doubt." From this moment on the collector will behave like Othello. He starts to repudiate his horse without really going to the heart of the matter.

Our collector has become a victim of a casual remark. May I say how deplorable such Iago remarks can be; they may produce unforeseen sequels, vitiate amateurs forever, cast doubts on genuine objects. What I am urging is a more careful pondering of thoughts and words on questions of authenticity before they are uttered and publicized. Determination of genuineness or falseness is a complex subject not to be treated lightly by professionals. At stake are the reputation of the museum curator, reputation and investment of the dealer, investment and love of the collector. Moreover, the question of whether to accept or condemn a work of art can be decisive and essential to many fields of our knowledge. I recall the Boston throne[6] and the standing goddess in Berlin.[7]

I shall therefore try to formulate a few recommendations, or perhaps rather admonitions.

1. "*Argumenta ad hominem*" should not be admitted in a discussion of forgeries. Example A: "This object comes from an excellent source — the collection of the Comte de la Rivière; therefore it must be genuine." The best collection can contain fakes. Example B: "This object is a fake because it comes from a bad source, Mr. . . . opoulos in Alexandria, well known for having sold fakes to American collectors." A perfectly genuine piece can emerge from a bad source. Example C: "I know the man who made this fake." This reasoning is particularly obnoxious. It can rarely be proved, and even if a testimony of the supposed forger is obtained, it can be false testimony. The moral is, examine and test an object on its own merits.

2. "Unknown, therefore impossible" — a view that should be weighed very carefully before being brought forward against an object. Of course, unusual phenomena should arouse suspicion, e.g., a Corinthian alabastron, intact but born without handle, or a bronze in the style of a terra-cotta figurine from Mesma are improbable. Imagine, however, one of the three finest works of Greek art dug up in these two last decades — the Vix krater,[8] the Piraeus kouros,[9] the Derveni krater,[10] — all three new and unique of their kind — appearing in a sale room. They would have little credit or credibility.

3. "Copied, therefore wrong." This is a very common view that can mislead us completely. Of course there are — to remain in the field of bronzes — aftercasts. Compared with the model, their size will be a bit smaller because of the shrinkage of the metal in casting after the given model. We find the same phenomenon in aftercasts of Renaissance medals. If you examine breaks, the surface of the break will be smooth on the modern aftercast. Yet we have to bear in mind that copies and aftercasts were made in antiquity, as well as duplicate casts from the same mold or molds, differing only in the cold work.

4. A false patina should not alone be a reason for condemning an object; it can cover a genuine bronze. Remove it before condemning the piece; often remnants of the genuine patina re-emerge after cleaning.

5. The stylistic argument. The ground on which we move here is most slippery. Naturally, you can condemn outright a work that does not present the stylistic features of the period it pretends to stem from or a work that lacks inner stylistic consistency.

But my purpose is not to discuss the obvious cases on which everyone agrees. Instead of discussing the method let me quote, as an example of a controversial approach to the question of forgeries, two eminent archaeologists, Carl Blümel and Adolf Greifenhagen, who state the following about the statuette in Fig. 1:

Fig. 1: Bronze statuette of Artemis, after AA *(1965), p. 122.*

E. Bielefeld has illustrated in *Ist. Mitt.*, XII (1962), pl. 5 the bronze statuette of an Artemis; he mentions it on page 20, footnote 7. It is referred to because of the position of the animal and would be indeed a most remarkable piece, if only it were ancient. The Berlin museums have known for a long time that it is a forgery of the twenties, as it had been offered to the Antiquarium in 1927 by C. T. Seltman and recognized at once as a fake. Therefore the purchase of the object was not considered. On this occasion photographs were made for the archives, under the number 4676/77. Bielefeld has reproduced them. A stylistic examination of the statuette would raise some objections ("allerlei Beanstandungen"). The style of the head, perhaps reminiscent of the Aeginetan sculptures, does not agree with the style of body and drapery. The latter seems to imitate East Greek terra cottas of the second half of the sixth century. On the whole, the figure has an "Etruscan" rather than an "East Greek" impact. The way the hands grasp the animal seems unusual, the right hand being turned outward. Normally, the animal should be cast separately, lying on the hands or fixed to the hands with a prong. We believe it is possible to ascertain related stylistic elements and the same hand in another well-known statuette offered in the Paris trade in 1920, that is, a few years before the Artemis figure appeared. This latter was the so-called Heilbuth bronze, the male counterpart to our Artemis, which even found its way temporarily into one of the most famous museums [the Ny Carlsberg Glyptothek is only named in a footnote], from which it has been long since eliminated, after being detected as a forgery. There is much to favor the view that both statuettes emanate from the same workshop, namely that of a forger of the twenties.[11]

Fig. 2 (left): Bronze kore, private collection. Photo DAI 41.1854.

Fig. 3 (center): Bronze kore, private collection. Photo DAI 38.416.

Fig. 4 (right): Bronze kore, Worcester Art Museum. Photo courtesy of the museum.

Let me add that this judgment obviously had been rendered from Blümel's memory (he already belonged to the Berlin museum staff in 1927) and from re-examination of the photographs. No one seems to have seen the original since 1927. The question I raise here is not whether the Artemis bronze is genuine or not, a case that I would refuse to judge from an illustration. What seems questionable to me is the combination of *argumenta ad hominem* and vague stylistic criteria presented in the article I quoted.

I may quote another German scholar, Ernst Homann-Wedeking, whose words gain some actuality as they refer to the bronzes in Figs. 2-3 and to No. 161 in the Master Bronzes exhibition (Fig. 4). In an article[12] memorable for its clear analysis of the difference between Greek and Etruscan art, he discusses some statuettes he considers dubious. I can only excerpt from a long passage. Homann-Wedeking compares two kouroi of the same type. Of the statuette in Figs. 5-6 he says,

> The small differences are remarkable. The back hair falls down without a chisel mark, the locks over the shoulders are missing, the nipples are inlaid in copper. One recognizes an attribute in the right hand, a staff broken off on both ends. Taken one by one these details would not exclude authenticity, but their combination is suspicious; if the insertion of the nipples in copper into the

Figs. 5-6: Bronze kouros, Swiss private collection. Photo D. Widmer.

bronze leads one to assume particularly careful workmanship, the lack of care in rendering the hair suggests, on the contrary, careless and summary work or simply the anxiety of the modern manufacturer not to reveal himself with incorrectly stylized detail. The fragment of an oblique staff which can only be completed as a spear would be an unusual attribute for a votive statuette of kouros type. It must be added that the patina adheres in layers, that it tends to flake off, and therefore forewarns us.

Without going into detail, I ask whether the flaking off of patina speaks for or against the piece. This is a question on which we should consult bronze technologists. In any case, this bronze, which belongs to a Swiss collector, still awaits a definite verdict of guilt or innocence. In the same article Homann-Wedeking speaks of a series of four bronze korai, two of which (Figs. 3, 4) are exact replicas of a statuette dug up in Marzabotto. A fifth, related piece, which he thinks genuine, is shown in Fig. 2. "The genuineness of the Marzabotto figurine is established; but because of the patina, which flakes off easily and consists of layers, the two other completely corresponding statuettes are in all probability modern copies of the former. It is not clear whether the fourth statuette, which further develops certain features of the first three, should be attributed to an Etruscan bronze founder or to a modern forger. Serious concern should arise when considering the rendering and arrangement of the hair over the forehead and the face as seen in profile and particularly in front view." The author continues with some other stylistic criteria, but he concludes, "All these features could have been bestowed upon the figure by a dry Etruscan master around the beginning of the fifth century. The credibility of this assumption should not be denied, but one does not feel comfortable with it. Comparisons which make a decision possible seem to be lacking. The statuette itself should be judged impartially." This is a courageous statement, as it admits a *non liquet* — on the borderline between yes and no.

Finally, let me discuss an important Etruscan bronze in a public collection which has been attacked by many archaeologists for some time. It is the archaic standing youth in the Toledo Museum (Fig. 7), solid cast, 16$^1/_2$ inches (42 cm.) high, unusual but not unique in size. A close examination of the surface revealed remainders of surviving incrustation in the corners between the legs and between arms and body, and patina which was flaking off and which interrupted the incised lines and the punchmarks indicating the border of the garment. Both observations speak in favor of the bronze. Again, this object should be submitted to a thorough technical examination, including microscopic inspection of the cold work, and then to a frank discussion, weighing all the pros and cons.

This characterizes the approach that seems to me the only logical, considerate, and responsible one for scholars, dealers, and collectors: (1) never to consult only one expert, as nobody is infallible or knowledgeable about all aspects of the field; (2) to judge an object by its own merits and to listen to and consult technicians.

This symposium has discussed the progress made in the field of technology. We are confident in the belief that close collaboration between science and archaeology will lead to tangible criteria for the detection of forgeries, as well as to answers for many other questions. The composition of the metal (and for marble, the age of incrustation), the consistency and structure of patina, the adherence of patina to the original surface, and the casting techniques are all fields of research to which we archaeologists, let us admit, have an amateurish approach. Of course we cannot unload our own responsibility on scientists, as we must know how to interpret their findings.

I conclude my thoughts on bronze collecting by alluding to a friend of mine, an eager collector and connoisseur. He does not allow anyone — including me — to touch his beloved bronzes, and he himself only touches them with gloves. I can only approve of this. The important collection of bronzes assembled by Winston Churchill's cousin, Capt. Spencer Churchill, suffered from serious ravages by being touched by too many people over the generations. The objects stood in the open on a table at his house in Blockley Park. A closed showcase, particularly with some chemical means to extract humidity from the air, would have preserved them better. Bronzes are delicate and fragile, although, to reverse a famous saying by Horace, "bronze is outlived only by poetry."

Fig. 7: Bronze youth, Toledo Art Museum. Photo courtesy of the museum.

Notes

1 J. W. Goethe, *Italienische Reise* (lst ed.; 1817), 123.

2 Rudolph Gaedechens, *Die Antiken des Fürstlich Waldeckischen Museums* (Arolsen, 1862).

3 Paul Arndt, "Die Sammlung antiker Bronzen des Fürsten von Waldeck," *Pantheon*, VII (1931), 78 ff.

4 Ulf Jantzen, *Bronzewerkstätten in Großgriechenland und Sizilien* (Berlin, 1937), 27, no. 28.

5 German Hafner, *Die Bronzen der Sammlung Dr. Heinrich Scheufelen in Oberlenningen . . .* (Mainz, 1958).

6 L. Alscher, *Götter vor Gericht* (Berlin, 1963).

7 C. Blümel, *Die archaisch griechischen Skulpturen der Staatlichen Museen zu Berlin* (2nd ed.; Berlin, 1964), 7 ff., no. 1, pl. 1.

8 R. Joffroy, *Le trésor de Vix* (Paris, 1954).

9 S. Meletzis and H. Papadakis, *Le Musée Archéologique National d'Athènes* (Munich and Zurich, 1964), 6, pls. 59-61.

10 G. Daux, "Chronique des fouilles . . . 1962," *BCH*, LXXXVII:2 (1963), 802, pls. 17-20.

11 C. Blümel and A. Greifenhagen, "Eine gefälschte Bronzestatuette," *AA* (1965), cols. 119-120.

12 E. Homann-Wedeking, "Bronzestatuetten etruskischen Stils," *RömMitt*, LVIII (1943), 87 ff.

Contributors to this Volume

Herbert A. Cahn was born in Frankfurt, studied classics in Frankfurt and Basel, and received his Ph.D. in Classical Archaeology from Basel University in 1940. He took part in the founding of Münzhandlung Basel (later to become Münzen und Medaillen A. G.) in 1933 and has been active in the commerce of ancient coins and classical antiquities ever since. The co-editor of two Swiss periodicals, *Antike Kunst* and *Schweizer Münzblätter*, he also teaches Greek and Roman numismatics at Heidelberg University.

Earle R. Caley was graduated from Baldwin-Wallace College in 1923 and attended the Ohio State University, from which he received a M.S. in chemistry in 1925 and a Ph.D. in 1928; he also holds an honorary D.Sc. from Baldwin-Wallace. He has taught at Princeton and at Ohio State, where he has been Professor of Chemistry since 1957. Professor Caley served as a chemist on the excavations of the Athenian Agora in 1937; he has been a consultant to numerous museums and since 1955 has been a member of the Advisory Board, Intermuseum Laboratory, Oberlin College.

Suzannah F. Doeringer earned an A.B. degree from Wellesley College in 1964 and an A.M. from Harvard University in the following year. As Assistant to the Curator of Classical Art at the Fogg Art Museum from 1965 to 1967, she took part in the organization of the Master Bronzes exhibition and the preparation of its catalogue. During 1968 she served as Assistant Curator of Classical Art at the Fogg, where she is currently the Executive Assistant to the Director.

Elaine K. Gazda received her A.B. from Marietta College in 1964 and her A.M. in art history from the University of Pennsylvania in 1966. She is currently working toward her Ph. D. at Harvard University. She has worked for the Fogg Art Museum during the summer of 1967, was draftswoman for the excavations at Sardis in 1968, and served as a teaching fellow in Fine Arts at Harvard in 1968-1969.

Rutherford J. Gettens received his B.S. from Middlebury College in 1923 and his A.M. in chemistry from Harvard University in 1929. He has taught at Colby College, Middlebury, and Harvard. He served as a chemist in the Conservation Department of the Fogg Art Museum from 1928 to 1951, being the Chief of Museum Technical Research during the last two years of this period. Since 1951 he has served on the staff of the Freer Gallery of Art in Washington, D.C. but retired from his post as Head Curator of the Freer Laboratory in 1968. He continues at the Freer as Consultant in Technical Research.

Mogens Gjødesen, born in Copenhagen, received his M.A. in 1940 from the University of Copenhagen. He has participated in several excavations, including those at Mylasa in Caria, Dendra in Argolis, and Tall Sukas in Syria. From 1940 to 1942 he served in the Department of Coins of the Danish National Museum. In 1943 he became an Assistant Curator at the Ny Carlsberg Glyptothek, in Copenhagen, where he has been Curator since 1951.

George M. A. Hanfmann, born in St. Petersburg, Russia, pursued his graduate studies in Berlin, where he received the Dr. phil. degree, and at Johns

Hopkins University, where he earned the Ph.D. In addition to extensive field work in Italy, Greece, Cyprus, and Turkey, he has published numerous books, articles, reviews, and exhibition catalogues. At present he is Professor of Fine Arts at Harvard University, Curator of Classical Art at the Fogg Art Museum, and Field Director of the Archaeological Exploration of Sardis.

Sybille Haynes studied classical archaeology, art history, and ancient history at the universities of Munich and Frankfurt am Main, receiving her doctorate from the latter university. Since 1951 she has worked as a voluntary assistant in the Greek and Roman Department of the British Museum. In 1964 she was elected a *membro straniero* of the Istituto di Studi Etruschi ed Italici. She has published a booklet on Etruscan bronze utensils and articles on Etruscan bronzes, silver, and sculpture, and on Greek and Roman bronzes and silver in a variety of journals.

Herbert Hoffmann, who was born in Berlin, received his A.B. (1951), A.M. (1952), and Ph.D. (1959) at Harvard University. From 1956 to 1958 he was a Prix-de-Rome Fellow at the American Academy in Rome. He has held the positions of Curatorial Assistant at the Metropolitan Museum of Art, New York, and Assistant Curator at the Museum of Fine Arts, Boston. He is now Curator of Ancient Art at the Museum für Kunst und Gewerbe, Hamburg. The author of several books on classical art, he is preparing a full publication of the Cretan bronze armor in the Schimmel Collection in cooperation with Antony Raubitschek, who is studying the inscriptions.

Hans Jucker studied classical archaeology, Greek and Latin philology, and ancient history in Basel and Zurich, receiving his doctorate and teaching certification; he pursued further study in Rome. Between 1950 and 1956 he taught in the gymnasia at Winterthur and Zurich. In 1957 he became Curator of the coin collection at the Bernisches Historisches Museum. He is presently a professor at the University of Bern. He has written extensively on ancient sculpture — particularly portraiture, Roman iconography, Roman coins, Etruscan art, and the minor arts.

Heather Lechtman holds an A.B. in physics from Vassar College and both an A.M. in Fine Arts and a Diploma in Conservation of Art and Archaeological Materials from the Institute of Fine Arts, New York University. She was a Fulbright Scholar at the Research Laboratory of the British Museum from 1964 to 1966 and has served as a conservator at archaeological expeditions to Mendes, Egypt, and Samothrace, Greece. Since 1967 she has been a Research Associate in Archaeology in the Department of Humanities and a staff member of the Laboratory for Research on Archaeological Materials at M. I. T.

Heinz Menzel has been a Research Fellow at the Römisch-Germanisches Zentralmuseum, Mainz, since 1948. His graduate study was done in Berlin, Budapest, and Mainz. In 1954 he published a catalogue of the ancient lamps in the Römisch-Germanisches Zentralmuseum. He is currently at work on a series of definitive catalogues of Roman bronzes from Germany, of which two volumes have appeared, Speyer and Trier.

David Gordon Mitten received his A.B. from Oberlin College and his A.M. and Ph.D. from Harvard University. He has participated in excavations in New Mexico, South Dakota, Isthmia in Greece, and Sardis in Turkey. He is the Assistant Director of the Sardis Expedition and project director of the excavation of the nearby prehistoric cemetery, Ahlatli Tepecik. A Professor of Classical Archaeology at Harvard, he also serves as the Associate Curator of Classical Art at the Fogg Art Museum.

Oscar White Muscarella holds an A.B. degree from the City College of New York and an A.M. and Ph.D. from the University of Pennsylvania. He has taken part in excavations in Colorado, South Dakota, Gordion in Turkey, and at five sites in Iran. He has published a number of articles on Near Eastern art and archaeology and a book, *Phrygian Fibulae from Gordion.* He has taught at the City College of New York and has served since 1964 as Assistant Curator and then Associate Curator in the Department of Ancient Near Eastern Art of the Metropolitan Museum of Art.

Robert M. Organ received his scientific education at the College of Technology, Birmingham, England, where at one time he lectured in physics. He joined the staff of the Research Laboratory at the British Museum in 1951 and became Chief Experimental Officer. Since 1957 he has been rapporteur for the study of metals to the ICOM Committee on Museum Scientific Laboratories. In 1965 he became Curator of Conservation at the Royal Ontario Museum; he serves at present as Chief of the Conservation-Analytical Laboratory, U.S. National Museum, Smithsonian Institution.

Harold J. Plenderleith has been the Director of the International Centre for the Study of the Preservation and Restoration of Cultural Property since 1959. He holds the B.Sc., Ph.D., and honorary LL.D. degrees from St. Andrews University. For a number of years he was Professor of Chemistry at the Royal Academy of Arts, London. From 1949 to 1959 he served as Keeper of the Research Laboratory at the British Museum. Among his many publications, *The Conservation of Antiquities and Works of Art* has become a basic handbook for conservators.

Cyril Stanley Smith earned his B.Sc. at Birmingham, England, in 1924 and his D.Sc. at M.I.T. in 1926. He also holds an honorary D.Litt. from Case Institute of Technology. His fields of research have been diverse, his most recent interests being the historical interaction between science and technology and the application of metallography to the study of archaeological artifacts. With various co-authors he has brought out edited translations of several early technical treatises. He has been an Institute Professor, Professor of History of Technology and Science, and Professor of Metallurgy at M.I.T. since 1961.

Arthur Steinberg received his A.B. at Harvard University in 1958. His graduate study was done at the University of Pennsylvania, where he earned the Ph.D. in 1966, at the American School of Classical Studies in Athens, and at the American Academy in Rome on the Prix-de-Rome fellowship. He has taken part in excavations at Sardis, Gordion, and Patnos, Turkey, and at Koroni in Attica, and has conducted a tour for the Archaeological Institute of America to North Africa and Sicily. Since 1964 he has been Assistant Professor of History and Archaeology at M.I.T.

Cornelius C. Vermeule, III, received his undergraduate education and his A.M. at Harvard University and his Ph.D. at the University of London. He has lectured at Smith College, Boston University, Harvard University, and Wellesley College, and has been an Assistant Professor at the University of Michigan and Bryn Mawr College. Since 1957 he has been the Curator of Classical Art at the Museum of Fine Arts, Boston, and since 1965 a Professor of Fine Arts at Boston University. He has recently completed an extensive catalogue of the classical bronzes of that museum, in collaboration with Mary B. Comstock.

William J. Young received his training at the Ashmolean Museum, Oxford University, and before coming to the United States was associated with the Pitt Rivers Museum and the Institute for Archaeological Research in London. He founded the Research Laboratory at the Museum of Fine Arts, Boston, in 1929 and now serves as its head. He has done considerable research in archaeology and in the conservation and preservation of works of art, along with analytical work by means of X ray, X-ray diffraction, X-ray fluorescence, and the optical spectrograph.

Index

Acetic acid, atmospheric pollution by, 81
Activated charcoal, to remove polluting gases, 81
Aesthetics, archaeological and art historical approaches of, 1
  link with technology, 52
Afrati, 168
Afrati armor, 129
  dating of, 138
  inscriptions on, 137
  Orientalizing decoration on, 140
  style of, 138
Afrati bronzes, compared to clay pithoi, 147
Afrati cut-out relief, 140
Aftercasts, ancient, 273
Agricola, Georgius, 252
Alexander the Great, coins of, 40
Alexander by Lysippos, model for Mars statuettes, 224
Alexander of Magnesia, 224
Alloy composition, under metallurgical microscope, 92
Alloy constituents, factor affecting corrosion rate, 89
Alloys, for bells, 251
  of copper, tin, and silver, 10
  first use of, 85
  in Greek bird (No. 25), 16
  for statues, 251
  tin-lead, 10
  use of different types of, 56
Alphabet, of Afrati inscriptions, 129
  Semitic or Phrygian, Greek borrowing of, 109
Altintepe cauldron, attachments on, 122-123
Ammonium sulphate, atmospheric pollution [by, 81
Analyses, chemical, 93
  laser-microscope, 3
  metallurgical, availability of, 4
  need for, 65
  paucity of, 3
  quantitative, on Greek bird (No. 25), 16
  sampling procedure for, 51
  slag, 4
  spectographic, 2, 56
  trace element, value of, 51
  uncertainty in, 51
  wet-chemical, 2
  X-ray fluorescence, 3
Ancona, horse from, composition of, 45
Annealing, on Greek bird (No. 25), 22
  oxidation during, 51
Antigonus Gonatas, coins of, 42
Antikythera, statue from, 39
Antimony, plated on bronzes, 97
Apollo, from Almenum, 222
  composition of Gallo-Roman, 45
  from Jardin du Luxembourg, 223
  from Volesvres, 223
Appliqué, silver, Vulcian origin of, 189
Ares Ludovisi, as prototype, 228
Arezzo, votive statuettes at, 236
Argive Heraeum, objects from, 40
Argive Heraeum female ("Eteocretan") figure, 153
  headdress of, 153
  relation to Crete, 154
Arkades, 129
Armor, technological context, 1
Armor from Afrati, 129
  dating of, 138
  inscriptions on, 137
  style of, 138
Armor from Axos, date of, 136-137
Armor from Crete, as archers' booty, 167
  low repoussé on, 105
  place of manufacture of, 168
Armor (Nos. 29-32), decoration of, 52
Armor in Schimmel collection, date of, 168
Arnaudon, analysis by, 43
Arsenic, action in copper, 98
  plate on bronzes, 97
  use of, 99
Art, relation to science, v
Artemis from Pagonda, lead content of, 41
Artist, involvement in technology, 54
  relationship with craftsman, 54
  relationship with foundryman and joiner, 32
Arts, metallic, written sources, vi
Atacamite, 61
Athena, armor dedicated to, 129
Athena of Euenor, 203
Athena Promachos, in Constantinople, 247
Athenian Agora, animal statuette from, composition of, 45
  female statuette from, composition of, 41
Athlete in British Museum (1907 10-20 2), Vulcian origin of, 185
Athlete (No. 83), repatination on, 79
Aurichalcum, use of, 248
Authenticity, 2
  condition of mineral as indication of, 95
  resolving questions of, 1
Auxerre statuette, compared to Eleutherna pithos fragment and *mitra* (No. 32), 149
Axos, 168
Axos armor, 136
Axos *mitrai*, compared to "Eteocretan" openwork plaques, 139
Axos poros head, 154
Azurite, 59-60

Bacchus, from Avenches, 222
  joins on, 236
  provenance of, 236
Ball player (Walters, No. 500), Vulcian style of, 184
Belgian Congo, tin mineral from, 61
Bell-casting industry, progress of, 250
Bells, mold-building techniques for, 241
Bern votive figures, composition of, 45
Bern youth, composition of, 45
Berthelot, M., research of, 62
Bibra, E. von, analyses by, 39-41
Bird, geometric Greek (No. 25), 14, 51
  mechanical join of tail, 15
  metallurgical join of tail, 15
  repairing procedure for, 16
Bird attachments, 112-114
Biringuccio, Vannoccio, 241, 252
Blacas collection boy, alloy of, 43
Blowpipe, 31
Bornite, 59
Botallacite, 63
Botryoidal malachite, 59
Boxer (Walters No. 526), 185
Boy adjusting sandal (Walters No. 449), Vulcian features on, 187
Brass, corrosion minerals on, 64
  at Gordion, 55
  in Roman coinage, 55
Braze, on Demeter bust, 54
Brescia Victory, composition of, 43
Brochantite, 62, 95
Bronze, importance of medium, 2
  instability of, 3
Bronze-caster, borrowing by, 231
  practices of, 221
Bronze-casters, Carolingian, 249
  early Renaissance specialization of, 242
Bronze-casting, development during Renaissance, 241
Bronze disease, 58
  cause of, 61
  microscopic detection of, 76
  outbreak of, 77
  use of silver nitrate on, 97
  use of silver oxide on, 97
  use of silver sulphate on, 97
Bronze industry, distinctions according to kinds of objects, viii
Bronzes, ancient, effect on later generations of, 252
  inspiration by, 252-253
  re-use of, 247
  survival of, 257
  time of reappearance of, 252
Bronzes, Greek, models for, 156
  procedure for study, 145
  statuary, technological context of, 1
  treatment of, before 1800, 271
Bronze-workers, Cretan, inventors of relief work, 150-151
Bronze-working, decline of, 249

Bührle Collection girl and boy, gesture of, 208
  sisters of, 210
  style of, 207
Bull attachments, casting methods, 106
Bull attachments, source of western examples, 112
  Urartian group, 111
  where found, 111
  winged, from Iran, 114
Bull protomes, places of manufacture, 167
Burnishing, 95
Bust, female, composition of, 45
By-products, analysis of, 1
Byzantium, bronze manufacture in, 248
  casting in, 241

Cahn, Herbert A., 55, 96, 236
Caley, Earle R., 51, 55, 62, 98
  analyses by, 40, 42, 44
Campanian fashion, 160
Campanian style, 168
Candelabrum figure (Walters, No. 500), Vulcian style of, 184
Candelabrum figures, compared to Spencer-Churchill youth, 178
  Vulcian, coiffure on, 204-207
Candelabrum top, compared to Spencer-Churchill lyre player, 179
Candelabrum youth, in Spencer-Churchill Collection, 177
Cannon, casting in fourteenth century, 250
Capua, dinos from, 160
Capuan dinos group, 157
Carbonated bronzes, locations of, 59
Carbonates, copper, 59
Carnelian in Leningrad, 224
Caryatid (No. 75), gesture of, 168
Cassiterite, 60
Casting, complications during, 6
  defective, 7, 9
  difficulties of, 5
  failures, 157
  interlock, 6
  methods, 250
  solid, Etruscan *kouros* (No. 167), 9
  without mold, 52
Casting methods, influence on conservation by, 74
  for siren attachments, 106
Casting of model, 174
Casting-on, on Greek bird (No. 25), 18, 22
Casting pits, in Athens, 4
Casts, ancient duplicate, 273
Caucasus, iron inlays from, 235
Cauldron, from Salamis, sphinxes on, 167
Cauldrons, arrival in Greece and Etruria, 103
Cauterization, bronze disease treatment, 97
Cellini, Benvenuto, 257-258
  account of casting, 251-252
Censer in Spencer-Churchill collection, significance of figures, 184
Censers, compared to Spencer-Churchill incense burner, 183
Censer shaft, 183
Cerbone chariot, decoration from, 195, 235
Cerussite, 63
Chalcocite, 59
Chalconatronite, 63, 64
Chalcopyrite, 59
Change, in appearance, 73
  visible evidence of, 79
Charcoal, activated, to remove polluting gases, 81
Chares, 54
Charioteer of Delphi, damage to, 245
Chariots, Cerbone, iron ornaments from, 195
Chemical analyses. See Analyses, chemical
Chinese bronzes, accelerated patina on, 97
  aesthetics of, 52
  article on corrosion on, by Gettens, 62
  percentage of lead in, 63
  study of, 95
  tin oxide patina on, 60
  water patina on, 58
Chinese vessels, percentage of tin and lead in, 56
Chisel from Jericho, microscopic study of, 76
Chiusi, objects from, 175
Christian zu Waldeck, Prince, 271
Christians, destruction by, 246
Chronology, archaeological and art historical approaches of, 1
Church, influence of, 242-243
Church doors, mold-building techniques for, 241
Cire-perdue. See Lost-wax casting
Cleaning, 80
  determination of process of, 3
  mechanical, 96, 258
Coinage, Roman, brass in, 55
  high zinc content of, 93
  zinc in, 55
Coins, analyses of, 41
  casting without mold of, 52
  composition of, 40, 42
  evidence for statuettes' composition, 55
  Lydian, 52
  weight of, 52
Cold work, on drapery fragment (No. 237), 24
  on Populonian slag heap figure, 199
Cold working, effects on, by mass production, 174
  slip bands resulting from, 30
Collecting, reasons for, 272
Collection, study, necessity of, 64
Collections, ancient, 259
  care of, 277
  quality of, 221
Collectors, xii
  bronze, motives of, 145
  contemporary, 271
Colossus of Barletta, 248
Colossus of Rhodes, 54
  destruction of, 245
Components of bronze, ratios of, 2
Composition, changes in, 55
  chemical, 38
  chronological changes in, 42
  modification of, by drossing, 51
  modification of, by reduction, 51
Compositions, differences in workshops, 3
Connellite, 63
Conservation, definition of, 73
  processes of, 80
Conservator, objectives of, 73
Constantine, collector of statues, 247
Constantinople, bronze-casting quarter in, 248
  destruction of bronzes in, 247
Construction of object, different materials in, 74
Contexts, technological and archaeological, 1
Coolidge, John P., v
  comments by, xi
  lion of, 256
Copies, ancient, 273
  of ancient bronzes, 260
  divergence from originals, 260
  of Marzabotto figurine, 276
  nineteenth-century, zinc content, 93
Copper, amount related to joining problems, 55
  Mycenaean search for, 195
  percentages of, 38
Copper carbonate, 58, 59
Copper oxide, 95
Copper resources, in Northern Latium, 195
Copper sulphate, on park bronzes and architectural trim, 62
Copper sulphides, 59
Core, 5
  refractory, on Greek bird (No. 25), 15
Coremans, Paul, conservation defined by, 73
Corinth, foundries at, 4
Cornwall, tin deposits of, 61
Corroded metals, methods for handling, 96
Corrosion, 51
  accelerated, experiment on, 98
  agents of, 89
  chloride, 62
  as electrochemical action, 91
  electrolytic, in join, 10
  end results of, 76
  on Greek bird (No. 25), 15, 20
  initial, under microscope, 92
  rate of, factors affecting, 89
  reorientation by fire, 97
Corrosion crust, examination of, under microscope, 74-75
  handling of, 79
  materials entrapped in, 61
  removal of, 77, 80, 83
Corrosion factors, economic implications, 57
Corrosion processes, causes of, 79
Corrosion products, 1, 3, 37
Corslet descriptions, C1, 135
  C2-C5, 136
Corslet (C3), location of, 129
Corslet from Olympia, compared to Afrati helmet (No. 29), 148
  Cretan origin of, 149
Cosimo, Duke, 258
Cosmetic treatment, 80
Cotunnite, 63
Covellite, 59
Craftsman, relationship with artist, 54
Cretan armor, hard working on, 167
  technique of, 104, 105
Cretan bronze-working, problems of, 104
Crusade, Fourth, destruction of bronzes during, 247

Crusts, removal of, 77, 80, 83
Crystal, observation of, 75
size of, 20
Cultural elements, Near Eastern, diffusion of, 103
Cumengite, 64
Cupric chloride, 77
Cupric oxide, 58
Cuprite, 58, 95
under malachite and azurite, 60
volume increase, 59
Cuprous chloride, on copper chisel from Jericho, 76
incomplete removal of, 77
Cuprous oxide, under microscope, 75
Curators, co-operation with collectors, xii
Cut-out, from Afrati, compared to helmet (No. 29), 148
in Louvre, hunters on, 148
Cut-outs, bronze, intermediary between smith and potter, 151

Daidalos, 139
Dating, methods of, 146
value of, 146-147
Daubrée, A., 59
Davies, O., analyses by, 40
Debris, foundry, at Enkomi (Cyprus), 4
Decay, chemical processes of, 77
Decorative bronzes, quality of, 173
Dedalic style, Cretan, 149
Delphi helmet, 136
Delphi *mitrai*, 136
Demeter bust, technology of, 54
Demon, on Afrati cinerary urn, 148
bearded, 148
winged, on clay pithoi, 147
Dendrites, on drapery fragment (No. 237), 30
under metallurgical microscope, 92
Dendritic structure, of athlete (No. 83), 79
Desert, effect of, on bronze, 61
Desiccants, for humidity control, 82
Destruction of bronze sculpture, causes of, 246
Development, stylistic, 2
Diana (No. 253), mechanical join with lead on, 8
X-radiograph of, 8
Diana from Toledo Museum, composition of, 45
Diodorus, 195
Dionysus in Philadelphia, 236
Dioskouros in Louvre, pose of, 224
Diskobolus (No. 176), cracked mineral crust on, 82
Diskophoros of Naukydes, model for Mercury, 229
Display case, selection of, 81
Dohrn, T., 2
Dolphin, Renaissance appliqué and Roman handle (No. 288), 254
Donatello, 251
ancient models known by, 253
casting by, 241
Doors, Byzantine, in Italy, 249
church, 249
metal analyses of, 249
Doryphoros by Polykleitos, influence of, 229, 231
as model for Mercury, 229
Dowels, use of, in mechanical joins, 7
Drapery fragment, microstructure of, 29
ovals and circles on join of, 23
patches on, 24
Roman (No. 237), fusion welding on, 22, 54
slip bands on, 30
stringers on, 29
Drapery, undercutting, on Demeter bust, 54
Drawings, Renaissance, of Etruscan bronzes, 259
Dreros, gorgoneion from, 136
helmet from, 136
mitrai from, 136, 139
Drescher, H., 10
Dross, 5
Drossing, composition modified by, 51
Duplication, 154
Dust, as cause of corrosion processes, 79
removal of, 80
as vehicle for ammonium sulphate, 81

Earrings, gold, from Athenian Agora, Near Eastern origin of, 124, n. 4
Elba, figure from, 199-212
Populonian interests in, 195
Eleanor of Castile, effigy of, 250
Electrochemical treatment, for stabilization, 82
Electrolytic corrosion, in join, 10
Electrolytic reduction, use of, 96
Electron-beam microprobe, use of, 65
Elving, P. J., analyses by, 40
Engraving, on pottery and bronze, 151
Enlargements, proportional, in Renaissance, 254
Environment, affecting rate of corrosion, 89
control of, 81
Ephesus athlete, analysis of, 41
Eros, in Kress Collection, 254
"Eteocretan," definition of, 151
openwork plaques, 138
Praisos, plate from, 154
Eutectoid, on drapery fragment (No. 237), 29
lack of, on Greek bird (No. 25), 20, 22
Evaluation, statistical, of Greek bronzes, 145
Exhibition, Master Bronzes, purpose of, 145

Fellenberg, L. R., von, analyses by, 41, 43, 44
Fettling, 74
Fibula, Boeotian or Thessalian, tool used on, 88, 89, 98
geometric (No. 26), tracing on, 53
gold, reproductions of, 53
Filarete, Marcus Aurelius by, 253-254
Finishing, involvement of artist in, 174
of metal object, viii
Finthen gilded statue, alloy of, 43
Fire, wood, impact on bronzes, 97
Flemings, Merton C., 55
Flight, W., analyses by, 43
Flux, in soldering, 10
Foce del Sele, metopes from, 160
Fogg Art Museum, xii
exhibit in, xi
Forger, extent of knowledge of, 87
Forgeries, detection by metallurgical examination, 87
detection of, 276-277
reflections on, 272-273
sources of, 273
Forgery, difference from copy, 256
early, 271
Fortetsa, lion-tamer on quiver from, 148
Foundries, excavation of, 4
Foundryman, relationship with artist and joiner, 32
Foundry Painter cup, 54
Frondel, Clifford, 63
Fufluna-Populonia, copper mining at, 195
Function, influencing bronze production,175
of Roman and Etruscan statuettes, 173
Furnaces, analysis of, 1
Fusion, of cast and weld metals, 29
Fusion weld, 27
on drapery fragment (No. 237), 22
Fusion welding, 9, 14, 24
definition, 7

Gangue, definition of, 85
Gas pockets, 5
Gases, freedom from in casting, 6
generation of in casting, 5
Gate, placement of, 6
Geilman, W., 60
Geneva Roman general, pose of, 224
Genuineness, proof of, 96
Gettens, Rutherford J., 10, 55, 95, 98
Ghiberti, 54
ancient figurines studied by, 253
foundry of, 251
Giamalakis collection, corslet (C2) in, 136
sherd with winged horse in, 148
Gjødesen, M., 168
Goat (No. 63), 154
Göbel, F., analysis by, 39
Gordion, 167
griffin-like creature from, 114
repoussé on situla from, 103
Tomb MMT, tin and zinc content in objects from, 55
Grado, statuette from, 224
Granulation, 52, 124, n. 4
Graver, use of, 88
Griffin, on corslet (C1), 135
Griffin attachments from Olympia, provenience of, 114
Griffin protome, in Teheran, 112
Griffin protomes, chronological development of, 103
failed casting of, 106
hammered, origin of, 109
high repoussé on, 103
iconography of, 103
lost-wax casting of, 103
on Salamis cauldron, 167
spectographic analyses of, 56
technique changes of, 104
Guilds, influence of, 242

Hagia Sophia, doors of, 248-249
Hairstyles, of Afrati workshop, 148
Halbherr, excavations of, 129
Hammering, 167
Hand, votive (No. 313), lead filler and tang in join of, 9
Handle attachment (No. 149), counterpart to, 154
Handles, from krater (No. 200), method of attachment, 14
Praenestine, characteristics of, 189
Hanfmann, George M. A., v, xi, 54, 55, 235, 236
Hard solder, difficulties in joins, 12
Hard soldering, 10, 25, 33
Hard working, 167
Harvard University, xi
Hasanlu, bird handle from, 114
repoussé from, 103
Haynes, D. E. L., 2
Heat, introduction in welding, 14
Helmet from Afrati (No. 29), compared to clay pinax, 148
compared to corslet from Olympia, 148
compared to cut-out relief, 148
date of, 149
decorative lines on, 52
linked to Gortyn pinax, 151
Helmet from Axos, 136
Helmet from Delphi, date of, 149
Helmet (H1), decoration of, 132-134
Helmet (H2) from Afrati, description of, 134
Orientalizing decoration on, 140
Helmet (H3) from Afrati, description of, 135
Helmet (H4), fragments of, 135
Hera in Constantinople, destruction of, 247
Herakles, on plate from Praisos, 154
Herakles from Vulci, compared to Spencer-Churchill youth, 177-178
Hermes, compared to Spencer-Churchill lyre player, 179
Hermes by Lysippos, as prototype, 226-228
Hermes of Polykleitos, as model, 229
Herodotus, 109, 116
Hildesheim, doors of, 249
Hirshhorn collection, *kouros* from, 213, 235
Hoffmann, Herbert, 167, 168
Hollow-cast objects, composition of, 46
Hoplite, on corslet (C1), 135
Horse, on helmet (H2), 134
Horse protomes, *mitra* (M1), 129
winged, on *mitra* (M2), 130
Horses, on clay pithoi, 147
winged, pithos with, 150
Humidity, control of, 81
Hydria, Greek (No. 109), handles soldered on, 14
Hydria, Greek (No. 110), restoration of, 80
Hydrozincite, 64

Idaean cave, techniques of bronzes from, 104
Ikaros, 140
Immersion, for stabilizing treatment, 82
Implements, technological context, 1
Impurities, in alloying elements, 51
in bronzes, 37
determination of, 38
Incense burner, in Spencer-Churchill collection, 182-184
Incision, determination of tool type, 87
Industry, bronze, distinctions according to kinds of objects, viii
Inscription, on Afrati armor, 129
on corslets (C3-C5), 136
dating of, 168
on helmet (H1) from Afrati, 134
on helmets (H2-H3), 135
on *mitrai* (M1-M2), 130
Interlock casting, 6
Iran, northern, repoussé in, 103
Iron, welding of, 14
Iron inlays, Etruscan use of, 235
Iron intarsia, 203
Iron ornaments, on Cerbone chariots, 195
Iron resources, in Northern Latium, 195
Italian bronzes, recognition of workshops of, 236
Itinerants, adaptations of style by, 106

Janson, H. W., 53
Jantzen, U., research by, 4
Joins, aesthetic requirements of, 33
on drapery fragment (No. 237), procedure for, 31
electrolytic corrosion in, 10
execution of, 8
hard-solder, difficulties of, 12
masking of, 32
mechanical, 6-9
mechanical, on Greek bird (No. 25), 20, 22
metallurgical, 6, 9-32
metallurgical, on Greek bird (No. 25), 19, 22
ovals and circles on, 23
silver-copper solder, photomicrograph of, 12
soft-soldered, photomicrograph of, 10
source of heat used for, 12
Joiner, relationship to artist and foundryman, 32
Joining, 5
problems of, related to copper amount, 55
Jucker, H., 235
Junghans, analyses by, 51
Jupiter, from Evreux, 231
influence of Lysippos on, 231
Justinian, statue of, 247-248

Kanephoros, from Paestum, 161
Käppeli collection boy, connection with Elba figure, 210, 235
Kennecott, support of, xii
Kesseltiere, attributions of, 115
Kleophrades Painter, calyx krater by, 203
Koine, decorative, in seventh-century Greece, 106
Kore, dancing, Etruscan, 235
Kore, in Schimmel collection, relation to Elba figure, 207
Kouros, Etruscan (No. 167), solid casting and radiograph of, 9
Kouros in Schimmel collection (No. 159), 235
Krater, by Kleophrades Painter, 203
Kress collection, Renaissance bronzes in, 254-256
Kythera, statue from, metal analysis of, 39

Labor, organization of, viii
Lacquer, black, 254
consolidation of patina with, 79
Lacroix, A., 59, 63
Lady, Etruscan (No. 185), use of dowel on, 7
Lasa (No. 184) in Fogg Art Museum, 235
Laser, optical, 93
Laser-microscope, 3, 93
Latium, northern, copper and iron resources of, 195
Lead, absence of, in Greek bronzes, 39-40
in Artemis from Pagonda, 41
in athlete from Ephesus, 41
in coins, 42
in female from Athenian Agora, 41
figurines mounted with, in Populonia, 199, 212, 235
high content of, in Roman bronzes, 49, 87
in mechanical join, 8
mineral alteration of, 63
percentage of, in Pliny's recipes, 48-49
quantity of, in drapery fragment (No. 237), 27
ratio of, to tin, 45, 46
in votive hand (No. 313), 9
Lead alloys, patina on, 55
Lead chloride, on plates from Mahdia, 63
Lead salts, cause of, 81
Lead segregation, 63
Lechtman, Heather, 2, 236
conclusions by, 51
Ledgemont Laboratory, xii
Leningrad, carnelian in, 224
Levi, Doro, excavations of, 129
Libethenite, 63
Lion head, from Populonia, 235
Lion protomes, iron intarsia on, 195-196
Lions, pair of, from Perachora, 154
rampant, on corslet (C1), 135
of Seattle Art Museum and John P. Coolidge, 256
Lion's head, cast, relative of Praeneste lion, 196
Lion-tamer, on Fortetsa quiver, 148
Localization, value of, 147
Lost-wax casting, cause of unidentical pairs, 154
description of, 87, 107
direct, 241, 250
of Greek bird (No. 25), 15
of griffin protomes, 103
indirect, 106 f.
in Middle Ages, 241
procedures for, 241
Lucanian fashion, 160
Lucas, Alfred, 96
Luristan, repoussé at, 103
Lyon, workshop in, 228

Lyre player in Spencer-Churchill collection, 178
Lysippos, influence of, 224, 231
Lyttos, alphabet of, 129
bust from, hair arrangement of, 153

McEwen, R. L., analysis by, 40
"Macro" scale, of bronze internal structure, 73
Maenad, on utensil stand (Walters No. 771), 189
Magna Graecia, Walters Gallery girl (No. 57), 157
Mahdia, chalcocite and covellite on nails from, 59
lead chloride on plates from, 63
Maintenance, of metal object, viii
Mainz, doors of, 249
Malachite, 59-61
botryoidal or mamillary, 59
Malachite crusts, with cerussite, 63
Male figure from Elba, 199-205
Mamillary malachite, 59
Man (Walters No. 680), Vulcian origins of, 185
Manufacture centers, 122
determination of, 146
Mariemont girl, origin of, 157
provenience of, 168
Market, demands of, influencing bronze production, 175
influence of, on appearance, 173
Mars, from Blicquy, difference in concept, 224-225
of Dronrijp, 226
of Mandeure, 226
from Neumagen, 224
from Reims, 224
from Tzum, 224
Mars statuettes, distribution of, 224
group of, model for, 223-226
pose of, 224
workshops for, 224
Maryon, Herbert, reproductions by, 53
Marzabotto figurine, authenticity of, 276
Massachusetts Institute of Technology, xi
Mass production, effects of, 173-174
influence of, on quality, 174
Roman, 221
site survey of, 247
Matrix, copper ore, 85
Mechanical join. See Joins, mechanical
Menzel, H., 236
Mercury, from Bar-le-Duc, 231
from Chalon-sur-Saône, 231
from Clermont-Ferrand, 231
from Fins d'Annecy, model for, 229
from Limoges, 231
from London, composition of, 43
in Lyon, 228
from Montorio Veronese, 226
in Munich, 226
in Munich (from Feurs), prototype for, 228
from Narbonne, 231
from Schwarzenacker, 226
from Sens, 231
in Toronto, 228-229
models for, 229
from Vaison, 231
in Walters Art Gallery, 231
from Wawern, 228
Mercury statuettes, influence of Lysippos and Polykleitos on, 231
seated, 226
standing, 228
Metal, processing, viii
sources of, viii
Metal coloring, 85
Metallurgical join. See Joins, metallurgical
Metallurgy, history of, 85
progress of, after eleventh century, 249
Metals, first used, 85
types corrodible, 91
Metal worker, itinerant, 106
interaction of, with potter, 105
Metaxas, Nikos, Afrati armor of, 129
mitra (M4) of, 131
"Micro" scale, of bronze internal structure, 74
Microscope, examination of Cretan helmet (No. 29) under, 52
laser, 93
metallurgical, 92
use of, to determine metallic structure, 74
Microstructure, of Greek bird (No. 25), 21
Mineral alteration products, 57
Mineral resources, influence of, on production, 173
Minerals, rare, reflecting environment, 64
Minerva, statuette, composition of, 45
Mines, metal, in Charlemagne's empire, 249
Mining establishments, 4
Minoan statuettes (Nos. 4, 5A, B), linked to sphinx (No. 41), 152
Mirror, in Spencer-Churchill collection, 180
Perugian origin of, 182
Mirrors, Chinese, tin content of, 87
Etruscan, tin content of, 87
Etruscan, tin oxide patina on, 60
mechanical joins on handles of, 7
Mitra from Olympia, date of, 149
Mitra from Rethymnon, 148
date of, 149
Mitra (M1), description of, 129
Mitra (M2), description of, 130
Mitra (M3), description of, 130
Mitra (M4), description of, 131
Mitra (M9), from Afrati, location of, 129
Mitra (No. 31), decoration on, under microscope, 52
malachite on, 59
Mitra (No. 32), date of, 149
Mitrai from Afrati, Orientalizing decoration on, 140
weight and shape of, 132
Mitrai from Axos, 136
compared to "Eteocretan" openwork plaques, 139
Mitrai from Crete, 136
Mitrai (M4, 5, 10) from Afrati, location of, 129
Mitrai, undecorated (M5-10), 132
Mitten, David Gordon, 167-168
Model, several statuettes from, 221
wax, 174
Modeling, effects on, by mass production, 174
Moisture vapor, as cause of corrosion, 79
Mold, 5-6
clay, for Greek bird (No. 25), 19
clay, in direct lost-wax casting, 107
multiple piece, 52
piece, on Demeter bust, 54
piece, in indirect lost-wax casting, 87, 107
Mold building, by Donatello, 241
distribution of labor affecting, 242
effects on, by mass production, 174
Molds marks, lack of, 87
Monteguragazza youth, compared to Spencer-Churchill youth, 178
Monumental sculptures, analogies to Cretan bronzes, 139
Moore, T. L., analysis by, 40
Morton, Thomas, 98
Motifs, Near Eastern, Greek borrowing of, 109
North Syrian, in local style, 120-121
sources for, 122
transmission of, 103
Multiplications, 154
Muscarella, Oscar, 103, 167
Museum of Fine Arts, Boston, xii
Museums, condition of bronzes in, 76
research in, xii
statistical survey of, xi

Nantokite, 61
Natterer, K., analysis by, 41
Near East, techniques and styles adopted from, 103
Nicetas Choniates, 247
Nichols, Henry, 97
Niello, use of, 98
Noble patina, on bronzes of high tin content, 60
definition of, 57
loss of, origin of change of appearance, 73
North Etruria, Orientalizing culture in, 203
North Syria, 167
exporting role of, 116
motifs from, 120-122
North Syrian bronzes, list of, 116-118

Object, bronze, designing, viii
Object, metal, finishing, maintenance, marketing of, viii
Oinomaos, 203
Onythe, helmet from, 136
Optical laser, 93
Ores, character of, 85
extracting metal from, 85
Organ, Robert, 62, 95, 98
Orientalizing art, sources of contact with Populonia, 196
Orientalizing bronzes, not imports, 118-120
Orientalizing culture, in North Etruria, 203
Orientalizing decoration, on Afrati armor, 140
Origins, controversial, bronzes of, 121-122
geographical, reflected by are minerals, 64
place of, 109
Ortiz, George, xii, 98, 235

Ovals, explanation for, 31-32
on drapery fragment (No. 237), 23, 31
Oxidation, during annealing, 51
Oxides, bronze, 14
copper, study of, 95
formation of, on iron, 14
removal of, in soldering, 10
tin, 38, 60

Paestum, Etruscan influences in, 168
marble head from, 160
terra-cotta antefixes from, 159
Pagonda, Euboea, analysis of a statuette found at, 41
Palaikastro, helmet from, 136
Panther, double-bodied, on helmet (H1) from Afrati, 133
on *mitra* (M4), 131
Paratacamite, 61
Parting, 91
Patches, on drapery fragment (No. 237), 24
Patera (No. 76), replications of, 154
Patina, accelerated, detection of, 97
cracking of, 79
definition of, 57
as evidence of environment, 58
false, 273
forged, detection under microscope of, 3
malignant, 58
noble, 60, 73
as part of bronze, 91
rate of formation of, 98
vile, 58, 62, 73
water, 58
Pausanias, 2
Pegs, in mechanical joins, 7
Peleus and Atalanta (Walters No. 748), cista handle, Vulcian origin of, 188-189
Peleus and Thetis, on mirrors, 180-181
on pottery, 181
(Walters No. 667), on candelabrum top, Vulcian origin of, 187-188
Perseus from Hamburg, relation to Cellini's Perseus, 258
Perugia, Fontana Maggiore, 250
mirrors from, 182
"Phaistos Group" of pithoi, 150
Phelps Dodge, support of, xii
Phillips, J. A., analysis by, 40
Philo Byzantinos, 54
Phosgenite, 63, 64
Photomacrograph, of drapery fragment (No. 237), 27
Photomicrograph, of drapery fragment (No. 237), 29
of modern joins, 10-12
Phrygia, as center for winged-bull attachments, 112
role in exporting, 116
Piece mold, 52, 87, 107
for casting models, 174
on Demeter bust, 54
use of, in fifteenth century, 251
Piece-mold casting, 106
Pinax from Gortyn, linked to Afrati helmet (No. 29), 151
snakes on, 149-150
winged demon on, 148

Pinax from Lato, winged youth on, 148
Piraeus bronzes, 2
Pitch, vegetable, preservation of bronzes with, 256
Pithoi, compared to Afrati bronzes, 147-151
Pithoi and bronzes, relief on, 150-151
Pithos, dating of, 149
method of decoration on, 147
Pithos fragment from Lyttos, winged horses on, 148
Pittioni, analyses by, 51
Plenishing, of armor, 167
Plenderleith, Harold J., 95
Pliny, vi, 2, 85, 197, 245, 251, 256
additional lead in formula of, 55
ambiguity in, 46
bronze recipes of, 46, 47
Plugs, 32
causes of, 31
on drapery fragment (No. 237), 23
Poggio della Porcareccia, lack of figurative bronzes from, 197
Pollis, 134
Pollutants, in air, 57
Pollution, atmospheric, control of, 81
Polykleitos, Doryphoros of, 229, 231
Hermes of, 229
influence of, 231
Pomerance, Leon, xii
Pomponius Gauricus, writings of, 251
Populonia, cold working at, 174
copper mining at, 195
figures from, 197, 212
iron intarsia in, 203
quality of bronzes from, 235
school, criteria for, 210
Porada, Edith, 56
Potter, interaction with metal worker, 105
Po Valley, decorative school in, 236
Praeneste, lion protome from, 195
number of workshops at, 175
Praisos, plate from, 154
Preservation, definition of, 73
Preservation of bronzes, with vegetable pitch, 256
Production, of bronzes, cultural conditions influencing, 175
division of labor in, 53
means and place of, 173-174
Products, values placed by society on, viii
Protomes, Cretan, possibility of, 167
places of manufacture of, 167
Prototypes, for Gallic bronzes, 231
Provenience, foreign, problems of, 109
Provinces, Roman, cultural legacy of, 221
"Provincial" bronzes, definitions of, 236
Pseudo-Aristoteles, 195
"Puddling," 31-32

Quantitative analyses. See Analyses, quantitative
Quiver, from Fortetsa, lion-tamer on, 148

Radiograph, of Greek bird (No. 25), 16
of Etruscan *kouros* (No. 167), 9
of Etruscan lady (No. 185), 7
Reactants with bronze, in air and soil, 57

Recipe books, influence of, 242
Recipes, color-making, vi
glass, vi
of Pliny, 46-49
on tablets from Nineveh and Babylon, vi
Reduction, composition modified by, 51
Refractory material, problems with, in casting, 5
Reims, Roman bronze from, connection with Apollo from Almenum, 222
workshop near, 222
Rejects, casting, analysis of, 1
on Samos, 4
Relative humidity, control of, 81
Relief, low, on corslet (C1), 135
on pithoi and bronze, 150
Renaissance, ancient subjects reintroduced in, 241
bronze-casting in, 241
refinement of techniques in, 242
techniques of mold building in, 241
Repatination, 76, 79
Replication, 154
Repoussé, on armor (Nos. 29-32), 52
on Cretan bronzes, 104
on helmet (H1) from Afrati, 133
high, on griffin protomes; at Gordion and Hasanlu, 103
low, on Cretan armor, 105
Restoration, definition of, 73
Renaissance, 256
Rethymnon, *mitra* from, 136
Rhodes, Colossus of, 54
destruction of, 245
Rhousopoulos, O. A., analyses by, 39
Richardson, Emeline, 168, 235, 236
Ridgway, Brunhilde S., 2, 54
Rivets, use of, in mechanical joins, 7
Roman bronzes, chronological sequence of, 221
workshops of, 221
Roman sculpture, dependence on Greek, 221
Rosenberg, Gustav A. T., cleaning method of, 62, 96
Rural centers, products of, 174

Sakkos, appearance of, 160
Salamis, cauldron from, 167
Samolin, William, 56
Samos, kneeling youth, origin of, 139
Sample, size of, 37
Sampling, procedure for, 37, 51
Sardis, bronze industry, end of, 247
lion lamp from, 248
Satyr (Walters No. 771), compared to Spencer-Churchill censer, 189
Scheufelen, Dr. Heinrich, collection of, 271
Schimmel, Norbert, xii
Schimmel, Norbert, collection of, 129
corslet (C3) in, 136
corslet (C5) in, 136
dolphin handle (No. 288) in, 254
spear thrower (No. 159) in, 210
Schools, Etruscan, nature of, 236
Science, relation to art, v
Scorper, rocking, on geometric fibula (No. 26), 53
use of, 88

Scrap, Roman, hoard at Augst, 4, 55
Scrap, bronze, 47, 48
Scrap metal, circulation of, 51
relation of, to rise of lead content, 55
use of, 2-3
Sculpture, ancient, Renaissance imitations of, 253
Sculpture, bronze, causes of destruction of, 245-247
Serpents, on helmet (H1) from Afrati, 133
Sheipline, V., analysis by, 44
Shellac, removal of, 80
She-wolf in Kress Collection, 254, 256
Shields, Cretan bronze, forerunners of Afrati bronzes, 139
Shrinkage, compensation for, 6
Silicon, 95
Silver appliqué, Vulcian origin of, 189
Silver chloride, sealing cracked mineral crusts with, 82
Silver inlay, Vulcian origin of, 189
Silver nitrate, use of, 97
Silver oxide, use of, 97
Silver salts, for stabilization, 82
Silver sulphate, use of, 97
Siren attachments, casting methods, 106
differentiating Oriental and Greek, 110
imported, sources of, 110
spectographic analyses of, 56
Situla, handle attachment from, replication of, 154
Situlae, at Gordion, repoussé on, 103
Slag, analyses of, 14
composition modification by reaction with, 51
Slag heap, at Populonia, 195
Populonian, figure from, 197
Slip bands, on drapery fragment (No. 237), 30
result of cold working, 30
Slush-casting, of liquid wax, 107
Smith, Cyril Stanley, xi, 55, 98
Smithsonite, 64
Snakes, on helmet (No. 29) from Afrati, 150
intertwining, motif of, 149
Snake tripod, Delphi, damage of, 245
Sodium chloride, 61
Sodium sesquicarbonate, immersion treatment with, 83
Soft-soldering, 10, 33
Solder, 10
hard, on Demeter bust, 54
hard, melting point of, 12
silver, 10
tin-lead, on Greek hydria (No. 109), 14
Soldering, 7, 10
hard, 9
soft, 9, 12
soft, utilized by Romans and early Greeks, 14
Soldering material, recognition of, 14
Solders, differences in, 10
Solid-cast objects, composition of, 46
Solid casting, of Etruscan *kouros* (No. 167), 9
Soxhlet extractor, use of, 80
Sparta figures, Eastern origin of, 203-204
Spear-holders, significance of pose, 203
Spear thrower, Schimmel collection, 210
Specialization by craft, effects of, 242
Spectographic analyses, 56
Spectography, use of, 65
Spectrochemistry, description of, 93
Spencer-Churchill, collection of, 177-184
Sphinx (No. 41), 153
date of, 152
style of, 151-152
Sphinxes, on Afrati cinerary urn, 148
on Chigi vase, 153
on clay pithoi, 147, 149
on *mitra* (M3), 130
on *mitra* (No. 32), 149
on pinax, 153
on Salamis cauldron, 167
Stabilization, methods of, 81-83
Stamps, to decorate clay pithoi, 147
Stannic oxide, 60
under microscope, 75
Statues, manufacture of, 2
Statuary bronze, Greek, 38
Greek, tin and lead content of, 40
Hellenistic, analysis of, 42
Roman, 43
Roman, zinc in, 55
Statue of Liberty, copper sulphate on, 63
Steinberg, Arthur, 2, 53, 55, 56, 167, 236
conclusions by, 51
Stringers, on drapery fragment (No. 237), 29-30
Study collection, necessity of, 64
Style, use of, for authenticity verification, 273
Styles, foreign, adaptation of, 103
influence of, 105-106
Subjects, transmission of, 103
Sulphide, atmospheric pollution by, 81
Sulphides, copper, 59
reaction with, 51
Sumerians, as metal workers, 85
Symposium, xi
purpose and value of, vi
sponsors for, xii

Tablets, recipes on, vi
Taste, factors influencing, 106
Technique, change of, on griffin protomes, 103-104
as criteria for workshop, 105
interest in, v
significance of, vii
transmission of, 103
Technology, bronze, challenge to sculptors, 251
in cultural context, vii
description of, viii
and link with aesthetics, 52
literary sources of, vi
as prerequisite for existence of work of art, v
reconstruction of history of, vi
relation of, to art, v
relation of, to society, viii-ix
sources for historical study of, v
study of, viii
Tel Rifa'at, 167
Tenorite, 58, 95, 98
Tension, surface, on coin shapes, 52
Terra-cotta *kore*, compared to caryatid mirror, 157
Terra cottas, reproduction of, from bronzes, 156
Tetrahedrite, 59
Theophilus, vi, 250
Tin, content of, 40
in ancient objects, 85
in athlete from Ephesus, 41
in coins, 42
mineral from Belgian Congo, 61
in objects from Tomb MMT, Gordion, 55
percentage of, in Pliny, 48
ratio to lead, 45-46
sources of, 55, 61
in statuette from Athenian Agora, 41
Tin dioxide, 60
Tin oxide, 58, 60, 61
Toledo Museum, archaic youth from, authenticity of, 276
Tool, bronze, fabrication of, 88
Tooling, superficial, on Greek bird (No. 25), 21
surface, 52
Tools, analysis of, 1
for cosmetic treatment, 80
types of, 53
Trace elements, 2
analyses of, 51
Tracer, use of, 88
Tracing, on armor (Nos. 29-32), 52
cause of unidentical pairs, 154
on corslet (C1), 135
on Cretan armor, 105
on geometric fibula (No. 26), 53
on helmet (H1) from Afrati, 132
on helmet (H2), 134
on pottery and bronze, 151
Tracing tools, 52
Trade routes, 2
Tripod, Etruscan (No. 195), radiograph of join on, 8
Tripods, Vulcian, groups on, 168
workshops making, 174-175
Turan (No. 168), 235
provenience of, 212
Tuscany, southern, copper and iron resources of, 195
Twinning, on Greek bird (No. 25), 21-22
Twins, on Afrati helmet (No. 29), compared to pithos decoration, 148
Types, Greek bronze, classification of, 145
unknown, 273
Tyrrhenian coast, Mycenaean search for copper on, 195

Ultraviolet rays, 94
Urartu, 167
Urban centers, products of, 174
Urn, cinerary, from Afrati, compared to Afrati bronzes, 148
Utensil stand, Walters (No. 771), 189

Varlamoff, N., 61
Varlamoffite, 61
Varnish, consolidation of patina with, 79
Vents, arrangement of, 6

Verdigris, identification of, 62
Vermeule, Cornelius C., 236
Vernon, W. H. J., 62
Vessel, lyre player from, 178
Vessels, attachments from, 178
  handles on, mechanical joins, 7
  technological context of, 1
  as votive offerings, cinerary urns, funerary gifts, 178
Victory from Brescia, composition of, 43
Vile patina, definition of, 58
  origin of change of appearance of, 73
Vix krater, tin oxide patina on, 60
Volutes, on sphinxes, 153
Von Bothmer, Dietrich, 167, 168
Votive bronzes, quality of, 173
Votive figures, from Bern, composition of, 45
  pairs of, origin of, 208
Votive hand (No. 313), lead in, 9
Votive statuettes, at Arezzo, 236
Vulci, decorative bronzes at, 236
  workshops at, 175
Vulci workshop, objects from, 177-189

Walters Art Gallery girl (No. 57), origin of, 157
  Paestan characteristics of, 161
  provenance of, 168
Warrior in Copenhagen, casting failure, 157
Warrior in Oxford, identical to Copenhagen warrior, 157
Water patina, 58, 61
Wax, as cosmetic, 76
  Greek bird (No. 25), 19
  liquid, slush-casting of, 107
  microcrystalline, as filler for mineral crust cracks, 82
  removal of, 80
  for saturation of corrosion crust, 77
Wax model, 174
  hair worked on, 174
Welding, 25, 33
  on drapery fragment (No. 237), 24
  fusion, 9, 14, 24, 27
  fusion, on Greek bird (No. 25), 22
Weld metal, 25, 27
  accretions of, 24
Whitby, L., 62
Wicinski, R. L., analysis by, 42
Wingham, analysis by, 44
Woman in Schimmel collection, Populonian origin, 199
Workshop, viii, 223
  Carolingian, at Aix-la-Chapelle, 249
  at Enkomi, Cyprus, 4
  in Lyon, 228
  North Etruscan, imitations in, 157
  Populonian, cold working at, 174
  near Reims, 222
  Vulcian, objects from, 177-189
Workshop attribution, archaeological and historical approaches of, 1
Workshop debris, 167
Workshops, distinctions between, 236
  excavation of, 4
  for Gallic bronzes, 231
  legionary, 173
  for protomes, 167
  question of organization of, 174
  of Roman bronzes, 221
  rural, producing imitations, 175
  social organization of, 2
  specialization of, 173
  study of, 173-175
  technique as criteria for, 105
  technological idiosyncrasies of, 236
  urban, producing masterpieces, 175
Writers, ancient, 2

X-radiograph, of Diana (No. 253), 8
X-ray, diffraction pattern of paratacamite, 62
  diffraction pattern of tin oxide, 60
  use of, 65
X-ray fluorescence, 3
  to measure parting, 91

Young, William T., 55, 95, 96
Youths, winged, identification of, 140

Zeus, by Lysippos, 231
  (No. 164), in Getty Museum, 212, 235
Zinc, alloy in late Roman bronzes, 64
  in objects from Tomb MMT, Gordion, 55
  in Roman coinage, 55
  in Roman statuary bronzes, 55
Zürich boy, connection with Elba figure, 210